Diffusion of Democracy

This book explores the course and causes of the worldwide diffusion of democracy via an assessment of the political and economic development of individual countries in the years 1800 to 2005. Using this extended range of data, and examining multiple variables, Barbara Wejnert creates a conceptual model for the diffusion of democracy and to measure national democratization. The author characterizes each nation's political system, its networking with other countries, level of development, and media advancement, in order to pinpoint what leads to national and regional progress to, or regress from, democratization. Her innovative findings challenge established thinking and reveal that the growth of literacy does not lead to democratization, but is instead an outcome of democracy. She also finds that networks between non-democratic and democratic states are more important to a nation's democratization than financial aid given to non-democratic regimes or the level of national development.

BARBARA WEJNERT is an Associate Professor in the Department of Transnational Studies at the University at Buffalo. Her interdisciplinary research is focused on the world-wide diffusion of democracy and globalization of the world and their effect on social inequality. She is an author and editor of ten books on issues of post-communist transitions, democracy, and global development, and their impact on social inequalities, including gender inequality.

Diffusion of Democracy

The Past and Future of Global Democracy

BARBARA WEJNERT

CAMBRIDGE
UNIVERSITY PRESS

CAMBRIDGE
UNIVERSITY PRESS

University Printing House, Cambridge CB2 8BS, United Kingdom

Cambridge University Press is part of the University of Cambridge.

It furthers the University's mission by disseminating knowledge in the pursuit of education, learning and research at the highest international levels of excellence.

www.cambridge.org
Information on this title: www.cambridge.org/9781107625259

© Barbara Wejnert 2014

First published 2014
First paperback edition 2016

A catalogue record for this publication is available from the British Library

Library of Congress Cataloguing in Publication data
Wejnert, Barbara.
Diffusion of democracy : the past and future of global democracy / Barbara Wejnert.
    pages cm
ISBN 978-1-107-04711-2 (Hardback)
1. Democracy.   2. Democratization.   I. Title.
JC423.W3643 2014
321.8–dc23   2013024740

ISBN 978-1-107-04711-2 Hardback
ISBN 978-1-107-62525-9 Paperback

Contents

Figures

Tables

Preface

Having lived for many years in communist Poland, the principles of democracy, human rights, and the opportunity for economic development were among my main concerns in life. My introduction to democracy as a political system and to democratic processes, however, was initiated by activism in the pro-democracy Solidarity Movement in 1980–1981. I was a student at that time and a member of the student section of the Solidarity Movement. Participation in occupational strikes at the A. Mickiewicz University in Poznan, my alma mater, was the best and the most important lesson for me on the nature and processes of democratization. This activism prompted eagerness to record the history unfolding before my very eyes. I collected copies of circulating documents, students' poetry and songs, as well as recorded interviews with striking students. I watched hours of video recordings of the student negotiations with Polish government members (a phenomenon equivalent to workers' negotiations). I also visited other campuses on strike across Poland. The documentation I collected and recorded was presented as a doctoral dissertation, and constituted a significant part of two books.

Participation in the Solidarity Movement taught me an unforgettable lesson about the power of individuals united by a common goal. I was able to witness how united citizens' concern about the future of their country could overpower totalitarian regimes (i.e., communist regimes) and initiate their breakdown. Consequently, the issue of democratization and democratic movements initially became the central focus of my research, and more recently, for comparative, empirical research on world democratic transitions over the past two centuries. I realize that democratization is a long process that starts with democratic political changes and democratic elections, and also that it takes many decades for its institutionalization. It requires the experience, knowledge, and skills of domestic politicians and the existence of certain economic, political, and cultural structures conducive to democratic growth.

Hence, democracies cannot be implemented solely by outside advisors or be a copy of democratic structures already established elsewhere. I also realize that democracies are sustainable only if they are born within countries and are mainly the outcome of grassroots initiatives or initiatives of governments responding to societal demands.

Not surprisingly, considering my professional and personal background, I joyfully welcomed opportunities to analyze democratic processes when teaching at Cornell University, being appointed as the editor of the journal *Research in Political Sociology*, and collaborating with international scholars on research concerning democracy and its outcomes. My interest in democracy and its importance to global development were enriched by an opportunity to create and to chair the Department of Global Gender Studies at the University at Buffalo, which led to an extension of my research networks across the globe and allowed me to teach on democracy to American and international graduate students.

Barbara Wejnert

Acknowledgements

I would like to express my thanks to those whose help was instrumental to the development of this volume. I owe a special gratitude to my uncle Mieczyslaw Szyk, Polish journalist, who tirelessly helped me with gathering press information about Eastern European dissident networks from communist and newly democratic Polish newspapers. Irreplaceable was the extensive help of Françoise Vermeylen, a methodologist at Cornell University, who shared her expertise and advice on statistical analyses of the democracy data. My most sincere thanks are addressed to the external reviewers for their endless effort in extensive reviewing and commenting on the submitted manuscript, with special thanks to the democracy scholars who shared comments on an earlier version of this work: John Markoff, Sidney Tarrow, Joseph Stycos, and Eunice Rodriguez. I want to express my warm thanks to Julie Ehlers, my over-worked copy editor, for her endless editorial assistance. Special gratitude is extended to graduate students from my class on democracy at the University at Buffalo, Bagula Buhendwa, Susanna Cardoso, Kayla Chan, Lauren Sordellini, Beth Delecki, and Jonah Burness, for their patient participation in discussions on democracy's development and for sharing comments on an earlier version of this book. My most special gratitude is extended to my commissioning editor at Cambridge University Press, John Haslam, for his endless help, encouragement, and support, provided in various stages of this volume's preparation, especially contacting and facilitating work with external anonymous reviewers and sharing important advice on the editorial process of this volume. My thanks are extended to the editors and managers of Cambridge University Press for their editorial assistance. Finally and most importantly, I want to thank my beloved family: husband Richard and son Camille for their patience, understanding, and care, without which this volume would not have been possible, as well as son Cyprian and his wife Kate for emotional support provided in the early preparation of this book.

1 | *Understanding democracy once more*

In place of an introduction

The worldwide growth of democracy

Most studies discussing the concept of modern democracy emphasize events following the French Revolution and the American Declaration of Independence, a time when democratic regimes started to spread across the world. Democratic systems, however, were preceded by various forms of pre-democratic government – representations of citizens' assemblies that made decisions about national or community developments. In smaller communities, such governing bodies were gatherings of either all free men or representatives elected by all free men, while in larger societies they were summoned by a ruler – a king or a monarch. While not democracies, these various forms of representative assemblies resembled democratic governments in form and in their process of decision making. Specifically, in the primeval, small villages of Scandinavia (Sweden, Norway, and Denmark) and in Italian towns, every male citizen could participate in the village/town meeting and could vote and decide on the main issues concerning their communities' development. This form of direct governing changed to indirect representation when the population in such communities grew. By the eleventh century, for instance, wealthy Italian towns such as Pisa, Siena, and Genoa, among others, established municipal councils with elected councilors that decided about the towns' development. The prior councils that included all citizens were replaced by councils of only wealthy merchants and nobility representing the needs or will of the whole population.

In states or countries headed by kings or monarchs, citizens' assemblies were rare; however, when they existed, such assemblies included only members of dominant social classes. For example, the thirteenth-century English parliament of Simon de Montfort comprised an equal number of representatives of each upper-strata social group: two knights as representatives from each county, two affluent city dwellers from each city, and two wealthy members of each borough that voted on decisions proposed by a ruling king. A little more inclusive was the English parliament summoned by King Edward I, who periodically added representatives of a lesser social rank to counterbalance the limited support shown by the nobility. Also more inclusive was the first European parliament established in fifteenth-century Poland by King John I Albert, called the *Sejm*. The *Sejm* was a national institution of considerable importance. It was an assembly of local gentry and burghers initially gathered by the king to raise funds for the country. However, it gained unusual and excessive power after the crown accepted a rule that no new law could be established without approval by the *Sejm*, the rule called *Nihil Novi*. Unfortunately this democratic-type rule tremendously limited the power of Polish kings and eventually, with an added right of veto given to each member of the *Sejm*, led to the country's partition and occupation.

The path to the development of modern forms of democracy was opened by the revolutions in France and in America in the late eighteenth century, and democratic systems were established in various parts of North and South America, in Europe and Africa and, by the end of the nineteenth century, in Asia. Although most of the first democracies were not consolidated or longlasting, a steady increase in the number of democratic transitions signaled the coming era of democracy (Gurr, Jagger, & Moore 1990; Fukuyama 1992). The remarkable growth in the democratization of countries over the past forty years has captured the political imagination of the world and, not surprisingly, there has been a relatively recent increase in the curiosity of scholars, policy-makers, and the public alike as to which factors contribute to, or modulate, democratic growth (Lipset 1994; Przeworski et al. 1996, 2000). So has democracy, at last, won the contest for the support of people throughout the world? Hardly. "Democratic governments (with varying degrees of democracy) exist in fewer than half of the countries in the world, which contain less than half of the world's population" (Dahl 1989, 1). Also, "Many young democracies emerge in the presence of challenging initial conditions such as widespread poverty and inequality, economic dependence on a small range of commodities and high levels of ethnic fragmentation among other social divisions ... initial conditions may also motivate politicians to centralize political and economic power, rather than distribute it more widely" (Kapstein and Converse 2009, 2, xv). Nonetheless, as Fukuyama and McFaul argue, the benefits of democracy and democratic coexistence significantly outweigh the costs; therefore, democracy's spread should be promoted and not discouraged (Fukuyama & McFaul 2007).

Some scholars believe that, even though there is no current alternative to democracy as a principle of legitimacy, democracy may stand unchallenged in principle and yet in practice be formidably challenged in its performance (Holbrook 2008). It is with this understanding that we need " ... to seek theories that integrate both spheres, accounting for areas of enlargement between them" (Putnam 1988, 433). Therefore, the first section of this book is devoted to the content of recent theoretical and empirical debates on democracy and democratic processes, including definitions of democracy and the meaning of democracy's interpretations, as well as analyses of the development, rate, and trajectory of democracy by means of factors that lead to the establishment and sustainability of a democratic system. Such research is particularly pertinent to our understanding of the contemporary world, especially research that considers that the descriptive studies accounting for current reality do not satisfy the curiosity about what contributes to the initiation of democracy, democracy's growth or its delayed development, or regression from a democratic system.

After an initial introduction to existing interpretations, the ultimate goal of this book is to provide an empirically driven "road map" that describes the processes of adoption of democracy by various countries, as well as countries' democratization and re-democratization, and that ultimately serves to design a *threshold model* of democracy's development and sustainability. To create the model, I integrate and empirically assess the contribution of external and regional influences, diffusion supported by accessible information, as well as development and modernization factors in democracy's growth. These factors that lead to the likelihood of the successful adoption and growth of democracy are called "development" (concerned with endogenous processes of a country) and "diffusion" (referring to exogenous factors).

The threshold model helps to design a prediction scheme for the world's democratic or non-democratic future. Thus, from this discourse on democracy's diffusion, which combines an account of worldwide democratization and factors leading to democratization, stems a proposition of a threshold model of democracy adoption. The threshold model is, in turn, applied to predict a future democratic or non-democratic world. Consequently, the volume concludes with a prognosis of the worldwide scope and rate of democratization until the second half of the twenty-first century.

Democracy: definitions and concepts

Democracy is an ancient political system that dates back more than two millennia; hence, over time, many scholars have analyzed and interpreted the concept of democracy, and "the very fact that democracy has such a lengthy history has actually contributed to confusion and disagreement, as 'democracy' has meant different things for different people at different times and places" (Dahl 2000, 3).

In general terms, democracy has been described as a political system that should guarantee to every adult citizen the right to vote, as well as "avoiding tyranny, essential rights, general freedom, self-determination, moral autonomy, human development, protecting essential personal interests, political equality, peace-seeking and prosperity" (Dahl 1989, 45). Two interpretations of the content and meaning of a democratic system have prevailed: first, democracy was viewed as an ideal, imaginary model, where the system is assessed as it should be; second, it was viewed as an existing reality, where the system is assessed according to what actually exists. Dahl calls the first interpretation an ideal type or a "value judgment," whereas the latter is an "empirical judgment" assessed according to an existing reality (Dahl 1989, 31).

In terms of particular characteristics, democracies vary significantly. The differences range from the degree of openness of ruling elites to inclusion of minorities within the governing body to the scope of guaranteed rights for social minorities. Thus, many of the oldest democracies that were generally considered to have had a consolidated democratic system were not always fully democratic (e.g., France in the 1950s was viewed as a weakening democratic state with limited civil rights). Also, in Western liberal democracies that are regarded as the most consolidated democratic systems, many citizens, including women and ethnic/racial minorities, were for decades excluded from the right to vote. Women received the right to vote a hundred years after most of the oldest liberal democracies were established: in the United States in 1920, in Canada in 1918, Britain in 1928, in France in 1944 and in the nearly 200-year-old democracy of Costa Rica in 1936.

This contradicts democracy's concept of the provision of equality to all citizens (Markoff 1996) and the fulfillment of the common desire of people to be recognized as equals (Tilly 2007). The treatment of Albanian minorities in Serbia or the Muslim population in Greece demonstrates the existence of other recent democracies that do not provide rights to minority citizens (Dinstein 1992).[1]

Similarly, many scholars perceive newly democratized African countries as weak because of a lack of unifying ideological principles, and because these contries do not embrace the concept of balance of power by their polity (Kissinger 2001; Kapstein & Converse 2009). In some of these democracies, the general laws and guiding principles of democratic rule are interpreted according to the convenience of the ruling elite, not democratic principles (Tilly 2005), making the African democracies weakly democratic in practice (Prempeh 2010, 19). Therefore, according to some academics, across periods of world history "democracy disappeared in practice, remaining barely alive as an idea or a memory among a precious few" (Dahl 2000, 3).

Thus, it may be puzzling to determine the causes of the development of democracy, particularly as many researchers and policy makers consider democracy the ultimate political system that is most beneficial to societal development. Scholars' curiosity could be also stimulated by the lengthy history of democracy and its diversified nature across countries and across time (Tilly 2007).

Causes of democracy's development

As the recent history of political thought suggests, academics have devoted equal attention to analyses of the development of democracy as to democratization processes. Starting with the powerful work of de Tocqueville (2009) through modern analyses, examinations incorporated theoretical investigations and pragmatic proposals that concentrated on several issues. Led by analyses of the taxonomy of democratic models (Held 1995) and democracy's prerequisites and

---

[1] Incidentally, in stark contrast were the communist countries and authoritarian government of the Soviet Union that granted equal rights to women from the time of inception of the communist political system in 1921. These rights included the right to vote and a quota system that guaranteed women election and representation in the top political offices of nearly one third of members (Tuttle 1986).

definitions (Dahl 1989, 2000), these examinations addressed the required responsiveness of a democratic government to its citizens (Dowding, Goodin, & Pateman 2004), development and sustainability of democratic governance (Tilly 2005, 2007), the concept of justice in relation to the democratic system and the importance of trust and rule of law (Rawls 1999; Tilly 2005), the honesty and integrity of the ruling elite (Kapstein & Converse 2009), citizens' inclusion in the governing process (Dahl 1989, 2000), and civil society and participatory citizenship (Skocpol & Fiorina 1999; Somers 1993). Other examinations concentrated on fairness in the distribution of economic and natural resources within democratic countries (Kapstein & Converse 2009, xix–xx) and across countries (Wallerstein 2001), and on social justice and its distribution (Dowding, Goodin, & Pateman 2004; Etzioni 2004). Studies on the factors that generate democratic growth (Schwartzman 1998; Skocpol 1998), the spread and diffusion of democratic systems (Huntington 1997; Wejnert 2005), and democratic movements (Tarrow 2005) concentrated on the assessment of worldwide growth in the number and strength of democratic systems.

Two distinct points of view dominated interpretations concerning the development and growth of democracy in the world. Some scholars believed that the prevalence of democracy is inevitable and thus marks an era of prosperity and human rights. Such an era is dominated by the cultural values of independence, individuality, and freedom (Fukuyama & McFaul 2007; Inglehart & Welzel 2005, 2009), values and appreciates individual achievement, and leads to the end of the world's history and the end of the last man (Fukuyama 1992; Mandelbaum 2004, 2008). A contrasting point of view is expressed by scholars who studied the crises of modern liberal democracies. These scholars believed that democracies are failing and hence, the time of worldwide democratization is coming to an end. Democratic supremacy will be replaced by authoritarian rule that, like democracy, supports a modernized market economy (Gat et al. 2009; Kagan 2008; Kaminsky 2013). The failure of democratic development was also perceived as resulting from the inequality of worldwide economic development, generated by the world-system dependency of under-developed countries on well-developed states (Wallerstein 2001).

Democracy as a political system is, therefore, far from the uniform political structure that most academics refer to as an ideal type of democracy. Rather, it is characterized by many divergences, changing its form and nature when oscillating between more and less democratic governing. Regardless of differences between countries, the goal and principle of democracy remains the same – countries are striving to obtain rule by people and equal rights to their fullest extent. The uncertainty, prolonged history, changing nature of democracy, and multiple, still-unanswered questions regarding democratic growth make the subject of this study particularly intriguing and worth addressing.

Democratic history is marching on: historical overview of the trajectory and rate of worldwide democratization

The assessment of trends and progress of democratic developments across the world over time required construction of a comprehensive database incorporating indicators characterizing the democratic system and nature of democratic/non-democratic countries. This study is based on the derived database *Nations, Development and Democracy: 1800–2005* (Wejnert 2007) that integrates socioeconomic and political factors related to democratization for 177 members of the international system (20 of which are historical, 157 of which are contemporary countries) for the years 1800–2005.[2] A total of 65 annually recorded socioeconomic, demographic, political, and diffusion variables are included in the dataset.

Database and measurements

The database *Nations, Development and Democracy: 1800–2005* (Wejnert 2007) is derived in large part from two major datasets: *Polity IV: Regime Authority Characteristics and Transition Datasets, 1800–2009* (Marshall, Jagger, & Gurr 2009, 2011) and indicators of *Freedom in the World 1994–2009* (Freedom House 2009). The socioeconomic, demographic, and political variables are derived and merged from Marshall, Jagger and Gurr (2009) and Banks' (1993) *Cross-National Time Series, 1815–1973*. In addition, variables were coded from descriptions of political, economic, and social institutions in volumes of the *Statesman's Yearbook*; the *World Handbook of Political and Social Indicators* (Taylor & Jodice 1982); Osmanczyk's (1982)

---

[2] Included are only those countries that are recognized as independent members of the international system with populations greater than 500,000 in the early 2000s (Gurr & Jagger 1995a; Marshall, Jagger, & Gurr 2009)

Encyclopedia of the United Nations and International Relations; and the journal *Freedom Review's* annual reports published by Freedom House (Freedom House 2009). Bollen's (1998) database *Liberal Democracy Indicators 1950–1990* was used to record data that were missing in the above datasets.

Included in the *Polity IV* dataset is an eleven-point scale developed by Jagger and Gurr (1995a); Marshall and Gurr (2012) that assesses level of democratization. The index is composed of major components that represent characteristics of democracy: (a) competitiveness of political participation, (b) regulation of political participation, (c) competitiveness of executive recruitment, (d) openness of executive recruitment, and (e) constraints on chief executives. These five components are in keeping with the definition of political democracy as the "extent to which the political power of elites is minimized and that of non-elites is maximized" (Bollen 1980), which is similar to an ideal model of democracy assessed according to its principles rather than performance (Dahl 1989, 38). Each component is weighted 0–3 or 0–4 on the basis of the presence of 2–7 characteristics per component, and a total democratization score is the sum of the five components' weights.

In Jagger and Gurr's system, a maximum score of 10 depicts a fully developed democracy, whereas a minimum score of 0 represents a lack of democracy. On the basis of their research, Gurr (1974) and Gurr, Jagger, & Moore (1990) designated a score of 7 or more as representing *coherent, stable democracies*, and scores ranging from 1 to 6 as *incoherent* or *transitional democracies*. Clearly, countries that have low levels of democracy also may have some level of autocracy. An index of autocracy is included in the *Polity IV* dataset and in the database *Nations, Development and Democracy: 1800–2005* (Wejnert 2007). However, given this study's focus on the prediction of the rate of democratization, autocracy scores are not considered, regardless of their potential enrichment of the understanding of polity development.

The significant advantage of using the *Polity IV* dataset (Marshall, Jagger & Gurr 2009) is its incorporation of longitudinal data from 1800–2008. No other available dataset provides an index of democratization level across all sovereign countries over a comparable time span. However, there are some disadvantages to using *Polity IV* indicators of democracy that are worth briefly mentioning. First, there is some degree of subjective interpretation of monographic and other source materials in deriving democracy scores. Second, Western liberal democracies are attributed very high democracy scores. For instance, France was awarded a score of 10 from 1930 until 1941 even though during this time French women did not have the right to vote (women received this right in 1944). Similarly, the United States has had a score of 10 since 1870, despite visible discrimination and lack of votes for women and people of color. And Costa Rica was considered to be highly democratic for nearly a hundred years before women obtained the right to vote in 1936 (Tuttle 1986). Furthermore, Switzerland has been given the highest score for democracy (10 out of 10) since 1848, although women received the right to vote only in 1971.[3]

In light of these problems:

(1) The authors of the database adopted rigid scores and rules of coding democracy in *Polity III* and *Polity IV* data as an attempt to limit subjectivity (see Jagger & Gurr (1995b) and Marshall & Gurr (2012) for details).

(2) Jagger & Gurr (1995a) tested the convergent validity of their democracy scale by comparing it against scales developed by other researchers, such as Gasiorowski (1993), Bollen (1980), Arat (1991), Vanhanen (1990), Coppedge & Reinicke (1990), and Freedom House (annual 1973–1994). Correlations ranged between 0.85 and 0.92 (p< 0.01), indicating comparability of the various scales with their own scale (Jagger & Gurr 1995a). Moreover, the Jagger and Gurr scale correlates highly with that of Bollen (1980), which is based on the two major components of political liberty and popular sovereignty (r = 0.89, *p*< 0.01; Jagger & Gurr 1995a).

(3) In this book, to assess the validity of the *Polity IV* dataset, the indicators were drawn from the broadly used *Polity III* dataset (Jagger & Gurr 1995b) for the years 1800–1994 and extended with the *Political Freedom Indicators* (Freedom House 2000) for the years 1995–1999. The comparability of *Polity IV* with *Polity III* was assessed with the extended scale by correlating data, and a correlation score of above 0.9 was obtained. High correlation scores indicate the similarity of *Polity IV* with the previously frequently used *Polity III* dataset, and attest to the validity of the *Polity IV* dataset, justifying its use in this study.

---

[3] Indeed, the significantly diminished importance of election outcomes is associated with Switzerland's collective executive that in great part relates to the long-term exclusion of women from the right to vote.

Nonetheless, the dataset of *Polity III* (Jagger & Gurr 1995b) and subsequently *Polity IV* of Marshall, Jagger & Gurr (2009) met with criticism. Przeworski et al. (2000) argue for correcting the weakness of the *Polity IV* scale through the inclusion of (a) an assessment of democracy focusing on competition for office via free election, (b) existence of more than one party, and (c) alteration of political power. At the same time Mainwaring & Pérez-Liñán (2001) propose to use a trichotomous measurement of democracy. They also argue that many existing scales violate major democratic principles, being biased toward leftist governments and being assessed too leniently in earlier years in comparison to the 1990s and 2000s. According to the authors, the definition of democracy should include assessment of the real power of elected officials, whether or not they rule *de facto*, and its focus on governmental protection of civil liberties, including freedom to elect. Hence, measurement of inclusiveness of franchise should be added to the scale, such as an assessment of whether or not elections trigger mass civilian protests. As another correction, the authors propose scales that include democracies with one-party systems where the electorate is satisfied with the party in power, as exemplified by Japan (Mainwaring & Pérez-Liñán (2001), 42–48).

Furthermore, Bowman, Lehaucq, and Mahoney (2005, 941) questioned the validity and accuracy of the existing, long-term datasets (such as the *Polity III* and *Polity IV* data), as incorporating data-induced measurement of democracy. The authors proposed measurements that rely on a broad range of data sources and experts' opinions. As such, substantive knowledge of countries would limit miscoding and biased selection of one measure over others. Consequently, regardless of high correlations between measures of democracy of different scales, Bowman, Lehaucq, and Mahoney (2005) believe that limited data or data inadequacy create substantive implications for the validity of many comprehensive, longitudinal datasets.

It is impossible to dispute the valid points of the raised critiques; nonetheless, considering the longitudinal nature of the study and its focus on the character of processes of democratization, I agree with Dahl (1989, 199) that "although at this point a complete, reliable, and current account of all democratic countries in the world appears to be unavailable, the two datasets *Polity III* and *Freedom House* allow fairly good estimates of democratization." In this study, therefore, an index of democracy was drawn from the datasets *Polity IV*,

Freedom House, and others that are incorporated in *Nations, Development and Democracy* (Wejnert 2007).

Index of democracy

To accurately interpret cross-world democratization, the database needed to incorporate a measurement of democracy that allows the ability to characterize and define the term "democracy" and the level of its development (Kapstein & Converse 2009; Kissinger 2001). Democracy could be understood simply as a dichotomy on a scale of 0–1 where a country is either democratic or not democratic. Countries thus can be viewed categorically, yielding a scaling of democracy as either "1" or "0." This is not in keeping, however, with the nature of democracy, which actually represents a continuous variable. Generally, states have accepted either some democratic principles while ignoring others, or have accepted most of the principles of democracy but differentially apply them across societal strata. Newly democratized African states, for example, claim to be democratic, but they do not follow unifying ideological principles or embrace a concept of balance of power by their polity (Kissinger 2001, 26). Many countries that are called democracies are unstable democracies, easily reverting to an autocratic system. Good examples are Russia (Politkovskaya 2011) and Belorussia (Alexievich 2006, xii), which embraced democratic principles only for a couple of years, as well as most sub-Saharan African countries, where corrupt elections prevent change in top leadership positions (Diamond & Plattner 2010, 47–50). Also, most democracies go through a cyclical process of democratization, a shift to autocracy and then re-democratization (e.g., Huntington 1992; O'Donnell, Schmitter, & Whitehead 1996) before reaching a point of stabilizing democratic system (Sawa-Czajka 2010; Wejnert 2010). For example, although at the end of the third wave of democratization in 1994 (Wejnert 2005), 114 out of 157 independent countries were considered to have some democratic principles in their polities (Karatnycky 1995), by the end of the twentieth century, less than 50 percent of all countries in the world were democratic, with male or full suffrage, and only about half of the world's population lived in democratic states (Dahl 2000).

Hence, democracy could be assessed as a process when one would speak of the *level of democratization* of a country that reflects on the actual nature of democracy as a developmental process, from non-democracy to some achieved level of democracy (Dahl 1989). Such a process is measured on a scale and, in this study, the indicator of democracy is formed as a continuous index that is based on scale of 0–10, where 0 means no democracy and 10 a fully developed democratic system.

Indeed, when presented graphically, the two divergent approaches to understanding the growth of worldwide democracy as a dichotomy (democratic/undemocratic system) vs the scale of the democracy level suggest diverse results – with the inclusion of the analysis of democracy scores for each sovereign country over time, the rate of democracy evolution significantly changes (see Figures 1.1a and 1.1b).

Moreover, the continuous operationalization of democracy creates a distinct statistical advantage (Bollen & Jackman 1985b), as the possibility of error in longitudinal assessment when using a dichotomous variable visibly increases in comparison to assessment with a continuous variable. It is also generally assumed that the temporal evolution of democracy follows a continuous, increasing trend across the last two centuries (Karatnycky 1997; Starr 1991).

Democratization of the world

Indeed, over the past two centuries we observed the upward curve in the growth of democracies (see Figure 1.2) and starting with the French Revolution and the American Declaration of Independence, democratic regimes have spread across the world. As early as the 1800s, democratic systems were established in various parts of North and South America, in Europe and Africa and, by the end of the nineteenth century, in Asia. Although most of the first democracies were not consolidated or longlasting, a steady increase in the number of democratic transitions signaled the coming democratization of the world (Gurr, Jagger, & Moore 1990; Fukuyama 1992).

Nonetheless, the relative number of democratic states as a ratio of the total number of sovereign states varied, suggesting recurring trends toward democratization in the contemporary history of the world. For instance, although the total number of democracies was the highest during the 1990s, following the end of World War I the ratio of democratic to non-democratic states reached 81 percent of all sovereign states (point *B* in Figure 1.2), exceeding the 75 percent of 1998 (point D in Figure 1.2). Similarly, while there were only twenty-nine

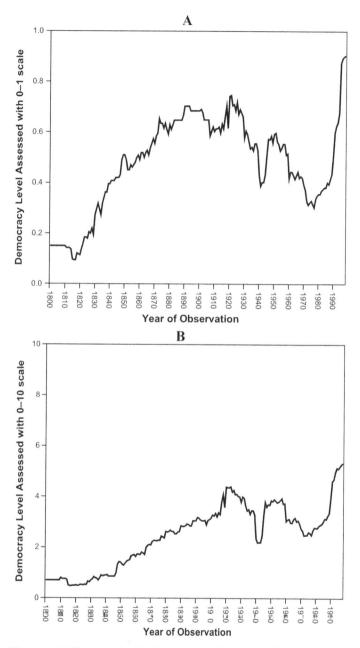

Figure 1.1 The mean level of democracy in the world, 1800–2005, assessed with scale 0–1 vs scale 0–10

Source: database *Nations, Democracy and Development: 1800–2005* (Wejnert, 2007). The mean level of democracy refers to the observed mean level of democracy in the world.

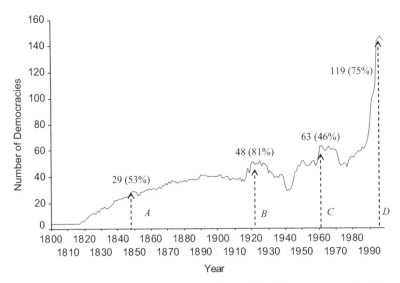

Figure 1.2 Total number of countries in the world exhibiting some principles of democracy across historical time, 1800–2000
Source: database *Nations, Democracy and Development: 1800–2005* (Wejnert, 2007). A, B, C, D – ratio of democratic to non-democratic countries in the world (in percentage). Countries are denoted as democratic if their democracy score is 1 or larger, which depicts acceptance of some democratic principles.

democracies in 1850, they constituted 53 percent of all fifty-five sovereign states (point A in Figure 1.2), which was a higher ratio of democratized states worldwide than the 46 percent in 1961 (point C in Figure 1.2), the era of global decolonization associated with democratization of newly independent states.

It appears that across the past two centuries, the steadily increasing but fluctuating growth in worldwide democratization and an increase in the number and the ratio of democracies in the world varied as a function of the world's *regions* and *time* (century). An accurate study, however, needs to incorporate additional explanations to illustrate the historical overview of the trajectory and rate of worldwide democratization: first, the conceptual meaning of a particular democracy level needs to be presented, i.e., whether a particular democratic system means stable, stabilizing, or unstable democracy and whether there is a threshold of the democracy score above which a system can be considered democratic or not, for instance, when a country is in the process of transition to democracy; and second, time-dependent variations and regional variations in democratization should be incorporated.

First, as Dahl (2000) argues, only congruent democracies with 7 or more out of the maximum 10 points on the 0–10 democratization scale designed by Marshall, Jagger, and Gurr (2009) in *Polity III* and *Polity IV* data are potentially sustainable. "Experience revealed that once democratic institutions were firmly established in a country, they would prove to be remarkably sturdy and resilient … Democracies express an unexpected capacity for coping with problems they confronted – inelegantly and imperfectly, true, but satisfactorily" (Dahl 1989, 188). In contrast, democracies that are weak (achieving a level of only a few points on the democracy scale of 0–10) easily retreat to undemocratic governing (Kapstein & Converse 2009). Subsequently, countries estimated to have at least 1 but not more than 7 points on the democratization scale are understood as having adopted some principles of democracy, but not as being stable and congruent. I propose viewing such countries as undergoing the process of transition to democracy, or simply, as *transitory democracy*. In the presented analyses (see Figure 1.1) of the two periods of the highest rate of world democratization – the early 1920s and the second half of the 1990s – none reached democratization at the level defined by Dahl (2000) as a *congruent democracy*. During both of these times, the attained level of democracy was at approximately 5 points on the democracy scale of 0–10 across the world. Moreover, as demonstrated in Figure 1.3, across the past two hundred years the average democracy level of all countries in the world did not achieve the level of sustainable, congruent democracy of 7 and above (on a scale of 0–10).

Second, according to the literature (Schwartzman 1998; Wejnert 2005), the rates and level of democratization varied between regions across the period. Indeed, in comparison to worldwide democratic growth, the temporal rate of cross-regional democratization reveals clear regional patterns of democratization (see Figure 1.4).

Cross-regional democratization

As Figure 1.4 illustrates, while in some regions democratization is steadily increasing, in others it is decreasing. Also evidently, periods of rapidly escalating democratization in some regions are in contrast to simultaneous periods of rapid democracy decline in others; e.g., during

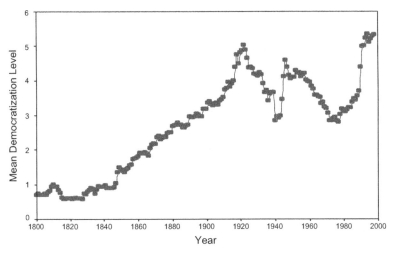

Figure 1.3 Mean level of democratization of the world, 1800–2000
Source: Research based on the database *Nations, Democracy and Development: 1800–2005* (Wejnert 2007).

the 1850s and 1860s, an increase of democratization in Europe and Asia vs a decline in Africa; or during 1900–1920, an increase in Europe and Africa vs a decline in Asia.

There are also noticeable differences in patterns of democratization in the nineteenth century as compared to the twentieth century. Evolution of democracy in the nineteenth century is characterized by three separate trends varying by region: a slow, steady upward trend towards democratization; an initial downward trend followed by an upward trend; and no democracy in the entire region. Across the nineteenth century, the newly established countries that were democratized were mainly in regions where the first democratic states already existed, namely France and the United States. Thus, only in Europe and the Western Hemisphere (i.e., North America and Latin America), did democracy reach a higher level than the mean democracy level of the world. However, while in Europe the democracy level was steadily increasing throughout the nineteenth century, in the Western Hemisphere, the democracy level rapidly declined in the 1810s and 1820s and only thereafter gained steady growth. In this region, most of the newly established, postcolonial countries initially became low-level democracies, with democracy scores of 1 during the first few decades

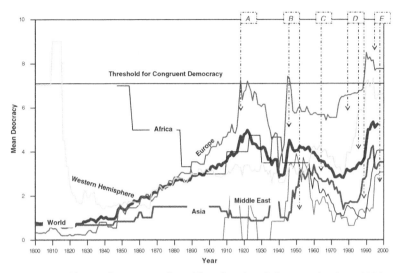

Figure 1.4 Observed patterns of world and regional democratization, 1800–2000

Source: database *Nations, Democracy and Development: 1800–1999* (Wejnert, 2000). *Notes*: A – the end of World War I and creation of many new states that were established as democracies in Europe. B – the end of World War II and liberation of many European and Middle Eastern countries correlated with the re-establishment of democratic systems in those countries. C – withdrawal from democracy trend in Africa that followed the rapid initial democratization of decolonized states. D – world oil crises and democratization of southern European and Latin American countries, the so-called first and second waves of democratization. E – collapse of the communist bloc and democratization in Eastern Europe and Russia, and return to democracy of many African countries. The steep decrease in democratization level in the Western Hemisphere 1810–1830 is a result of the rapid growth of the number of sovereign but not democratic countries in the region in which in 1800 there existed only one strongly democratic country, the United States of America.

of their existence (in most cases that meant that in these countries the only democratic practices were instituted but not fully free elections). For example, Mexico, Ecuador, Venezuela, Nicaragua, El Salvador, Honduras, Guyana, Peru, Bolivia, Chile, Argentina, and Uruguay had democracy scores of only 1 during the first few decades of their existence. Since the high democracy level of the region was generated mainly by the strongly democratic United States (with a democracy score of 7 in the nineteenth century), the addition of low-level democracies lowered the overall mean democracy level in the region. By the end of the nineteenth century, the gained democracy by some countries, accompanied by maintenance of low-level democracy by others, led to a slow increase in the mean of regional democratization.

Congruently, in Africa the democratic trend over the nineteenth century was downward, reversing to an upward trend only in the last two decades. At the beginning of the nineteenth century there was only one independent country – Liberia, which was also a relatively stable democracy (it had a democracy score of 7 on a scale of 0–10 where 0 means no democracy, 10 well-developed democratic system). With the establishment of new countries in the mid nineteenth century that were low-level democracies (e.g., Ethiopia, established in 1855, had a democracy score of 5; South Africa, established in 1856, had a score of 3), the average democracy level in the region declined. In addition, Liberian democracy declined to a score of 1 by the end of the century. At the same time, in the entire region of the Middle East, there were no democracies throughout the nineteenth century. Similarly, in Asia, the initial years had no democratic states, but this was followed by the emergence of low-scoring democracies (e.g., Japan) in the late nineteenth century (see Figure 1.4).

In contrast, an examination of world democratization in the twentieth century demonstrates that democratic trends across all regions were more strongly correlated with world-scale historical events rather than with the initial character of newly established countries, as was the case in the nineteenth century. For instance, as shown by point A in Figure 1.4, the end of World War I led to a mean increase in the level of European democratization that generated a rapid increase in the overall world democratization level in the years from 1910 to 1925. Eleven new countries – one third of the total number of countries in Europe at that time – were established as democratic states, in part due to political pressures during post-war negotiations and peace treaties. Among them were Poland, Czechoslovakia, Ukraine, and Lithuania. Conversely, the Great Depression of the 1930s led to the outbreak of totalitarianism and retreat from democracy, and eventually to the onset of World War II. Foreign occupation of a vast number of European, Asian, Northern African, and Middle Eastern countries by the totalitarian regimes of Germany, Italy, Japan, and their allies inhibited democratic development. Indeed, literature discussing the conditions suitable to democratic transitions and the development of democracy frequently addresses the impact of totalitarian regimes on the suppression of democratic processes in occupied territories, as "democratic institutions are less likely to develop in a country subject to intervention by another country hostile to democratic government in that country" (Dahl 1989, 147). As scholars suggest, sovereignty is one of the conditioning indicators of democratic existence (e.g., Karatnycky 1995). Hence, as shown in Figure 1.4, the rate of worldwide expansion of democracy was negative until the end of World War II, when stability was obtained and a new geopolitical map of the world was drawn.

The end of World War II witnessed a significant increase in the level of world democratization, which was reflected in the level of democracy of most regions (see point *B* in Figure 1.4). The upward trend in the rate of world democratization at the end of the 1940s through the 1950s was associated with the re-establishment of democratic systems in many liberated European and Northern African countries, and with a period of extensive decolonization (mainly in Africa) and initiation of democracy in post-colonial states. This worldwide growth of democracy was followed by a sharp decline when democratic regimes subsequently reverted to authoritarian rule in many of the fragile post-colonial states of Africa (see point C in Figure 1.4).

As shown in point D in Figure 1.4, the decades of the 1970s and 1980s witnessed slight increases in world democratization associated with democratic transitions that occurred in southern Europe and Latin America, a result in part of the world oil crises (Higley & Gunther 1992; Huntington 1992; O'Donnell, Schmitter, & Whitehead 1996, Tilly 2007). Also connected with these historical events was the democratization of Asia assisted by Western economic aid. However, as shown by point E in Figure 1.2, the rapid upward trend in world democratization did not start until the 1990s, corresponding to the collapse of the Soviet bloc in 1989–1990 and to the spread of democratic transitions across former Soviet bloc states (Bermeo 1991; Havel 1985; Huntington 1992; Ost 1992; Szelenyi 1996; Stark & Bruszt 1988; Wejnert 2002a), and the re-democratization of many of the African countries (Kapstein & Converse 2009; Kissinger 2001; Tilly 2006).

The questions remain: why do countries adopt democratic systems, and what characteristics of countries contribute to the democratization processes?

2 | Factors contributing to democratization

An overview

Starting with initial studies many relevant analyses have focused on countries' socioeconomic characteristics as predictors of their level of democracy (Bollen 1983, Lipset 1960; Neubauer 1967). In this study it is proposed to call such predictors *development indicators* of democracy adoption and growth. In this case, the majority of studies have explored the role of socioeconomic conditions of countries, such as GNP, education, economic crises, the level of urbanization and industrialization. Accordingly, it was believed that democratic transitions and successive temporal growth in a country's *democraticness* (the achieved level of democracy that attests to the level of strength of a democratic system) result from countries' development. Therefore democratic transitions were believed to be slow and monotonic and typically to occur randomly in various parts of the world. Comparing the number of democracies with the level of countries' democratization the world did not look very democratic regardless of the rapidly growing number of countries that were considered as having a democratic system (compare Figure 1.2 and Figure 1.3).

Recently researchers who have focused on groups of democratizing countries have become interested in factors that lie outside of development. For instance, initiated in the aftermath of World War I, imposition of a democratic system on many of the newly created European states – called engineered democratic experiment – changed the character and the temporal rate of democratization in the world (Gurr 1974). Since that time, as scholars believe, countries have tended to democratize in clusters within regions of the world, where increases in democratization have occurred as *waves*, each of which having its own characteristics and growth rate (Doyle 1983, Huntington 1992, Markoff 1996). For instance, the most recent clustering is considered the *Third Wave* of democratization (Huntington 1992), and included southern Europe in the 1970s (Pridham 1990; Tarrow 1989), Latin America in the 1980s (Higley & Gunther 1992; Linz & Stepan 1996; O'Donnell, Schmitter, & Whitehead 1996), the former Soviet-bloc countries in the 1990s (Bermeo 1991, Stark and Bruszt 1998; Wejnert 2002a, 2005), followed by South Korea, Taiwan and re-democratization of many post-colonial African states in the late 1990s and 2000s (Bratton & Mattes 2001; Spears 2003).

The very existence of clustering within regions, and the resulting complex temporal nature of regional democratization, suggests that endogenous socioeconomic conditions may be modulated by *diffusion factors*. Such factors would influence the democratization processes of a country via forces at work (a) globally, e.g., due to a spread of modern media communication, (b) within the region in which a country resides, e.g., influence of high regional density of democratic countries, and (c) within a group of countries forming a network, e.g., role modeling of democracies on non-democratic members. Therefore, in the search for diffusion predictors of democratic growth, leading scholars on democracy such as Dahl (1989), Lipset (1994) and Markoff (1996), suggested that factors influencing global democratization might operate in the form of *diffusion processes*. Diffusion factors would include the impact of global media information, spatial and temporal proximity or structural equivalence to democratic countries, and the hegemonic imposition of a democratic system by economic powers on less developed states, as in the influence of the British Empire on colonial dependencies or of the promotion of democracy by the United States on recipients of its economic aid and partners of trade (Fukuyama & McFaul 2007). Consequently, diffusion might operate via several mechanisms, including provision of information about democratic systems, demonstration of how democratic systems work, modeling of existing democracies, or an imposition of democratic regimes.

The great majority of relevant studies show that indicators of countries' levels of development are sufficient and most significant predictors of those countries' democratization. Using studies that included only one type of indicators (only socioeconomic predictors), however, it is impossible to challenge the well-established belief and to test whether the popular argument about *development* predictors being the key determinants of change in countries' level of democracy holds.

Competing conceptual frameworks explaining
the development of democracy

The very existence of clustering within regions, and the resulting complex temporal nature of regional democratization, suggests that development socioeconomic conditions may be modulated by diffusion factors.

Three major frameworks – the theory of *modernization*; *class conflict* theory; and the *world system/dependency* theory – dominated most previous interpretations of democracy development. Interpretations were less frequently enhanced by investigations of the impact of diffusion processes on democratic and democratizing countries (Huntington 2011; Wejnert 2005). Less often, studies of democratization concluded with supporting analyses of other factors crucial to democracy's development, such as development of societal trust and fair laws (Tilly 2005), or citizen unrest (Tarrow 2005) or analyses of the effects of global events.

Modernization framework

Following the earlier studies of Lipset (1960), Nebeurer (1967) and Schumpeter (1950), scholars who applied the theoretical framework of modernization believed in the inevitable development of democracy and worldwide democratization due to progressive economic advancement of countries. According to these interpretations, the development of democracy is facilitated by factors of modernization, such as increase of GDP, literacy and education, formation of a middle class; establishment of democratic laws, separation of the political system from the economy and from religion, transformation of people's values, citizens' political participation, prevention of corruption, and an increase in the legitimacy of the ruling elite.

Since the end of World War II, socioeconomic factors have been considered to be strong predictors of democratic growth, and modern democracy was believed to be "a product of capitalistic processes" (Schumpeter (1950 : 297). Indeed, Merritt and Rokkan's (1996) cross-national study illustrated the dependency of democratic growth on the level of countries' literacy and education, showing that high illiteracy rates (higher than 80 percent) and low levels of access to schooling (where less than 40 percent of children completed primary education) inhibit democratization. Similarly, very low levels of economic development limited democratic growth because less-developed countries were incapable of overcoming the economic difficulties that emerged during the societal restructuring that accompanied the democratization process (Neubauer 1967).

The dominant argument of modernization theory is that since the industrial and post-industrial revolution, the modern development of countries is expressed by expanding urbanization and industrialization, an increase in GNP, societal prosperity, and a broader income distribution (e.g., Bollen & Appold 1993; Boswell & Peters 1989; Inglehart & Welzel 2005). With these developments, the level of societies' education, literacy and media technology advance all facilitate the formation of *a middle class* of intellectuals and educated professionals. The expanding middle class challenges groups that hold social and political power, demanding civil rights and inclusion in political decision-making (Maravall & Santamaria 1986; Markoff 1996; McAdam 1988; Moore 1966, Porter & Alexander 1961; Stephens 1989) which leads to the development of inclusive government and decision-making systems that characterize democracy. Also, traditional agrarian societies (except for the free farmers' economy) are too constrained to develop diverse social classes and essentially are outside the possible adoption of democracy (Crenshaw 1995, expanding the argument of Russett 1964). Proto-modernity has determining effects, as a modern market economy becomes one of the favorable conditions for the creation of democratic institutions (Dahl 2000).

Also, democracies, in contrast to undemocratic governments, offer advantages in terms of economic and other resources to a large share of the population and create systems of extraction and allocation that are publically controllable. Therefore distribution of privileges and resources is broader and more equal, as it includes vulnerable population (Tilly 2007, pp. 106–133). The resulting undisturbed increase in the standard of living prevents the growth of anti-democratic political opposition that potentially could abolish nascent democratic reforms (Burton, Gunther, & Higley 1992, Sawa-Czajka 2010). On the other hand, lack of, or delayed, increase in the standard of living detracts from democracy, facilitating grounds to establish or to strengthen non-democratic regimes; such a process occurred in Belorussia two years after the initiation of democracy in 1991 (US Department of State 2010).

Once modernization and development is set in motion, it penetrates all aspects of life, bringing specialization in occupations, rapid economic growth, and rising education levels and life expectancy. It transforms social life and political institutions, intensifying mass participation in politics. It also gives direction to societal differentiation and specialization, allowing for a separation of the political system (e.g., governing institutions) from other social systems (such as the economy and religious institutions), which creates societies that are ready to proceed to democratization (Dahl 2000, Tilly 2007). Societies in which religion is not separated from politics can rarely institute democracy; e.g., this category would include Muslim states and Orthodox Christian or Judaism-based states. To be sustained, democracy requires the separation of religion from politics (Lipset 1994). As a result, many Middle Eastern countries are undemocratic, since the religious freedom, human rights, and economic and political openness towards the Western democracies and democratic principles do not exist in these countries, and are not understood in them (Coleman & Wittes 2008, Mayer 2007).

Modernization affects not only economic spheres, but also societal culture. As Lipset states, "capitalism has been a necessary, but not a sufficient, condition" for democracy (1994:1). Cultural factors appear to be even more important than economic ones. Also, development is conducive to democracy because an educated and articulate society becomes accustomed to independent thinking. Modernization then brings social and cultural changes: changes in the societal lifestyles that transform people's values and motivations (Inglehart & Welzel, 2005). Among these conditions are individual autonomy, self-expression and belief in individuality, freedom of choice that leads to growing emancipation from authority, and emphasis on self-expression that spills over into the political realm. The new belief system makes people more trusting, tolerant and willing to actively participate in decision-making (Tilly 2005). Citizens actively participating in politics require transparency and accountability from the ruling elite, which prevents corruption (Deudney & Ikenberry 2009) and augments trust in and legitimacy of government that is necessary for establishing a successful and sustainable democracy (Tilly 2007). Participating citizens also demand a mechanism to sufficiently protect social minorities from the rule and infringement of the majority (Dahl 2000; Lipset 1993), further building societal trust and legitimacy of democratic government (Tilly 2005). Cultural changes add to the emergence and prospect of democratic institutions and societies with the discussed characteristics. Overall, economic development generates sociopolitical, social and cultural transformations that are conducive to democracy. Concluding the discourse, some authors have believed that democracy is the only route to countries' modernization and sustainable development (Fukuyama 2004; Mandelbaum 2004, 2008).

Critique of the modernization framework: why economic growth and modernization does not always lead to development of democracy

The question remains, whether modern development is the only route to the establishment of democratic rule and whether economic development leads to development of democratic system. Of course, there are limits or exceptions to the power and influence of socioeconomic development and modernization on democratic growth. For instance, Przeworski & Limongi (1993) and Przeworski (1997) believed that economic prosperity could not only lead to stability of democratic regimes, but to sustainability of any political regime, including undemocratic rule that prevents democratic development. A similar perspective was shared by other scholars (Przeworski et al. 1996). Hence, socioeconomic development affects democratization, as well as the growth of non-democratic systems.

Following the same logic, others argue that the stability and sustainability of new democracies are contingent upon the level of economic development preceding the initiation of democratization processes (Przeworski & Curvale 2006). The more developed countries of Eastern Europe sustained democratic processes, while the less-developed reverted to authoritarian regimes, e.g., Belorussia (US Department of State 2010), Russia (Hersbring 2003; Politkovskaya 2007) or Albania (World Bank 2011). Similarly, Latin American states embraced democracy in principle; but in practice, the democratic system quickly become unsustainable and easily reverted to low-level or non-democratic status (Przeworski 2009). Another highly respected argument is that economic growth does not necessarily lead to democratic transition or the *onset* of democracy, but relates to democratic stability (Przeworski & Limongi 1997; Przeworski et al. 2000). A typical example is a major world power – China, that never in its glorious history was democratic and it does not look as if it will democratize any time soon. Although some scholars citing the Chinese public opinion polls argue that political rule is legitimate in China hence the country is not authoritarian (Bo 2010), the questionable and non-existent freedom of press and expression, and questionable human rights, distort the positive portrayal of the evolvement of a supposedly unique Chinese democracy that is different from any Western democracy.

Other scholars have also raised concerns regarding the uniformity of social and cultural changes that stem from modernization, believing that changes do not follow a linear process but rather follow phases. The industrialization phase is associated with secularization, bureaucratization and development of rational values, while post-industrialization is associated with an emphasis on individual autonomy and values of self-expression leading to emancipation from authority (Deudney & Ikenberry 2009; Inglehart & Welzel, 2005). We can hence conclude that modernization advances social and cultural changes during industrialization and post-industrialization alike and, in turn, helps democracy to develop and prosper; but the development of culture that secures sustainable democratic development is more characteristic of the post-industrialization period.

Modern development is synonymous with individual choice, e.g., the science industry that is needed for modern economic development is formed and facilitated by freedom of individual thinking. Therefore a country without democratic regimes does not guarantee that freedom of choice, and could be destined to inhibit progression of economic growth (Inglehart & Welzel 2009). Furthermore, without freedom of individual thinking, societies are driven by internal contradiction between the freedom of development and politically constrained lack of freedom of choice and prohibition of individualism in decision-making. Such countries are at risk of instability and failure of the existing political system (Mandelbaum 2008). As was concluded, although it is unrealistic to assume that democratic institutions can be established anywhere in the world and in any preceding conditions, progress toward modernization inevitably leads to democratization and it is only a matter of time before a modernizing country will eventually become democratic (Inglehart & Welzel 2009). The contemporary regimes of China and Russia "will not be viable for a long time" (Deudney & Ikenberry 2009). Although the prior argument is contradicted by some researchers (Bo 2010) inevitably the journey to establishing sustainable democracy is long and difficult, as it requires building the legitimacy of the ruling elite, the emergence of a set of beliefs in freedom, tolerance, and independence, and a separation of religion from political decision-making.

Nonetheless, not all scholars and policymakers are firm believers in the theory that economic growth – and especially a global, free market economy – can enhance development of a democratic system. Gat et al. (2009), for instance, argue that market-oriented democracies are overwhelmed by contradictions between the economic inequality generated by capitalism and democratic egalitarianism. The irreconcilable discrepancy stimulates tension within democratic societies that will diminish the power of democracies and ensure their eventual replacement by undemocratic states. Even welfare programs introduced in some democratic capitalistic countries will not reconcile these differences, allowing for the exacerbation of tensions and anti-democratic protests that eventually will weaken or destroy democratic systems.

Furthermore, debating recent worldwide economic crisis, Azar Gat and others have argued that non-democratic countries develop a stronger economy and their GDP growth rate is faster than that of democratic states; therefore, the path toward worldwide democracy will soon revert to authoritarian revival (Gat et al. 2009, Kagan 2008). To document this position, Gat et al. indicated that the recent decline in the growth of the GDP in the United States symbolizes the decline of its economic influence and power (2009). This argument was echoed by scholars analyzing the recent wave of economic interventions by the state in democratic and non-democratic countries alike. Accordingly, they indicated that long-term control of the economy by the state jeopardizes the separation of the economy from the political system and, in turn, eliminates the preconditions instrumental to the development and stability of democracy (Bremmer 2009; Bremmer & Keat, 2009). The political and economic dominance of democratic states (like the United States) will eventually diminish, being suppressed or substituted by the economic and political power of authoritarianism. Contrasting arguments take into account government spending on development, education, science and technology, and the military. According to such a point of view the lineal interpretation of the impact of GDP growth on a country's world influence is unreliable because a country's power is defined by multiple and complex indicators (Joffe 2007). Accordingly, the United States with enlarging education and welfare spending still holds a position of unmatched economic power in the world (Joffe 2007). The United States also asserts its world political domination by

contributing to world security and leadership in international negotiations (Joffe 2009), but to hold its influence, the United States needs to
counter-balance the Sino-Muslim influence on world affairs and align
with Western democracies (Saban Center at Brookings 2008).

Furthermore, the minimal spending by non-democratic states on the
knowledge industry, the military, university input, research and development, social security, and health benefits will require an increase in
government spending that most likely will slow present economic
growth (Joffe 1999). Since investment in social benefits cannot be
postponed because it would generate social conflict that could lead to
democratic transitions, the possibility of imminent world dominance
by a non-democratic regime is, at best, limited (Joffe 2007, 2009).

Will Putin's Russia be a good example of such potential development? Just as in the former communist period, Russia's recent dependency of economy on political institutions and constrained societal
freedom, with privileged positions for members of authoritarian structures, allowed for a retreat from democracy to totalitarianism
(Politkovskaya 2007). A weak democracy was easy to change into a
non-democratic system at a time of economic hardship associated with
the restructuring of the economy into a market system. Authoritarian
rule by promising better economic conditions was initially broadly
approved and accepted by society (Fish 2005). It is however questionable whether Russian's economic development formed on the basis of
GDP generated by the petroleum industry will continue for long, in
face of the rapidly increasing development of sources of alternative
energy. Lack of political freedoms combined with enlarging economic
inequalities between the members of the political system and workers
has already led to numerous protests that are controlled by terror and
injustice. Understanding the history of the political development of this
region, the short-term taste of democratic rule in the 1990s most
probably will lead to large-scale unrest of the working masses deprived
of human rights and economic stability. The history of contemporary
Russia might repeat the situation in the Middle Eastern countries in
2011, where the abolition of undemocratic rule by desperate masses of
protesters risking life, imprisonment, and torture for democratic causes
was a common phenomenon (e.g, the case of Libya in 2011).

Finally critics of the "modernization" approach have questioned the
influence of the global market economy and foreign multinational
corporations that are supposed to enhance modernization and lead to

the development of democracy in developing states. Accordingly, scholars analyzing cases of Latin American countries observed that to protect their own economic gains, foreign multinational corporations harm potential democratization by supporting autocratic rulers who suppress democratic upheaval and individual rights (Huntington 2011; Kolodko 2011; Rueschemeyer, Stephens, & Stephens 1992). Przeworski and others support this, though showing that prosperous development equally leads to the stability of democratic as well as non-democratic regimes (Przeworski et al. 2000).

The power of an authoritarian regime to withstand democratization was documented much earlier by Skocpol (1979). She showed that in the agrarian aristocracies of China, Russia, and France, landowners were too provincial to introduce democratic reforms, regardless of pro-democracy international economic and military pressure. Similarly, in many contemporary developing countries, autocratic rulers stay in power and inhibit internal pro-democratic dissention. Autocratic leadership gains public support because it is able to exert control over the influence of multinational corporations, whereas democratic governments are too weak to wield such control (Chirot 1996). Autocratic regimes also increase their power by effectively stimulating economic growth by announcing the prospect of warfare. In this situation, autocratic rulers gain societal support by military spending that increases development and enlarges the work force, promising better living conditions; e.g., the pre-World War II history of Europe.

World system and dependency framework

The world-system theory presents an enhanced critique of the modernization approach. Its central argument is that on the world scale, the increase of a country's urbanization and industrialization stems in part from the country's historically determined position in the world system (Wallerstein 1974).

Arguing for countries' historically determined geo-positioning in a global economy of the world system, scholars representing this approach categorized countries as core (affluent), a category that includes former colonial powers and the countries of Western Europe, the United States, Canada, and countries of the British Commonwealth including Australia and New Zealand; semi-peripheral (semi-affluent), which includes countries that are approaching the status of well-developed states, but are at the developmental level of middle economies; and peripheral (marginal), including under-developed states, many of which are former colonies. The semi-peripheral and peripheral countries are exploited economically by developed democratic states, which use their raw material through the means of market. Consequently, the semi-peripheral and peripheral countries develop more slowly, are dependent on developed countries, and are disadvantaged in world trade. This dependent economic position limits and slows modernization and economic development (Bollen 1983; Snyder & Kick 1979). Consequently, delayed or minimal modernization that leads to economic disadvantages in the world trade system contains democratization processes in peripheral or semi-peripheral countries, significantly lowering the acceptance of democracy, as well as the level and rate of democratic growth (Wallerstein 2001).

Moreover, limited and stagnant modernization correlates with inefficiency, unprofessional business management, deters market competition and prevents progression toward democratization. It also constrains the likelihood of a country's acceptance of the democratic system. Such conditions are common phenomena in the state-controlled market economy of less-developed countries.

Not all researchers, however, are convinced that its world-system position conditions a country's development or democratization. For instance, Bollen (1983) states that a peripheral position – and to a lesser extent semi-peripheral position – depressed the level of political democracy. However, Bollen & Appold (1993) believe that position in the world system has little direct effect, per se, on the structure of industrialization and, in turn, on democratic growth, in spite of the advantages of trade. Undemocratic states are known for limited participation in a global free market, growing poorer and less advanced than those democratic states participating in global trade. Even if overall development is highly advanced, as in the case of China, social inequality in those states is also much higher (Fukuyama & McFaul 2007), but social inequality also threatens liberal democracies (Fukuyama 2012). Increasing poverty and social inequality may eventually contribute to societal tensions, and may generate pro-democracy demands and the abolition of an authoritarian system (Inglehart & Welzel 2009, Politkovskaya 2007). In less-developed countries, democratic processes could be challenged by the rebirth of totalitarianism and a state-controlled economy, such as was the recent case of Belorussia (Wejnert 2010).

Critique of the world-system framework: why the world-positioning of countries does not affect development of democracy

The evidence regarding the effects on democracy of countries' positions in the world system is mixed. Any negative influence of the structure of the world system on democratization of peripheral and semi-peripheral countries is balanced by positive effects. For instance, the development of Latin America strongly relied on foreign loans and so stagnated during the world oil crisis. Economic problems generated distress in a society disappointed with the ruling elite, eventually leading to a transition from non-democratic to democratic systems in Latin America during the 1980s (e.g., Rueschmeyer, Stephens, & Stephens, 1992; Stephens 1989; Higley & Gunther 1992; Huntington 2011; O'Donnell, Schmitter, & Whitehead 1996).

Other critics of the world-system framework have noted that democracy is effective only when political officials respect law and are ruled by law. In less-developed states, regardless of the political system, the ruling elite is known for disregarding the law (Fish 2005), and is riddled by corruption and cronyism (Madaha & Wejnert 2011) that inhibits economic growth and limits the possibility of becoming an economic power (Deudney & Ikenberry 2009). It is not the semi-peripheral or peripheral position that contributes to limited democratization but disrespect for law and an ill-functioning system of societal control combined with lack of a control mechanism to restrain corrupt members of political governance that limits countries' development and in turn the development of democracy (Wejnert 2002d).

Considering these existing critiques, why has the world-system theory become so powerful and influential? As some have argued, the justification, rationale and popularity of the dependency theory in part relates to its popularity among authoritarian leaders who conveniently use the theory to redirect the blame for poverty caused by corruption to the geo-historical structure of the world system (Joffe 2009).[1] Others believe the world-system approach was essential to the development of neocolonial theory and an application of Marxism to international

---

[1] Polemically, Gat presented examples of two non-democratic counties (Prussia and Singapore) with a ruling elite respecting law and not being corrupted. Expectedly, these countries were also economically prosperous (Gat et al. 2009).

relations (Wallerstein 2001, Lord & Harris 2006). Regardless of the rationale, the world-system framework designed earlier by Wallerstein (1998) and others as an explanation for the underdeveloped south (the underdeveloped countries of Africa, Latin America, and Asia) in comparison to the well-developed North of Western European and North American countries, still presents a valid used up-to-date explanation of unequal world development and world-wide democratization.

The class conflict framework and its critics

The next perspective represents a *class-conflict* approach to democratization. According to Rueschemeyer, Stephens, & Stephens (1992) capitalist development is associated with democracy because it transforms class structure – strengthening the middle and working classes while weakening the landed upper class. The contradiction of interests between classes raises class conflict and advances the cause of democracy. To overcome the power of the ruling elite, workers and intellectuals, often in partnership with capitalists, organize political movements aimed at abolishing authoritarian regimes; for instance, such political movements were organized in Latin America (Przeworski 2009); in Eastern Central Europe against communist, autocratic rulers (Herspring 2003, Przeworski 2010, Wejnert 2002c, 2010), and in re-democratizing countries of sub-Saharan Africa (Kapstein & Converse 2008). Newly rich capitalists also use other methods than protest mechanisms to win this struggle for power. To challenge the ruling elite, they may merge with foreign capital, creating interrelated, multi-country economic production (Kolodko 2011, Maravall & Santamaria 1986; Huntington 2011). This broad and complex global economy is more difficult for authoritarian regimes to control and, as conflict over political power escalates, ruling regimes are forced to accept democracy (Herspring 2003; Schwartzman 1998, 167; Tilly 2005).

The enlarged middle class, in addition to challenging the established political status quo, also develops laws that facilitate public participation in governing (Somers 1993, Tilly 2007). Consequently, political culture forms on democratic principles, rules of law and social trust (Tilly 2005), with the middle class as the principle carrier of democratic values (Dahl 2000; Lipset 1960, Sawa-Czajka 2010). Summarizing, as analyses attest, the increase of urbanization and industrialization stimulates development of the social classes of intellectuals and workers that are supportive of democratic principles (Huntington 2011, Kolodko 2011). Those classes challenge the established social groups, demanding inclusion in political decision making and civil rights (Moore 1966, Sawa-Czajka 2010, Stephens 1989). As a result, a political culture based on democratic principles evolves.

Democratization is an outcome of high levels of economic development, the formation of new classes and institutions, and new cultural values that accompany industrialization. Pluralistic social structures become economically and socially interdependent, fostering competition for political power and pushing the ruling elite to adopt civil and political rights (Crenshaw 1995). Political involvement, coupled with the enlargement of a middle class of educated professionals, enhances individuality and the request for freedom of choice stimulating emergence of a societal culture compatible with democratic principles (Inglehart & Welzel 2005). Class conflict thus in part generates the establishment of a democratic culture supporting societal aspirations for political inclusion and respect for human rights and individual values.

In contrast, to the world-system framework that stressed conflict between social groups, rather than competition, while also recognizing the importance of industrialization, the ruling elite within countries, or dominant countries within a world system, were seen as using economic or political pressure and violence to preserve their power. At the same time, powerless countries or deprived social groups also used pressure to gain political and economic influence. As a result, a struggle for power dominated relationships within economic and social structures of countries (Moore 1966, Stephens 1989). Conflict between classes became an inevitable part of the democratization processes.

Thus, while focusing on means of action of conflict in the world-system and conflict frameworks versus competition in modernization frameworks, all presented explanations agreed that socioeconomic forces are the underlying impetuses for establishing democratic rights and rules of governing.

Summary of theoretical frameworks

Regardless of differences in assessment and explanations of democratization as caused by modernization, or class conflict, or countries' positioning in the world-system, scholars were able to reach the consensus that democratization, regardless of often being considered to be the best political system of the world that exists (Fukuyama 1992, Fukuyama & McFaul 2007) has not reached its end point (Gat et al. 2009, Dahl 2000). Summarizing the presented theoretical approaches we also need to agree that a level of sustainable democratic stability is rarely obtained from the moment of institution of democracy, because the process of democratization is prolonged and it takes enormous human, economic and political resources to build sustainable democracy. Western European democracies, as well as the democratic system in the United States, are vivid examples of the protracted and problematic history of the development and growth of democracy (Schmidt 2006).

This study explores two alternative understandings of democracy's development generated by the theoretical frameworks applied to analyzed democracy growth: (a) frameworks emphasizing external influences on countries, which could be named diffusion factors and may apply independently of the sociopolitical, endogenous process of a country, and (b) frameworks that focus on a country's characteristics, such as its politics, socioeconomic factors, or culture, that could be named development factors. In fact, the very nature of the clustered and recently remarkably rapid spread of democratization (Huntington 1997, Wejnert 2005), raises the possibility that perhaps the effect of the socioeconomic conditions specific to each country may be enhanced by *diffusion* processes that contribute to democratization, as "diffusion, contagion, or demonstration effects seem operative" (Lipset 1994:16).

Frameworks focusing on diffusion factors

The presented empirical and theoretical research on democracy suggests analysis of clusters of major factors determining the adoption and temporal rate of democratization that may apply independently of the sociopolitical processes of a country and refer to *diffusion factors*.

The study of diffusion began with Tarde's 1903 book on *The Laws of Imitation*; however, a more concerted development of this approach did not occur until forty years later, when Ryan and Gross (1943) published results on the spread of hybrid corn use among Iowa farmers. Since that study's publication, more than 4,000 research papers have appeared on the diffusion of such diverse endeavors as agricultural practices (Fliegel 1993), new technologies (Burt 1987; Coleman, Katz, & Menzel 1966; Palmer, Jennings, & Zhou 1993), fertility control methods (Rogers & Kincaid 1981; Rosero-Bixby & Casterline 1994), policy innovations (Berry & Berry 1992; Boli-Bennett & Ramirez 1987; Valente 1995), and political reforms (Meyer 1987; Starr 1991). Analyses of the respective sets of diffusion variables are associated with different concepts and methods involving diverse processes, principles, and determinants of diffusion. Consequently, the literature associated with each of these factors often tends to analyze diffusion in isolation from the insights of the others (exceptions include Rogers [1962, 1995] and Strang & Soule [1998]).

As a means of correcting this situation, this chapter examines how diverse concepts, variables, and processes related to diffusion can be integrated to give information about the impact of diffusion on countries' democratic growth. Since the goal is to establish a conceptual framework of variables influencing diffusion, rather than to provide an exhaustive review of the literature associated with each variable, the discussion focuses on the nature of each variable and its importance to the process of democratization, and not on every detail of its effects. Moreover, because democracy processes are different for individual countries and for collective entities within which countries operate (e.g., political organizations, political/economic blocs of countries, or regional clusters of countries), the different nature of diffusion involved in democracy processes that depend on these distinctions is noted throughout.

Generally, diffusion indicates the spread of a practice within a social system, where the spread denotes flow or movement from a source to an adopter typically via communication, role modeling, and/or coercion. Mechanisms of diffusion are frequently employed to analyze social changes characterized by temporal processes (Meyer & Rowan 1977; Rogers 1995; Rogers & Shoemaker 1971; Thomas et al. 1987).

Remarkably, the impact of diffusion on change towards democracy has been rarely tested. Some exceptions are: an empirical study on the effect of neighboring democracies on non-democratic countries (O'Loughlin et al. 1998); work on the imposition of democracy on colonial or economic dependencies (Crenshaw 1995; Bollen & Jackman 1985a); and the influence of modern media on the recent spread of democracy (Gunther and Mughan 2000). Some scholars have discussed the potential relevance of diffusion processes to democratization; for example, Przeworski and Limongi (1997) argued that international conditions predict the survival of a democratic regime better than does the level of socioeconomic development,[2] and Whitehead's (1996) findings attested that the vast majority of countries did not generate democracy through independent innovation.

Moreover, few empirical studies on democracy assessed a single variable that could indicate diffusion processes. Among those few are studies on the imposition of democracy on colonial dependencies by colonial empires (Crenshaw 1995; Bollen & Jackman 1985a), influence of modern media (Gunter and Mughan 2000), and structurally equivalent socioeconomic characteristics of countries (Huntington 1992). To some degree, the understanding of diffusion was enriched by studies focusing on the introduction of the diffusion concept to analyses of democratic movements (Tarrow 1989, 1998) and by longitudinal assessments of democracy's growth in the world (e.g., Huntington 1992; O'Loughlin et al. 1998). Furthermore, Wejnert (2005) empirically tested the predictive power of *development* versus *diffusion* variables on countries' democratization and showed a stronger impact of diffusion on democratic growth than variables referring to countries' development.

Following Dahl (1989), this study suggests that although "diffusion cannot provide the whole explanation of the expansion of democracy, it probably significantly accounted for the diffusion of democratic ideas and practices" (Dahl 1989, 9). Consequently this study provides a comprehensive, conceptual framework of variables contributing to processes of diffusion of democracy. This framework summarizes, categorizes, and organizes diffusion variables derived in prior studies, and offers a conceptual guide to the ongoing discussion of exogenous influences on countries' democratization that may operate as diffusion.

First, a major set of factors that have been largely neglected in empirical studies on democracy are *communication modes* reflecting democracy's outcomes and determinants of communication about democracy. Among them are cost and benefits, countries' networks, density and proximity of democratic countries to non-democracies,

---

[2] Przeworski and Limongi (1997), however, did not statistically distinguish different mechanisms by which the international climate is transmitted to particular countries. They also did not assess the predictive power of the international climate relative to the socioeconomic conditions of a country, which this chapter focuses on.

and the impact of media on the spread of information about democratic principles and goals. Mechanisms of networks, spatial density, and media have been applied to many different phenomena characterized by temporal processes, but to only a few studies on the trajectory and rate of democracy's development. Second are *regional characteristics* affecting democratic changes, among them distinct political, socio-demographic, economic, and geographic conditions of regions that may control: (a) the susceptibility of countries to democratic transition, (b) openness toward acceptance of democracy as political system, and (c) countries' rate of democratic growth. Third are major *historical events* that alter the rate of countries' economic development, promoting or discouraging the growth of democracy. Finally, fourth and fifth are factors that reflect the *global uniformity* of the world, including institutionalization, cultural Westernization, and the *environmental context*. These factors incorporate processes that modulate democratic growth via the structural characteristics of the modern global world.

Communication modes

As the literature suggests, strongly relevant predictors of countries' democratization are factors denoting communication channels, external promotion of models of democracy, and facilitators and barriers to the spread of democracy. Examples of studies on democracy that discuss variables indicating these predictors include discourses on the influence of international networks on the democratization of their members, for instance the European Union on countries opting for inclusion (Sawa-Czajka 2010; Kolodko 2011); the imposition of democratic practices by colonial powers on former colonies (Bollen & Jackman 1985b); and analyses addressing the adoption of democratic principles as a condition for receiving financial aid (Fukuyama & McFaul 2007; Karatnycky 1997). These factors are potential sources of the spread of democratic ideas, especially in affecting the democratization of countries that developed during the post-industrial era (Gunther & Mughan 2000).

Accordingly, I propose to name these indicators the *communication mode* of diffusion and categorize them as: (a) *barriers to communication* deterring or promoting the spread of democracy; (b) *communication channels* (coercion, network connectedness and horizontal/vertical channels); and (c) *media*. When considering democratic processes I thus derive the conceptual framework by grouping variables of communication modes into three major components, depicted according to:

(1) barriers to communication: democracy's public versus private consequences; benefits versus costs;
(2) communication channels;
(3) media.

Each component offers a different lens for understanding how variables influence a country's decision to accept and sustain a democratic system. The first of these components is associated with the characteristics of democracy, which encompasses two sets of variables, public versus private consequences of democracy and benefits versus costs of democratic transition. The second component involves characteristics of countries that influence the acceptance and sustainability of democracy, i.e., characteristics of countries relative to communication about democracy, called here communication channels, and incorporates three sets of variables: hegemonic imposition, network connectedness, and horizontal/vertical channels of communication. Each of these sets of variables is associated with sub-variables described in the text. And the third component refers to the global spread of media communication with its delineated sets of sub-variables introduced in the text.

Barriers to communication

While most analyses of diffusion have emphasized countries and their perceptions of democracy, along with variables of environmental context influencing the democratization process, relatively few scholars have studied the barriers to democracy's adoption relating to the nature of the democratic process per se as determinants of democracy's diffusion. In the available literature on the diffusion of various innovations, authors have most commonly considered two factors associated with diffusing entities that are applicable to studies on diffusion of the democratic system: public vs private consequences (e.g., Meyer & Rowan 1977; Strang & Meyer 1993), and benefits versus costs (Greve 1998).

Public vs *private* consequences refers to the impact of democratization on entities other than the individual person as a citizen of a country (public consequences) versus the individual person themself (private consequences). When democracy results in public consequences, it involves collective actors – countries, states within countries, countries' institutions, and organizations including global international organizations, such as the United Nations – mostly concerned with general issues of rights, societal well-being, justice, equality, and the like. Among the processes involved in countries' democratization are the adaptation of political models of governing (Uhlin 1995; Wejnert 2001a), welfare and education policies (Thomas & Lauderdale 1987) and state laws (Berry and Berry 1992). Public consequences concern macro-goals of democracy and refer to broad, often historical, issues, appealing to and engaging a broad audience, and leading to reforms that are historical breakthroughs, such as laws protecting civil rights, patent laws, global concern for human rights, or international regulations protecting the natural environment. Such studies, for example, address involvement of the international community in the issue of decolonization (Strang 1990), worldwide promotion of democracy (Fukuyama & McFaul 2007), and concerns about global warming (Gore 2009).

Private consequences are reflected by the micro-goals of democracy that focus on the needs of an individual person, such as improvement of standards of living, improvement of health, or enhancement of the social position of a person. Micro-goals therefore affect the well-being of individual citizens of a particular state. These goals intend to improve the quality of individual lives or reform organizational and social structures of which individuals are a part. Examples include welfare policy (Karger & Stoesz 2009), access to new medical practices, or management styles and new technologies (Oakley, Hare, & Balazs 1992; Palmer, Jennings, & Zhou 1993).

Although both types of consequences of democracy result in societal changes, the manner of channeling information from a democracy source (a country that is a precursor of democracy or a democracy model) to a country considering democracy adoption differs depending upon the democracy's consequences. The importance of this distinction lies in the fact that different mechanisms of interaction between the model of democracy and a potential adopter country result in diffusion processes that differ in nature. Democracy's characteristics with public consequences are mainly adopted when information and imitative models are uniformly distributed around the world. This process is most effective when norms, values, or expectations about certain forms or practices become deeply ingrained in society – institutionalized – and reflect widespread and shared understandings of social reality (Meyer & Rowan 1977, 343), as, for example, was the case with the rapid spread of mass education, social security systems, and models of nation-states among the world's political states (Thomas et al. 1987).

Media has a strong influence on goals with public consequences (Gunther & Mughan 2000). Media becomes a channel of influence on democracy primarily when the concerns are target-like, well-defined societal issues. For example, Strodthoff, Hawkins, and Schoenfeld (1985), in a study on the diffusion of ideology in environmental movements, argued that the media covered information about the movements only after their goals had become well-established public concerns. In this respect, media effects support the role of broadly accepted behavioral patterns called institutionalization, spreading information about those institutionalized practices that captivate public interest. As Uhlin (1995) argued in his study on the diffusion of democracy models, media is effective in providing information about democracy models with public consequences, but the persuasive role in the adoption of democracy is country-to-country interaction. It seems, however, that there would be limited international interest in the adoption of democracy if the democracy models were not institutionalized, meaning broadly approved (the next section of this book explains the notion of institutionalization in a greater detail).

As other studies suggest, the spread of democracy pertaining to private and public consequences occurs largely due to spatial and temporal contiguity between a source of democracy's model and a country which is a potential adopter. A few effects are particularly substantial here: *spatial effects*, such as geographic proximity; *interpersonal communication*, institutional or individual coercion; and the pressure of *social networks*. For instance, studies argue that close relationships and strong ties between government members of two distinct countries (formed when countries are members of the same networks) serve a socialization-like role, familiarizing governments with democratic principles (Davis 1991; Lord & Harris 2006). Of course no factor affects the democracy process in a vacuum, without interaction with other factors. As this study suggests, there is a vast web of interactions between the effects of the public/private consequences of democracy and the various processes of communication and worldwide global unity, and these processes are delineated in the next sections of this chapter.

There are many cases where the consequences of democracy are not so dichotomous because in practice, many democratic changes simultaneously reflect direct (*manifested* function) and indirect (*latent* function) consequences. For instance, while the adoption of fertility control methods by Korean village women resulted in the private consequences of reduced family size, it also promoted the democratization process of building civil society through the organization of a women's movement that influenced national policies and led to the adoption of less traditional gender roles, reduction of violence against women, and enforcement of human rights (public societal consequences) (Rogers & Kincaid 1981).

Evaluation of *benefits* vs *costs* of adoption of democracy involves consideration of risks or costs that should be expected by countries–potential adopters, since the process of transition to democracy inevitably involves a restructuring of the political system, which may include the education of the political cadre about principles of democratic governance, establishment of a voting process, establishment of new political institutions and organizations, and/or passing amendments to constitutions. Such risks relate to the possibility of harm governed by more or less known probable outcomes of democracy (Douglas 1985). Since adoption of democracy is often associated with some degree of risk (Brown et al. 1992), countries are likely motivated to reduce uncertainty by gathering "innovation-evaluation information" (Rogers, 1995, 168) and generally estimate the acceptability of certain levels of risk within the framework of a safety principle (Douglas & Wildavsky 1982; Kahneman & Tversky 2003a). In judging risk, countries must estimate the similarity between the current *expected* outcome of their action and an ideal outcome they believe to be associated with democracy on the basis of the external sources of information defining its nature. The variable of risk is often treated as a component of the probability of achieving the expected outcomes, either private, public, or both, of the adoption of democracy (Wejnert 2010), and countries appear to combine the costs and benefits of democracy in judging the degree of reward associated with acceptance and development of democracy (DeSoto & Anderson 1993).

Cost variables relate to monetary and non-monetary *direct* and *indirect costs* or risks associated with the adoption of democracy. Direct costs, or financial uncertainties, are typically clear and are relative to the economic situation of a country. These include such costs as the reform of social policies or institutions, reorganization of government, restructuring of the economy, reorganization of the voting system, implementation of public safety practices, and secure social equality (Bakardjiva 1992; Gore 2009; Kapstein & Converse 2009; Tilly 2007, 117).

While *indirect costs* are not often clearly identifiable as outcomes of democracy, they can add markedly to the cost or risk of democratization, and can significantly modulate the rate of democracy's growth. Modifying governing styles needed to enact democracy includes, for example, an indirect cost of restructuring the government (Herspring 2003) and organization of the voting system (Fish 2005). Indirect costs may also be non-monetary, called "technical uncertainty" by Gerwin (1988), such as time spent on retraining volunteers who check voters' registration or help during voting (Gill & Markwick 2000). These costs are especially onerous for new democracies in developing countries, relative to their current direct costs of political governing.

Another form of indirect costs has to do with *social costs* related to the outcome of the adoption of democracy and its growth, called "social uncertainty" by Dewar and Dutton (1986). One example of social cost is democracy-induced social conflict, as with unions organizing workers to oppose labor-saving technology that reduces employment (Gerwin 1988; Kolodko 2000), societal opposition to tax laws (Berry & Berry 1992), or an outbreak of societal protests demanding higher salaries (Kolodko 2011).

Direct and indirect costs of democratic changes inhibit democracy adoption, especially when costs exceed a country's resource potential. As exemplified by analysis of the introduction of democratic freedom in Russia, the costs of economic restructuring led to a retreat from democracy to an authoritarian system (Herspring 2003), called by Politkovskaya (2007) a *fallen democracy*, because the introduction of a market economy system was unaffordable for an average citizen in this post-socialist country (Gill & Markwick 2000). Under such circumstances, society opted for a return to the assured outcomes of communism rather than the slow building of uncertain democracy.

Communication channels

Since the timing of the adoption of new ideas typically depends on the interaction of social units in a process of communication (Rogers 1995), a major focus in diffusion research has been on variables that mediate communication processes – including both the transmission and the absorption of information – between countries within societal macro-structures. Interactions can occur between individual countries, between countries and the media, or via international organizations. In this context I examine channels of communication reflecting a country's position in networks in relation to their interactions within three major spheres: (a) *hegemonic imposition/coercion*, (b) *network connectedness and openness*, and (c) *horizontal/vertical channels of communication*.

Hegemonic imposition

It would be impossible to understand globally spreading democratization without analysis of the character of communication between countries within networks of countries. For instance, across many cohesive networks, such as colonial networks, military pacts, or economic unions, hegemonic imposition of a democratic system by the democracies that are the economic powers is visible. At least across the past century, such was the influence of the British Empire on its colonial dependencies and the United States on recipients of its economic aid (Dahl 2000; Karatnycky 1995; Fukuyama & McFaul 2007). In the case of Great Britain, before granting independence Britain established democracy in its former colonies during the decolonization era (Bollen & Jackman 1985b; Crenshaw 1995). This regional coercion was frequently supported by economic aid when effecting democracy; e.g., post-colonial British dependencies in West Africa (Kapstein & Converse 2009, 39–46) seemed to be effected by coercion.

In contrast, other colonial powers, such as France, Portugal, Spain, Belgium, or The Netherlands, adopted a position of non-intervention and left their colonies ill prepared for democratic transition (Emerson 1960, 230–237; Theobold 1960, 37; Porter & Alexander 1961, 9–19). Hence, Fukuyama and McFaul (2007) argued that coercion and mimicry among democratic governments belonging to a mutual organization leads to isomorphism of the governments' practices.

Examples of networks that influence the temporal rate and trajectory of democratic growth also include coercive networks of strongly cohesive economic and/or political pacts. Many such networks demand the acceptance of democracy by all members that are sovereign and independent countries. This imposition of democracy includes international economic networks such as the European Union, the Nordic Council, and the Council of Asian Industrial Development. Similarly, the imposition of a political system occurs in military pacts when only stable or stabilizing democratic countries are able to be accepted, for example, in the recent incorporation of Eastern European countries into the North Atlantic Treaty Organization. This is a challenging condition for many newly democratizing countries of Eastern Central Europe (Wejnert 2005) that in their recent history have needed to accept the anti-democratic ideology of communism.

Similarly, but related to coercion to adopt anti-democratic principles, the Soviet Union imposed and controlled the implementation of a hostile-to-democracy, communist ideology throughout the entire bloc of countries – members of the highly integrated economic and political networks controlled by the Soviet Union in post-World War II Europe. For instance, membership in the Warsaw Pact required adoption of the communist system across all of its countries, many of which were formerly democratic (Havel 1985).

As studies have shown, highly centralized, stratified networks (such as colonial networks, communist networks, or the economic network of the European Union) use coercive pressure on their members to achieve conformity of democratic practices, causing homogeneity and modulating rates of democracy's adoption.

Countries' connectedness/openness

It is significant to notice that the channels of communication and influence on the growth of democracy within networks differ depending on the networks' structure (Wejnert 2002b). Two sets of variables that influence the impact of networks on individual countries have been defined. The first is *countries' connectedness* (i.e., closeness of communication between members). The second concerns characteristics of countries that influence *openness to novel information*.

The most significant *countries' connectedness* within a network variable predicting adoption are inversely related to network *size* (Schmidt 2006), but directly related to network *closeness*, measured as the number of friends and collaborating states each country has within the network (Starr 1991). Both variables – network connectedness and network closeness – reflect interactions between countries. In small, well-connected groups of countries, direct interactions between members of governments frequently account for the adoption of democracy. This impact appears to be related to the fact that adoption by some countries has a cumulative effect on the adoption decisions of other countries within the same international network, such that the number of adoptions of democracy follows an exponential progression until only avid opponents of adoption remain (Starr 1991). Thus, in many cases, adoption of democracy is better explained as a network-based decision, where exposure to new political ideology through a network of peers has a cumulatively increasing influence on a country's adoption, as pressure towards conformity builds and perceived costs or risks of negative outcomes of democracy decrease (Schmidt 2006). Important indicators of network connectedness are *frequency of interactions* between member countries, measured, for instance, by the rate of visits of a head of a country to other countries in a network, or the rate of meetings between representatives of members of a network. Closeness of connections is also determined by *openness of communication* within a network that refers to the level of privacy of shared information (Abdalla Salem El-Badri 2010).

The channels of influence on diffusion of democracy from a country's position in organizational, international networks can be viewed as twofold – *horizontal* and *vertical* communication channels – and are somewhat similar to those operating in interpersonal networks. One channel is *horizontal*, where upper-level integrative bodies of different but competing networks, like the the United Nations or NATO, influence the spread of democracy *across* regional networks such as the European Union. A second channel is *vertical*, where the flow of information is from upper-level executives down to members within a particular network. For instance, as Schmidt's (2006) studies of the political behavior of large European countries indicated, variables related to the degree of central structure and central authority of the European Union substantially enhanced the effectiveness of a *vertical* channel of influence on the democratization of Europe.

Within vertical and horizontal channels of influence, organizational networks can affect the rate of adoption of democracy via multiple effects. They can, for example, be *informative*, as when members learn of the principle of democracy (Herzog 2002); or *conductory*, facilitating contact with former democracies, such as in meetings with representatives of countries that have already adopted a democratic system (Kolodko 2011) or with groups of political scientists that developed a paradigm of democracy (Tilly 2007). Another kind of effect is *educational*, such as providing professional advice on new developments, workshops dedicated to democracy's promotion, publication of experts' opinions in newsletters, and discussions with academic consultants on the beneficial aspects of democracy (Dahl 2000). Still others are *coercive*, using explicit or implicit rewards or negative contingencies for producing conformity and compliance with respect to adoptive behavior (Schmidt 2006) (the coercive effects were discussed above); and *modeling*, providing standard, uniform models of *correct* decisions (Wejnert 2010). For example, high-status governments can affect adoption of desirable behaviors by individual citizens, such as when adoption of agricultural innovations by farmers in developing countries was induced by governmental policy intervention in the form of subsidies and financial credits to farmers who adopted innovative practices while withdrawing support from farmers who continued old practices.

Media effects

Finally, m*edia effects* are viewed by some authors as affecting the global spread of democracy. When convincingly presented with sufficient frequency, media exposure by itself has been associated with increased rates of democratization (Dahl 1989; Lipset 1994; Karatnycky 1995). With media exposure, the need for actors to interact directly to provide information about democracy is markedly reduced because modern communication promotes democracy, thereby acting as a major channel of communication in the diffusion of democracy process (Gunther & Mughan 2000; McColm 1990). For example, the increase in the growth of democracy in Bulgaria after the introduction of satellite antennas suggests that gained societal knowledge about the standard of living in Western European democracies provided additional incentives to create a sustainable democracy (Bakardjiva 1992).

Of course, media exposure interacts with the characteristics of countries and characteristics of social networks to influence adoption. Countries that are privileged in the world market have higher positions in the world system and, therefore, are more conducive to democratic growth; and, as the earliest adopters of democracy, they influence subsequent adoption by other countries (e.g., the more modernized countries of Eastern Europe, such as East Germany, Poland, the Czech Republic, and Hungary, democratized sooner and spread democratic principles) (Wejnert 2010). In well-developed countries, the adoption of new principles and ideology about the democratic political system is equally spread throughout a country, as in the case of the interactive influence of modernization and modern media influencing the spread of internet communication technology (Computer Aid International 2000). In contrast, countries with a lower position are more economically dependent and, hence, are later adopters of democratic models and are low-level democracies (Wallerstein 2001). In these countries, the spread of new media technology takes place mainly in urban areas, while rural, underdeveloped environments are relatively less exposed to the newest information technology.

Thus, the impact of media is also a sign of the level of modern development; therefore, the media indicator needs to be analyzed separately as a level of availability of media technology vs the level of access to media information. The number of modern media devices per capita in each country (i.e., the number of computers, TV sets, radios, or satellite antennas) could symbolize the availability of media that is highly related to the level of countries' modernization and partly related to diffusion. However, enhancing the spread of information about the democratic system would depend on public *access* to media information. This indicator could be determined by the interactive influence of other societal characteristics, such as the literacy rate, level of education, and urbanization of a particular country.

For instance, it is argued that computers require skills that are more easily learned by more highly educated people (Galbraith 2000), such as those who have completed secondary or tertiary school (Computer Aid International 2000). Thus, an illiterate population or a population without sufficient education would not be able to use computers and would be excluded from access to media. In other words, regardless of multiple information sources about democracy included on web pages, a person has to be able to use computers and navigate the internet to utilize existing information.[3]

---

[3] Moreover, adding computers to the skill kit for educated people raises the worth of the skill on the labor market (Galbraith 2000, 31). As Krueger (1991) calculated, computer skills added 10–15 percent of wage premium in the United States. The benefit of using computers to increase skills of workers has been recently recognized by many African countries that are trying to build a highly skilled, computer-literate labor force. With the help of international aid organizations, e.g., the European Computers for African Schools Project (CFAS) or Computer

Thus, when the interactive indicators of "literacy x computers"; "education x computers" are high, the access of the population is greater, whereas when the indicators are low, access is limited. The populations of regions where computers are not available would be partly excluded from social accessibility to spreading information about democracy.[4] Depending on the contextual situation, the media indicator could answer questions with the varied conceptual meanings of either social availability or social access to media. The meaning would measure development due to modernization or world-system position (depicted by social availability), or measure diffusion of democracy (depicted by social access).

A primary effect of media exposure is the dissemination of information about democracy directly to potential adopters, thereby acting as a major channel of communication in the diffusion process (Rogers 1995; Rogers & Shoemaker 1971). Democratic goals with public interest that diffuse in loosely connected, large organizational networks of countries, such as NATO or the European Union, may be predominantly influenced by primary media effects.

In a secondary effect, media information interacts with countries' networks, where some countries may actively select information and transmit it across a network of countries. The process of adoption of democracy appeared to involve media communications in interaction with countries' networks, and both factors seemed to complement and support each other, in promoting the spread of democracy across Eastern Europe (Sedaitis & Butterfield 1991). The classic example is the activity of the American network of the *Media and Democracy Coalition*, which aims especially to support first adopters that are initiators of democracy within a non-democratic network of countries. Citizens in initiator-countries affected by the media's primary effects often seek out communication channels to promote information retrieved from the media about democracy and its principles to a broader audience and to stimulate discussion about freedom of the press and telecommunication policies, further extending the impact of

Aid International, recycled computers are delivered to African schools, and post-educational training in computer operation is offered. The trained students, upon returning to their own communities, are in turn obligated to educate the local community in computer use (Computer Aid International 2000).

[4] In Swaziland, Africa, 90 percent of state high school graduates have never used or seen computers (Computer Aid International 2000).

primary effects. Similarly, the interaction of media with the sociopolitical characteristics of a country can significantly alter the potential effect of media on the diffusion of democracy. In countries with a political climate hostile to democracy, governing constituencies may ban access to certain media forms, as in the recent case of China closing access to the Google search engine.

In some analyses, the indicator of media is considered an indicator of technological advancement and thus an indicator of economic development (Lipset 1994), while in others it is one of the most powerful indicators of diffusion (Rogers 1995). This study measures societal access to media and thus societal exposure to information channeled via media, rather than the mere existence of media technology in a country. Following investigations on media as a channel of societal communication that promotes diffusion and studies on the positive effect of media on democratic growth, exposure to media information is treated as a mechanism of diffusion.

Framework of regional characteristics

The complex temporal nature of regional democratization suggests that country-specific influences may be modulated by factors that impact the democratization processes of a country via forces at work: (a) within the region in which a country resides, e.g., due to a close regional *proximity* or a high regional *density* of democratic countries relative to undemocratic countries, (b) within the region in interaction with a non-democratic country with structural equivalence to democratic countries, and (c) spreading waves of regional democratization.

A separate chapter is needed to discuss the rich literature on the specific regional characteristics that led to the adoption of democratic systems during various historical periods. Due to this book's focus on the portrayal of the trajectory of democratization across the world and across the world's regions, I will specify a few regional indicators that seem to be most relevant to worldwide democratic trends.

Some analysts have emphasized *regional spatial density* and *proximity* that stimulates greater frequency and intensity of contacts between non-democracies and democracies and, in turn, increases the likelihood of the acceptance of democracy. Extensions of this approach are analyses suggesting *structural equivalence* of countries within regions, or within regional networks, that facilitate greater role modeling of non-democracies on structurally similar democratic countries. Countries use spatial factors and structural equivalence (a) to avoid mistakes when adopting democracy by learning from the mistakes of prior adopters, and (b) to copy solutions to the problems of democratic development that have been tested by democratic countries. Other scholars indicate *regional waves of democratization* as a factor affecting democracy. These regional waves occur when transitions to democracy and democratic growth sweep across most or all countries of a region.

Consequently, when using literary sources one needs to notice that the temporal rate of democratization varies across regions: countries within regions democratize in clusters, and some regions democratize much sooner than others, depending on differences in historical development, socioeconomic growth, natural and economic resources, and a region's connection to the world's hegemonies. Patterns of regional democratization differ, from slow and randomly occurring in various parts of the region to temporally and spatially clustering within sectors of regions. Importantly, however, regional variance in the temporal rate of democratic growth affects worldwide democratization.

Regional spatial density and proximity

As argued by Tolnay (1995), the probability of the transmission of an idea from one country to another is enhanced by the density and proximity of democratic countries within a region. The effects of density of potential adopters are a function of geographical proximity or distance between social units, e.g., countries, and hence, spatial effects are best estimated as a joint function of distance and density. Extending the understanding of spatial proximity to *adoption potential* (measured as the *distance x density* of adoptions in interacting units), Tolnay (1995) estimated adoption rate in relation to adoption potential, where, when nonlinear, or linear with a slope not equal to unity, diffusion is assumed to have occurred.

Adopting Tolnay's (1995) findings, this study argues that the importance of proximity rests in its effect on the frequency of communication and the close nature of interactions between potential adopters, which enhance the spread of ideas and facilitate imitative behavior. In other words, the closer countries are to each other, the greater the number of possible linkages through which democracy can be promoted and spread. The effect of geographical (spatial) proximity is visible in cases of the adoption of policy reforms by countries or by large communities, such as adoption of municipal reform by American cities (Knoke 1982); new administrative programs and policies across American states (Walker 1969); state lotteries and innovative tax policies by neighboring American states (Berry & Berry 1992); and principles of democracy by countries located within the same geographical region in the world (Huntington 1992). Hedstrom (1994) assessed that geographic distance between centers of trade unions added velocity and frequency to labor strikes. Frequently, the effect of geographical proximity is visible in cases of the adoption of democratic principles by countries located within the same geographical region in the world (Huntington 1992), especially when these countries share cultural characteristics and are engaged in mutual capital flow and trade.

Thus, across the globe, the geographic as well as numeric expansion of democratic countries increases the capacity to observe and to model democratic states. Congruently, according to Rasler (1996), during the Iranian revolution the escalation of political protests across the country was a positive function of a density of protestors within a certain geographical area as well as the geographical proximity of centers of protest. The high density of democracies within one region influences the adoption of democracy by countries that are non-democratic within this region, as well as influencing the adoption rate in another region (Starr 1991). When spatial factors are estimated as a joint function of distance and density (O'Loughlin et al. 1998), the adoption potential indicates that the larger the proportion of democracies in the region during a particular year, the more likely democracy is to survive in any particular region (Przeworski et al. 1996, 42; Schwartzman 1998). Indeed, studies of the 1989–1990 democratization of Eastern Europe observed that the probability of transmission of democratic ideas from one country to another was closely related to the two strongest variables – the spatial proximity and density of democratized countries (Wejnert 2002a, 2002c).

Finally, *spatial density* refers to the density of existing democracies within an organizational network, where the lesser the density of democracies, the more the perceived risk of adopting by non-democracies (Abdalla Salem El-Badri 2010). Because each democratic state also subsequently serves as a transmitter influencing other potential democracies that are in close social proximity, the density of countries that have already adopted democracy may be an important influence on the adoption rate within a network (Schmidt 2006). However, it is argued that the cumulative number of adoptions within a unit of an organization or bloc of countries promotes new adoptions up to a critical point of exhaustion of resources, after which the adoption rate decreases (Hannan & Freeman 1987). This finding indicates that the effect of density is not temporally static but rather varies over time, depending on the density of prior adoptions of democracy and on the duration of time intervals between former and new adoptions.

Structural equivalence

Estimating the complexity of spatial effects is further complicated by the need to consider countries' structural equivalence as potentially affecting the impact. *Structural equivalence* of members in a network or in a region, particularly in terms of comparable economic and social status, stimulates a country's perception of concordance with other countries. Awareness of the sameness of countries' status in the international arena modulates the adoption of democracy by stimulating homogeneity in countries' behaviors (Tuma, Titma, & Murakas 2002). Countries assess their own structural equivalence with other countries by judging (a) economic factors, i.e., the level of wealth or economic system a country possesses (Burt & Talmund 1993; Palmer, Jennings, & Zhou 1993; Kolodko 2011); (b) culture, such as similarity of language, cultural traditions, religion, self-identity, values, and norms (Abbott & DeViney 1992; Brown & Bandlerova 2000); (c) common historical background (Uhlin 1993); and (d) similarity of prior political behaviors aimed at changes to the political system, such as using similar strategies or political actions (Abdalla Salem El-Badri 2010; Oberschall 1989).

The structural equivalence of countries most likely enhances the effect of distance and density by stimulating communication about democratic principles, as was the case with the formation of the suffrage and women's rights movements in Sweden in the late nineteenth century, which were inspired by successful suffrage movements in structurally similar Switzerland and France (Markoff 2003; Vallinder 1962). Similarly, in Finland in 1890, women gained voting rights after rights were gained not in one of the European great powers, but in structurally similar Norway, Denmark, and Iceland (Markoff 2003). Moreover, the Indonesian government modeled its democratic system on the Netherlands' rather than the popular American democratic model, only because the Netherlands' economy more closely resembled that of Indonesia and more contacts were established between the two countries (Uhlin 1993, 1995). Moreover, Mizruchi (1993), studying the behavior of large corporations, showed that equivalence between firms better predicted homogeneity of behaviors in highly stratified networks than the level of cohesion between firms.

Thus, weighting countries by their structural equivalence may lead to a more accurate prediction of democracy's adoption and rate of democracy growth than focusing solely on direct interactions between countries within networks and on communication links, particularly since structural equivalence may facilitate adoption by activating countries' competition. This was exemplified by the former Soviet-bloc countries competing for the earliest adoption of democracy, which was a required condition for acceptance to NATO (North Atlantic Treaty Organization) and the European Union.

Looking at the adoption of welfare policies across various countries, Abbott and DeViney (1992) demonstrated that structural equivalence between states contributed more than twice as much as all other selected variables to the predictability of the adoption of welfare policy in a country, adding, furthermore, that geographic proximity alone does not have a very significant effect on a country's adoption of welfare policy unless it is supported by close interaction between countries, e.g., comparability in trade, capital flow, language, or religion.

This finding by Abbott and DeViney (1992) was extended by the argument of O'Loughlin et al. (1998), showing not only that neighboring with a democratic country increases the democracy level of a country, but also that merely being located in a sub-region containing at least one democracy is an equally important predictor. Sub-regional structural similarity of countries generated by such factors as a similar culture or economic structure, trade relations or religious ties, strongly affects democratic growth. An example of the significance of structural similarity can be found in the democratization of the former Soviet bloc in the early 1990s, when Poland initiated the wave of transitions to democracy followed not by one of its neighbors but structurally similar Hungary. East Germany, which shared a border with Poland, democratized after Hungary, Czechoslovakia, and Yugoslavia. Following the logic of this argument and the results of Wejnert's (2005) study, it would be correct to assume that democratized Iraq will enhance future democratization processes in other Muslim countries throughout the Middle East in addition to its positive effect on neighboring Iran. The Arab Spring events are perhaps the first signals of the coming democratic future in the Middle East. Although the countries in this region share a culture that is unlike the culture of Western democracies, and thus the character of developed democracies will most likely be modified, the activated civil society demonstrated in the Arab Spring should provide roots for future stable democratic institutions.

Regional waves

Another useful concept for understanding the wide-ranging conditions leading to regional democratization is the notion of waves of democratization (Huntington 1992). Accordingly, in Wave I, from 1828 to 1926, industrial revolutions and post-World War I pro-democratic tendencies led to the democratization of many countries, among them the newly independent European states. Wave II in the 1940s to 1960s (during and after World War II) saw the democratization of Asian countries (e.g., India), but was unstable and reversible. In the 1970s, democratization in southern Europe was ignited, in part, by the worldwide spread of decolonization and the oil crisis (O'Donnell, Schmitter, & Whitehead 1986), while a decade later, the inability to repay foreign loans caused by repercussions of the oil crisis initiated democratic processes in many Latin American countries (Higley & Gunther 1992). Similarly, the economic downturn and collapse of the Soviet Union added the countries of the Soviet bloc to the next wave of worldwide democratization. Thus, the most recent clustering of democratizing countries – Wave III – includes the democratization of southern Europe in the 1970s (Pridham 1990; Tarrow 1989), Latin America in the 1980s (Higley & Gunther 1992; Linz & Stepan 1996; O'Donnell, Schmitter, & Whitehead 1996) and the former Soviet bloc countries in the 1990s (Bermeo 1991; Stark & Bruszt 1998; Wejnert 2002a), followed by South Korea and Taiwan, and the re-democratization of many post-colonial African states (Bratton & Mattes 2001; Spears 2003).

Communication and regional factors concern a broad array of variables that modulate the process of democracy's adoption. For instance, a democratic system could be perceived as higher in benefit if it is considered to bring economic progress (Sawa-Czajka 2010) or involves justice (Rawls 1971; Tilly 2005). It is also more likely to be adopted if has been adopted by structurally equivalent countries (e.g., the common explanation of waves of democratization in Latin America, or Eastern Europe [Huntington 1992]); if it has been adopted by countries in close spatial proximity such as the neighboring states of Eastern Europe (Wejnert 2002a); if it involves pressure from powerful international networks or economically/politically dominant states, such as the European Union or the United States (Huntington 1992; Markoff 1996; Wejnert 2010). Also, when democracy is highly approved across the world and is perceived as associated with an increase of standard of living, or when information about democracy was obtained from a social/organizational network that a country belongs to rather than from objective sources such as media or scientific evaluation (a similar process was observed by Rogers [2003] in the case of adoption of technological innovations), it has a greater chance of adoption by many countries. All of these variables may be seen as *broadly acting* influences in the processes of adoption, for example influencing attention to external information about democratic principles, and may be conceptualized as variables that *modify* a country's estimation of the benefits and potential positive outcomes of democracy. Learning through observation of the adoption outcomes of other countries builds confidence in the expected outcomes of democracy, increasing democracy's value, and has more weight than information obtained from objective sources (Rogers 2003).

Framework of worldwide historical events

According to the theories of democratization that emphasize a world historical perspective, *worldwide historical events* are distinguished as either causing marked changes in the global economy, such as a worldwide recession/economic depression or worldwide economic boom, or leading to the rapid development of civil society. Examples of historical events include: (a) major wars, e.g., World War I and World War II; (b) rapid changes on the financial market, generating worldwide depression and/or economic crisis, e.g., the 1997 Asian financial crisis; and (c) a global oil crisis altering the established patterns of world trade, e.g., the 1973 oil crisis, which started when members of the Organization of Petroleum Exporting Countries (OPEC) proclaimed an oil embargo.

Global historical events affect the spread of democracy, because they affect countries' economic growth. In a situation of progressive economic development, a country becomes more open to the global market and to contacts with the democratic world. Frequent contacts facilitate societal exposures to democratic principles and societal awareness of democratic freedoms, leading to the strengthening of a civil society that demands inclusion in political processes. Economic downturn, on the other hand, generates dissatisfaction with the existing political system (Przeworski & Limongi 1997) and leads to the growth of a civil society protesting and calling for change in the existing ruling elite or existing political system. Economic hardship is perceived by society as an outcome of irresponsible governing; therefore, ruling elites are asked to step down. Consequently, scholars argue that an active civil society constitutes an inevitable part of the democratization process (Tarrow 1989).

Some scholars, therefore, have argued that the vast majority of countries did not generate democracy through an independent innovation (Whitehead 1996). First, it is argued that the 1980 democratization in Latin America in part resulted from worldwide economic decline caused by the world oil crisis (Higley & Gunther 1992; Huntington 1992, 51; O'Donnell, Schmitter, & Whitehead 1986). Second, in the challenging economic conditions after World War I, an increase in the democracy level of Western countries was observed when women were granted the right to vote, in part because of their direct involvement in war efforts (Markoff 2003; Skocpol 1992; Tuttle 1986). Third, major, global-scale wars also influence the development of democracy when victorious democratic countries impose their democratic system on liberated countries. Good examples are the newly established or liberated countries of East and Central Europe at the end of World War I. Indeed, eleven new countries were established as democratic states, in part due to political pressures during post-World War I negotiations and peace treaties. Among them were Poland, Czechoslovakia, the Ukraine, Hungary, Estonia, Latvia, and Lithuania. Fourth, ironically and contrastingly, an anti-democratic, communist system was imposed on the same countries when the communist Soviet Union won World War II a few decades later.

Therefore, Przeworski and Limongi (1997) attested that international conditions may better predict the survival of a democratic regime than does the level of socioeconomic development. Although Przeworski and Limongi's (1997) analysis was short on assessments of the scope of international effects and of the predictive power of international effects relative to the socioeconomic conditions of a country, the impact of international conditions was mentioned by other authors studying processes of democracy, for example, factors that led to the creation of Balkan identity (Vickers & Pettifer 2000), or national democratic politics in the united Europe of the 2000s (Schmidt 2006).

Global uniformity framework

Variables related to global uniformity reflect the view of the contemporary world as one cultural community, characterized by collective development grounded in a synchronized, cohesive process of societal evolution. This uniform evolution is thought to be a function of three exogenous variables: a process of *cultural McDonaldization* of the world, mainly due to the influence of Western Europe and US culture; indicators of *institutionalization*, rule-like behavioral or policy patterns that are assessed by experts and hence followed by many countries; and *global technology*. Thus, it has been frequently concluded that "modern democracy is a product of capitalist processes" (Schumpeter 1950, 297) that render socioeconomic factors strong predictors of democratic growth.

Cultural McDonaldization

The accounts of global uniformity in diffusion have often emphasized a process of cultural Westernization of the world, mainly through the influence of Western Europe and the USA, referred to in social science literature as Cultural McDonaldization (Ritzer 2007). This is concordant particularly with the dominance of Western cultural characteristics that generate standard practices and behaviors. Western practices often connote symbolic meanings of socioeconomic advancement and elevated status. For less-developed countries progressing toward economic prosperity, the characteristics of modernity and Western culture are some of the strongest stimuli eliciting the adoption of practices, including those of an ideological nature, such as a democratic system (Fukuyama 1992; Pellicani & Volpacchio 1991). Such a process has been cited, for example, as contributing to a favorable environment for the triumph of US and Western cultural values and norms across South American societies in the 1980s (Higley & Gunther 1992) and Eastern European societies in the 1990s (Karnoouh 1991). Despite the depleting effect of these values on national cultures, and the degradation of national cultural roots due to the influence of Western mass culture (Koralewicz & Ziolkowski 1993), the Western values of individuality and materialism were broadly adopted.

Conversely, characteristics of modernity and Western culture can also invoke great antipathy and serve as barriers to the adoption of democracy. The critical assessment of and opposition to diffusing Western models is visible especially among societies with cultures that do not share European cultural roots. The Japanese preservation of cultural identity through selective adoption of practices and, preceding these adoptions, modifications of Western styles of political decision making, is a strong example of cultural opposition to Western models (Kissinger 2001). The animosity of countries in the Middle East toward Western cultural and economic relations is another (Kurzman 1996).

The impact of Western cultural patterns, therefore, does not develop in a socio-cultural vacuum, but rather is modulated by the societal culture specific to each country. Such modulating effects would be at the level of national populations, or at least at the level of large subgroups of populations in cases where heterogeneity of culture is found within countries.

A study by Herbig and Palumbo (1994b), comparing the patterns of adoption of novel industrial practices in American (representing the Western McDonaldization) and Japanese societies (opposing cultural Westernization), supported the possibility of the modification of spreading cultural models by national cultural characteristics. Accordingly, an American culture that supported the values of independence, risk-taking, and individual success resulted in an adoption pattern in which, once exposed to a new political ideology or a new behavioral pattern, Americans rapidly adopted novelty. Their eventual rate of adoption, however, was temporally prolonged due to a relative paucity of collective interaction and collaboration. The adoption process in Japan manifested an opposite pattern. Individual Japanese citizens were generally slow to adopt innovative policies or behaviors, resulting in a relatively long time to initial adoption compared to the American population. Nevertheless, as the authors suggested, the temporal rate of adoption, once the adoption process began, was significantly shorter than for Americans, probably because Japanese culture was socialized to be strongly competitive but also to value collectivism.

When Straub (1994) examined comparability in adoptive behaviors between Japanese and American companies he found that in Japan, private companies adopted fax technology more frequently than email, the reverse of the pattern in America. Fax, being a more official means of communication, was more compatible with Japanese culture, which promotes more formalized social relations, while email, a more casual form of communication, was more congruent with American culture, which endorses less formalized social relations. Similarly, Herbig and Miller (1991), analyzing the change of behavior in large companies, argued that companies have been found less likely to adopt new behaviors that conflict with cultural mores and systems of belief, or that are discordant with local customs, norms, and tradition, because such incongruence increases the costs of adoption (too high potential risk of societal disapproval).

On the other hand, when a behavioral pattern is consistent with local cultural traditions, belief system variables have been one of the strongest factors in determining the adoption ceiling, i.e., the number of actual adoptions to the number of potential adopters. For example, welfare policy was adopted more rapidly among countries that had similar religion and language (Abbott & DeViney 1992).

This could explain the strong modifier of democracy adoption across the Middle East as resulting from the animosity of Middle Eastern countries toward Western forms of political and economic relations (Kurzman 1996). This characteristic could also explain why India, introduced to Western political philosophy and Western culture by Great Britain – its former colonial power – became democratic at the moment it gained independence, while the neighboring traditional and culturally constrained society of China has endured controlling political authority throughout its history. A high degree of *cultural traditionalism* is often associated with social inertia in adopting new practices and ideas, adversely affecting a country's adoption of novel developments and extending the time between early and late adoptions. Myrdal (1968), for example, thought that these factors explained the unproductive economic behavior of India's poor peasants, where the strong cultural constraints on the societal positions of most of the poor population eliminate the potential of upward social mobility and may have gradually reduced incentives to adopt novel approaches to agricultural production.

Institutionalization

Institutionalization is the spread of rule-like behavioral models that are supported by common recipes and an implicit structure of incentives for the adoption of approved forms of government, practices, programs, or policies. Standardization of those models elicits the adoption of institutionalized practices (Meyer & Rowan 1977). Strang & Meyer (1993) extended this view through the notion that the decisions of potential adopters are not completely dependent on observation of the actual experiences of early adopters of new behavioral patterns or new ideologies, but are also an outcome of imitations of rule-like models analyzed by experts. In this view, the imitative behavior of democracy adoption is influenced by the *theoretical* information provided by experts about the expected outcome of democracy (Dahl 2000).

As the initial studies on institutionalization (Meyer & Rowan 1977) and a number of other studies have emphasized, *institutionalized* practices mainly affect adoptions by groups of countries. Two separate sources appear to contribute to the process of institutionalization of democratic principles in societies and, hence, to the adoption of democracy. The first is a base of scientific knowledge in which the costs, benefits, and outcomes of democracy are specified, attracting potential adopters and encouraging countries to comply with new models (Whitehead 1996) as when the institutionalization of the world's opinion about the benefits of democracy increased democracy's expansion (Linz & Stepan 1996). The second is the introduction to the public of new practices by interest-group politics, which, through selective legitimization and rationalization of particular institutional forms and practices, contribute to their normalization. This latter case is illustrated by the 1960 United Nations declaration that de-legitimized imperialism in global political discourse and led to an increased rate of decolonization (Strang 1990).

Moreover, countries often identified institutionalized practices as being *modern*, and as most central and relevant to mainstream societal evolution. Under these circumstances, individual citizens and/or political authorities in a country believe that it is advantageous to comply with accepted, modern behaviors that have gained rule-like status because those who adopt established practices are more likely to be rewarded with rapid advancement. Many modern political models such as nation-state models (Meyer 1987) are adopted based on this premise.

According to some studies, *institutionalization* is promoted when the similarity of countries' external conditions leads to similarity in their behaviors. In this sense, institutionalization would be understood as a response to the same external conditions rather than countries' internal processes leading to democratization and, hence, would be unrelated to diffusion. The literature on democracy suggests, however, that countries that have similar external conditions often pursue different actions. For instance, holding external conditions constant, countries select different political systems when two or more alternative systems are available (Coleman & Cofman Wittes 2008; Gill & Markwick 2000; Politkovskaya 2007), or try a new idea before its adoption (Lord & Harris 2006; Vickers & Pettifer 2000). The argument, then, is that institutionalization plays an important role in the diffusion of democracy, stimulating and enhancing the processes of democratization. Therefore, as argued by Wejnert (2001a), institutionalization due to broad imaging of democracy in the media, role modeling on existing democracies, and rule-like information about democracy's outcomes promoted by experts, complemented by other mechanisms of democracy promotion, is one of the factors stimulating democracy's diffusion.

Institutionalization, thus, is frequently enhanced by the spread of *global technology* and global adoption of technological innovations, including modern internet communication, worldwide connectedness of societies via online communication, and broad access to modern media that facilitates the growth of multinational connections between countries and between individual citizens of various countries, enhancing the spread of democratic principles. Similarly, global trade and economic markets lower the threshold of diffusion of various practices and policies (Stark & Bruszt 1998).

Uniform evolution is also markedly enhanced by the fact that the process of diffusion per se often promotes the development of similar societal structures, which, in turn, facilitates diffusion of *additional* practices and ideas (Thomas et al. 1987). For example, the temporal rate of diffusion for computer use in American public schools, begun in the 1970s, grew so rapidly that by 1988 over 97 percent of schools had one or more computers. The ratio of computers per student increased from one for every twelve students in 1993, to one for every eight students only a year later. The adoption of external networking, through the internet or area providers, was equally rapid but took a different path, determined by the density of computers a school already owned (Anderson & Magnan 1996). Therefore, schools' initial adoption of computers facilitated the adoption of external networking and, in turn, exposure to institutionalized practices and policies, including the practices of democracy.

Environmental context framework

A fundamental element in adoption theory is the recognition that innovations are not independent of their environmental context; rather, they evolve in a specific ecological and cultural context and their successful transfer depends on their suitability to the new environments they enter during diffusion (Ormrod 1990). Environmental context variables fall into two subgroups: *geographical settings* and *global political positioning*. The variables refer mainly to the spread of ideologies with private and public consequences that are adopted by countries. In his analysis of the worldwide diffusion of technological innovations, James (1993) refers to contextual factors as "externalities," and suggests that they affect the practicality and benefits of adoption, as well as an adopter's willingness and ability to adopt democracy. Following James's (1993) argument, externalities would have a *permissive* effect, where their presence or absence would largely determine a country's decision to adopt or not adopt a democratic system.

Geographical settings

Many studies of diffusion are concerned with a specific category of geographical settings: the effect of the spatial factor of proximity (distance) on democracy's adoption. This variable refers to an automatic spread of democracy between individual countries that are in close geographical contiguity, such as within groups of countries located within the same geographical region. Geographical proximity is generally estimated as the relative rate of adoption between geographically spaced actors. Because proximity can affect the frequency of communication and the direct nature of interactions between countries, it enhances the spread of information and ideas, and facilitates imitative behavior (Rogers 1995). Abbott and DeViney (1992), discussing the diffusion of welfare policy across the world, added that geographic proximity alone does not have a very significant effect on a country's adoption of welfare policy unless it is supported by countries' closeness in interaction, e.g., comparability in trade, capital flow, language, or religion. Frequently, the effect of geographical proximity is visible in cases of the adoption of the principles of democracy by countries located within the same geographical region in the world (Huntington 1992), especially when these countries share cultural characteristics and are engaged in mutual capital flow and trade.

Thus, Tolnay (1995) argued that the effects of density of potential adopters of democracy are a function of geographical proximity or distance between states, and, hence, spatial effects are best estimated as a joint function of distance and density. Extending the understanding of spatial proximity to *adoption potential* (measured as the *distance x density* of adoptions of democracy in interacting regional units and networks), he estimated adoption rate in relation to adoption potential: when nonlinear, or linear with a slope not equal to unity, diffusion is assumed to have occurred. Congruently, Rasler (1996) posited that during the Iranian revolution the escalation of pro-democracy political protests across the country was a positive function of a density of protestors within a certain geographical area as well as the geographical proximity of the centers of protests.

Global political positioning

Global political positioning can be detrimental to the development of democracy. The leading factors are colonial occupation and the establishment of groups of colonial dependencies, and large-scale wars where occupied or colonized countries are losing independence and sovereignty. Since only sovereign countries can become democratic, occupation and domination by a foreign power eliminates the possibility of democratic transition. Another factor is a structure of regional or global parliaments or regional political organizations, like the European Parliament, the Arab League, or the Organization of African Unity, where cohesive political structures potentiate the effects of the diffusion of democratic principles, respect for human rights, and liberty, whereas a fragmented parliamentary system inhibits tolerance, mutual support, and unity in decision making. Fragmented political structures inhibit democratic transition and democracy adoption or stimulate withdrawal from democracy because a strongly fragmented parliamentary system prolongs decision making, shared advising, and mutual support and cooperation. It also prohibits unity in voting or informed judgment on common decisions pertaining to countries that are members of the networks.

Global political networks provide means of diffusion of democracy that are independent of direct country-to-country interactions. For instance, Fukuyama & McFaul (2007) argued that coercion and mimicry between democratic governments leads to isomorphism of the governments' practices. Political positioning could inhibit or postpone the adoption of democracy in a federation of countries. For example, in the case of the adoption of democratic movements and transformative ideas of a political system, political conditions appear to be important variables affecting the diffusion of new ideas, as was the political situation inhibiting the development of democratic movements in the former Soviet Union (Sedaitis & Butterfield 1991).

Finally, political positioning is enhanced by interaction with global cultural trends. According to Mayer (2007), and Brown (2005), spreading popular culture matters for the worldwide development and diffusion of democracy, similar to the clash of civilizations that dictates the remaking of the world's order according to characterization by pro- or anti-democratic principles (Huntington 2011). Moreover, global religious orientations significantly impact citizens' pro- or anti-democratic attitudes and values (Chu, Diamond, & Shin 2001; Tessler 2002).

The discussion presented above has focused on the diffusion characteristics that modulate the process of development and adoption of democracy, relatively ignoring the characteristics of countries. Similarly, much of the literature that attended to the characteristics of countries has paid little attention to the influence of a country's characteristics on other components of democracy adoption. However, as much as diffusion influence may alter the process of democracy development, the characteristics of countries may also substantially influence a country's assessment of the potential benefits and the potential negative outcomes of democracy adoption, thereby interacting with the characteristics of democracy per se. The discussion, therefore, turns to these specific country characteristics, which in this study are called development factors.

Frameworks focusing on development factors

Four sets of variables concerning the characteristics of countries' development appear to modulate the adoption of democracy: (a) familiarity with democracy, (b) status characteristics, (c) socioeconomic characteristics, (d) societal culture – characteristics that are associated with cultural variables that modify a country's receptiveness to democracy – and (e) a country's political conditions.

Familiarity with democracy

The level of familiarity associated with democracy relates to the degree of "radicalness" embodied therein (Dahl 2000). Because countries are naturally cautious in approaching *novelty*, the rate of adoption of democracy – all other factors being equal – is amplified by decreasing its novelty (Wejnert 2005). A major influence in altering the notion of "radicalness" of democracy for a country is prior experience the country has had with the democratic system. This prior experience generates knowledge about the outcomes associated with democracy, a process that reduces the estimate of the potential negative consequences of democracy adoption by increasing the apparent *familiarity* of a new idea and by building confidence in the ability to control societal anxiety resulting from unexpected outcomes of democratization. Such a situation was discussed by Gardawski (1996), who analyzed the process of democratization and the outcomes of democratic transition in Poland.

When the apparent familiarity of democracy is increased, for instance by media information and the opinions of experts (Meyer 2002), the perception of risk held by a country is substantially reduced, facilitating adoptive behavior. For instance, countries that are re-adopters of a democratic system because of previous experience with democracy had significantly higher rates for adopting democracy than countries without such previous experience (Wejnert 2010). Familiarity with the outcome of democracy can be also acquired by observing the outcomes of other actors, since learning through such observation lowers the risks associated with adoption by eliminating the novelty of or uncertainty regarding democracy's outcomes (Schmidt 2006).

A classic example is contemporary Russia, which attempted to adopt a democratic system prior to the presidency of Vladimir Putin. Due to lack of experience and limited knowledge, the economic costs of these democratic changes formed a negative image of the democratic system that was used by Putin to revert Russia to authoritarianism. A similar process took place during the initial hardship of newborn democracy in Belarus in the 1990s, also stimulating retreat from democracy. Rogers noted that a "negative experience with one innovation ... conditions a potential adopter to reject future innovations" (1995, 227).

The process of familiarity is, however, more complex. In extreme cases, familiarity can lead to the false belief that risks are under control; e.g., Polish workers were over-confident about the prosperity of democracy, which led to political errors and initial dissatisfaction with the long-awaited democratic system (Kolodko 2011; Sawa-Czajka 2010). Moreover, the effect of familiarity is further extended by "anchoring" to the first experience a country had with a democratic system, where a negative first experience creates distrust and disbelief of positive results, which deters the potential adoption of democracy. Negative experience with democracy could condition a future decision not to democratize again.

There are a number of factors that reduce novelty and increase familiarity with democracy. As Rogers (1995) demonstrated, information obtained from close peer-countries located in social and organizational networks has more weight than information obtained from objective sources, such as the media or scientific evaluations of democracy. Moreover, familiarity with democracy that results in public consequences is increased by non-relational sources of information (institutionalization and media) (Lord & Harris 2006), while familiarity with democracy that results in private consequences comes primarily from spatial and/or temporal interaction between the country that is a democracy model and the adopting country (Wejnert 2010). Thus, it seems that a country's familiarity with democracy not only is a function of the source of information about democracy (e.g., media, institutionalization, direct interaction or observation), but also depends on the private versus public consequences of democracy (which were delineated earlier in this chapter, in the section on communication and diffusion).

Status characteristics

The status characteristics of a country refer to the prominence of a country's relative position within a population of actors. In the most general terms, variance in these characteristics is a function of a country's social structure and the homogeneity of a country's networks. Countries with *high status*, i.e., those who control either political power or economic resources or both, usually adopt democracy first, and then impose the adoption of democracy on lower-status countries, as in the case where coercion by economically dominant European countries with large populations and geographical area significantly promoted the adoption of democracy by smaller, less prominent European countries in the aftermath of World War I (Gordon Ash 2005).

A country's high international position significantly modulates the likelihood of democracy's adoption within culturally homogenous countries, such as when the adoption of democracy could spread across Middle Eastern countries as soon as one country becomes a precursor of democracy (Saban Center for Middle East Policy 2008), or a single powerful country could inhibit or postpone the adoption of democracy in a federation of countries. For example, in the case of the adoption of democratic movements and ideas transformative of a political system, political conditions appear to be an important variable affecting the diffusion of new ideas, as was the political situation inhibiting the development of democratic movements in the former Soviet Union (Sedaitis & Butterfield 1991). Furthermore, a high-status collective group of countries can also affect the adoptions of individual countries, such as when the adoption of democratic models by non-democratic developing countries was induced by the United Nations' support for human rights (Mingst & Karns 2007).

High-status countries, such as the USA and the countries of Western Europe, increase the rate of democratic growth in the world by inducing adoption within their networks, coercing dependent nations to become democratic and conditioning the provision of economic aid to democratic growth. On the other hand, the low economic status and relative lack of technological advancement of third-world countries dramatically slows the worldwide diffusion of democratic practices (Tilly 2007).

Thus, the predictive power of an individual country's status on the adoption of democracy varies positively with the prominence of a country's position in a network, such as in the case of coercion of less influential countries by stronger states (Fukuyama & McFaul 2007), or the adoption of democracy by countries when the high-status countries with whom they frequently communicate have also adopted a democratic system (Tilly 2007). Consequently, on the global scale, the impact of the low economic status of third-world countries dramatically slows the worldwide diffusion of democratic practices, while the advanced technological and high economic status of Western Europe and the United States enhances the adoption of democracy (Tilly 2007).

In a study on the effect of the media, Weimann and Brosius (1994) argued that an actor's status characteristics interact with media effects, mainly because media affects high-status members who identify novel ideas and then vertically spread them within a group of lower-status members. If media exposure interacts with the characteristics of countries and the characteristics of social networks to influence adoption, countries that are privileged in the world market have higher positions in the world system and therefore are more conducive to democratic growth and often are the first adopters of democracy. As the earliest adopters of democracy, they influence subsequent adoption by other countries. For example, the more modernized countries of Eastern Europe, e.g., East Germany, Poland, the Czech Republic, and Hungary, democratized sooner and spread democratic principles to Bulgaria, Romania, and Albania (Wejnert 2010), whereas Albania, the least influential of these countries, was the last country within the Eastern European bloc to undergo the transition to democracy. In addition, in well-developed countries, the adoption of democratic ideology is equally spread throughout a country due to the interactive influence of modernization and modern media (Computer Aid International 2000). In contrast, in less-developed countries with a lower global position, the spread of new principles of governing takes place mainly in urban places (the result of the interaction of global political positioning and the effect of media), while rural, underdeveloped environments are relatively less exposed to the principles of democracy. Countries with a lower global position are later adopters of democratic models and are low-level democracies (Wallerstein 2001).

These findings are modulated by the fact that high-status adopters initiate the adoption of ideas that are mainly non-controversial and are consistent with established norms. Therefore, under these particular circumstances, the processes of the adoption of democracy by countries that are within the affluent countries' network most likely are similar, and network members with the lowest ranking in status adopt democracy last. Moreover, under these particular circumstances, countries that have a high global position but reject Western culture may delay the adoption of democratic principles that are incongruent with their cultural norms, thus either not adopting or delaying the adoption of democracy. Examples of such countries include Singapore and China.

Socioeconomic characteristics

Overall, the rate of diffusion appears to be confined within the characteristics of countries that create "objective feasibilities" of democracy adoption. For example, the rate of diffusion of practices and policies, even ideological ones such as democracy, has been correlated with a country's overall economic development, measured by development indicators, relative position in the international trade market, and standard of living (Hyojoung & Morrison 2010; Tuma, Titma, & Murakas 2002).

Particularly strong is the effect of economic variables that have both potentiating and inhibiting effects on diffusion, such as in cases of unsuitable economic policies (Herspring 2003) and of poor economic conditions. The economic conditions of a country, along with its cultural and political circumstances, determine the *accessibility* of potential adopter-countries to innovative democratic practices, market economy, or technological advancement. For instance, some technologies are not available to citizens of developing states because these countries are too poor to introduce them into domestic markets (Rogers 1995). Some studies suggest that economic variables often account for more variance in the adoption of democratic policies than sociodemographic variables such as race, gender, marital status, and education level (Nazir & Tomppert 2005); adopters' social position, education, and cosmopolitanism (DiMaggio & Powell 1983); or a country's international position or cosmopolitanism (Dahl 2000). For countries, economic variables accounted for more variance in the adoption rates of various practices and policies than spatial factors (Hedstrom 1994). Similarly, economic variables carried more weight than institutionalized models in the adoption of occupational practices by states (Zhou 1993).

As broadly described in key literature (e.g., Dahl 1989; Tilly 2005), the main elements of a country's characteristics relevant to democracy are its *socioeconomic* and *political* conditions (see Figure 1.2). The most influential economic variable is a country's level of economic development, which is frequently measured by GNP or GDP per capita, and where too low a level of development delays democratization (Bollen & Jackman 1985a). Another variable is the GINI index, which indicates the degree of economic gap between social strata, where a large economic gap is more typically found in non-democratic regimes. Countries with large economic inequalities (large GINI index) are usually unprepared to pursue democracy, because the transparency and inclusiveness of democratic governing would inhibit the preservation of the status quo of the economically dominant group (Kolodko 2011).

Economic conditions also include the development of industrial or more advanced forms of economy that are the most conducive to democracy adoption. The variable *labor force*, representing a country's distribution of labor force, measured, for instance, as the percentage of society working in the industrial or service economy, depicts a country's level of industrialization. Industrial/post-industrial countries are characterized by a class of workers demanding inclusiveness in the governing process and democratic rights, and facilitating pro-democratic movements (Tilly 2007). On the other hand, it is more difficult to organize a democratic movement in agricultural societies; hence, democracy is often out of reach for those societies (Boswell & Peters 1990).

Another economic variable is the level of education and the writing and reading abilities of a country's population. Educational attainment permits the development of a well-informed civil society that is adequately prepared to be involved in democratic processes. The knowledge base of a civil society influences a country's governing and decision making and the establishment of an intelligentsia – social strata crucial to democracy promotion (the variable *education* could be measured as the percentage of a country's population that completed high school). As presented in the discussion on democracy, highly educated societies are characterized by an intelligentsia, a social stratum instrumental in promoting democratic freedom, liberty, and human rights.

In addition to economic conditions, political characteristics can be detrimental to the development of democracy. Leading among them is a country's sovereignty, since occupation or domination by a foreign power strongly limits or eliminates the possibility of democratic transition. The second political factor influencing the feasibility of democracy's development is the inclusion of a wide-ranging society in the process of governing. The very essence of democracy is inclusiveness of minorities, regional groups, or regional governments in political participation; countries with large disparities in political rights are rarely democratic and are less likely to become democratic (Herspring 2003; Mayer 2007). Finally, a fragmented parliamentary system inhibits tolerance, mutual support, and unity in decision making. This leads to a withdrawal from democracy or inhibition of the democratic transition, because a strongly fragmented parliamentary system prolongs decision making. It also prohibits unity in voting or informed judgment.

Among cultural characteristics, some studies on democracy assert that the type of civic culture matters in terms of democracy adoption. In some societies, the clash of civilizations prevents the remaking of the world's order that is characterized by anti-democratic principles (Mayer 2007).

For an individual country, other countries' characteristics may influence indicators of *countries' development*, such as reactivity to novelty and uncertainty, global status, past experiences with democracy, and an adequate level of "how-to knowledge" (Rogers 1995). For example, in the case of a country's adoption of the newest media technology, which generally enhances the adoption of democracy, tolerance might be measured as a degree of prior use of domestic technology (e.g., a microwave, computer, cellular phone, fax machine, iphone); familiarity with technological equipment (the number of journals devoted to modern technology a person has read or subscribed to); average social and economic status of citizens (the level of education, annual income for the past five years, home ownership, job security); and how-to knowledge (the number of years a person has used computers, the number of computer programs a person is familiar with, the number of years a person has used any other digital equipment). All of these predictors, however, support, and modulate a country's socioeconomic characteristics.

Societal culture

A broad spectrum of variables in global societal culture is studied in diffusion research – *belief systems* (values, norms, values, language, religion, ideologies), *cultural tradition, cultural homogeneity*, and *socialization* of citizens – as influencing the adoption of democracy. In addition, studies emphasize countries' adoption behaviors as a function of the impact of culture on *societal values*, characteristics that confer high status and the composition of networks.

The impact of belief systems on countries' decisions has been described in a number of studies. The democratic transition in the culturally similar communist countries of the former semi-colonial network of the Soviet alliances follows paths of democratic growth that were more typical of postcolonial than non-colonized states (Evens and Whitefield 1995; Havel 1985; Holmes 1997). Tolnay's (1995) work on the diffusion of behavioral patterns in the American South that follow common linguistic and religious contours is one example.

Belief systems constitute culture, but culture also affects *societal values* and, in turn, influences the adoption of democracy. For example, Mayer (2007) and Arat (1991) examined how comparability in culture-induced systems of values affected variability in adopting democracy behaviors between Islamic and Western countries. In European countries where the United Nations' concept of human rights prevails, countries more frequently adopted democracy, the reverse of the pattern in Arabic countries. The Islamic interpretation of human rights was more compatible with Arabic culture, which promotes more formalized social relations; while the United Nations human rights system, which endorses freedom of expression, personal freedom, and a more casual form of social interaction, was more congruent with American and European culture, which endorses less formalized social relations (Arat 1991, Mayer 2007). Moreover, Wejnert (2010) argued that countries have been found less likely to adopt a political system that conflicts with their societal cultural mores and systems of belief, or that is discordant with local customs, norms, and tradition, because such incongruence increases the costs of adoption (unacceptably high potential risk of societal disapproval). On the other hand, when a political system is consistent with local cultural traditions, belief-system variables have been one of the strongest factors in determining the adoption of democracy ceiling, i.e., the number of actual adoptions to the number of countries at risk of adoption.[5]

The perception of difficulties in the adoption of democratic principles that are incongruent with local cultural values seems to be higher for individual countries than for groups of countries. Therefore, democracy conflicting with cultural norms is adopted only by a relatively small

---

[5] Countries at risk of democracy adoption are non-democratic countries that could become democratic under suitable conditions. For more information on the potential adopters at risk of adoption see Wejnert (2002d).

percentage of individual countries that are at risk of adoption. For instance, individual Eastern European countries under a socialist economic system would not adopt democracy because it conflicted with their norms of commanded economics (Szelenyi 1988). Middle Eastern countries rarely adopt democracy as it contradicts the Islamic interpretation of human rights (Arat 1991). Thus, individual countries usually express higher degrees of congruence with societal cultural values than groups of countries, consequently following societal norms more strictly in their adoptive behaviors. On the other hand, marginal countries, outsiders in a community of countries who are free from societal norms, adopt unconventional systems sooner than their conventional neighbors, which could serve to explain why it was easier for Israel to adopt democracy than for Palestine.

Culture also affects two further variables: characteristics that confer high status, thereby having a significant impact on individual adoption behavior; and the composition and/or structure of social networks that are conducive to more rapid adoption. For example, favorable attitudes toward democracy and its freedom of media, belief system, and personal freedom, embedded in the local culture of European communities, conferred higher status on adopters of human rights practices. In turn, this should have a significant direct effect on the adoption of democracy by Eastern Central European countries (Slownik 2007).

With respect to social networks, Kristof & WuDunn (2009) observed that the adoption of women's empowerment practices through maternal health policies occurred within the networks of countries with similar social practices. Moreover, the effect of culture on the structure of the networks of countries is most notably visible in isolated networks, such as communities that are established by homogeneous states (Smith & White 1992). In such networks, the adoption of democracy by a network's most prominent country induces adoption across the community of countries; for example, when United States adopted the democratic system, the new democracy affected the democratization of Canada and consecutively the democratization of South American states. Moreover, the effect of culture on the composition of social networks strongly affects whether decisions to adopt are made by individual countries or, for example, by leading countries within a network that leads to the democratization of all countries within the network, as in the post-colonial societies of the British Empire (Crenshaw 1995).

This finding supports as well as extends the argument of O'Loughlin et al. (1998), showing not only that neighboring with a democratic country increases the democracy level of a country, but also that merely being located in a sub-region containing at least one democracy is an equally important predictor. Sub-regional structural similarity of countries generated by such factors as a similar culture or economic structure, trade relations, or religious ties, strongly affects democratic growth. An example of the significance of structural similarity can be found in the democratization of the former Soviet bloc in the early 1990s, when Poland initiated the wave of transitions to democracy followed not by one of its neighbors but by structurally similar Hungary. At the same time, East Germany, which shared a border with Poland, democratized after Hungary, Czechoslovakia, and Yugoslavia. Following the logic of this argument and the results of Wejnert's (2005) study, it would be correct to assume that democratized Iraq will enhance the democratization processes in other Muslim countries throughout the Middle East in addition to its positive effect on neighboring Iran.

One additional aspect of culture can affect adoption rates: the degree of *cultural homogeneity* of a country's population may be positively related to the adoption of democratic ideology, because it increases the degree of structural equivalence between transmitters and potential adopters (Finn 2003). As Herbig and Palumbo (1994a) argue, for example, the cultural homogeneity of Japanese society might have increased the rate of adoption of industrial innovations, while American cultural heterogeneity might have slowed it down. In another study, these same authors also argued that particular attributes of societal culture have had a causal effect on the speed of diffusion of new policies across societies, and on the differential rate of adoption of new practices by American vs Japanese industry. Japanese culture, resistant to change and risk-averse, promotes collective decisions, which prolongs the rate of adoption of new practices. American culture, on the other hand, shortens the time for adoption by promoting authoritarian, aggressive, and competitive behaviors. When considering the adoption of a democratic political system, cultural traditionalism and cultural homogeneity are important determinants of such adoption. Extending Herbig and Palumbo's (1994a) argument, we may expect that culturally traditional China is delaying the adoption of democracy, but after democracy is adopted its growth rate will be rapid due to China's relative homogeneity and sense of collectivism.

There is one additional way in which cultural variables may influence adoption rates: pro-democracy *socialization* of individual citizens within countries, which is influenced strongly by culture, may mobilize the available societal talents of entrepreneurship, perseverance, determination, and liberal thinking required of societies who consider the adoption of democratic practices or policies (Rothwell & Wisseman 1986; Ruttan 1988). Socialization also includes the marketing skills required of countries that consider the adoption of a market economy, which is highly recommended for a democratic system (Finn 2003). Socialization contributes to the development of such characteristics as tolerance and cooperation (Kristof & WuDunn 2009), which are needed for the enactment of democratic principles and the transition toward a market economy (Finn 2003). It also contributes to the development of such characteristics as competitiveness and proficiency, voluntary service, perception of social equality, and respect for human rights, which are needed for the enactment of many types of democratic practices, including vast ones such as the transition toward a market economy, inclusiveness in the political process, and political participation of the broad society (Meyer 2007). Although the United States' democracy is not perfect, these qualities of American society were found by de Tocqueville (2009) to be important stimulants to early democratic development in America.

Political conditions

Diffusion studies concerned with the impact of *political conditions* on the adoption of democracy have primarily analyzed the character of political systems, along with the regulations and norms inherent in the legal systems that control citizens' behaviors. Researchers analyzing the adoptive behavior of countries have found strong effects of states' political stability on the adoption of new policies (Berry & Berry 1992) and of bureaucratic efficiency on the cross-national adoption of welfare policies (Abbott & DeViney 1992). Similarly Gurr, Jagger and Moore (1990) and Sedaitis and Butterfield (1991) found political conditions to be a strong prerequisite for the potential democratic transition of non-democratic states.

For a single country, the variables of political conditions include national policies, the structure of government, bureaucracies, the political character of a state, and the existence of political freedoms and laws. Particular emphasis has been placed on the extent to which state policy, by supporting traditional national practices, affects adoption. Here it has been demonstrated that the rate of adoption is strongly influenced by distribution of concessions and repressions among various political, corporate, and social groups (Rasler 1996). Several studies suggest that the rate of the adoption of democracy by states is a function of state legislative systems. For instance, prior to decolonization, Britain reacted to colonial discontent with the gradual introduction of a representative form of rule, which aided the transition to a more democratic form of government across the British colonies (Bollen and Jackman 1985b; Crenshaw 1995). The recent conditioning of US aid on the introduction of democratic principles in economically dependent countries resembles British policy (Robinson 2004).

Another political factor influencing the feasibility of democracy's development is the inclusion of society in the process of governing. With respect to individual countries, the adoption of democracy seems markedly determined by states' ideological doctrines and by political censorship. For example, Bakardjiva (1992) demonstrated that, due to political reasons and fear of exposure to Western advanced technology, items such as satellite antennas, fax machines, and cellular phones were not available to citizens of former Soviet-bloc countries until the 1990s, when changes in political conditions led to the diffusion of communication technology to this region. Correspondingly, political censorship and ideological doctrines in former communist states that rejected Western philosophical thought appeared to have limiting effects on adoption of scientific knowledge by members of academic communities (Wejnert 1996c). Furthermore, strong censorship severely limits the freedom of the press that is frequently the only platform where civil society can express its pro-democratic tendencies (Politkovskaya 2007).

Summary of diffusion and development frameworks

The above discussion illustrates that studies of democratization have identified a broad array of variables that can significantly influence the probability of whether a country will adopt democracy. Most prior accounts have focused on the characteristics of countries' development that serve a gate function, opening and closing possibilities for the successful adoption of democracy. Some more recent studies have emphasized the sources and nature of information about democracy

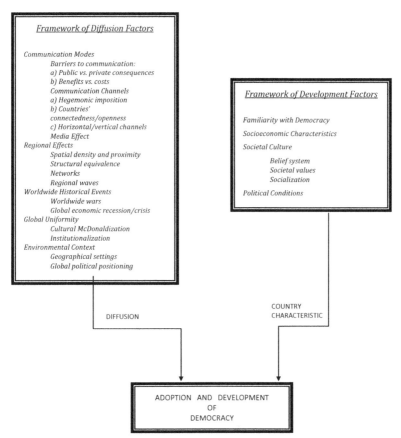

Figure 2.1 Conceptual frameworks of factors contributing to the adoption and development of democracy

that are available to a country and that modulate countries' receptiveness and openness to democratic principles in their political behaviors, the diffusion factors. The combined effect of the two sources of factors influencing countries' democratization is presented in Figure 2.1.

Implications of the conceptual frameworks for future research on democratization

The above discussion illustrates that studies on democratization have identified a broad array of variables that can significantly influence the probability of whether a country will adopt democracy and/or further develop a democratic system. Most accounts have focused on the sources and nature of information about democracy that are available to a country. The main process underlying these accounts is generally one of modeling or learning, whereby the experience of early adopters of democracy influences the behavior of potential adopters of democracy (Wejnert 2002b). From this standpoint, it could be ascertained that the growth and spread of democracy is dependent on a rational process of adoption understood in the Weberian tradition, similar to the rationalization of cultural norms, values, or structures.

What has received much less attention in democracy research is the interaction of countries' characteristics with a larger societal context, where among the contextual influences most likely to interact with countries' characteristics are network connectedness, spatial proximity of other democracies, structural equivalence with democratic countries, and a global pro-democracy culture that stimulates the promotion of democratic transitions. A country's characteristics, on the other hand, involve factors determining the actual feasibility of democracy's adoption, such as a country's socioeconomic situation, cultural characteristics, or political position. The implication of a salient role for a country is that the country's characteristics will modulate both the process of information intake and the process of decision making concerning the adoption of democracy.

Taken together, the process of countries' democratization integrates the diffusion influences on adoption, arrives at value V of democracy that accounts for potential difficulties or risks associated with democratic transition or development adoption, and provides an overall estimate of the probability of a positive expected outcome of democracy adoption, or successful democratization (S_{vr}). The country must then weigh the value of probable successful democratization S_{vr} against the level of countries' development denoting the feasibility of acceptance of democracy by a country, the A_t value, in a manner to be described below.

The theoretical threshold model of democracy adoption

Accordingly, as quantified in the empirical research on democracy, the diffusion factors referring to democracy value and the difficulties (risks) of its adoption, defined by the sets of variables of global historical events, regional effects, communication modes, global uniformity

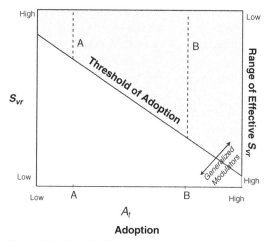

Figure 2.2 Threshold model of democracy adoption

effects, and environmental context, could be specified as leading to and guaranteeing the successful adoption of democracy as a function of value and risk of adoption and depicted as (S_{vr}). Also, a country's characteristics defining *ability* to adopt democracy in a t time, depicted herein as A_t, can be identified. Taken together in an interactive, heuristic manner, countries' S_{vr} and A_t generate the empirically derived threshold model of adoption of democracy, where the effect of S_{vr} interacts with A_t.

Hence, the framework based on decisional processes allows for a formal modeling of adoption, i.e., where all variables above can be integrated in an attempt to predict adoption. For any country, whether adoption occurs at any point in time will depend on the current relative values of three variables: S_{vr}, A_t, and a *threshold of adoption* (T) (see Figure 2.2) within a population of countries at risk of democracy adoption.[6]

Threshold of adoption is a hypothetical construct that represents a weighted value of all country characteristics, previous experiences, and external factors that modulate a decision to adopt democracy. Within

---

[6] Population at risk is best defined in the literature on the adoption of innovations where such a population is a group of actors with characteristics that predestine them to make the decision of adoption, but which has not adopted a particular behavior yet (Rogers 2003).

the combinatorial weighting of these factors, the threshold is viewed as being weighted most strongly by the joint function of two main variables: S_{vr} and A. In future research, other variables that contribute to an adoption threshold need to be defined, and their relative influence along with the variables of S_{vr} and A_t needs to be statistically evaluated. In any case, a country would have a characteristic threshold value that is subject to modification as a function of changing country characteristics, previous experiences with democracy, and external influences of diffusion.

Also, it is possible to model the interaction of S_{vr}, A_t, and T more formally. The relation between S_{vr} and A_t is represented in Figure 2.2 as a trade-off function, where pairs of values of S_{vr} and A_t (depicted as line A and line B) specify a diagonal representing the minimum threshold value for adoption. Thus, for any country, a decision to adopt democracy at any point in time is dependent on whether the interaction of S_{vr} and A_t produces a value that exceeds the T value of the country. Because the two input variables (S_{vr} and A_t) are interactive, independent variation in either one of the variables modifies the probability of adoption. Therefore, if there was a change in the value of A_t, e.g., a change in a country's level of economic development, the country might adopt innovations at lower S_{vr} levels than previously. Thus, as implied by Kolodko (2000), describing the influence of Western democratic states on the adoption of democracy in Eastern Central Europe in the 1990s, an increase in countries' economic prosperity stimulates the adoption of democracy and promotes trade relations with developed Western democracies, simultaneously enhancing learning about the principles of the democratic system. In this situation, an increase in the value of S_{vr} would increase the probability of adoption for countries of a specific range of A_t values. This is illustrated by the economically unstable and economically fragile democracies of the post-colonial British states in Africa, where a democratic system was imposed by Britain (see Figure 2.2).

On the other hand, an increase in countries' economic prosperity encourages the adoption of democracy even under conditions of moderate values of S_{vr} (Dahl 2000). A good example is the relatively stable democratic development of the more economically advanced India, compared to the African states that had a similar British colonial history. The functional implications of this model will now be considered.

Differences between countries

As noted by many scholars (Dahl 2000; Tilly 2005), initially the focus of research on democracy and democratic transitions has been almost entirely on the effects of individual differences in countries and not on population-based models, such as blocs of countries. Therefore, it is particularly important that the interactive relationship between S_{vr} and A_t provides a means of representing individual variation in adoption. Thus, if the value of S_{vr} for any particular country is held constant across countries, variation between countries in the adoption of democracy would be highly dependent on a country's value of A_t. To illustrate this, a dimension of A_t values is represented on the horizontal axis of Figure 2.2, where two countries with divergent A_t values are demarcated: A (low A_t level) and B (high A_t level). In this example, country A has a lower level of development than country B and, therefore, country A will, on average, require higher values of S_{vr} in order to adopt democracy. That is, for any given value of S_{vr}, country B is more likely to adopt than country A. Interestingly, this proposition appears to be the equivalent of Rogers' (2003) suggestion that it is a *country* and a *country's characteristics* which account for the difference in time of adoption between first adopters of novel ideas (innovators) and laggers (the last adopters in a group of countries) (see Figure 2.2).[7] Applying Rogers' (2003) explanation, a country's characteristics will account for differences in the timing of the adoption of a democratic system.

Conversely, in the case of relatively *stable* differences in the A_t values of countries (e.g., due to the same culture or a similar level of economic development), the effects of a country's differences in S_{vr}, the diffusion effects, become more pervasive. There are at least two major effects of stable differences in A_t values. First, stable differences in A_t values may have marked effects on the *range* of S_{vr} values that lead to a decision to adopt democracy. This interaction is illustrated in Figure 2.2, where the right vertical axis represents the range of *effective* S_{vr} values (i.e., S_{vr} values that lead to democracy's adoption). Increasing A_t levels (horizontal axis) are associated with an increasing efficacy of *weaker* S_{vr} values, and thus with an increasing range of effective S_{vr} values that

---

[7] An explanation about laggers is provided, e.g., by Palmer, Jennings, & Zhou (1993).

will result in adoption. Continuing the above example, country A and country B in Figure 2.2 are shown to have a narrow (A) vs broad (B) range of effective S_{vr} values, respectively. Therefore, the broader range of effective S_{vr} values for country B suggests that, *on average*, country B will likely adopt democracy sooner than country A.

Second, if there are stable differences in the A_t levels of *individual* countries, it is possible that the effect of the magnitude of variables that contribute to S_{vr} estimates could result in stable differences in assessing the risk of adopting democracy, as suggested by others (Dahl 2000; Tilly 2007). In this case, country A in Figure 2.2, which has a lower A_t level, may manifest a general reduction in the positive values perceived for S_{vr} variables and, hence, a general reduction in the probability of adopting democracy. For instance, countries that are low in development could be found to have reduced responsiveness to the value of democracy (Kapstein & Converse 2009), suggesting that adoption by highly resistant countries is achieved only by high values of S_{vr}. Such a variable could contribute, for example, to the marked differences found between innovators and laggers in time of democracy adoption, where laggers decide to adopt only after a critical mass (a high density of democratic states within a region)[8] has the effect of reducing the novelty of this system, limiting the potential of failure of democracy due to modeling effects and communications and, thereby, increasing the value of S_{vr}. For example, poorly developed Albania adopted a democratic system last within the democratizing Eastern European bloc in the 1990s.

Modulatory variables

A threshold model of democracy has an additional important implication. One of the tasks for democracy research is to identify variables that have a generalized modulatory effect (either increases or decreases) on the threshold of adoption for a *population* of countries. Such modulatory variables should significantly increase the prediction of adoption rates for a group of countries because the S_{vr} and A_t values required to reach a threshold of adoption will be altered by that variable for all countries. Figure 2.3 illustrates the effects of generalized

---

[8] A comprehensive discussion on critical mass provided Rogers (2003) and Valente (1995).

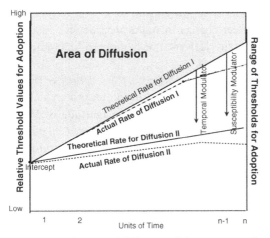

Figure 2.3 The rate of diffusion of democracy within a population at risk

modulators on the threshold of adoption, an effect that, by increasing or decreasing the threshold, simultaneously modifies the S_{vr} and A_t values required to reach the threshold of adoption for an entire population of countries.

One group of modulator variables would be those that have a strong, generalized effect on A_t values. An example of such an effect is when significant changes occur in global trade relations that lead to a rapid decline in the economic situation of all the countries in the world regardless of their initial level of development. The effect of the Great Depression of the 1930s was such a case: when facing economic difficulties, previously democratic countries became totalitarian regimes that resulted in the birth of fascism, totalitarianism, racism, and the initiation of World War II. The impact of the oil crisis of the 1970s on the economic recession and decline of democracies in Latin America could serve as another example of such a situation. That is, these variables' presence or absence can have such a marked effect on A_t values that the decision to adopt can become practically a dichotomous one. Thus, for instance, global pro-democracy changes or liberal leadership of non-democratic countries might have significant modulatory effects on the threshold of adoption of democracy, as was observed in the case of the rapid spread of the adoption of principles of democratic governance during the Gorbachev era (Sedaitis & Butterfield 1991) versus the Putin era (Herspring 2003) in Russia. Such a susceptible modulatory variable could affect change in political leadership, e.g., from totalitarian to democratic or vice versa, or from hard-line totalitarian to liberal totalitarian leadership.

Similarly, a variable that could markedly affect S_{vr} values is the density of democratic countries. When the density of adopting countries reaches a critical mass, the perception of the magnitude of S_{vr} values can increase (rewards for democracy adoption are seen as highly plausible, while expectancy of difficulties is reduced due to learning processes from globally spreading democracies, and hence, the threshold of adoption could be reduced for all remaining countries who have not yet adopted). Density introduces temporal modulatory effects into the prediction of adoption rates, effects that are likely to be complex and which were discussed above and by others (Kolodko 2011; Wejnert 2005).

Predictive perspective on the threshold model of the rate of democracy adoption

An important implication of the model concerns the potential to investigate democracy adoption from a predictive, as opposed to a solely retrospective, perspective. As variables that are associated with significant country characteristics are more formally defined empirically, country characteristics can theoretically be measured prior to any act of democracy adoption. At the level of populations of countries, this has implications for predicting the rate of adoption. When the value of the diffusion factors, diffusion influences S_{vr} for democracy, is held constant across countries, variation between countries at the time of the adoption of democracy will be highly dependent on a country's development value of A_t. Thus, with reference to Figure 2.3, just as country B would be predicted to adopt democracy *sooner* than country A, two populations of countries having different *mean* values of A would be predicted to have different rates of adoption.

A critical goal for democracy research will be to identify which types of variables affect the *rate of adoption*. As explained above, current research suggests that at least three variables – diffusion factors depicting the success of democracy adoption due to external influence S_{vr}, country characteristics A_t, and threshold of adoption T – may significantly modify the rate of adoption and, hence, contribute to rate predictions. To illustrate these effects, the distributions of adoption threshold (T) values for two hypothetical groups of countries as a function of three variables – *mean*, *kurtosis* (peakedness), and *skew* of the distribution – are illustrated in Figure 2.4 – A, B, and C, respectively. The corresponding rate of adoption curves (percent adoption as a function of time) associated with each distribution of T values is shown in the lower left corner of each section of Figure 2.4. For simplicity, all distributions in the figure represent populations of an equal number of countries; in this case, kurtosis strongly reflects the impact of the range of T values of each distribution on the rate of adoption.

In Figure 2.4A, the two distributions of T values, labeled 1 and 2, are of normal distribution and have equal kurtosis and skew; only their means are significantly different. As shown in the graph in the lower right corner, all else being equal, Distribution 1 – with the lower mean, earlier initial adoptions, and lower extreme high values – is predicted to have a faster rate of adoption than Distribution 2. Figure 2.4B illustrates the effects of kurtosis on predicted rate of adoption in populations that are otherwise normally distributed and have equal mean and skew. In this case, Distribution 2 is predicted to have a faster rate of adoption, despite the fact that the time of initial adoptions is later than in Distribution 1. This is because the range of T values in Distribution 2 is much lower, as are the extreme high values, than in Distribution 1. Moreover, differences between Distributions 1 and 2 of Figure 2.4B in the predicted rates of adoption may be magnified if an additional variable is considered. In Distribution 2, an increase in the density of adoptions will occur much more quickly than in Distribution 1 due to its greater kurtosis in T values, thereby reaching a critical mass of adoptions much sooner in time than in Distribution 1. Once reached, the critical-mass effect should significantly increase the rate of adoption of the remaining actors in the population (Rogers 1962; Wejnert 2002b).

Finally, Figure 2.4C illustrates the predicted rate of adoption in two populations that are equal with respect to mean, kurtosis, and skew, but which have opposite *direction* of skew (Distribution 1 = right skewed; Distribution 2 = left skewed). This pattern of distributions is particularly interesting. It might be predicted that Distribution 2 has a faster rate of adoption than Distribution 1, because of (a) the tail of lower T values and hence an earlier beginning of adoptions for

86

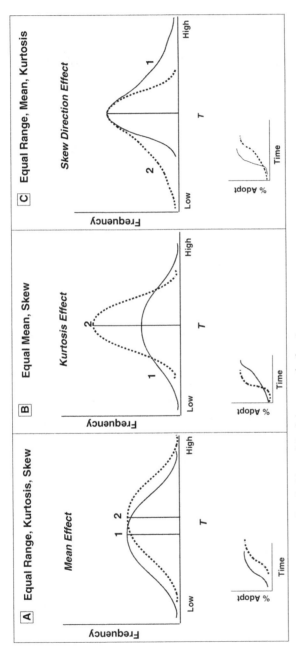

Figure 2.4 A predictive threshold model of the rate of adoption

Distribution 2, and (b) the tail of higher T values in Distribution 1. But again, the introduction of a density variable may alter this prediction. In Distribution 1, although a later start of adoptions would be predicted, it would be characterized by a faster increase in the density of adoptions earlier in the distribution of T values and in time than in Distribution 2, thereby reaching a critical mass (the number of democracies in a region that is needed for an almost spontaneous, automatic adoption of democracy by remaining non-democratic regimes) of adoptions earlier in the range of values in Distribution 1 relative to Distribution 2. Again, the critical-mass effect would be expected to rapidly decrease the threshold of adoption for actors in the upper tail of Distribution 1, thereby producing an overall adoption rate that is faster than in Distribution 1. Interestingly, the latter scenario appears to characterize the shape of the distributions described for the adoption of democracy in Latin America vs Eastern Europe, even though democracy is believed to have equal value for the two groups (Przeworski et al. 2000; Wejnert 2002b). Due to the special density, geographical closeness, and political and economic cohesiveness of Eastern European countries versus the spatial disparity, geographical distance, and political and economic variability of Latin American countries, Eastern Europe manifested an adoption distribution similar to the skew of Distribution 1 in Figure 2.4C (slow to initiate adoption, but a faster subsequent rate due to high cohesion), whereas the Latin American adoption of democracy was similar to the skew of Distribution 2 (sooner to initiate adoption, but a slower subsequent rate due to low cohesion). Importantly, as research indicates, the overall rate of adoption was faster for Eastern European than Latin American countries (Markoff 1996; Wejnert 2010). Considering the impact of the variables S_{vr}, A_t, and T on the adoption of democracy and democratic growth, the present theoretical model of decision making is illustrated more formally in an empirical study where each indicator of S_{vr} and A_t is presented as an interactive component of the threshold model of democracy adoption in Eastern Europe in 1989 and the early 1990s.

In future research on democratization and on the assessment of predictive models of democratic growth, groups of development and diffusion factors need to be taken into account that emphasize differing sets of variables expected to influence a country's democratization. Therefore, the next part of this book constitutes the research section that provides:

(a) an illustration of the adoption of democracy process, using as an example the democratization of Eastern Central European countries in the early 1990s, that includes (i) empirical research on the direct networking of dissidents in pro-democratic movements across the Eastern European regions and (ii) empirical analyses of the temporal rate and variability of democratic changes across Eastern European countries;

(b) a comparison of the relative predictive power of the groups of development and diffusion factors in accounting for countries' variations in democratic growth, where the relative effect of exogenous factors incorporates diffusion as well as the historical events and regional factors that may alter the growth of democracy; and

(c) the provision of predictive analyses of worldwide democratic growth through the first half of the twenty-first century.

In assessing the predictive power of indicators, I view democratic growth as a joint function of characteristics of countries and of regions. Country and regional characteristics are analyzed with hierarchical models that simultaneously assess the impact of indicators on an average country's democratic growth (the level and rate of growth) and on three types of variance: (a) variance in the level and rate of democratic growth among regions; (b) variance in the level and rate of democratic growth among countries; and (c) variance in the democratic growth within countries (residual). The hierarchical models are expressed in the form of growth models (Singer and Willett 2003). These models provide a more comprehensive view of democratization processes than has been possible in the simple regression models used in most previous studies.

Moreover, although much more research is needed, in order for democracy to be adopted and the process of the growth of democracy to occur, the benefit of democracy's adoption must exceed its potential cost – in other words, the adoption of democracy must be profitable. Not surprisingly, some theorists of democratization consider profitability to be one of the major advantages of democratization (Kolodko 2011). This concept, however, is disputed by researchers studying the outcomes of a shock therapy strategy designed by Goldman Sachs for democratizing underdeveloped third world countries (Klein 2007).

The important questions are how the theoretical parts presented above inform understanding of the empirical processes of worldwide democratization, and in what way the presented framework influences future research on democratization. The next section of the book, therefore, contains empirical studies that attempt to statistically evaluate predictive schemes of democracy adoption as a stepping stone to understand (a) the complexities of the process of democracy adoption, (b) the complexities of the process of worldwide democratization, especially in terms of the linkage of political interrelations with countries' economic performance, and (c) global trends that modify the temporal rate and countries' openness toward democratic principles. Ideally, future studies should bridge the subfields of comparative (relying on domestic characteristics) and international (referring to shifting international trends) analyses.

An illustration of a threshold model of the adoption of democracy: the case of Eastern Europe

Is the adoption of democracy a diffusion process? It is generally recognized that political change is an outcome of multifactorial rather than unitary influences. The process of democratization in former communist states could be accurately viewed as the dynamic interplay of at least three factors: (1) the external, international conditions of European unification, the reforms within Soviet Union, and the global institutionalization of democracy – the diffusion variables, (2) the variables of the development of a country that include countries' economic situation and reforms of governmental structures, and (3) a threshold of democracy adoption, derived from the external diffusion factors interacting with the internal development of countries' domestic environment of malleable political institutions.

Contribution of diffusion factors

Most frequently, scholars believe that the factors of countries' development are the necessary conditions that contribute to a domestic environment suitable to the adoption of democracy (Tilly 2005), and to the feasibility of the implementation of democratic reforms (Bruszt & Stark 1991; Marody 1991; Opp & Gern 1993). Later investigations added that shifting international influences (which are called, in this study, factors of diffusion) constituted the enabling factor in the process of transition from communism by accommodating the development of democratic movements and the pro-democratic agendas of political organizations (Brown et al. 1992; Bunce 1990). According to some researchers, democratic reforms in Eastern Central Europe can only be understood within the framework of external, global conditions, because these conditions would have an enabling effect on the influences of domestic conditions in communist states (Banac 1992; Bunce 1990). Directly preceding democratic transitions in Eastern Europe, one of the major international factors was Gorbachev's politics (Bunce 1990; Holmes 1997), which led to the East–West *détente* (Banac 1992; Pridham 1990). At the same time, the expansion of global communication systems (Huntington 1992), shifts in world hegemonies (Wallerstein 2004), and the institutionalization of democracy (Wejnert 2005) caused the snowballing effect of worldwide democratization (Huntington 1992).

Hence, the international factors could be viewed as enabling in nature, modulating the degree to which domestic conditions can express themselves and exert an influence on existing authoritarian regimes (Pridham 1990; Schwartzman 1998). Furthermore, changes in international relations and international political circumstances intensified exposure to the principles of freedom and equality, and to the existence of economic co-dependency in the world, encouraging communist leaders to cooperate with capitalist Western democracies.

In particular, Gorbachev's politics were an important enabling or disinhibitory factor affecting domestic forces, because his political position, expressed in political speeches, significantly reduced the degree of threat and control exerted by the central authoritarian power of the Soviet bloc. For example, in January 1987, during a Central Committee Plenum to discuss progress on reforms in the Soviet Union, Gorbachev introduced a new slogan into the reform debate: *dimocratizatsia*, by which he meant competition among candidates during elections and elections by secret ballot. After disapproval by the Party hierarchy, Gorbachev quickly withdrew from this radical stance. But it was too late: the introduction of democratic concepts had already occurred, and it undermined future political statements by Gorbachev. Thus, when in 1988 the Polish Communist Party requested that the Central Committee of the Soviet Communist Party assist them in an anti-Solidarity campaign, Gorbachev restated the need for leniency toward democratic movements in Eastern Europe (Zakowski 1991). Sedaitis and Butterfield (1991) suggest that it was the Gorbachev era opportunity structure that improved the chances for the introduction of democracy in communist countries. Holmes argues that Gorbachev's criticism of socialism and his own proposed reforms "helped to undermine the legitimacy of communists everywhere" (1997, 26). Political liberalization in the Soviet Union and the Gorbachev era were, then, precipitating factors that led to a breakdown of authoritarian regimes in former communist countries (Bunce 1990).

The regimes of Eastern Central Europe were also vulnerable to the fluctuations of interest and support provided to communist allies by the Soviet Union. The "compromised integrity of the communist Moloch was exacerbated by the dependence of the East European communist parties on a powerful but capricious Soviet Union that provided their political and economic livelihood" (Bunce 1989, 235). For instance, as a result of Gorbachev's policies and of Gorbachev's critical speech of April 1987 (which legitimized the independence of all Communist parties and called for reforms throughout the bloc), several Communist parties replaced their top political executives. In Czechoslovakia, Husak was replaced by Milos Jakes as general secretary of the Party in December 1987; in Hungary, the relative hard-liner Karoly Grosz, leader of the communist party since 1956, the time of the Hungarian revolution and political changes within the communist leadership, was replaced by Janos Kadar. Frequent regime adjustments and political changes weakened the communist regimes, making it difficult for them to implement policies and to exercise political power (Banac 1992; Havel 1985; Sedaitis & Butterfield 1991). Gorbachev's policies stimulated the East–West *détente* in economic and political spheres, opening Soviet–American relations that broadened cooperation between the two superpowers (Bunce 1990) and increased the frequency of contact between Western democracies and communist countries.

Opportunities for adopting democracy also opened with the global promotion of democracy by Western countries. This intense promotion was often associated with financial aid and eventuated in the development of a pro-democracy era and the institutionalization of democracy as the most modern and most desirable political system. Taken together, the Gorbachev effect, open East–West relations, and the effect of the institutionalization and promotion of democracy provided opportunities and support for initiating democratic reforms in communist states.

Another factor of diffusion that opened the possibility of democratization was the advancement of global economic development and the economic need of the Soviet-bloc countries to collaborate with Western democracies. For example, the organization of the European Community (EC), as well as the elimination of the politics of separate East- and West-European economies within the framework of trading relations, channeled the merging of Eastern Central Europe and the Soviet Union with a capitalistic world (Klingemann, Fuchs, & Zielonka 2006; Lovenduski & Woodall 1987). Some of the communist countries became successful rivals of industries in the capitalist world market, and complemented capitalistic economies as subcontractors (e.g., Hungary, German Democratic Republic, and Poland) and as producers of the raw materials and agricultural products indirectly demanded by the world market (e.g., Asian regions of the Soviet Union) (Kulluk 1993). By the end of the 1980s, the economic exchanges intensified calls for the reunification of Germany, a critical issue in Western politics (Graf, Hansen, & Schulz 1987).

Importantly, this economic and political cooperation increased *dissident activity* within Eastern European countries that prepared these countries for an implementation of democratic changes and the eventual replacement of the communist rulers. As the events of the recent Arab Spring in the Middle East suggest, dissident activity is commonly developed in countries with totalitarian regimes. Interestingly, however, in the case of Eastern Europe, networks of political dissidents from various countries acted in unison. Their leaders held frequent meetings – most often in secret places – jointly undertook actions promoting democratic principles and civil rights, and shared educational material about corruption and the abuse of power by communist authorities. The educational material was mainly printed by the Polish underground press and transported across borders for distribution in other Eastern European countries. During meetings and via printed material, leaders of dissident networks shared plans for anti-government activity and exchanged strategies for political action (Marody 1991; Opp & Gern 1993; Zakowski 1991). Indeed, Tarrow (1991a, 1991b) has proposed that political changes in Eastern Europe in the 1990s may be viewed as a *wave of mobilization* for collective action in response to generally expanding political opportunities, which lower the costs and risks of collective action yet secure higher potential gains. Cohesion and connectedness of dissident networks active in various Eastern European countries evolved as a by-product of shared material and actions aimed at the planning and projecting of a post-democratic political and economic future.

The evolved grassroots mobilization in Eastern European countries strengthened political opposition in the republics of the Soviet Union. The violent and non-violent protest demonstrations and ethnic conflicts of the 1980s constituted the foundation of social and political change in the former Soviet Union (Beissinger 1990), accounting for "perestroika from below" (Sedaitis & Butterfield 1991).

From this perspective, the political changes and democratic transition in Eastern Europe could be seen as consequences of the waves of mobilization for collective action that were present in communist countries prior to the beginning of democratic initiatives (Tarrow 1998). What was most threatening to communist regimes, then, was not the breakdown of legitimacy, since this process started prior to the 1990s reforms, but "the organization of counter hegemony: collective projects for an alternative future" (Przeworski 1991, 54).

The collective project of implementation of democratic changes across the Eastern European countries, guided by unified dissident activity, was further enhanced by the *structural equivalence* of all communist Soviet dependencies. Structural similarity accounted for each country's sameness of political structures headed by the communist party leaders, and the uniformity of the centrally planned economy. This structural equivalence allowed for an increase in the temporal rate of change, where the domino effect of democratic reforms in one country stimulated reforms in the most connected and most similar communist country.

At the most general level, transformation in global political and economic conditions during the second half of the twentieth century stimulated democratic movements, which, in turn, rapidly sensitized the masses and political dissidents to democratic ideas. Thus, the international political and economic trends (diffusion factors) influenced the economic and political conditions (development factors) of each former communist country, lighting a path for the transition from communism. A combination of international events, led by the strong permissive effect of Gorbachev's politics, coalesced and to different degrees coincided with the expression of the domestic forces of Eastern Central European countries. In the process of democratization, the international diffusion factors interacted with domestic political and economic conditions.

The contribution of development factors

Several investigators have emphasized the impact of development in Eastern Europe and the economic situation of the 1970s and 1980s on the formation of democratic movements (Huntington 1992; Przeworski 1991; Stark & Bruszt 1998). Increasing industrialization, urbanization, and literacy were contradicted by the economic crisis and poverty, leading to growing public awareness of social inequalities and economic deprivation, and setting nations on the path to demand democratic reforms. Unequal distribution of scarce goods and benefits was magnified by social inequalities and the special privileges of the ruling elite, and abused the citizens' rights. Eventually, such conditions awakened citizens' need for freedom from authoritarian repression (Goldfarb 1991; Vladislaw 1987), or, in the poetic words of Vaclav Havel, "communism exhausted itself, had proven to be inhuman, its dream of utopia fully dissipated and bankrupt" (Havel 1988, 42). Thus, Eastern European democratization had its roots in despair and in an awakening imperative for change that would guarantee social equality and social freedoms (Havel 1988), a view congruent with Dahl's (1989) concept of citizens' frustration taking the form of public opposition to monocratic regimes.

A declining economic situation was, however, not only a phenomenon of the 1980s. As demonstrated by Stark and Bruszt (1998), economic difficulties were visible long before the democratization of Eastern Central Europe. Moreover, the difficulties and the economies varied in nature. Therefore, comparing countries' economies, authors described various paths of extrication from monocratic state socialism. Depending on the geopolitical and economic situation, the paths produced different institutional outcomes to the 1990s transitions; nonetheless, the resulting reforms were democratic in nature.

Pro-democracy reforms also resulted from the rapid development of modern mass communication. Mass communication inhibited the prohibition of publication and the withholding of information about democracy by the ruling elite (Huntington 1992; Markoff 1996). An increase in education led to the formation of and growth of the middle class intelligentsia. According to the literature, the intelligentsia was an important factor in the Eastern European democratic transition, as it supports human rights, liberty, and democratic principles, and often leads democratic movements (Rueschmeyer, Stephens, & Stephens 1992).

In addition to economic and media factors, the political processes of *regimes' liberalization* were among the influential contributors to post-communist transitions (Dahl 2000; Tarrow 1991a). Despite popular notions about the authoritarian, repressive nature of communist regimes, these regimes varied in the degree of their liberalization and in their attitudes toward political opposition (Bunce 1990; Przeworski 1991; Wejnert 1988). It is believed that the variability in the degree of liberalization was partly due to internal conflicts and divisions that plagued the authoritarian power of Communist parties (Banac 1992; Havel 1985). On the basis of a qualitative assessment, compared to Poland and Hungary, Czechoslovakia and East Germany were two of the more hard-line Stalinist countries (Bunce 1990), while the Yugo-slavian regime was considered to be one of the most liberal (Gredelj 2002; Vodopivec 1992; Woodward 1995). For instance, the more liberal regimes responded to societal grievances by replacing members of the ruling elite and making adjustments in the composition of the government. The more liberal regimes were also less punitive toward the developing civil society and its democratic mobilization, thus themselves setting up more suitable conditions for a transition from communism. At the same time, the regimes that were perceived as strong, measured, for example, by the severity of sanctions against political opponents, prevented or significantly limited grassroots actions aimed at democratic reforms, as in the Ceauşescu regime in Romania, the regime in Albania, and the Brezhnev regime in the Soviet Union (Beck 1993; Bunce 1990). Degree of liberalization could be considered the foundation for the potential development of collective protests and also the foundation of changes within communist governments.

In sum, a broad spectrum of domestic determinants – economic development, access to media, education, and the degree of regimes' liberalization – contributed to democratization processes in Eastern Central Europe. Taken together, these factors serve as an indicator of domestic readiness, or what this study calls development factors, to political democratic change. Democratic change, hence, was an effect of the level of countries' socioeconomic development and the degree of the stability and strength of communist regimes.

This study hypothesizes that the interaction between international and domestic influences significantly determined the potential and the feasibility of processes of democratization in Eastern Central Europe. To prove the hypothesis, this study assesses the effects of international (representing diffusion) and domestic (representing development) factors as components of democratic processes of each country. The international factors are represented by the activity of the political opposition that was generated in large part by permissive international changes and by networking of political dissidents across communist regimes. The effects of development factors are represented by countries' socioeconomic conditions, and the political conditions of the strength and stability of communist regimes.

An analysis of the breakdown of the communist regimes of Soviet bloc countries and the replacement of communism by democracy serves a threefold goal. *First*, it provides an understanding of the required suitable international conditions that sparked and initiated the breakdown of communism. These sparking events were Gorbachev policy, the East–West *détente*, and East–West collaboration that facilitated the first occurrences of democratization. *Second*, it provides an understanding of the multiple influences stimulating each country's adoption of democracy. *Third*, it applies the research findings to the presented conceptual model of the threshold of democracy adoption as determining each country's timing and temporal rate of democratic transition.

Research design: methods and data

To assess the process of countries' adoption of democracy, I used data on (a) the perceived potential benefits of democracy and perceived potential negative outcomes of democracy adoption to illustrate the S_{vr} of each Eastern European state, (b) A_t depicted as each country's level of economic development and domestic political situation, and derived (c) the T threshold of democracy adoption. The data were extracted from five sources: (1) indicators of political mobilization in Eastern Europe and on changes within communist governments between the late 1940s and 1982 from the *World Handbook of Political and Social Indicators* (Taylor & Jodice 1982), the *World Polity III* (Jagger & Gurr 1995a), and *Cross-Nation Indicators of Liberal Democracy, 1950–1990* (Bollen 1998); (2) indicators of the political system preceding communism from the Bureau of European and Eurasian Affairs of the United States government (Osmanczyk 1982); (3) indicators of economic and political development from the database *Nations, Development and Democracy: 1800–2005* (Wejnert 2007); (4) data files containing interviews with Eastern European dissidents and members of democratic governments that were conducted by the author in 1992–1993; and (5) descriptions of democratic transition presented in newspaper articles 1980–1993 and recorded by the author. While all countries were communist prior to the transition to democracy, they vary significantly by (a) the level of economic development, (b) their openness toward political change, (c) the existence of prior democratic experience, (d) the degree of civil disobedience calling for freedom and equality, as well as (e) the strength of their political regimes (see Tables 2.1 and 2.2).

Diffusion indicators of democracy adoption

In the literature on Eastern European democratic transitions of the 1990s, pro-democratic tendencies expressed by various forms of anti-communist protest and dissident activity are frequently depicted as one of the factors determining the success of the adoption of democracy (S_{vr}). As scholars argue, according to the framework of diffusion factors described in Figure 2.1 (above), such tendencies result in part from two variables in: (a) the communication channels of diffusion, especially the variables of countries' openness towards democracy and (b) the regional networks depicted by the variable of countries' connectedness.

Communication channels: countries' openness towards democracy

To represent factors indicating S_{vr}, variables were selected that depicted the degree of countries' openness towards democracy or expressed desire for democracy, measured by pro-democracy collective actions. Collective actions are represented by collective protests, defined as a combination of strikes, riots, political protests, armed attacks aimed at the existing regime, and the irregular transfer of political power associated with violence (e.g., *coups d'état*). Countries' openness toward democracy is also depicted by the variable of political demonstrations. Ties between dissident networks are indicated by frequency, place of meeting, the number and rank of interacting dissidents, and the content of shared agendas.

This study hypothesizes that the occurrence of protests and demonstrations attested to the express need for democratic freedom, and the openness was in large part facilitated by the worldwide institutionalization of democracy and the general belief that democracy means

Table 2.1 *Change to democratic system as a function of a country's prior experience with democracy*

Country	Political system prior to communism	Political system prior to democracy	Year(s) of democratic collective protests	Time of democracy adoption
Poland	Parliamentary democracy	Communist system	1956, 1968, 1970, 1976, 1980–1981	June 1989
Hungary	Regency-monarchy, regent Miklos Horthy	Communist system	1956	August/September 1989
Czechoslovakia	Parliamentary democracy	Communist system	1968	September/October 1989
East Germany	Republic (Weimar Republic) 1918–1933 Dictatorship 1933–1945	Communist system	1953	October/November 1989
Yugoslavia	Constitutional monarchy, Kingdom of Yugoslavia	Federal socialist system	No major movement	November 1989 disintegration of the state
Romania	Monarchy, King Carol II	Communist system	1970 small scale miners' protests	December 1989/ January1990
Bulgaria	Monarchy, Tsar Boris III	Communist system	No major movement	December 1989/June 1990
Albania	Constitutional monarchy: 1925–1938 Parliamentary republic prior to 1925	Communist system	No major movement	December 1990

Sources: E. Glenn Curtis. 1991. *Yugoslavia*. Washington, DC: Federal Research Division of the Library of Congress.
History of Albania, Area Handbook of the US Library of Congress. (http://motherearthtravel.com/albania/history-10.htm)
Background note: Bulgaria, Bureau of European and Eurasian Affairs. May 3, 2011. www.state.gov/r/pa/ei/bgn/3236.htm#history
Background note: Romania, Bureau of European and Eurasian Affairs. April 26, 2011. www.state.gov/r/pa/ei/bgn/35722.htm
Background note: Hungary, Bureau of European and Eurasian Affairs. May 19, 2011. www.state.gov/r/pa/ei/bgn/26566.htm
Background note: Poland, Bureau of European and Eurasian Affairs. February 18, 2011. www.state.gov/r/pa/ei/bgn/2875.htm
Background note: Czechoslovakia, Bureau of European and Eurasian Affairs. April 12, 2011. www.state.gov/r/pa/ei/bgn/3237.htm
Background note: Germany, Bureau of European and Eurasian Affairs. November, 2010. www.state.gov/r/pa/ei/bgn/3997.htm
Data retrieved on June 1, 2011.
Additional source: Wejnert (2002a).

Table 2.2 *GDP per capita in Eastern European countries, 1980–1989*

Country	1981	1982	1983	1984	1985	1986	1987	1988	1989
Albania	1099	1111	1101	1065	1060	1091	1054	1013	1092
Bulgaria		2450	2260	2150	2040	2170	2560	2750	2320
Czechoslovakia		2980	3000	2860	2740	2790	3030	3360	3460
East Germany								12500	9679
Hungary	2150	2260	2150	2050	1940	2020	2250	2450	2580
Poland		1540	1800	2060	2080	2030	1850	1850	1780
Romania	2417	2408	2096	1687	2073	2233	2484	2558	2283
Yugoslavia	3450	3230	2640	2270	2040	2290	2510	2720	2920

Sources: Making the History of 1989. Economies in Transition 2007–2011. Roy Rosenzweig Center for History & New Media. http://chnm.gmu.edu/1989/exhibits/economies-in-transition/introduction (Accessed June 1, 2011).
World Bank national accounts data, and OECD National Accounts data files (for Albania) www.indexmundi.com/facts/albania/gdp-per-capita (Accessed June 1, 2011).
East Germany a victim? SciForum.com. www.sciforums.com/showthread.php?t=32423 (Accessed June 1, 2011).
World Economic Outlook (WEO) data, IMF (for Romania) www.econstats.com/weo/V008.htm (Accessed June 1, 2011).

modern and desirable (Brown et al. 1992), as well as the effect of the media, especially the introduction and rapid spread of satellite TV antennas across Eastern Central Europe (Bakardjiva 2002), and the structural equivalence of economic and political systems across the former Soviet bloc countries (Bunce 1990; Kavan 2002; Kolodko 2000). Each category of variables was weighted according to the degree of magnitude and frequency of a particular action for the announced purpose of protesting against the established regime. The weights of each variable were determined using the literature (Dahl 2000; Tarrow 1989; Tilly 2005) and the description of variables included in Taylor & Jodice's *World Handbook of Political and Social Indicators* (1982). Hence, each variable of expressed value was assigned a scalable, weighted rating. For example, for each Eastern European country, the variable *collective protest* was weighted by the rate and scope of actions (strikes, political protests, and armed attacks against the existing communist regime) across the years 1948–1982. In 1948, the consolidation of the communist system in all Eastern European countries took place, whereas the year 1982 marked the end of major protests before the ultimate transition to democracy in the late 1980s (see Table 2.3).

Similarly, the rate and scope of the variable *political demonstration* was measured as an average number of political demonstrations across these years for each country. Taken together, the scores of collective protests and political demonstrations represented the pro-democratic tendencies that were expressed by each country, where the greater the rate of collective protests and political demonstrations, the higher the expressed openness toward democracy.

Once the scales were defined, each country was assessed on the same attribute-rating scales to estimate the degree of a country's openness toward democracy (see Table 2.3). To depict small changes within the collective protest and to focus on the processes of organization of collective protests, especially the one preceding the period of democratic transitions of the early 1990s, the statistical measurement of the events of 1948–1982 is enhanced by data of the author's interviews with the leaders of democratic movements in 1992–1993, and analyses of newspaper articles published in 1980–1993.

Countries' familiarity with the democratic system

In addition, since the institutionalization of democracy has a strong impact on countries' democratization processes, institutional models of democracy would more strongly affect countries that had a political system similar to democracy, or incorporated principles of democratic governing. Thus, a country's prior system of governance was also used to assess a country's familiarity with a political system similar to democracy. Since all Eastern European countries were communist states prior to the adoption of democracy, I assessed the type of political system a country had before becoming a communist state. Similar to the assessment of liberalization, each variable was assigned scalable, weighted ratings as determined by an analysis of variables provided in the *World Handbook of Political and Social Indicators* by Taylor & Jodice (1982) and by an analysis of the relevant literature (Higley & Gunther 1992; Held 1995; Evans, Rueschemeyer, & Skocpol 1985; Tilly 2007). The prior political systems of parliamentary democracy, regency, republic, constitutional monarchy, and absolute monarchy (see Table 2.1) were rated on the degree of closeness to democracy, with higher scores assigned to systems closer to democracy (Tilly 2007). Hence, a score of 4 refers to a parliamentary democracy, 3 to a republic, 2 to a constitutional monarchy, 1 to a monarchy/regency, and 0 to an absolute

Table 2.3 *Value of democracy and risk of democracy adoption as expressed by each Eastern European country, 1948–1982*

Country	Democratic collective protests	Openness to political demonstra-tions	P	Familiarity (F) Prior political system**	$S_{ur}=$ $S_{ur}=$ P±F	Liberalization (L) Political adjustment*	Economic conditions*** GDP/c	$A_t =$ L±E	Threshold of democracy adoption**** $T=S_{ur} \times A_t \times 10^{-2}$
Poland	29.5	5.12	34.62	3	37.62	12.7	1	13.7	5.2
Hungary	5.7	1.05	6.75	1	7.75	22.7	3	25.7	2.0
Czechoslovakia	17.7	8.2	25.9	3	28.9	14.6	4	18.6	5.4
East Germany	13.8	2.17	15.97	2	17.97	24.5	4	28.5	5.1
Yugoslavia	3.8	1.0	4.8	1	5.8	12.3	3	15.3	.89
Romania	3.7	1.05	4.75	0	4.75	9.9	2	11.9	.56
Bulgaria	1.03	0.2	1.23	0	1.23	6.6	2	8.6	.11
Albania	0.6	0.05	0.65	1	1.65	3.5	1	4.5	.07

The score of collective protests and political demonstrations were assessed as a ratio of rate and scope of collective protests that is described in the text above. Since the higher score of political adjustment and prior political system represent lower R, inverted score of R is used in the analyses of S_{ur}.

* The higher the number of political adjustments the greater is the familiarity with political transitions and hence the lower is the R. The rate and scope were measured as an average political adjustment across the years.

** The score depicts degree of closeness of pre-communist system to democracy where the higher score represents the closer system and therefore the greater experience with democratic governing and lower R of democracy adoption, thus score 3 represents parliamentary democracy, 2 – republic, 1 – constitutional monarchy and regency, and 0 – monarchy (see also Table 2.1).

*** Countries' A_t was measured on scale 1–4 where 1 represents countries with GDP per capita with GDP/c less than 2000($); 2 countries with GDP/c of 2000–2499 ($), 3 countries with GDP/c of 2500–2999 ($), and 4 countries with GDP/c of more than 3000 ($) (see also Table 2.2).

**** To simplify the T scores, the numbers are divided by 100, while scope was measured on scale 1–3 with score 3 when a country had a maximum of over 30 adjustments in any year, score 2 for 15–29 adjustments and 1 when the maximum number of adjustments was less than 15 in any year.

monarchy. Once the scales were defined, each country was assessed on the same scale to estimate the degree of familiarity with democracy of a country making the decision to adopt democracy (see Table 2.3).

Regional networks: countries' connectedness

Moreover, in addition to the variable of openness toward democracy, this study assesses the diffusion indicators of the regional connectedness of dissident networks (Bloom 2002) that reflect regional connection and ties between communist states. These variables measure the bond between members of dissident networks. The data are derived from interviews with leaders of democratic movements conducted by the author, 1992–1993, and analyses of newspaper articles from underground and new democratic Eastern European presses published 1980–1993. The newspaper articles were analyzed by the author with the application of Tarrow's (1991b) and Tilly's (2008) methodology of analyses of newspaper material.

Indicators of countries' development

Importantly, indicators of countries' development (A_t), especially countries' political and economic conditions, are essential determinants of the democratization process. In this study, regime liberalization and familiarity with democracy were measured to assess the political situation, while countries' economic situation was represented by a measure of Gross National Product per capita (GNP/c).[9]

Liberalization of communist regimes

In a manner similar to that used in operationalizing S_{vr}, I measured the liberalization of communist regimes that each communist country entertained using the sub-variables of the length and number of terms the same elite served in political offices, the number of executive adjustments within the same elite, and the regular transfer of political power from one political group to another via conventional legal or customary procedures (non-violent change of political authorities),

---

[9] The description of variables is provided in Appendix 1.

based on literature describing the degree of a regime's changeability (Bermeo 1991; Burton, Gunther & Higley 1992). These variables, which were determined using Taylor & Jodice's *World Handbook of Political and Social Indicators* (1982) and denoted together as regime adjustments, represent familiarity with the changes within a political system, where the greater the familiarity the lower the risk of adoption. The weights of this variable were assigned according to the rate and scope of changes in the top executive positions, and for each Eastern European country I measured the number of political adjustments within the top political offices over the years 1948–1982.

Countries' economic conditions

Each country was also assessed on indicators of the level of economic development. Those countries that were the most economically developed would be predicted to have a higher chance of democracy adoption (high A_t). Each country's A_t was measured as GDP per capita across a decade prior to democratic changes. Using a scale of 4–1, each country's level of development was assessed, with score 4 representing countries with GDP above 3000 ($), 3 representing countries with 2500–2999 ($), 2 representing countries with 2000–2499 ($), and 1 representing countries with GDP below 2000 ($) (see Table 2.2).

Comparative analyses of successful democracy adoption due to diffusion (S_{vr}) and countries' development indicating countries' tolerance of democracy adoption (A_t) yielded the assessment of countries' predisposition to adopt democracy, or threshold of adoption (T).

Research results

Analyses of the empirical data demonstrate that Eastern European countries vary substantially in their degree of expressed openness toward democracy (P) as well as in the degree of liberalization of political regime (L). Accordingly, countries with the greatest frequency and number of collective protests and political demonstrations (high P), leading to high S_{vr}, were Poland followed by Czechoslovakia, East Germany, and Hungary. Changes within the top political offices that frequently followed demonstrations or protests were also highest in Hungary, East Germany, Czechoslovakia, and Poland (high L) leading to high A_t (see Figures 2.5, 2.6, and 2.7 and Table 2.3).

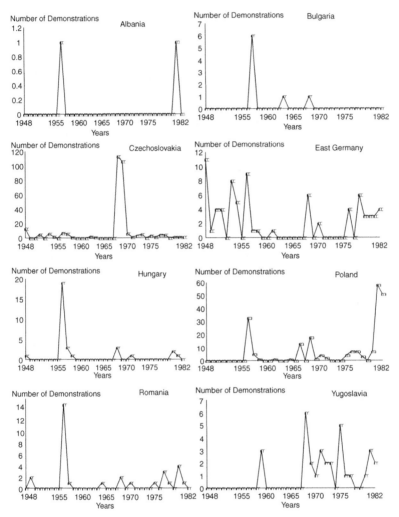

Figure 2.5 Number of political demonstrations in Eastern Europe per country per year

Changes within the top political offices attest to the level of regime liberalization that a country would be exposed to when it decides to change its political system to democracy (Wejnert 2002a, 2002d). A higher number of adjustments, regardless of the same main political line, would increase the likelihood of adoption; therefore, the standing

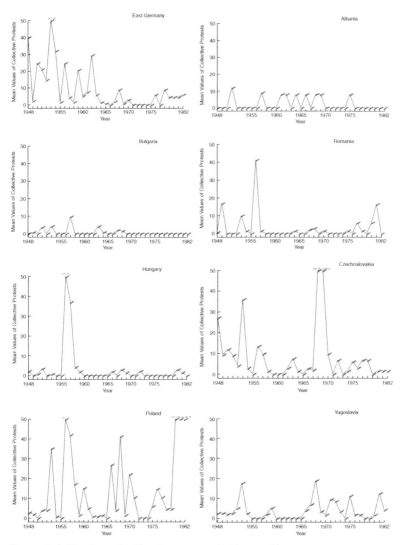

Figure 2.6 Number of collective protests in Eastern Europe per country per year

score of political adjustment represents higher liberalization, contributing to A_t. Countries with the smallest number of changes in political office were Albania, Romania, and Bulgaria. The possibility of democracy adoption in those countries would be the smallest (see Figure 2.8).

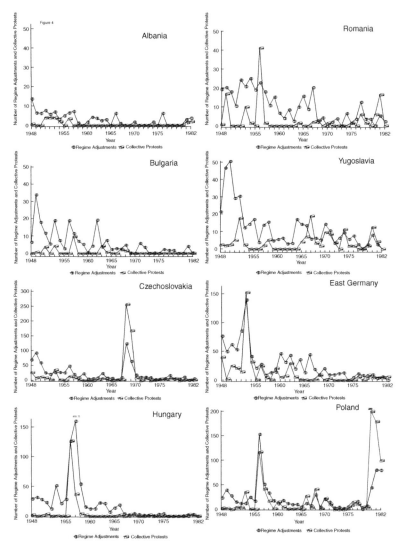

Figure 2.7 Number of executive adjustments in Eastern Europe per country per year

Moreover, considering familiarity with democracy (F), the second variable of S_{vr}, only Poland and Czechoslovakia, followed by East Germany (as part of Germany before the Nazi movement), experienced democratic governance prior to communism (high familiarity). Poland and Czechoslovakia were parliamentary democracies, while

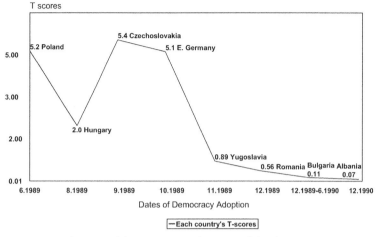

Figure 2.8 Adoption of democracy as a function of the threshold of democracy adoption in Eastern Europe
The T-scores were measured with an application of the threshold model of democracy adoption incorporating decisional processes.

Germany was a republic in the 1920s but became an authoritarian state in 1933. Hungary was a regency after the abdication of the last king (Charles IV); similarly, Albania, after few years of political instability, became a constitutional monarchy, as was Yugoslavia. Romania was a kingdom, and the Bulgarian monarchy was ruled by the Tsar (see Table 2.1).

The economic development of Eastern European countries, regardless of a similar economic structure of a centrally planned economy across communist dependencies, varied in its characteristics. The most economically developed were East Germany followed by Czechoslovakia and Yugoslavia, leaving Poland, Bulgaria, Romania, and Albania far behind (see Table 2.2).

Thus, summarizing the impact of the variables of S_{vr} and A_t on a country's democratization, indicators representing S_{vr} and A_t constituted interactive components of the Threshold (T) of the adoption of democracy of each country in the late 1980s and early 1990s. The adoption of democracy depicts a time of countries' movement from being non-democratic to achieving some level of democracy (see Table 2.3 and Figure 2.9).

COMPONENTS OF SUCCESSFUL DISSIDENT MOVEMENTS

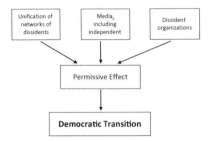

Figure 2.9 Components of successful dissident movements in Eastern Central Europe, 1970–1980
The figure presents a hypothetical network based on empirical data from interviews conducted by the author with leaders of dissident movements.

Accordingly, the first country to adopt a democratic system was Poland, which had the highest number and magnitude of collective protests and demonstrations (high S_{vr}) across its communist history. Prior to the communist period, Poland was a parliamentary democracy, increasing its familiarity with democracy outcomes (high S_{vr}). Across post-World War II history, Poland also had a high number of political changes within the communist polity (high A_t). In the 1980s this country, however, had one of the worst economic situations within the Eastern European bloc (low A_t). Nonetheless, the very high S_{vr} (the highest of all Eastern European countries) apparently so strongly affected the threshold of adoption that the low A_t (significantly lowered by economic crisis) was sufficient to pass the threshold. Hungary, which before the communist period was a constitutional monarchy, was the next country to adopt a democratic system. It had the fourth largest economy and the second highest number of political adjustments following political protests, although these phased out in the early 1960s, negatively affecting the S_{vr} value after that time. Nonetheless, the initially high number of political adjustments combined with the relatively high number of political protests was supported by the impact of a relatively stable economy. Combined, the interactive effect of these factors was sufficient to affect the threshold of democracy adoption.

Almost simultaneously with Hungary, democracy was adopted in Czechoslovakia. Czechoslovakia had some political protests and demonstrations before the 1960s and a large number of protests during the 1960s. Political adjustments visible until the 1980s resulted from these protests. Prior to the communist period, Czechoslovakia was a parliamentary democracy, which increased its familiarity with democratic principles. By the end of the 1980s, it was the second most economically developed Eastern European country after East Germany.

Bulgaria adopted democracy next to last. It was one of the poorest economies, relatively inexperienced in terms of political protests, and had only minor regime adjustments, only in the early communist period (until the mid 1950s). Prior to communism, Bulgaria was ruled by the authoritarian regime of the Tsar.

Finally, Albania was the last Eastern European country to adopt democracy. It had the smallest number and magnitude of political protests, very few political adjustments until the mid 1950s, and no adjustments after that time. Albania was also the least economically developed country of all the former communist Eastern European states. A lack of past democratic experience was magnified by the country's monarchic history prior to the communist period. According to our conceptual model, with the exception of Poland and Hungary, countries with higher T adopted democracy sooner, while the laggers had low T scores (see Figure 2.9).

Summary and concluding comments on democracy adoption

Although these results are tentative and mainly for illustrative purposes, they suggest that, in the case of democracy adoption, the impact of the internalized democratic values of the citizenry and prior experience with democratic governing substantially increase a country's vulnerability to democratization. In fact, pro-democratic experience, familiarity with changes within top governmental offices, and knowledge about democracy outcomes (e.g., Poland and Hungary) seem to be even more significant factors than the economic circumstances that are frequently seen as the primary promoters of democracy. For example, for Poland, which first adopted democracy, the S_{vr} score was much higher than for any other country in Eastern Europe, but the country had low development and was undergoing economic difficulties. Similarly, the A_t score of middle-developed Hungary was matched only by East Germany. Poland, with the highest S_{vr}, had lower T scores than Czechoslovakia but adopted democracy sooner. Thus, it seems that the threshold that is mainly derived by an impact of S_{vr} has a very strong impact on the adoption process. At the same time,

East Germany, with the highest A_t among these countries, adopted democracy after Poland, Czechoslovakia, and Hungary, again attesting that S_{vr} has a stronger impact on democratization than A_t.

With the exception of two precursors of democracy adoption (Poland and Hungary), however, the higher T matched the earlier timing of democracy adoption. Even though the model is supported by illustrative analyses only, it does help to identify the relevant categories of variables that contribute to predicting the adoption of democracy and its rate. Hence, the theoretical model presented in the section above makes an attempt to guide the understanding of the manner in which these variables interact when applying a theory of diffusion to estimate the value of successful adoption of democracy S_{vr}, its probability of being successfully instituted, and its relative importance compared to a country's propensities.

Interestingly, regardless of all these countries being members of the same structurally similar Soviet bloc, their values of T are clearly divided into two groups of scores: of above 200 (or 2.0×10^{-2}) and below 100 (or 1.0×10^{-2}). In the first group are Poland, Czechoslovakia, Hungary, and East Germany, and in the second are Bulgaria, Romania, Yugoslavia, and Albania. It could be that the economy of these two sets is vastly different; however, the Yugoslavian economy was as high as that of Hungary, while Romania and Bulgaria had a higher GNP/c than Poland. Again, it is difficult to attribute the timing of the transition primarily to countries' development; rather, it seems that the diffusion factors of S_{vr} affected the transition time to a greater extent than the economy, and the higher T (above 200) that matched the earlier timing of democracy adoption was mainly generated by factors of S_{vr}.

Nonetheless, in the group of the first adopters Hungary is an outlier with relatively low S_{vr} scores and lower T scores than Poland, Czechoslovakia and East Germany. Also Hungary's T scores, unlike those of Poland and Czechoslovakia, were generated mainly by regime adjustment that resulted from the influence of the democratic movement of 1950s and early 1960s. The grouping of countries and the interesting case of Hungary suggests that processes other than openness toward democracy and familiarity indicators may enforce the S_{vr} and the timing of democracy adoption. Since countries' development seems to be less influential, the additional indicators most probably reinforce processes of diffusion.

In search for additional indicators, the study relies on the empirical analysis of the outcomes of democratization factors in the years directly preceding democratic transition, believing that such analyses should shed more light on the democratization processes and democracy adoption.

An illustration of personal ties, networks, and institutional links in building democracy in Eastern Europe: studies of dissident movements

The Arab Spring of the people's revolution in the Middle East renewed scholarly interest in the development of democracy within grassroots movements that incorporate the activity of political dissidents. Although there are many journalistic accounts of ongoing pro-democratic or anti-authoritarian movements, such as strikes, riots, and protest letters, not many scholarly analyses devote attention to the longitudinal study of the events that lead to such protests. In particular, there is a relative paucity of scholarly empirical accounts of the activity of political dissident movements that are often hidden, purposely censored, and concealed from the public eye. Most frequently, the degree of the spread of dissident activity within a country is unknown to scholars, in contrast with the rather well-developed accounts of events during strikes and city riots. It is equally difficult to find information about the national and international networks that political activists formed to gain support for acclamations, propositions, and calls for political or economic reforms. Information about these hidden political topics becomes available mainly during a time of transition from authoritarian to democratic government, or during a break in the strength and a temporary or unexpected weakening of a totalitarian government. Most of the research on political dissidents, therefore, is conducted decades after the events, when the information has only historical meaning, or at the time of an open window of opportunity that allows access to politically sensitive data. Contrasting with this trend, this study presents data from research conducted during the time of transition from a communist to democratic system, and during the formation of a new democratic government in Eastern Central Europe in early 1990s, posing a question about the importance of dissident activity to the adoption of democracy within this region.

Generally, in scholarly studies, the term *dissident* defines a person who actively challenges an established political government, its ideology, or existing political doctrine. The term dissident was formed in the early 1960s in the former Soviet Union, and initially it referred to the political, anti-government activity of individual citizens. Shortly thereafter, however, the name began to be used for the anti-communist groups and organizations, the uncensored, independent Samizdat Press, and anti-government actions that collectively formed the dissident movement.

The need to analyze the processes of dissident activity is important, as it provides first-hand understanding of the political background, social and economic conditions, and societal structure that are contributory components of the formation of dissident activity as a grassroots response to totalitarian rule. Some of this information is provided by the dissident press, allowing a researcher a glimpse of the activity of existing dissident organizations and their networks. "Do you, Adam Michnik, Jacek Kuroń and Jan Lutyński, remember our first secret meeting in the mountains on the Polish–Czechoslovakian border? We were then, you and us, so called dissidents, which meant people who were chased by the police, arrested, sent to prison, and publicly ridiculed" (Czech President Vaclav Havel in his Presidential Address in Polish Parliament on January 25, 1990).[10]

Research on anti-communist dissident activity in Eastern Central Europe

To fill the gaps in existing research on the processes of the development of societal response to totalitarian rule and the grassroots building of democracy, this book is devoted to longitudinal, historical analyses of dissident movements across Eastern Europe in the 1970s and 1980s that, as this study claims, were the building blocks of the democratic transitions in formerly communist Eastern Europe in the early 1990s. This work results from the author's analyses of newspaper interviews and speeches delivered by political dissidents who frequently became politicians during the post-communist era. The

---

[10] *Trybuna Ludu* (January 25, 1990). Czech president Václav Havel in his presidential address in the Polish parliament on January 25, 1990.

articles were published in Polish, Czechoslovakian, Bulgarian, and Russian newspapers in 1989–1991, the period of the democratic transitions. Among the newspapers are the Polish dailies *Zycie Warszawy*, *Gazeta Wyborcza*, *Trybuna Opolska*, *Trybuna Ludu*, *Gazeta Poznanska*, and the Bulgarian newspaper *Tpyd* (*Trod*). The newspaper articles are supported by face-to-face interviews with Bulgarian, Polish, and Czech leaders of the anti-communist opposition conducted by the author in 1993. The collected data are complemented by data from an anthology of political dissidents of the regimes of the Soviet Union published by the Polish independent press Karta in 2007, and other available literature. For instance, a significant part of the data derives from direct interviews with prominent Eastern European political dissidents, some of them democratically elected presidents, ministers, and members of post-communist parliaments, and from an analysis of "The Paper Ammunition," a collection of over 3,000 volumes of material published by the independent Polish press Nova and other independent presses of Eastern Europe, collected and donated to the Cornell University Special Collection at Olin Library by Cornell Librarian Wanda Wawro. The collection was smuggled to the United States during the Solidarity time and period of martial law in the 1980s.

The research analyses were organized according to three categories of variables that characterized political dissident activity in Eastern Europe and Russia and that described the processes that led to transitions from communism to democracy. The first are *network* variables incorporating: (a) direct contacts between political dissidents within and outside their own country – interpersonal networks of dissidents and (b) institutional links between networks of dissident organizations. The second are *media*, representing the influence of Western and domestic media communication on processes of dissident activity, such as the broadcasting of Radio Free Europe, Radio Svoboda, the BBC, Voice of America, Deutsche Welle, and the live broadcasting of round table negotiations or pre-election rallies by the media of communist countries. The third are *organizational support* variables that encompass the help and support of foundations, international organizations, and anti-communist associations in organizing meetings between the oppositions' members and in publication or dissemination of dissident material, e.g., the Ford Foundation, Batory Foundation, and International Labor Organization.

Research results

The leading factors of dissident movements in Eastern Europe contributing to democracy changes are presented in Figure 2.9. As demonstrated there, the spirit of liberty expressed in the slogans "anticommunism," "freedom," and "democracy" was transferred during face-to-face meetings of dissidents; through exchanges of literary material and political analyses published in the independent press, e.g., the publications of the independent, underground Polish publisher Nova; information disseminated by the uncensored publications of Samizdat across the Soviet Union; Western media broadcasting of anti-communist protests and interviews with protest organizers and witnesses; and via unification of dissident networks, media – including the independent press – and the institutionalized goals and demands of human rights supported by the international appeal for human rights signed by many countries. It is perhaps most important to start analyses of these three channels, or factors: interpersonal and organizational networks, independent media, and organizational support of pro-democratic activity, as they constitute the permissive effects for the activity of dissident organizations.

The conceptual framework of the analyses of the leading factors of dissident movements in Eastern Europe is presented in Figure 2.9.

Network connectedness of political opposition

"The principal goal of discussion between leaders of the Polish opposition with Cardinal Tomášek, with activists of Karta 77, and with Alexander Dubček, was to find the best way to 'push' Czechoslovakia towards Polish-type reform ... that would eventually result in the breaking off from communism," commented the communist newspaper *Rude Pravo*, criticizing the July 1989 meeting of Solidarity members with Czechoslovakian dissidents (Lubiejewski 1989).

As some researchers have explained, among the most influential factors that affected the development of the democratic opposition are *liberalization* and the level of *repressiveness* of communist regimes (Ost 1990). Accordingly, Polish and Hungarian communist regimes were perceived to be more liberal than regimes in East Germany and Czechoslovakia (Bunce 1990). The relative freedom of a strong Polish Catholic Church, its cooperation with the political opposition, and the international authority of the Polish Pope John Paul II added pertinence to anti-communist mobilization. "Poles discovered the strength of the opposition when the Pope's visit in June 1979 brought two million people into the streets," wrote Przeworski (1991, 59). John Elson added: "Tadeusz Mazowiecki, a Solidarity intellectual who was Poland's first post-communist prime minister, this month told *Time* [in an interview for the newspaper *Time*] something that church officials in the past frequently denied. 'After the communist regime imposed martial law in 1981, the Pope wrote letters of counsel to Solidarity activists interned by the communists; priests and bishops served as couriers because they were not subjected to body searches ... and their robes carried more mail than many workers in our postal service,' said Mazowiecki" (Elson 1994, 64).

The more liberal regimes were less punitive toward the developing civil society and its democratic mobilization. Regimes that were perceived as strong, due to their own stability and sanctions against political opponents, prevented protest actions aimed at democratic reforms, e.g., the Ceauşescu regime in Romania and the Brezhnev regime in the former Soviet Union (Beck 1993; Bunce 1990). But each communist regime underwent changes in regard to its degree of more open, lenient attitudes toward political opposition that affected the punitive nature of the regimes; e.g., the Polish regime under Bierut during Stalin's time was much more punitive than the regime of Edward Gierek of the 1980s (Ost 1990), or the Czechoslovakian regime of liberal reformist Alexander Dubček during the Czechoslovakian Spring of 1968 vs centrists and Soviet sympathizer Gustáv Husák. Such changes influenced the organization and activity of dissident movements within Eastern European countries as well as these movements' connections and mutual support.

The most significant building blocks of pro-democratic, Eastern European movements were interpersonal contacts between the political dissidents of the former Eastern European states that dated from long before the breaking of the communist regime in Poland in June of 1989. Members of Polish Solidarity, Czechoslovakian Karta 77 (Card 77); the Bulgarian opposition movement Confederation of Labor Подкрепа (Podkrepa); Hungarian dissidents and dissidents of the Ukraine, Russia, White Russia, and Lithuania met on various occasions starting in the 1970s. As Václav Havel describes, he came to Poland the for first time "as a student with a student tourist group in

1957. It was shortly after your famous October [workers protests in Poznan, Poland, in October 1956] and your country was full of hope ... I was fascinated with everything that was Polish. I read Hlasko, Milosz, Herbert and Kolakowski, Brandys and Rudnicki [Polish writers who were censored and banished from publishing houses]" (*Gazeta Wyborcza* 1990, June 8).[11] Polish Solidarity activist Helena Wujec, also a member of the democratically elected parliament in Poland, added in an interview with the author, "Before 1968 [organized anti-communist student protests and opposition movement in Poland] we were fascinated by the activity of Soviet dissidents, listening to the ballads of Bulat Okudzawa and soulful Russian protest songs. Very popular among Polish students was the Russian independent literature from Samizdat smuggled to, or published in, the West."[12]

Hence, the links between individual dissidents were established more than a decade prior to the democratic transitions but intensified in the 1980s. In 1984 and 1985, the Polish political dissident Zbigniew Janas organized more frequent contacts with the Czechoslovakian opposition, after his release from several years' imprisonment for political activity. Meetings of Polish dissidents with leaders of the Czechoslovakian political opposition Karta 77 (Vaclav Hável and János Kis), aimed at dislodging the communist regime (Lityński, 1992).

Dissidents held their meetings in remote, secured mountain huts and on mountain hiking trails, hidden from secret service and police activity. Among other "convenient and secured" sites of dissident meetings were cars crossing the main cities of Hungary, Romania, or Czechoslovakia. One such meeting was described by Zbigniew Boni, former Solidarity activist, who became the democratically elected vice-Minister of Labor in the first democratic government of Poland in 1990. As Minister Boni described, to avoid detection and surveillance by the secret police, he and political dissidents from other Eastern European countries would drive on Prague's and Budapest's streets while discussing political programs. "At the end of the 1980s I had a

---

[11] Speech of the President of Czechoslovakia, Václav Havel, addressing the Polish parliament on October 1, 1990. Polish daily newspaper *Gazeta Wyborcza* (October 1, 1990): 1.

[12] Interview with Helena Wujec was conducted by Barbara Wejnert on July 20, 1993 in Warsaw's chapter of the the Polish Solidarity party that was formed from the Solidarity movement.

secret meeting with Václav Havel. We were sitting in a car driving around Prague to secure ourselves and to protect the privacy of our conversation."[13] Such strategic meetings facilitated by face-to-face communication were the basis of programs to implement democratic principles and democratic reforms; and of plans and strategies that led to the break-up of the communist regimes. Dissidents discussed and shared plans for how and when to disarm communism and implement democratic reforms.

As the media of democratic Poland reported, a month after the collapse of communism in Poland, Solidarity members visited members of Karta 77 in Prague as members of the Polish parliament. It was "the first legal meeting of the members of the Polish and Czechoslovakian opposition. Previous meetings were organized in conspiracy, often attracting the intervention of the secret police." (Lubiejewski 1989). According to interviews conducted by the author, before the Polish Round Table negotiations of spring 1989, members of the Polish Solidarity movement established contacts with Russian political dissident organizations and their Samizdat publishing operation, as well as with the Lithuanian opposition that was organized around dissident periodicals such as the *Chronicles of the Catholic Church* in Lithuania, or the *Chronicle of Contemporary Events.*[14] The interview data were confirmed by notations in the published *Dictionary of Dissidents* (Slownik 2007, 334–337).

Individual contacts, however, served also as a channel of exchange of Samizdat literature, published and often printed by Soviet dissidents. This literature contained data about unspoken events in the modern history of the communist states that, under communist regimes, were forbidden to be discussed or remembered. Such uncensored material also provided information about the cruelty of communist regimes toward political opponents; described cases of violations of human rights and prisoners' rights that were supposed to be respected due to international conventions (e.g., the Helsinki accord), such as prisoners' living conditions and cruelty committed in Russian Gulag camps; as well as the imprisonment of political dissidents in mental hospitals

---

[13] Interview with Zbigniew Boni, vice-Minister of Labor in the democratically elected Polish government, former activist of Solidarity. The interview was conducted by the author of this book on July 3, 1993.
[14] Described by Zbigniew Boni, July, 1993.

specially designed to interrogate and incarcerate political opposition – as sources in The Paper Ammunition explain.[15]

Uncensored books and other material were printed mainly by the Polish independent press Nova. This press was established in 1977 and was the longest and most active independent press within the Eastern European bloc. Its advantageous location in Poland, the most politically free country within the Soviet system, allowed for the longest functioning until the collapse of the communist regime in 1989. Some of the materials were also printed in languages other than Polish, such as Czechoslovakian, Lithuanian, Russian, and Ukrainian. "After the first meeting of Havel, Michnik, Lityński, and Jacek Kuroń,[16] the Polish underground press was smuggled to Czechoslovakia thorough the mountains," said Ludmila Wujec,[17] Solidarity activist and member of the Polish democratic parliament. "Printed by Nova, material was illegally delivered to members of Karta 77 across the Polish–Czechoslovakian mountain border. Karta 77 in turn distributed it internally among Czech and Slovak dissidents," according to information from a direct interview with Henryk Wujec, a former member of the National Committee of Solidarity and a former member of the NSZZ "Solidarity" Mazowsze Region Management Board, who in 1993 became a deputy of the *Sejm* (Parliament) of democratic Poland, and from 1997 to 1999 a co-chairman of the Committee for Agriculture and Rural Development.[18]

To demonstrate the extent and importance of interpersonal and organizational networks to the adoption of democracy in Eastern Central Europe, as well as the significance of the media, the next section delineates dissident networks and the influence of the media across historical events prior to, during, and after the democratic transitions of the early 1990s.

---

[15] "The Paper Ammunition" collection of material published by the independent Polish press Nova and other independent presses of Eastern Europe, smuggled to the United States during the Solidarity time and martial law in the 1980s, collected and donated to Cornell University Library's special collection. The collection is described above.

[16] Jacek Kuroń was a Minister of Labor and Social Policy in 1989–1990 and 1992–1993. Among other parties he belonged to the post–Solidarity Citizens' Parliamentary Club (OKP).

[17] Interview with Ludmila Wujec, Solidarity activist and member of the Polish democratic parliament, conducted on July 23, 1993, by the author.

[18] The interview with Henryk Wujec was conducted on July 19, 1993, in the Warsaw headquarters of the OKP (Citizens' Parliamentary Club), by the author.

Interpersonal networks of dissidents: contacts before the Polish first democratic election in June, 1989

But the most significant were the interpersonal secret meetings between dissidents that were initiated in late 1970s. For instance, in 1978, Havel from the Czechoslovakian Opposition Group Karta 77 and Adam Michnik, Jacek Kuroń, and Jan Lityński from the Polish KOR (Committee of Workers' Defense) initiated the mountain meetings. "Do you, Adam Michnik, Jacek Kuroń, and Jan Lityński, remember our first secret meeting in the mountains on the Polish–Czechoslovakian border ... And later years of carrying backpacks full of illegal publications across our joint mountains?" asked Czech President Václav Havel (Havel 1990). Henryk Wujec added: "after the first meeting of Havel, Michnik, Lityński, and Kuroń, the Polish underground press was smuggled to Czechoslovakia through the mountains."[19] As a continuation of these meetings, in 1984 the Polish Solidarity designated Zbigniew Janas to organize more frequent contacts with the activists of Karta 77 (Lityński 1992). From this time Zbigniew Janas " ... frequently met with Václav Havel and János Kis, and smuggled books and other material across the Polish–Czechoslovakian mountain border. Some of which were published in the Czech language," described Henryk Wujec.[20] "I had a secret meeting with Václav Havel in the Fall of 1989. We were sitting in a car in Prague," said Solidarity activist and democratically elected vice-Minister of Labor, Zbigniew Boni.[21] Adam Michnik traveled to Budapest to meet Gelza Jasienki, the Hungarian reformer elected as Minister of Foreign Affairs in the postcommunist government. The meeting took place in a car parked on the streets of Budapest in the summer of 1989.[22] Also, Fidelsz from Solidarity visited Budapest dissidents and had a meeting in a car in the spring of 1988.[23]

From the early 1970s, the role of dissident meetings was twofold: (1) they facilitated direct contacts, and (2) they served to exchange and

---

[19] Interview with Ludmila Wujec, Solidarity activist and member of the Polish democratic parliament, conducted on July 23, 1993 by the author.

[20] This interview with Henryk Wujec was conducted on July 5, 1993, in Warsaw, in the headquarters of OKP, by the author.

[21] Interview with Zbigniew Boni, July 4, 1993.

[22] Interview with Zbigniew Boni, July 4, 1993.

[23] Interview with Zbigniew Boni, July 3, 1993.

distribute printed dissident material. Both the interpersonal meetings and the printed material created channels of communication between members of democratic movements that facilitated the exchange of ideas about principles of democracy and the planning of democratic reforms. The independent press provided true information about the unspoken modern history of communist countries and the cruelty of communist regimes, and published censored literature (The Paper Ammunition).[24] By the end of the 1980s, initiated by the Solidarity movement, the Solidarity Information Service (SIS) had published information about the Polish national strikes in the summer of 1988, the Round Table talks between the representatives of the Polish communist government and members of the central committee of the Solidarity movement in the Spring of 1989, and the Polish free democratic election of June 1989 that led to the breakdown of communist rule. SIS also published banned books, such as Wojciech Maziarski's book about the independent student movement, and a book about Lech Wałęsa by the same author; essays about Polish dissidents written by Hungarian reformist Janos Kiscosz; and Janos Kiscosz's book about Polish economic reforms. The SIS's primary goal was to inform Polish society and to address the Hungarian political opposition.[25]

Starting in 1988, the Polish Klub Inteligencji Katolickiej (KIK; Club of Catholic Intellectuals), which was founded at the start of Gomulka's political softening era in 1956 and later evolved into a mild Catholic-centered opposition group in communist Poland, established contacts with the East German political opposition, supporting the idea of the unification of Germany. At the same time, KIK also established contacts with the Hungarian opposition, and activist Fidelsz from KIK visited Budapest in the spring of 1988.[26]

To plan more frequent and organized contacts with members of the political opposition, Solidarity appointed "special tasks" members responsible for contacts with dissident groups in selected countries.

---

[24] "The Paper Ammunition" is a collection of over 3,000 volumes of material published by the independent Polish press Nova and other independent presses of Eastern Europe, collected and donated to the Cornell University special collection libraries by Cornell Librarian Wanda Wawro. The collection was smuggled to the United States during the Solidarity period and the period of martial law in the 1980s. The author of this book studied almost the entire collection, supported by a grant from the Humanity Institute in 1994.

[25] Described by Zbigniew Boni, July 3, 1993.

[26] Interview with Zbigniew Boni, July 20, 1993.

Beginning in the mid 1980s, Zbigniew Bujak was the primary person responsible for contacts with Hungarian dissidents, Zbigniew Janas organized contacts with the Czechoslovakian Karta 77, and Grzegorz Kostiewa-Zorbas was designated to establish contacts between Solidarity and dissidents of democratic movements in the Ukraine; among them were Czarnowil and the brothers Choryniow – as Henryk Wujec explained.[27] At the same time, Václav Havel and Karta 77 established contacts with Hungarian reformers; for example, Havel had a secret meeting with Imre Pozsgay in the fall of 1989 (*Gazeta Wyborcza* 1989e) as well as establishing face-to face contacts with the leaders of the Bulgarian Confederation of Labor Подкрепа (Podkrepa).

Podkrepa, founded on February 8, 1988 by the Bulgarian intellectuals Konstantin Trenchev, Boyko Proychev, and Nikolay Kolev-Bossia, was, as its president Konstantin Trenchev described, "a Solidarity child ... we shared the idea for an independent trade union of intellectuals like the Polish KOR, which was the predecessor of Solidarity ... Podkrepa had particularly friendly relations with the Polish trade union Solidarity" (Komitov 1991a, 1). Also, Solidarity established contacts with, and sent a congratulatory letter to, the Podkrepa founders within weeks after its proclamation.[28] Podkrepa copied its strategy of protest from KOR and from Solidarity.

First, Podrepa, like KOR, sent information about its establishment to the Western media: "On February 11 we sent information to the Western broadcasters about the new formal organization. Deutsche Welle, Radio Free Europe, and the BBC immediately reported the news" (Komitov 1991a, 3). Second, like KOR and Solidarity, Podkrepa founders called Western radio stations from private homes. The first person to overcome the fear of the Communist police and call from a private home was Jacek Kuroń from the Polish KOR. His initiative was later copied by many dissidents from Poland and other Eastern European countries. Third, similar to the Polish political oppositionists, Podkrepa leaders signed their names and phone numbers to printed material and information submitted to Western broadcasters. Again, the first dissident who signed his name, phone number, and address under articles

---

[27] Interview with Henryk Wujec, secretary of OKP and president of Unia Demokratyczna (Democratic Union Party), conducted by the author in the Unia Demokratyczna office in Warsaw on July 30, 1993.

[28] Interview with Dr. Trenchev, president of Podkrepa, in the Podkrepa office in Sofia, on August 6, 1993, conducted by the author.

published in the underground press was Jacek Kuroń.[29] His model of communication was also copied by other Eastern European dissidents. This direct form of communication served a double purpose; it was the fastest way to inform the world about dissident activity in any communist state, and it was also a channel for informing the citizens of communist countries about anti-communist activity in their own states. For example, after the transmission about the establishment of Podkrepa, "the telephone didn't stop ringing. People from all over the country expressed their desire to join us. I remember that within the first fifteen minutes after the transmission, the first to give us a call were Zoja and Stefan Komitovi from Veliko Tarnovo in Bulgaria. The list of names of those who joined the organization increased with every passing day," said Podkrepa president Konstantin Trenchev (Komitov 1991a, 3).

Networks of dissident organizations after the Polish Round Table negotiations and the Polish democratic election in June 1989

"The events in Poland are the role model for Czechoslovakia. If Poland sustains the change, revolution in Czechoslovakia is inevitable," said Pavel Tigrid, director of the Czechoslovakian section of Radio Free Europe after the Solidarity victory in the June 1989 election.

The Polish Round Table talks and the Solidarity victory in the first free democratic election held in a Soviet-bloc country initiated the outburst of mutual contacts and exchange of information between Poland and the members of other democratic movements. Interestingly, following these events, dissident contacts changed their character from face-to-face, interpersonal meetings to organizational contacts with dissidents representing anti-communist organizations.

The Polish Round Table negotiations[30] as well as the Polish free election in June 1989 were closely observed by the anti-communist opposition in all East European countries. After winning the free election, Solidarity's goal was to help dissident movements in other communist countries to establish democratic elections and political reforms in their own countries. "During the Polish Round Table we created

---

[29] Interview with Ludmila Wujec, Solidarity activist and member of the Polish democratic parliament, conducted on July 23, 1993 by the author.

[30] Negotiations between the democratic movement Solidarity and the Polish communist government regarding political and economic reforms in Poland.

four- to five-person groups of sociologists and political scientists who daily listened to Western broadcasting and analyzed each step in the progress of negotiations ... Our model of organization of a round table was copied from Poland," said Kristo Petkov, president of the former Bulgarian communist trade union that in 1989 became the Confederation of the Independent Trades Unions of Bulgaria (CITUB) and one of the representatives of the Bulgarian political opposition at the Bulgarian Round Table negotiations with the communist government.[31] "We borrowed from Solidarity the following strategies: waves of strikes that the government could not control, lists of demands submitted to the government, and petitions to initiate round table negotiations between the Bulgarian government and Podkrepa, to discuss needed political and economic reforms. We also called for a free election that could overthrow the communist government," said Konstantin Trenchev, President of Podkrepa.[32] Prior to the formal initiation of Podkrepa, the Bulgarian movement was organized secretly: "the idea of its establishment had often been discussed, as early as the years 1983–1984," said Trenchev (Komitov 1991a). Plamen Darakchiev shared similar information in an interview with Stefan Komitov (1991a).

Members of Polish Solidarity visited the Czechoslovakian, Bulgarian, Hungarian, Ukrainian, and Mongolian political opposition. Shortly before Ukrainian independence, Adam Michnik, Dracz, and Zbigniew Bujak traveled to the Ukraine for a rally in Kiev, delivering greetings from Solidarity and teaching about the Polish free election, explained Zbigniew Boni in an interview in 1993.[33] Maciej Jankowski, head of the Mazowsze region of Solidarity, visited Mongolia, advising on democratic elections and helping the Mongolian opposition to prepare its first free election in 1990. Solidarity contacted Romania, but since there were no established opposition groups, it provided humanitarian help to non-communist Romanian citizens, said member of the central committee of Polish Solidarity Janusz Palubicki in 1993.[34]

---

[31] Interview with Kristo Petkov, president of the Independent Trade Union of Bulgaria, conducted in Sofia at the headquarters of CITUB by the author on August 4, 1993.

[32] Interview with Konstantin Trenchev conducted in Sofia at the headquarters of Podkrepa by the author in August 8, 1993.

[33] Described by Zbigniew Boni. The interview was conducted by the author on July 3, 1993.

[34] Interview with Janusz Palubicki, member of the Polish parliament and Solidarity member, conducted by the author on July 26, 1993.

More frequent contacts were established between Polish Solidarity and the Czechoslovakian, Hungarian, and Bulgarian democratic dissident movements. Indeed, a few weeks after the election, the newly formed Obywatelski Klub Parliamentarny – OKP (Citizens' Parliamentary Club) consisting of 169 Solidarity members who were also members of the democratically elected parliament of Poland, fully developed actions aimed at providing help to other Eastern European pro-democratic opposition movements. Such help was openly declared by the president of OKP, Bronisław Geremek, in his manifesto addressed to all political opposition groups active in the Soviet-bloc states (*Gazeta Wyborcza* 1989e).[35] As Zbigniew Boni explained in an interview conducted in Poland, the primary goals of OKP were twofold: first, to maintain existing contacts between members of the opposition via private face-to-face meetings and official visits of members of the Polish parliament, and second, to help to prepare other societies to break with communism and to organize democratic elections.[36]

Within OKP, two clubs were established to support opposition movements in Czechoslovakia and Hungary: Polish–Czechoslovakian Solidarity, presided over by Zbigniew Janas, and Polish–Hungarian Solidarity, presided over by Zbigniew Bujak. On July 18, 1989, Polish–Czechoslovakian Solidarity issued its first document, the Seven-Point Program supporting democratic reforms in Czechoslovakia. The program was a response to the manifesto "A Few Words" that was sent to the Czechoslovakian government by Cardinal František Tomášek. "A Few Words" demanded freedom of religion and citizens' rights. On July 21, three days after the manifesto, a delegation from Polish–Czechoslovakian Solidarity, consisting of Adam Michnik, Zbigniew Janas, Jan Lityński, Zbigniew Bujak, and Mirosław Jasiński, traveled on diplomatic passports to Czechoslovakia to discuss the Seven-Point Program with the Czechoslovakian opposition. They met with a priest, Václaw Maly, and other members of Karta 77, Ana Hromatkova and Peter Pospichal. The Polish delegation also had an audience with Cardinal Tomášek and met with Alexander Dubček in his mountain dacha and again in his home in Bratislava, and had talks with Václav Havel (*Trybuna Ludu* 1989; Lubiejewski, 1989; *Gazeta*

[35] *Gazeta Wyborcza* 1989b, "Polska Zaraza" (Polish Disease) (September 3–5): 2.
[36] Interview with Zbigniew Boni, July 20, 1993.

Wyborcza 1989a). It was "the first legal meeting of members of the Polish and Czechoslovakian oppositions. Previous meetings were organized in conspiracy, often attracting the intervention of the secret police" (*Trybuna Opolska* 1989). As the Czech communist newspaper *Rude Pravo* critically assessed, the goal of these meetings was to define a strategy to abolish the communist system in Czechoslovakia (*Trybuna Opolska* 1989).

The frequency of contacts between the Czechoslovakian and Hungarian opposition and OKP intensified in the summer of 1989 after the victory of Solidarity in the Polish free election. The OKP members frequently traveled to Czechoslovakia and Hungary in the summer of 1989, concealing their true purpose by traveling with theater groups for drama festivals or with academics and artists to universities for art exhibitions and conferences, and illegally crossed mountain borders, all with one goal: to maintain close contacts with groups of dissidents from neighboring Eastern European countries. For example, in August 1989, Krystyna Kruaze and Mieczyslaw Piotrowski from Polish–Czechoslovakian Solidarity were stopped on the Polish mountain border (*Gazeta Wyborcza* 1989e).[37]

In the fall of 1989, member of the newly elected Polish government and former dissident Zbigniew Bujak visited Budapest with the theater group "Gardziejowice," and Adam Michnik (another member of the post-communist Polish government and a former dissident) visited Budapest as a representative of the Polish parliament. Michnik met with reformist Gelza Jasienski, who was later elected Minister of Foreign Affairs in the post-communist Hungarian government, to discuss democratic political and economic reforms.[38] In August 1989, Krystyna Kruaze, and a month earlier, Mieczyslaw Piotrowski from Polish–Czechoslovakian Solidarity, traveled to Prague. They were both stopped at the border by the Czech police (*Gazeta Wyborcza* 1989b). The Czech police attempted to halt communication between Solidarity and Czechoslovakia and Hungary. In October 1989 in Prague, they arrested Zbigniew Janas, who had traveled to Hungary on a diplomatic passport (*Gazeta Wyborcza* 1989c). In December 1989, two members of Polish Solidarity, Grzegorz Kmita and Robert Prus, were released

---

[37] Gazeta Wyborcza, 1989d. Kometarz Wiadomosci (Commentary News) (August 21, 1989): 2.
[38] Interview with Zbigniew Boni, July 20, 1993.

from a Czechoslovakian prison after being arrested for "illegally cross-ing the border" with Poland (Polska Agencja Prasowa 1989).[39]

It is assumed that meetings with Polish Solidarity members and dissidents from other Eastern European countries facilitated the devel-opment of a new strategy to promote democratic principles in Czecho-slovakia and Hungary that reflected the distinct character of the democratic movements in these countries. In Czechoslovakia, political protests were expressed via alternative, independent art: music, movies, poetry, and material published in the underground press, a method of protest borrowed from the Russian underground organiza-tion Samizdat. The newly developed strategy represented a response to the repressive nature of Czech regimes that included severe punishment for political activity, significantly more severe than in Poland.

To bring together scattered alternative-culture groups, Czech and Slovak dissidents, in cooperation with Polish Solidarity, organized the Symposium of East European Cultures that included the Festival of Independent Czechoslovakian Culture in Wrocław on November 10–12, 1989. This symposium was organized in cooperation with the Czechoslovakian Karta 77 and was directed by Polish activists Zbigniew Janas and Mirosław Jasiński. Regardless of the sealed-off border between Czechoslovakia and Poland, 5,000 Czechs and Slovaks came to Wrocław, representing forty different dissident groups (Pelikan 1989). They traveled through Germany and the Soviet Union. Many well-known dissidents delivered speeches at the symposium, including Stanislaw Baranczak, a Polish dissident of the 1968 student movement who emigrated to the United States; Jirzi Pelikan, a hero of the Prague Spring who emigrated to Italy; Václav Havel, former dissident and later president of the Czech Republic, Adam Michnik, Kiryl Podrabinek, Karl Johann von Schwarzenberg, Milan Simecka, Wolfgang Templin, and George Urban. It was the largest meeting of scattered opposition groups and individual dissidents from Czechoslovakia, and, as the Solidarity press jokingly described it, "the largest CIA convention" referring to the common communist accusation of political dissidents being agents of the American Central Intelligence Agency (*Gazeta Wyborcza* 1989g). The Wrocław Festival informed Czechoslovakians about the number of political opposition groups that were active in

---

[39] The Polish Press (Polska Agencja Prasowa) was informed about this arrest by "Citizens Forum," a Czechoslovakian opposition organization.

Czechoslovakia, and their strength. As Václav Havel observed, the " Wrocław Symposium ... was unexpectedly the prelude to our Czecho- slovakian Revolution" (Havel, 1990).

The Polish–Hungarian Solidarity organized a similar event at the University in Pesc, Hungary, called "Polish Days." The Polish Days in Pesc, however, brought only limited success. First, the Hungarian opposition, unlike revolutionary Poland, Czechoslovakia, or Bulgaria, chose a *reformist* road of transition from communism, mainly con- cerned with economic changes (Bruszt and Stark 1991), using Polish experiences as examples of potential Hungarian reforms.[40] Subse- quently, in the fall of 1989, Janos Kiscosz, a member of the Hungarian opposition, published a book about Polish economic reforms. And second, it was difficult to develop contacts with Hungarian dissidents because Hungary is located farther away than Czechoslovakia and does not share a border with Poland. Also, the Czechoslovakian secret police arrested dissidents traveling for the "Polish Days" and confiscated smuggled anti-communist publications. For instance, Solidarity members Tomasz Gadula-Zawratynski, Andrzej Miastowski, Pawel Polester, and Piotr Zlosnicki were arrested at Prague airport, and police confiscated Solidarity posters, videos, and photographs prepared for the festival in Pesc (Borkowicz 1989). They were released after twenty hours of police interrogation.[41] Therefore in October 1989, Zbigniew Bujak, traveling with the theater group "Gardziejowice," visited Buda- pest to continue discussions, maintaining collaboration but focusing on economic changes.[42] Also, to counteract the limited success of "Polish Days," the independent trade union of Hungary visited Warsaw by official invitation of the Polish democratic government, to learn about Polish reforms.[43]

In the fall of 1989, the Bulgarian democratic movement Podkrepa invited members of the parliamentary club OKP of Polish Solidarity to deliver a series of lectures on the preparation of democratic elections. In the winter of 1989, a delegation from Solidarity, presided over by Wnuk Lipinski, Maciej Jankowski, and Henryk Wujec, visited Bulgaria to meet representatives of Podkrepa. "We assured them that they could

---

[40] In the fall of 1989, the Hungarian opposition published a book about Polish economic reforms, by Janos Kiscosz.
[41] *Gazeta Wyborcza*, 1989a. "Polacy Niemile Widziani" 9.11.1989.
[42] Interview with Zbigniew Boni, July 20, 1993.
[43] Interview with Zbigniew Boni, July 20, 1993.

win the election, although not believing it ourselves," commented Henryk Wujec.[44] The delegation from Polish Solidarity delivered printed material from the independent press describing the Polish Round Table and its free election, and also printing equipment (Zakowski 1991).[45] Just before the June 10 and 12 election, Zhelyu Zhelev, President of the Bulgarian Union of Democratic Forces representing the Bulgarian opposition at the Round Table, called for a rally on the Liberty Square in Sofia. One million people (nearly one-sixth of the Bulgarian population) gathered in the square to listen to the speeches of Zhelyu Zhelev and invited Polish Solidarity members Maciej Jankowski, Adam Michnik, and independent movie producer Andrzej Wajda (*Gazeta Wyborcza* 1990). Polish Solidarity members read a letter from Lech Wałęsa to the gathered Bulgarians. On June 5, the Bulgarian democratic newspaper *Trud* published a speech delivered by Adam Michnik at this meeting (Michnik 1990). Zhelyu Zhelev, soon to be the democratically elected president of Bulgaria, said to the Polish president Lech Wałęsa: "My country follows Polish footsteps because Poland is the most advanced and the most experienced in political and economic reforms. The common factor of Poland and Bulgaria is that they are both liberated from communism ... We have often used the Polish model in our activity" (Informacja PAP 1993). Pavel Giergica from the Polish communist trade unions (Zwiazki Zawodowe) visited CITUB in March 1990 to help the Bulgarian opposition to prepare for the free election (CITUB 1991). "No government could resist Podkrepa's strength ... We even tried to assist and help the incipient democratic movements in the Soviet Union and Albania," said Konstantin Trenchev (Komitov 1991a, 12).

"The delegation of Polish Solidarity also delivered printing equipment and printed material from the independent press describing the most recent democratic events in Poland: the Round Table and the free election," said Henryk Wujec.[46] Trenchev said, "We did not have

---

[44] Interview with Henryk Wujec, Solidarity activist and member of the democratically elected Polish Parliament. Interview was conducted by the author of this book in Warsaw, on July 18, 1993.

[45] Interview with Henryk Wujec, July 18, 1993. Also: interview with Emilian Abadzejew, secretary of the Central Committee of Bulgarian Independent Trade Union (CITUB), conducted in the CITUB office in Sofia by the author on August 10, 1993.

[46] Interview with Henryk Wujec, July 18, 1993.

any information about Solidarity in 1980–1981 or any contacts with Solidarity. We listened to Radio Free Europe and other Western broadcasting, so there were limited opportunities to learn about Solidarity. But we met with Wałęsa and other Solidarity members during international congresses and conferences numerous times. The name and the idea of a round table was copied from Poland but the structure of the Bulgarian Round Table was different."[47] "From May 1990 Solidarity supplied Podkrepa with printing equipment and material about the organization and setting up of a free election," recalled secretary of the central committee of CITUB, Emilian Abadzejew.[48]

Maciej Jankowski from Mazowsze Solidarity and Henryk Wujec from the OKP visited Podkrepa, helping in preparations for the free election (Zakowski 1991). Similar contacts developed with the Ukraine dissident movement, aimed at the preparation for a free election and the establishment of democratic government. Shortly before Ukrainian liberation from Soviet dependency and abolition of communism, members of the central committee of Solidarity Dracz, Michnik, and Bujak traveled to the Ukraine for a rally during which they delivered greetings from Solidarity and gave speeches in Kiev.[49] Maciej Jankowski, head of the Mazowsze chapter of Solidarity, visited Mongolia to advise democratic forces on democratic elections and to help prepare for the first free election in 1990.

The leaders of Polish Solidarity also established contacts with Romania; however, since there were no dissident movements or established opposition groups in Romania, Solidarity contacts with Romania focused on the provision of humanitarian help to non-communist Romanian citizens. Nonetheless, as member of Polish parliament Janusz Palubicki explained, due to information shared during such contacts, the new communist elite that replaced the previous communist elite in the Romanian government had to respond to societal requests for reforms; among them was the introduction of a free market economy and democratic ideology.[50]

---

[47] Interview conducted by the author with Dr. Trenchev, President of Podkrepa, in the Podkrepa office in Sofia, on August 6, 1993.
[48] Interview with Emilian Abadzejew, August 10, 1993.
[49] Interview with Zbigniew Boni, July 20, 1993.
[50] Interview with Janusz Palubicki, member of the Polish parliament and member of the Solidarity movement, conducted by the author on July 26, 1993.

After the waves of Bulgarian national strikes at the end of 1989 and the overthrow of the last communist government of Lukanov, plans for the Bulgarian Round Table and free election solidified. This coincided with the free election won by Czechoslovakian democratic forces and the election of former dissident Václav Havel as president in January 1990. From this point in early 1990, contacts between the democratic oppositions of Eastern European states reshaped their character, and the direct contacts, anti-communist publications, and preparations to abolish communist governments were replaced by dissidents' concentration on the implementation of democratic reforms and the creation of a solid and stable base for sustainable democracies.

As during the period of dissident activity, the models of economic and political reform and models of democracy were not individually invented by each country or borrowed from the Western democracies, but rather the newly elected democratic governments of East European countries followed the model established by the first post-communist, democratic government of Poland and the first Polish economic restructuring plan of Balcerowicz. To implement democratic freedom Václav Havel, for instance, sent a letter to Tadeusz Mazowiecki, Solidarity prime minister in Poland, and to the leader of the Hungarian opposition Imre Pozsgay, asking for intervention to release the arrested dissident Ján Čarnogurský from prison.[51] At the same time, the Czechoslovakian Civil Forum informed the media about the arrest of Polish dissidents by the Czech police, which led to their release.

Frequent meetings of former Eastern European dissidents who became members of newly elected governments also concentrated on the post-communist economic reforms.

Democratic networks after the victories: the first democratic elections in the countries of Eastern Europe

Diffusing democratic transitions initiated the spread of information about democratic reforms in the Soviet Union. Although throughout the 1980s contacts were maintained between Solidarity (mainly KIK), the Russian and Lithuanian opposition Samizdat, and the Ukrainian and Belorussian opposition movement, the free election won by

---

[51] Daily newspaper *Gazeta Wyborcza*, 1989a. "News." October 3, p. 3.

Solidarity intensified prior links.[52] Adam Michnik traveled to Moscow, where he spoke before a group of reformist deputies to the Supreme Soviet and Solidarity parliaments. "Weeks later, Michnik went again to the Soviet Union [the Ukraine], this time to Kiev, where he spoke to the founding conference of the Ukrainian National Movement shouting 'Long live Ukraine!' *Komsomolskaya Pravda* then ran an extensive interview with Michnik in late September, allowing him to present his view freely to the paper's several million Soviet readers" (Ost 1990). A few months later, in the fall of 1989, Bogdan Borusewicz was sent by Solidarity to the striking workers in the oil fields of Donbas (Russia) to help with the organization of their strike.

Contacts between the democratic opposition movements of East Europe and the Solidarity movement reshaped their character when Czechoslovakian democratic forces won the free election;[53] Václav Havel became president of Czechoslovakia in January 1990; the Bulgarian Round Table and free election were organized in the spring of 1990; and the Hungarian communist party officially renounced Leninism, legalized all political parties, and announced a free election for spring 1990. The illegal secret visits became official visits of the members of democratic parliaments, and discussions about the abolition of communism transformed into discussions about the implementation of democracy, a market economy, and merger with the countries of the European Union, which so far had incorporated only Western European democracies.

In the fall of 1989, the Independent Trade Union of Hungary made an official visit to Warsaw by invitation of the members of the Polish democratic government and the Solidarity trade union. The discussion centered on using Polish democratic reforms as a model for reforms in Hungary.[54] Three weeks after the victory in the democratic election in Czechoslovakia, on January 3, 1990, Václaw Claus, Minister of Finance of the Czechoslovakian democratic government, visited Leszek Balcerowicz, Polish finance minister, to confer about Polish economic strategy.

---

[52] Interview with Zbigniew Gadaj, Office of Cooperation with Trade Unions, Polish Ministry of Labor and Social Policy. The interview was conducted by the author on July 21, 1993.

[53] In 1992, because of growing nationalist tensions, Czechoslovakia was peacefully dissolved by parliament. On 1 January, 1993, it formally separated into two completely independent countries: the Czech Republic and the Slovak Republic.

[54] Interview with Zbigniew Boni, July 20, 1993.

A week later, Jirzi Dienstbier, the Czechoslovakian Minister of Foreign Affairs, visited Warsaw by invitation of the Polish foreign minister and the Polish parliament, discussing problems of European unification. And that same month, Václav Havel and his cabinet visited the Polish parliament, taking counsel on political reforms, the Balcerowicz plan of economic reconstruction, and on "seeking to achieve ... the return to Europe" (Havel 1990). As Havel announced in his presidential speech, delivered in the Polish parliament on January 10, 1990, "a perfect coordination of measures and actions with those taken by Hungary is required" for merger with the European Union (Havel 1990).

Role modeling on Polish reforms was also visible in Bulgaria. During the Bulgarian Round Table negotiations between the political opposition and the Bulgarian communist regime, economic reforms and the political situation in Poland as well as in Hungary were discussed (CITUB 1991, 8). Also, shortly after the Bulgarian democratic election in the spring of 1990, Kristo Petkov, President of CITUB, traveled to Warsaw to meet Leszek Balcerowicz, Minister of Finance, Jacel Kuroń, Minister of Social Policy, Tadeusz Mazowiecki, Prime Minister, Maciej Jankowski, head of the Mazowsze region of the *Solidarity* movement, and Alfred Miodowicz, president of the Polish communist trade union. The discussion mainly focused on Polish economic reforms.[55] In addition, a group of Bulgarian parliamentary members, presided over by Ivan Kostov from the Bulgarian Union of Democratic Forces, visited members of the Polish parliament in September 1990. "We returned to our country believing that we would be able to avoid many mistakes in the transition to a market economy," said Kostov, commenting on the discussions about privatization and market economy (Informacja PAP 1993). In May 1989, Bulgarian students who studied at Lodz University in Poland invited Henryk Wujec to give lectures to the Bulgarian opposition on the Polish Round Table negotiations and Polish preparations for the democratic free election of June 1989.

After the victory of the Polish Round Table negotiations, Polish Solidarity also intensified contacts with the oppositions from the Soviet republics.[56] Since 1986, Grzegorz Kostiewa-Zorbas had been responsible for contacts with the Ukrainian opposition. In 1988, the Ukrainian

---

[55] Interview with Kristo Petkov, President of the Bulgarian Independent Trade Union CITUB, conducted by the author in the CITUB office in Sofia on August 12, 1993; interview with Emilian Abadzejew, August 10, 1999.

[56] Interview with Zbigniew Boni, July 20, 1993.

dissident Czarnowil renewed contacts with Polish Solidarity activists after being released from a Ukrainian prison. According to Henryk Wujec, a member of the central committee of the Polish Solidarity movement, and later president of the Party of the Democratic Union, contacts between Polish Solidarity and Ukrainian dissident movements were also maintained through the three Choryniow brothers.[57] At the end of the Polish Round Table negotiations, a member of the national committee of Solidarity, Bogdan Borusewicz, discreetly visited striking workers in the oil fields of Donbass in Russia and initiated contact with the opposition of Russian workers, remembered Janusz Palubicki.[58]

Following the Romanian revolution in December 1989 that overthrew the communist government of Nicolae Ceauşescu,[59] a delegation from the Romanian post-communist government headed by Dr. Alexander Atanasis (vice-Minister of the Romanian Ministry of Labor) visited the Polish Minister of Labor and Social Policy on September 3, 1990, to discuss a strategy for transition to a market economy, particularly reforms within the labor force, unemployment benefits, privatization policy, and new wage and salary policies (Polish Ministry of Labor and Social Policy 1990). In November 1991, the Albanian government also visited the Polish government by invitation of the Minister of Foreign Affairs, and two months later the Albanian vice-Prime Minister Abdul Dxhaja had a meeting with Polish government members: the vice-Prime Minister, the Minister of Economy, and the Minister of Finance, to discuss the problems of a market economy (PAP 1991).

The impact of the media on democratic transitions in Eastern Central Europe

"Once or twice they lied, that it would be possible for me to see my wife Kojana, but we managed to see each other after they took me to the militia headquarters. There I gave her a message with a short

---

[57] Interview with Henryk Wujec, July 30, 1993.
[58] Interview with Janusz Palubicki, July 26, 1993.
[59] The Romanian Revolution started in December 1989 in the city of Timisoara and soon spread throughout the country, becoming the only one of these revolutions that forcibly overthrew a communist government and executed the country's head of state. The Revolution marked the end of the communist regime of Nicolae Ceauşescu and his family, who were tried in a show trial by a military tribunal on charges of genocide, and immediately executed on Christmas Day, 1989.

summary of what had happened to me in prison. The Western information services broadcast it immediately," said Konstantin Trenchev, president of Podkrepa (Komitov 1991a, 3).

From the initial stages of the anti-communist opposition expansion until the implementation of the first democratic reforms in communist countries, the most influential factor on the development of democratic movements was Western radio broadcasting, such as Radio Free Europe, Voice of America, the BBC, Radio Svoboda, and Deutsche Welle, while the national media were rather silent. Among a few exceptions was the Information Service about Solidarity (SIS) established by Wojciech Maziarski the summer of 1988, which, among other goals, monitored the waves of Polish national strikes in the summer of 1988 that led to round table negotiations between the Communist government and members of Solidarity regarding democratic reforms in Poland and to the first free democratic election in June 1989. Solidarity also initiated an information campaign about Polish dissidents and Polish political activity in Hungary. This campaign was organized in cooperation with members of the Hungarian democratic opposition. Wojciech Maziarski from Solidarity published a book about the Hungarian independent student movement, as well as the first book ever written about Lech Wałęsa. Janos Kisza published essays about Polish dissidents that were also distributed in Hungary. Moreover, in Czechoslovakia, due to similarity of language, the newspapers of independent-thinking intellectuals and religious groups were also broadly distributed. These newspapers, such as the Polish *Common Weekly* (*Tygodnik Powszechny*), a Catholic newspaper with limited censorship, often defeated the formation and creation of an underground press in Czechoslovakia because Czechs broadly subscribed to the Polish publications. Also, many political dissidents subscribed to Polish underground publications, partly compensating for the lack of a Czechoslovakian independent press, explained Ludmila Wujec during an interview with the author.[60]

The democratic reforms in Poland in June 1989 provided the political opposition with access to national media. The independent and legal press, and radio and TV stations, were able to inform Eastern European societies about democratic changes, further promoting

---

[60] An interview with Ludmila Wujec conducted by the author in Warsaw on July 23, 1989.

pro-democracy ideas. Thus, the role of the media was diverse and corresponded to the degree of development of a democratic movement in each country. First, the system of mass communication intensified the exposure of East European societies to the principles of freedom and equality, undermining the totalitarian character of communism. This role was mainly provided by Western broadcasting. Second, it stimulated the growth of democratic opposition by enhancing internal communication within the democratic movement, as in Poland, where the re-broadcasting of information about the 1980 summer strikes in shipyards by international radio and TV stations helped to mobilize workers and provided support from other social strata (Verdery 1993; Wejnert 1988); or in Bulgaria where enrolment to Podkrepa was initiated after Radio Free Europe's broadcasting (Komitov 1991a). Third, considering that telephone communication was censored access to phone lines limited, postal mail correspondence was controlled, and the possibility of international travel was highly controlled and very limited, for general societies the media were the only available source of information about dissident activity in other communist countries. "We did not have any direct contacts with Solidarity leaders prior to 1989. But we listened to Western broadcasting, Radio Free Europe, Radio Svoboda, and learned about Solidarity," said the the president of Podkrepa in an interview.[61] Fourth, the media, by informing the international community about the violations of human rights committed by communist rulers, actively defended arrested dissidents. As Darakchiev said, "other active assistants in defense of those arrested were Deutsche Welle, the BBC, and the other Western information services" (Komitov 1991b, 8).

Summarizing, across Eastern Central Europe prior to the Round Table negotiations and the democratic elections, the media affected democratization processes mainly via Western European and other foreign broadcasts, connecting dissidents and providing channels of information about their activity. During the democratic negotiations, the national media were allowed to provide live broadcasting of round table negotiations and pre-election rallies in communist countries, thus becoming a transmitter of information about the the first victories over communist regimes, and sending a message about the democratic

---

[61] Interview with Konstantin Trenchev, President of Podkrepa, conducted on August 3, 1993, by the author.

reforms implemented by the newly democratic governments in each country. Last, the media brought international and national attention to the unified efforts of dissident movements, discussing mutual support and frequent meetings between reformists and members of Eastern European democratic governments. Thus, the impact of the media on the occurrence and temporal rate of democratic transition in Eastern Europe was visible during all stages of the breakdown of the communist regimes.

Foreign intervention: the role of foreign organizations in the processes of democratization of Eastern Europe

Foreign organizations influenced the spread of democratic movements in communist countries in two ways: (a) by inviting political dissidents from communist countries to organized international conferences, seminars and, workshops that became platforms for discussions about democracy and the implementation of democratic reforms in the communist states, and (b) by sponsoring meetings of the newly elected members of Eastern European democratic governments with the dissidents of communist countries. The international conferences, in addition to their purpose of learning about free trade unions, democracy, and human rights, provided the opportunity to meet dissidents from other communist countries and activists of the Western labor unions. "I met with Wałęsa and other Solidarity members during international congresses and conferences numerous times," said Trenchev in an interview.[62] These initiatives were particularly valuable in the initial phases of the development of democratic movements, when the fledgling democratic movement needed public support for their activities. "This declaration was sent to all the mass media in our country, and abroad, to the Committee for Human Rights, to the Standing Committee for Defense of Citizens' Social Interest and Rights in the United Nations, to the independent trade unions of some European countries and to some international law defense organizations," said Trenchev, discussing the declaration submitted to the Bulgarian communist government that proposed economic and political reforms in Bulgaria (Komitov 1991a).

---

[62] Interview with Konstantin Trenchev, August 3, 1993.

Moreover, international organizations intervened on behalf of arrested dissidents, as when the Human Rights Committee requested the release of the arrested founders of Podkrepa (Komitov 1991a), or when the Polish democratic government of Mazowiecki negotiated with the Czech government for the release of the arrested Slovakian dissidents Ján Čarnogurský and Miroslav Kusý (*Gazeta Wyborcza* 1989c). International organizations also sponsored consultation-type meetings on the implementation of democratic reforms between newly elected governments and dissident movements in still-communist countries. Such meetings were organized by the Ford Foundation, the Batory Foundation, and the International Labor Organization, in 1989–1993.

For example, after the Polish democratic election of June 1989, the Batory Foundation, a branch of Soros's Open Society Institute, sponsored a meeting in Warsaw between the Czechoslovakian and Hungarian opposition and the newly elected members of the Polish democratic government. Among the participants were Havel, Balcerowicz, and Mazowiecki. The meeting facilitated future contacts between political dissidents and provided an opportunity to exchange views about economic and political reforms.[63] In May 1990, the Batory Foundation sponsored Zhelyu Zhelev and Petyr Beron (the president and secretary of the Bulgarian Democratic Forces, which represented unified prodemocratic movements) and Konstantin Trenchev (President of Podkrepa) in their visit to Lech Wałęsa (Polish president, and former head of the Solidarity movement), Tadeusz Mazowiecki (the prime minister in the newly elected government), and members of the Presidium (central committee) of the OKP.

Starting in 1990, the International Labor Organization (ILO) supported a Polish initiative to become a supplier of printed material about the Polish free election, Round Table negotiations, and agreements signed between Solidarity and the Polish government. This material was sent to other Eastern European countries. By 1993, "Poland had become a model country sharing its experience with Eastern European neighbors."[64]

The ILO also helped the Polish Ministry of Labor and Social Policy to organize a training center on the management of labor and on social

---

[63] Interview with Zbigniew Boni, July 20, 1993.
[64] Interview with Henryk Wujec conducted by the author in Warsaw on July 4, 1993.

policy in Molino, Poland, that trained members of new governments and policy makers on new strategies and styles of management of labor resources, and helped to establish new regulations on social policies in a free market economy. The center was equipped with modern technology, and world-renowned labor experts gave workshops on the social and economic policies of the emerging market economies. In October 1993, among the trainees were ministers of labor in Estonia, Lithuania, Latvia, the Ukraine, Russia, and Belorussia.[65]

In addition, the ILO, together with the Polish Ministry of Labor and Social Policy, opened the International Training Centre of the ILO in Turin, Italy, to "provide training at national and regional level to meet the needs of labour and social policy on the basis of modern methods and programs, and experience of Western European countries and international organizations, particularly the ILO ... The training programs of the Centre correspond in large degree to current needs of Central and East European countries" (International Labour Organization 2014). The seminars, supported by the Brussels Fund of the ILO, were particularly addressed to the Estonian, Lithuanian, Ukrainian, Belorussian, and Russian ministries of labor and social policy, regional social policy makers, and labor unionists. Similar working meetings were organized by the ILO in Geneva.

Consequently, the initiatives of Western organizations helped dissidents and, later, new democratic governments to coordinate economic and political cooperation and exchange experiences on political and economic reforms. Clearly the closest cooperation and most frequent exchange of ideas in the initial stages of transition took place between Poland, Hungary, and Czechoslovakia. This cooperation culminated with a signed agreement on mutual cooperation between the Czechoslovakian, Hungarian, and Polish ministers of labor and social policy, in Visegrad in October 1991.[66]

---

[65] Interview with Remigiusz Henczel, Director of the International Cooperation Department, Polish Ministry of Labor and Social Policy, conducted in Warsaw, July 27, 1993, by the author.

[66] The *Visegrad Agreement* was signed by the *Visegrad Group* formed by the newly democratic governments of Poland, Hungary, and Czechoslovakia on February 15, 1991. The main goal of the group was the development of cooperation with the European Union and NATO in order to become members of these organizations. On January 1, 1993, the new countries of the Czech and Slovak Republics replaced Czechoslovakia.

The significant role of international organizations in the institutionalization of democracy and in the implementation of democratic reforms in former communist countries was expressed in Podkrepa's Constitution, which began: "Bearing in mind the fundamental rights and needs of people stemming from their human nature and the norms of civilized behavior endorsed and proclaimed by the United Nations in the Universal Declaration of Human Rights ... guided by a sense of civic and human solidarity and by a sincere desire to aid the building of a fair, humane and civilized society based on the principles of democracy and pluralism, we have decided to hereby found the Confederation of Labor Podkrepa" (Podkrepa 1990, 1).

The rise of dissident movements met with the approval of societies dissatisfied with their economic situation: increasing inflation, uncontrolled amounts of private savings with no possibility of spending, scarcity of all consumer goods, long lines of consumers in front of grocery and other retail stores, and lack of freedom and liberty. Lack of political freedom combined with economic difficulties attested to the inability of communism to sustain itself (Havel 1988).

Cohesion of dissident activity: an overview and conclusion

In conclusion, regardless of many studies arguing that democratic transitions are products of the conditions of each country's development of primary economic difficulties and the weakening of communist regimes, it would have been impossible to achieve the rapid tempo of democratic transitions in Eastern Europe without the impact of a variety of diffusion factors: interpersonal networks of dissidents and networks of dissident organizations, media, and institutionalization of democracy. This group of diffusion factors interacted with the malleable conditions of countries' development. Hence, historical changes would not have taken place without the support of interpersonal and organizational networks of political opposition, the influence of global and national media, and assistance of international organizations supporting and promoting an institutionalized model of democracy. The timing of the transition was also influenced by the global Gorbachev effect and his reforms and new policies implemented in the Soviet Union. Visible also was the impact of a leading democratic movement in Poland on democratic movements in other Soviet-bloc countries.

Anti-communist activity was initiated by dissident networks cascading with webs of connections between European countries of the Soviet bloc. For example, starting in 1988, the Polish Klub Inteligencji Katolickiej (KIK; Club of Catholic Intellectuals), established contacts with the East German political opposition, as well as with the Hungarian opposition – activist Fidelsz from KIK visited Budapest in the spring of 1988.[67] Simultaneously, dissident Václav Havel from Czechoslovakia established contacts with the Hungarian political opposition, particularly with Imre Pozsgay (*Gazeta Wyborcza* 1989e).[68] The same year dissident organizations of Polish Solidarity and Czechoslovakian Karta 77 jointly established contacts with the Bulgarian Podkrepa soon after its establishment. On April 13, 1988, Solidarity sent a letter to the founding committee of Podkrepa congratulating it on its organization (Komitov 1991a). From spring of 1989, Zbigniew Bujak from Polish Solidarity maintained contacts and visits with the Hungarian opposition. In the spring of 1989, Solidarity activist Irena Lasota traveled to Prague and Budapest to meet Czech and Hungarian dissidents.[69] In May 1989, Zheli Zhelev from Bulgarian Podkrepa visited Solidarity in the Mazowsze region and conducted a meeting with the head of regional Solidarity in Mazowsze.

After the victory of Solidarity in the first free democratic election in June 1989, the contacts between dissident organizations exploded. In addition to direct visits of dissident leaders, contacts were maintained via meetings at the international conferences sponsored by Western European organizations and fully publicised by broadcasting in the global as well as national media. Such intensity of contact between Polish, Czechoslovakian, Bulgarian and Hungarian oppositions, as well as oppositions in other countries, stimulated the exchange of material, experiences, and knowledge among dissidents and unified opposition in the struggle against communist power.

The visible unity of the Eastern European dissident movements and the ties between dissident networks significantly contributed to the rapid adoption of democracy across the communist regimes of Eastern Europe. In this study, the temporal rate and the consecutive order of these adoptions are called the *domino effect* of democratic transitions.

---

[67] Interview with Zbigniew Boni, July 20, 1993.
[68] *Gazeta Wyborcza*, 1989a. Premier Solidarny z Havlem (Solidarity of the Prime Minister with Havel) (October 3): 1.
[69] Interview with Zbigniew Boni, July 20, 1993.

Together with the contributors of diffusion and development analyzed in previous sections of this study, the domino effect of democratization shaped all the Soviet regimes within Eastern Central Europe as well as within the countries of the Soviet Union. Thus, the network ties of dissident movements and the role modeling of the first democratic transition of Poland, combined with the permissive effect of the Gorbachev policy and shared information on reform strategies, contributed to diffusion factors, facilitating cross-state unity and solidarity of these movements and eventually leading to the change from communist systems.

Consequently, when in 1988 the Polish communist party requested that the central committee of the Soviet communist party assist them in an anti-Solidarity campaign, Gorbachev restated the need for leniency toward democratic movements in Eastern Europe (Zakowski 1991). Thus, the "Gorbachev era of structural opportunities" and a conviction that the Soviet Union would not intervene in Eastern European domestic affairs, enhanced the emergence of amenable conditions for Eastern Europeans to introduce democratic political reforms and market economic systems (Bunce 1990; Holmes 1997; Sedaitis & Butterfield 1991). Financial support to newly emerged Eastern Central European and Russian democracies was provided by the World Bank, the International Monetary Fund, and the Bank for Development and Reconstruction. The financial aid, however, was conditional upon the sustainability of the new democratic rule by governments of the former Soviet states (Graf, Hansen, & Schulz 1993; Kolodko 1996; Lovenduski & Woodall 1987).

Summarizing, the permissive effect of Gorbachev's politics combined with (a) ties and frequent contacts between dissident networks, (b) support provided by the institutionalization of democracy as the most desirable political system, and (c) the help provided to new democracies by global financial institutions, set up ideological and philosophical trends that coalesced in the mid 1980s, leading to the mobilization of domestic democratic movements in Eastern Central Europe and the former Soviet republics (Dahl 1990; Deacon 1992; DeSoto & Anderson 1993; Havel 1988, 1985). Democratic opposition that included the activity of anti-communist groups, democratic movements, violent and non-violent protest demonstrations, and ethnic conflicts is often credited as the main constitutor of political changes in the Soviet-style regimes (Beissinger 1990; Marody 1991; Opp & Gern 1993; Sedaitis &

Butterfield 1991; Zakowski 1991). These waves of mobilization for collective action (Tarrow 1991a) exemplify regimes' democratic transitions: "psychologically frustrated opponents to a government who could not openly and legally organize into political parties took the form of public opposition" (Dahl 1989, 170).

What are now needed are empirical studies that attempt to statistically evaluate predictive schemes of democracy adoption and growth as a stepping stone to understand (a) the complexities of the process of worldwide democratization, especially in terms of the linkage between political factors and countries' economic performance, (b) predictive power of the contribution of endogenous versus exogenous factors to the world's democratization, (c) the temporal rate and growth of democracy, and (d) the global and domestic trends that modify the temporal rate and countries' openness toward democratic principles. Such empirical analyses are presented in Chapter 3.

3 | Trajectory and temporal rate of democratization

Worldwide democratization, 1800–2005

The fact that there is no current alternative to democracy as a principle of legitimacy does not imply that democracy becomes unassailable. Democracy may stand unchallenged in principle, and yet in practice be formidably challenged in its performance. (Giovanni Sartori)

This empirical chapter expands on the theoretical findings presented in Chapters 1 and 2, and is grounded in the existing theories of democratization. The majority of studies on democracy have explored the role of the socioeconomic conditions of countries, such as GNP, education, economic crises, and the level of urbanization and industrialization. Additionally in this study, diffusion indicators of networks (socioeconomic, political or colonial), institutionalization, and media communication expand this theoretical framework and turn the focus of analyses to global as well as regional patterns of democratization. Further, the factor of major historical events is used as a controlling factor in the analyses. The hypotheses of this study are tested using multi-level regression analyses. For illustrative purposes, before providing an empirical explanation of the potential causes of variation in democratization processes within a country, a region, or across regions, this study first turns its focus to illustrating the *descriptive statistics* supported by a longitudinal, historical account of the development of democracy within each region and across the regions of the world.

Measurement of democracy

Descriptive and inferential statistics analyze democracy using the constructed database *Nations, Development and Democracy: 1800–2005* (Wejnert 2007) that was introduced and described in Chapter 1. As mentioned there, the database incorporates 65 annually recorded socioeconomic, political, and diffusion factors related to the democratization of 177 countries that are members of the international system (20 of which are historical, and 157 of which are contemporary countries) for the years 1800–2005.[1] The factors were derived and merged from Marshall, Jagger and Gurr's *Polity IV: Political Regime Characteristics and Transitions, 1800–2008* (2009); *World Development Indicators 1960–2009* (World Bank 2009); Social and Economic Indicators of Freedom House (Freedom House 2009); Banks' (1993) *Cross-National Time Series, 1815–1973*; and Bollen's (1993, 1998) database *Liberal Democracy Indicators 1950–1990*. The missing variables were supplemented by coded data from the descriptions of countries in the *Statesman's Yearbook*; the *World Handbook of Political and Social Indicators* (Taylor & Jodice 1982); Osmanczyk's (1982) *Encyclopedia of the United Nations and International Relations*; and the journal *Freedom Review*'s annual reports published by Freedom House (Freedom House 2009). Detailed information on the dataset is provided in Wejnert (2007).

Index of democracy

As mentioned above, the statistical part of the study analyzes the trajectory and temporal rate of democratization using an inferential statistical study in which the core variable is an indicator of democracy. As explained in Chapter 1, the index of democracy is assessed on a scale of 0–10 to add validity to the analyses (see Figures 1.1a and 1.1b), not only because the nature of democracy is continuous but also because the character of such an index of democracy is similar to the character of other predictors. Thus, considering that the ultimate aim of this study is to determine the development and growth of democracy over time, as well as to depict predictors of democracy – predictors that are continuous variables themselves – use of a continuous index of democracy provides substantially more statistical power, because the outcome variables have enhanced variation relative to a categorical index, allowing stronger relations to continuous predictors to emerge.

Although some scholars have critically assessed and proposed replacing the existing measurements with new scales (information

---

[1] Included are only those countries that are recognized as independent members of the international system with populations greater than 500,000 in the early 2000s (Jagger & Gurr 1995a; Marshall, Jagger, & Gurr 2009).

about critical debates on this issue is presented in Chapter 1), in view of the longitudinal advantage, high correlations with other available scales, and widespread use of datasets that were incorporated in *Nations, Development and Democracy: 1800–2005* (Wejnert 2007), I conclude with Dahl (1989, 199) that "although at this point a complete, reliable and current account of all democratic countries in the world appears to be unavailable, the two datasets *Polity* and *Freedom House* allow fairly good estimates of democratization."

Analysis of the observed data: observed worldwide democratization

Prior to the statistical assessment of the growth of democracy in the world and across world regions, the study conducted analysis of the observed development of democracy since 1800. As shown in Figure 1.4, observation of the total number of democratic states in the world suggests that the 1990s was a decade of rapid worldwide democratization, where 114 countries out of 157 sovereign countries were considered to be democratic by 1994 (Karatnycky 1995), and this number increased to 119 countries that had adopted democratic principles by 1998. Accordingly, the temporal evolution of democracy follows a steady, upward curvilinear trend; nonetheless, the level of world democracy has never achieved the high level of a minimum score of 7 on the democracy scale of 0–10 that is considered to indicate a stable democracy. Moreover, from 1800 only the region of Europe, and only at the end of the twentieth century, had a mean democracy level above the threshold of a stable, coherent democracy score of 7 and above.

Observed regional democratization

A comparative assessment of democracy across regions in the last two centuries demonstrates a differential temporal rate and the potency of democracy development within regions, where in some regions the periods of escalating democratization are in contrast to periods of democracy decline in others (e.g., Europe vs Africa in the first decades of the twentieth century). The temporal rate of regional democratization also varies across the past two centuries. In the nineteenth century the level of worldwide democracy was relatively low and determined mainly by the

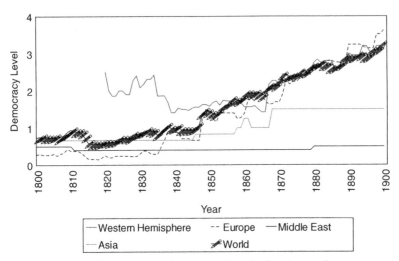

Figure 3.1 Mean democracy level across regions in the nineteenth century
Source: Research based on the database *Nations, Democracy and Development: 1800–2005* (Wejnert 2007).

higher democracy level in Europe and the countries of the North America (as part of the Western Hemisphere) (see Figure 3.1).

Thus, the worldwide expansion of democracy was generated by a spread of democracy within only two regions (Europe and the Western Hemisphere), and the temporal rate of world democratization followed the rate of European and American democratization combined. This development could suggest role modeling on the first democracies by non-democratic states, processes that are discussed in Chapter 4. Analysis of the observed data across the nineteenth century shows that no region of the world achieved a high, sustainable level of democracy. In fact, most regions were very low democracies, with the mean democracy score under 4 on the scale of 0–10.

In contrast, the democracy level across the twentieth century is determined by democratization taking place across all major regions of the world, signalizing the coming of the democratization era across the world, from the Americas and Europe to Africa and Asia. Moreover, the large-scale, highly politically important historical events that directed the development of the world's affairs coincided with a visible increase in the number of democratic states. These events, such as World War I, World War II, the period of decolonization, and the world-scale oil crisis, redirected the history of many states, granting independence and democracy to many newly liberated states in post-World War I Europe, post-World War II Europe and Asia, and the newly born post-colonial states in Africa and Asia (see Figure 3.2). Interestingly, economic crisis generated a substantial increase in transitions from autocratic regimes to democracy.

Similar to the nineteenth century, across the twentieth century most regions of the world were on average democratic but only at the low democracy level. The exceptions are Europe and the Americas, which achieved a higher democracy level mainly determined by the high democracy score of the North American countries and Western European countries. Regardless of the democratization of many South American countries after the 1960s, the average democracy level of the region was below a score of 7 on the scale of 0–10, which means the countries were below a threshold of democratic sustainability and stability (see Figure 3.2).

Using the scale of democracy of 0–10 developed in this study, and selected years, the study observed a longitudinal rate of democracy growth across regions and compared it to the overall rate of democracy growth in the world (see Figure 3.3).

As presented in Figure 3.3, a comparison to the observed worldwide democracy level of the observed scores of democracy level in each region across the past two centuries demonstrates that the overall growth of democracy in the world did not arrive at the level of sustainability. Regardless of the long-term development of democratic systems, this level was also not obtained by the majority of the world's regions.

Statistical analyses

Prior to performing these analyses, the time variable first was rescaled to make the year 1950, when about half of the countries existed as sovereign states (87 countries out of the total 177), the centered time (1950 = 0), rather than 1800, the initial year of this study, when only 16 countries were independent. Hence, to provide a more meaningful interpretation of the results, the intercept in the growth model was specified to represent the average status of world democratization in 1950.

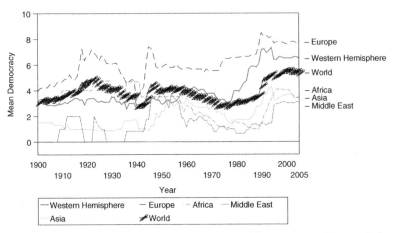

Figure 3.2 Mean democracy level across the world's regions in the twentieth century

Source: Research based on the database *Nations, Democracy and Development: 1800–2005* (Wejnert 2007).

Notes: A – the end of World War I and creation of many new states that were established as democracies in Europe. B – the end of World War II and the liberation of many European and Middle Eastern countries correlated with the re-establishment of democratic systems in those countries. C – withdrawal from democracy trend in Africa that followed the rapid initial democratization of decolonized states. D – the world oil crises and the democratization of southern European and Latin American countries, the so-called first and second waves of democratization. E – the collapse of the communist bloc and democratization in Eastern Europe and Russia, and the return to democracy of many African countries.

Second, this study assessed the descriptive validity of the database as the initial means of evaluating the validity of the constructed database and the method of measurement of democracy level. If the database and measurement methods are valid, the plotting of democracy-level scores for each country for all years 1800–2005 for (a) the world as a whole (collapsing across all countries) and (b) various world regions (collapsing across countries within specified geographic regions) should produce differential temporal patterns of democratization. The differential regional pattern is a function of regional historical events known by historians as factors influencing democratic development (Stephens 1989; Wallerstein 2001). The initial establishment of

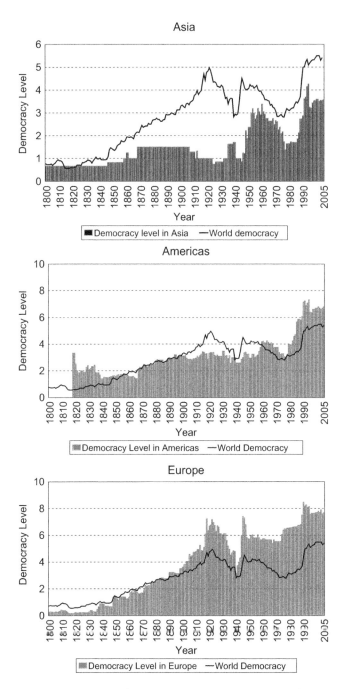

Figure 3.3 Observed democracy scores across regions and time in comparison to worldwide democracy score across the same time

The two regions of the Americas (or Western Hemisphere) and Europe, with democracy scores above an average worldwide democracy level, are depicted in differing frames of their graphs.

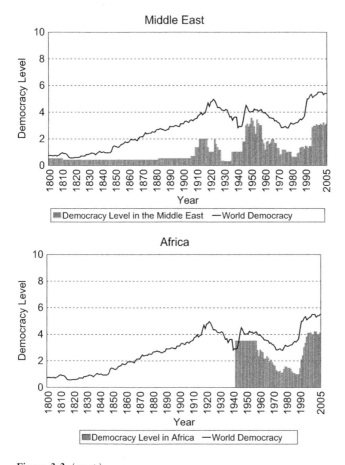

Figure 3.3 *(cont.)*

descriptive validity is crucial if subsequent statistical modeling of democratic growth is to be derived from the observed data. Statistical modeling is required to determine the effects of predictor variables on democratization patterns.

Third, this study views democratic growth as a joint function of the characteristics of countries and of regions. Country and regional characteristics are analyzed with hierarchical models that assess the impact of a predictor on an average country's democratic growth (the level and rate of growth) and three effects of variance: (a) variance in the level of democratic growth between regions; (b) variance in the level and rate of democratic growth between countries, and (c) residual. The hierarchical models are expressed in the form of growth models to characterize longitudinal datasets (Singer & Willett 2003). Although this methodology has not been the most frequently used in prior research on democratization, according to this study, the assessment of democracy with hierarchical data provides a more comprehensive view of democratization processes than has been possible in simple regression models used in most previous studies. The hierarchical models account for the effects of within-country, country-level, and region-level characteristics on democratic growth.

Fourth, to allow the intercept and the slope to vary across countries and across regions, this study selected a structure of variance-covariance using goodness-of-fit statistics where the UN (unstructured) structure was indicated as the best-fitting data in this study (Singer and Willett 2003).[2] A comparison of the results of the UN model with the simple model, which did not impose additional structure on the error covariance matrix (beyond the heteroscedastic structure of the intercept and slopes as outcome models), indicates that, once the covariance of the intercepts and slopes has been introduced, no additional autoregressive error structure needs to be added.[3] Accordingly, a three-level hierarchical Model D accounting for a variance between countries as well as between regions of the world, and for a variation within countries, indicates the lowest value of unexplained variance in democratic growth (the intercept) and hence fits our data best (see Table 3.1).

Nonetheless, one more test of fit statistics was performed, with results leading to the same conclusion (see Table 3.2).

Finally, prior to deriving the most predictive model of democratic growth, valid time spans of democratic growth and the slopes of the temporal rate for the world and each region were identified. Two main criteria were employed in selecting these time spans, the application of which can be seen by reference to the observed data in Figure 3.3:

---

[2] The UN model was selected out of the tested CS, CSH, HF, ARH, AR, and UN, using the goodness-of-fit statistics of Akaike's Information Criterion (AIC); Akaike's Information Criterion was corrected for sample size (AICC); Bayesian Information Criterion (BIC); and a subsequent Likelihood ratio test (–2 RLL).

[3] The validity of the model was also assessed statistically (see Table 3.2).

Table 3.1 *Fixed effects estimates and variance/covariance of the evolution of democracy in the world, 1800–2005, obtained while using multilevel growth models with data centered on 1950*

World	Fixed effects estimates			Covariance parameter estimates						
	Intercept	Year	Year^2	Variation between regions' intercepts	Variation between regions' slopes	Regions' covariance intercepts/ slopes	Variation between intercepts of countries	Variation between slopes of countries	Countries' covariance intercepts/ slopes	Residual
Model A within-country variation	3.8074 $p <.0001$	.008877 $p <.0001$	−.00012 $p <.0001$							13.9003 $p <.0001$
Model B within-country & regional variation	4.1675 $p =.01967$	.01172 $p =.2191$	.000034 $p =.0029$	9.1106 $p = 0574$	.000537 $p =.0589$	−.00267 $p =.9329$				10.6329 $p <.0001$
Model C within-country & countries' variation	3.2128 $p <.0001$	.01581 $p =.002$	.000092 $p <.0001$				14.3447 $p <.0001$	.00322 $p <.0001$	−.09822 $p <.0001$	3.1925 $p <.0001$

Model D within-country, regional & countries' variation									
5.7095	.01014	.000093	6.2311	.0002	.000983	10.9957	.0029	−.1046	3.1879
$t = .018$	$p = .247$	$p < .0001$	$p = .10$	$p = .1934$	$p = .9754$	$p < .0001$	$p < .0001$	$p < .0001$	$p < .0001$
(1.07)	(.008)	(.0078)	(4.871)	(.0003)	(.03194)	(1.302)	(.0004)	(.02257)	(.03968)

Model A: Individual growth model in which democratization is predicted by time.

Model B: Two-level growth model while controlling for variance in the intercept and slope between regions.

Model C: Two-level growth model while controlling for variance in the intercept and slope between regions.

Model D: Three-level growth model while controlling for variance in the intercept and the slope between countries, and the intercept and slope between regions.

Goodness of fit parameters of Akaike's Information Criterion (AIC).

Akaike's Information Criterion corrected for a sample size (AICC), Bayesian Information Criterion (BIC), and Log Likelihood (−2LL):

Model A: AIC = 72583.6, AICC = 72583.6, BIC = 72591.1, −2LL = 72581.6

Model B: AIC = 69096.4, AICC = 69096.4, BIC = 69095.7, −2LL = 69090.4

Model C: AIC = 54526.9, AICC = 54526.9, BIC = 54539.5, −2LL = 54518.9

Model D: AIC = 54488.9, AICC = 54488.9, BIC = 54487.4, −2LL = 54474.9

The smaller the obtained value, the better the fit of the model to the data. −2LL is used to assess probability p by comparing the difference in −2 RLL between two competing models to a χ^2 distribution (Singer 1998).

Table 3.2 *Goodness of fit parameters of Akaike's Information Criterion (AIC), Akaike's Information Criterion corrected for a sample size (AICC), Bayesian Information Criterion (BIC), and Log Likelihood (−2LL)**

	AIC	AICC	BIC	−2LL
Model A	72583.6	72583.6	72591.1	**72581.6**
Model B	69098.4	69098.4	69097.5	**69090.4**
Model C	54526.9	54526.9	54539.5	**54518.9**
Model D	54488.9	54488.9	54487.4	**54474.9**

* The smaller the obtained values, the better is the fit of the model to the data (Little et al. 1996). −2LL, depicted in bold letters, is used to assess 2 distribution, by comparing the difference in 2 RLL between two competing models to a χ^2 distribution (Singer 1998; Singer & Willett 2003).

(a) existence of sufficient variability in democratic level; and (b) the number of sovereign states as a percentage of the total number of states existing at the end of the 1990s. The years prior to the time when sufficient variability in the average democratization level was observed and the years prior to when at least one-fourth of the states in the world, or in a particular region, received independence were omitted, and the slopes that best fit the observed data as year, year squared, or cubic year were selected. Accordingly, for the world analysis, the years 1860–2005 and the slope of year squared were selected; for the Americas, the years 1820–2005 and the slope of year squared were selected; for Europe, the years 1800–2005 and the slope of year were selected; for Africa, the years 1949–1999 were selected; for the Middle East, the years 1917–2005 were selected; and for Asia, the years 1900–2005 and the slope of cubic year were selected. Oceania, which includes a small number of countries and no variability in democratization (only four states in the region are democratic, two of which have been highly democratic for over a century) was excluded from the regional analyses. The assessment of slopes is presented in Table 3.3.

Neither the hierarchical models nor their variation of polynomial growth models have been frequently used in longitudinal studies on democracy's growth. Therefore, using the depicted time span and the slope for the world and each region, the validity of the derived unconditional growth model was assessed by evaluating the estimated rate and level of democratic growth in the world and in each world region against observed data.

To test the hypotheses of this study, I used the constructed database *Nations, Development and Democracy* (Wejnert 2007) that was introduced in Part I. Accordingly, the database assesses 187 sovereign countries from 1800–2005 on indicators that represent (i) level of democracy, (ii) socioeconomic characteristics, and (iii) diffusion process.[4] Nineteen countries for which substantial data on indicators of socioeconomic development and/or of diffusion were missing were dropped from the analyses, yielding 168 countries in this study. The list of countries is included in Appendix 1.

Most studies of democracy have used a categorical variable of democracy, where countries are viewed as democratic or not, yielding a scaling of democracy as either "1" or "0." As explained in Part I, from a measurement perspective, however, it is more accurate to view democratization as a continuous variable, where one would refer to the *level of democratization* of a country rather than its existence, because states frequently either accept some democratic principles while ignoring others, or accept most of the principles of democracy but differentially apply them across societal strata. The continuous index of democratization detects small gradations of change in democracy level over time that are missed by the categorical index and, I argue, it yields results that are more accurate. Prime examples are democratizing African states that claimed to be democratic in the 1990s but were strongly corrupted, had limited rights, and governmental elections were not inclusive (Kissinger 2001, 26), or European and American liberal democracies at the time of the exclusion of women and ethnic/racial minorities from the right to vote (Tuttle 1986).

Indeed, as demonstrated in Figure 1.2 in Chapter 1, across the past two centuries the observed mean level of democracy in the world substantially differed when assessed with the scale of 0–1, where one means fully democratic, versus the scale of 0–10, where ten means fully democratic. Across all years, the mean level of democracy is lower when assessed with the 0–10 scale (the world looks much less "democratic"), and the magnitude of change in democracy level is more gradual, e.g., slopes of the growth of democracy for the years 1820–1900 or 1980–1999. In addition, the relation of predictors to

---

[4] Following Gurr, Jagger, & Moore (1990), a sovereign country was defined as an independent member of the international system that had a population greater than 500,000.

democracy growth should be stronger when assessed with the scale of 0–10 because predictor variables are also continuous (increased predictive validity).

In this study, the level of democracy was assessed using Marshall, Jagger, & Gurr's (2009) index of democracy, depicted on a continuous scale of 0–10. The index component of democracy level that is included in the database defines a democratic regime according to its principles rather than its performance (Dahl 1989, 38), reflecting the competitiveness and regulation of political participation, competitiveness and openness of executive recruitment, and constraints on chief executives. Marshall, Jagger, and Gurr's index is highly correlated with the other democracy scales of Gasiorowski (1993), Bollen (1980), Arat (1991), Vanhanen (1990), Coppedge and Reinicke (1990), and Freedom House (annual 1973–2009), and the correlations ranged between 0.85–0.92, $p < 0.01$ (convergent validity of the scale) (Jagger & Gurr 1995a). Moreover, a three-level model of multilevel regression (Model D in Table 3.1) was selected to assess the worldwide growth of democracy from 1800–2005.

Statistical modeling of contrasting definitions of democratic growth within regions

To analyze patterns of regional democratization, in this study longitudinal analyses were conducted that assessed democratic growth from 1800–2005 by applying multilevel linear growth modeling (a type of multilevel regression modeling). Conceptually, the multilevel model can be viewed as a hierarchical system of regression equations, where longitudinal hierarchical data with one dependent variable is measured at the lowest level but some of the explanatory variables are measured solely at higher levels (Bryk & Raudenbush 1992; Marsh, Hau, & Konk 2000). Multilevel analyses allow researchers to simultaneously consider multiple units of analysis within the same analysis.

This methodology offers an attractive approach to the analysis of the longitudinal data of democratic growth, as growth trends are allowed to vary within each country and across countries within each region, and the growth modeling does not require all units to have the same number of data points over time (Goldstein 1995). Since values of predictors are not always available for all years, multilevel growth modeling is ideally suited to our investigation.

The goal of this statistical modeling is to select the best model for an assessment of regional democratization. To reach this objective, in this study three increasingly complex multilevel linear growth models were applied to the analysis, and their fit to our data was comparatively assessed with the fit statistics of Akaike's Information Criterion (AIC), Akaike's Information Criterion corrected for sample size (AICC), Bayesian Information Criterion (BIC), and a performed Likelihood ratio test (–2 RLL) (Singer 1998). Based on the conducted tests, unstructured (UN) models were selected as best fitting the data. An approximate test of the null hypothesis that the difference between the models is 0 was given by comparing the difference in the obtained –2 RLL between the two competing models to a χ^2 distribution (Singer 1998). In addition, I used Bryk & Raudenbush's (1992, 65) method to compute how much variation in democratic growth within each country is explained by each model (the residual), and how much of the variance component for the intercept and the slope terms have diminished with each added consecutive model.[5] The modeling was implemented in "SAS proc mixed," a procedure that allows multilevel hierarchical modeling (Singer 1998).

Before these analyses were performed, I first rescaled the time variable to make the year 1950, when about half of the countries existed as sovereign states (87 countries out of the total 173), the centered time (1950 = 0), rather than 1800, the initial year of our study, when only 22 countries were independent. Hence, the intercept in this growth model is specified to represent the average status of the world's democratization in 1950, assessed with the 0–10 democracy scale (see above), which would allow for a more meaningful and easier interpretation of the results.

As the first approximation, I applied a linear regression model with a predictor of time and obtained one regression line for all the countries representing the status and the rate of democratization of an average country in each region (Model A). The obtained average status of

---

[5] As discussed by Bryk & Raudenbush (1992, 65), I compute this by subtracting the intercept variance of one model from the intercept variance of the other model, divided by the value of the first variance. However, following Singer, I want to explain that this percentage is not the same as the traditional R^2 statistic because it only talks about the fraction of explainable variation that is explained. If the amount of variation between countries in the world is small, this could be explaining a part of very little (Singer 1998, 333; Snijders & Bosker 1994).

democratization in the regions – the intercept values – ranged from
23.5 (Africa) to 7.7 (Middle East) and was statistically significant. In
each region, an average country's yearly democratic growth was
depicted as a linear slope that fit a *function of time* (year). The obtained
residual, representing the amount of unexplained variance in democratic growth within each country, was very significant (for each region
$p<.0001$), indicating an inadequate fit of Model A to the observed data
(see row 1, Table 3.3).

In this analysis, all the countries in each region were forced to
have the same regression line (the same intercept and slope of
democratic growth), regardless of their historical development, an
assumption that has little validity in the observed data. Countries
typically differ in economic, political, and cultural development, i.e.,
some countries were independent states in 1800, while others gained
independence during the twentieth century; some countries are historically industrial states while others are regional bread baskets;
some countries are religious states while their regional neighbors are
traditionally secular. Thus, I argue, it would be inappropriate to
treat yearly changes in countries' level of democratization as if they
were a random sample without regard to the type of country the
changes are occurring in or what region the countries are located in.
Observations in the same country are more similar than observations between different countries and countries with similar historical development are typically more similar to each other than they
are to countries with different historical backgrounds. I express this
lack of independence as a correlation coefficient: the intra-class
correlation. Multilevel modeling allowed me to take these correlations into account when modeling democratization as a function of
variables that change within each country (country-year level covariates), in addition to variables that depict historical characteristics
of each country (country-level covariates).

In the second approximation, this study allowed each country
regression line to vary, assessing democratization as predicted by time
while controlling for variance between countries' intercepts and slopes.
In constructed two-level regression modeling (Model C), the democratic growth was predicted by time in level-1, while level-2 expressed
variation in the intercepts and the slopes of democratic growth
between countries in each region. Model C was applied to research
on democratization across regions.

Table 3.3 *Models for the estimates of slopes and slopes' terms in world and regional analyses*

WORLD AND REGIONAL MODELS	FIXED EFFECTS ESTIMATES				COVARIANCE PARAMETERS ESTIMATES Country Region						FIT STATISTICS			
	Intercept	Year	Year²	Year³	Residual	Intercept variance	Slope variance	Intercept/ slope variance	Intercept variance	Slope variance	− 2RLL	AIC	AICC	BIC
World Year: 1860–2005														
Model A	3.8548** (1.1252)				6.2048* (.8625)	10.7395* (1.287)			6.9385** (5.251)		46388.1	46398.1	46398.1	46397.0
Model D : Year	3.8246** (1.0245)	.0113 (.16) (.00813)			3.4372* (.0437)	10.7632* (1.291)	003077* (.00042)		6.7851** (5.141)	.0002 (.2) (.000294)	46394.3	46404.3	46404.3	46403.2
Model D: Year²	3.7612** (1.0915)	.0089 (.32) (.00902)	.00016* (.00002)		3.4023* (.0465)	10.8661* (1.305)	.003218* (.00044)		6.485 (.09) (4.994)	.0003 (.2) (.00036)	46311.8	46321.8	46321.8	46320.8
Model D: Year³	3.8184** (.0134)	−.025** (.0126)	.00065* (.00003)	.0086* (.0) Infinity[1]	3.2592* (.0446)	11.2194* (1.349)	.003576* (.00047)		5.559 (.1) (4.6056)	.0007 (.1) (.00065)	45897.0	45907.0	45907.0	45906.0
Western Hemisphere Year: 1817–2005														
Model A	8.8505* (.5949)				3.4091* (.0815)	8.8664* (2.606)					14666.1	14674.1	14674.1	14679.0
Model C: Year	4.0433* (.5872)	.0187* (.0045)			3.4109* (.08158)	8.5510* (2.4982)	.00047* (.00015)	.0119 (.41) (.01441)			14662.2	14670.2	14670.2	14675.1
Model C : Year²	3.8806* (.5895)	.0273* (.0049)	.00015* (.00002)		3.3093* (.07918)	8.6086* (2.5182)	.0005* (.00018)	.008 (.6) (.01554)			14579.5	14587.5	14587.5	14592.4
Model C: Year³	3.5064* (.6072)	.0228* (.0057)	.00059* (.00004)	.0040* (0) Infinity[1]	3.1507* (.07545)	9.1099* (2.6750)	.00073* (.00026)	−.003 (.89) (.01904)			14442.8	14450.8	14450.8	14455.7

159

Table 3.3 (*cont.*)

WORLD AND REGIONAL MODELS	FIXED EFFECTS ESTIMATES				COVARIANCE PARAMETERS ESTIMATES — Country Region						FIT STATISTICS			
	Intercept	Year	$Year^2$	$Year^3$	Residual	Intercept variance	Slope variance	Intercept/ slope variance	Intercept variance	Slope variance	−2RLL	AIC	AICC	BIC
Europe Year: 1800–2005														
Model A	4.5546* (.499)				4.2832* (.09439)	11.506* (2.602)					18438.8	18446.8	18446.8	18454.5
Model C: Year	5.054* (.4791)	.0290* (.0054)			4.2862* (.09451)	10.6797* (2.2903)	.001112* (.000263)	.0395** (.01824)			18425.2	18433.2	18433.2	18441.0
Model C: $Year^2$	5.0414* (.4761)	.0306* (.0055)	.00003 (.00002)		4.2830* (.09444)	10.5188* (2.2523)	.001138* (.00027)	.0379* (.01816)			18442.1	18450.1	18450.1	18457.8
Model C: $Year^3$	5.1439* (.475)	.0313* (.0055)	−.00003 (.06) (.00002)	−.0004 (0) Infinity[1] (.4) (.00004)	4.2832* (.09446)	10.2777* (2.1974)	.001112* (.00026)	.0368*** (.01773)			18468.0	18476.0	18476.0	18483.7
Africa Year: 1949–2005														
Model A	2.2574* (.3925)				2.9277* (.1122)	23.5372* (5.8759)					5941.6	5949.6	5949.7	5956.5
Model C: Year	.9824 (.19) (.7527)	.032** (.0162)			2.9279* (.1122)	22.0057* (5.4373)	.009777* (.00245)	−.4269* (.1152)			5944.3	5952.3	5952.3	5959.2
Model C: $Year^2$	5.5421* (.7799)	−.317* (.0262)	.00584* (.0004)		2.4508* (.09394)	20.6643* (5.1365)	.008906* (.002206)	−.3605* (.0989)			5710.3	5718.3	5718.3	5725.1
Model C: $Year^3$	1.92** (.8643)	.2031* (.0583)	−.01214* (.0022)	.00025* (.000025)	2.2892* (.0878)	21.1068* (5.331)	.00874* (.00219)	−.3632* (.1012)			5634.4	5642.4	5642.4	5649.2

Middle East Year: 1917–2005

Model												
Model A	1.4636* (.5306)				2.5123* (.1146)	7.7719* (2.5739)			3913.6	3921.6	3921.6	3925.7
Model C: Year	1.25** (.64)	.0074 (.55) (.0124)			2.5118* (.1145)	7.932* (2.646)	.0027* (.00097)	−.0761 (.07) (.04165)	3920.2	3928.2	3928.2	3932.3
Model C: Year^2	1.2923** (.6369)	.00002 (.9) (.014)	.0001(.3) (.0002)		2.5119* (.1146)	7.8239* (2.6079)	.00269* (.00096)	−.0743** (.041)	3934.7	3942.7	3942.7	3946.9
Model C: Year^3	1.967* (.603)	−.026* (.0136)	−.0016* (.0003)	.00005* (.000006)	2.3677* (.108)	6.8656* (2.2759)	.00228* (.0008)	−.0556 (.1) (.03428)	3895.2	3903.2	3903.3	3907.4

Asia Year: 1900–2005

Model												
Model A	2.5885* (.5182)				2.628* (.1002)	12.388* (3.609)			5650.7	5658.7	5658.7	5664.2
Model C: Year	2.879* (.7121)	−.009 (.5) (.0153)			2.6282* (.1002)	12.5316* (3.6895)	.00557* (.00168)	−.1708** (.06738)	5656.9	5664.9	5664.9	5670.4
Model C: Year^2	2.8751** (.7463)	−.0357** (.0171)	.00076* (.00009)		2.4822* (.0947)	13.6903* (4.0411)	.00684* (.00206)	−.2084** (.07886)	5599.1	5607.1	5607.1	5612.5
Model C: Year^3	3.4023* (.7801)	−.0865* (.0189)	.0006* (.00008)	.00003* (.000003)	2.3078* (.08809)	14.8915* (4.4003)	.00793* (.00241)	−.2435* (.09014)	5525.4	5533.4	5533.4	5538.8

* $p < .005$

** $p < .05$.

Bold numbers depict the insignificant p values.

Values in parentheses depict standard errors of parameters.

I t-value equals infinity.

The estimates of the variance/covariance in the intercept and the slope between countries in addition to the estimates of variance in democratic growth of each country were obtained. In Model C, the study explained only .5 percent more variation in democratic growth within each country over time in Africa and .1 percent in Asia (than we were able to explain in Model A [Table 3.3, see first and second row of each region]; none in other regions).[6] However, significant variance between countries' intercepts and slopes was depicted in each region. The null hypothesis, that the country parameter was 0 in the population, was rejected.[7] Importantly, Model C, having smaller values of AIC, AICC, and BIC, better fit observed data than Model A and, with an additional degree of freedom, the difference in –2LL compared to χ^2 distribution was significant, with a probability of $p<.0001$ (Little et al. 1996; Singer 1998). The only exception was the region of the Middle East, where obtained values of AIC, AICC, BIC were almost the same, but Model C depicted strong variance in the intercepts and slopes of countries' democratic growth.

The significantly better fit of Model C than the simple regression models (Model A) leads to the conclusion that predicting democratization level by time while accounting for variation between countries' intercepts and slopes would explain the most variance in each region's democratic growth. These findings were supported and validated in my prior study on worldwide democratization (Wejnert 2005). Therefore, in this analysis, I applied a two-level linear growth model (Model C) in which level-1 constitutes growth of democracy within each country (each country's changes in democratization as predicted by time), while controlling for variance between countries' intercepts and slopes (level-2). Each of these levels added a source of variability into the analysis (see Table 3.3).

The goal of statistical modeling in this study is to select the best model for an assessment of democratic growth in each region. Since the observed data indicate strong variance in the curve of the slope of democratic growth across regions (see Figure 3.3), and the above two-level models still left a great portion of the residual unexplained, in the next step this study increased the complexity of the two-level model by

[6] As discussed in Bryk & Raudenbush (1992, 65), the variation in countries' democracy scores is explained by regional effects as $(13.915 - 10.6329)/13.915$, which yields .235 or 23.5%.

[7] The standard error for variance between countries' intercepts was large, resulting in smaller t-statistics but significant p-values (for all regions $p<.0001$).

adding an operationalized time variable. In each region three increasingly complex models with a variable of time that fit a *simple* (year), *quadratic* (year^2) or *cubic* (year^3) *function of time* were tested to select the best model to represent our data (see Table 3.3–Model C: Year, Model C: year^2 and Model C: year^3 for each region).

Multilevel regression models

In view of the high variability of regions' historical development, for each region a specific model was specified in which first, a time span of study was selected to obtain a more balanced dataset. The selected period depended on the number of established independent countries in a region, i.e., I selected a time since at least one-third of all sovereign countries were established in a region. Second, I applied Model C of Table 3.3 to each region where the 2-level regression model was adjusted for each region's data and time span of analysis. This model validity was attested with the –2LL, AIC, AICC, and BIC fit statistics and is presented in Table 3.3.

The results in Table 3.3 as well as in Figure 3.4 indicate variability between democracy scores at time = 0 (i.e., year 1950) across countries and across regions, and variability of regions' and countries' within-region slopes of temporal rate of democratic growth. To control for this variability, specific indicators of change in democracy development were selected in consecutive models. Prior to these analyses, however, to control for the correctness of the selected regional multilevel regression models, I compared regression models assessing the rate of growth of democracy across the world regions of the Americas (North and South), Europe, Asia, Africa, and the Middle East with the observed rate of growth of the average level of democratization of countries in each region. I used the dataset and index of democracy defined on a scale of 0–10 to assess the estimated analysis and the observed rate. As shown in Figure 3.4, across 1800–2005 the observed democracy level in each region closely resembles the estimated level of democratic growth across regions over time. As assumed, the similarity of the observed and estimated results attested to the accuracy of each selected statistical model of each region and the world.

Also as shown in Table 3.3 and Figure 3.4, in addition to the obtained residuals as well as the curvilinear slope of the temporal rate of democracy growth depicted either as a quadratic or a cubic function

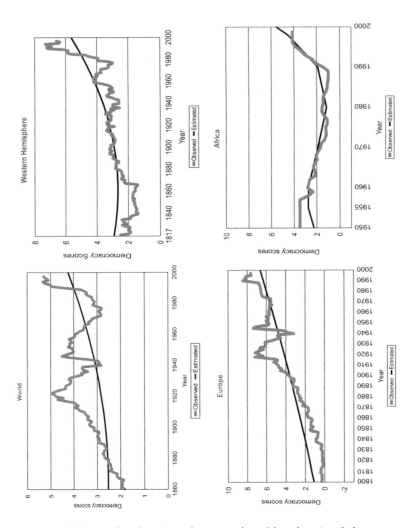

Figure 3.4 Observed and estimated scores of world and regional democratization, 1800–2000

of time in each region, significant correlation between countries' intercepts and slopes was observed, suggesting that in most regions the temporal rate of democracy development depended on the democracy score at the time of origin (which was selected as 1950, see above). Only the region of the Western hemisphere could be considered an exception.

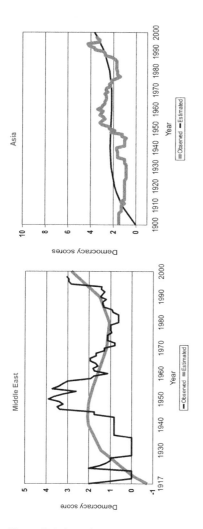

Figure 3.4 (*cont.*)

Across all regions, the residual obtained in the two-level hierarchical Model C selected for regional analyses was significant, indicating that a portion of variance in the democratization pattern is still not explained. Also, in each region strong variation between countries' intercepts and between countries' slopes was depicted, indicating that the application of additional variables to the model might reduce the variance and result in intercept and slope values that are closer to the observed data. Thus, additional variables were added to better explain the variance in democratic growth within regions over time.

The significant variation between countries (in terms of slopes and rate of democratic growth) also demonstrates that, contrary to some prior investigations focusing on one group of factors, e.g., geopolitical history (Wallerstein 2001) or economic development (Gat 2008), world democratization is a complex multilevel process, of which temporal, country, and regional effects are important components. Hence, the assessment of the democratization pattern only across the world or only as determined by one type of factor could serve mainly as the first approximation in the study, while evaluation of regional patterns of democratization, being influenced by multiple variables, could lead to more parsimonious analysis.

The two-level hierarchical regression model specification permitted the addition of covariates that change yearly for each country, as well as covariates that characterize each country across time. Similar to the analysis of the world democratization level, in regional analyses were depicted each country's urbanization level, literacy, regional agricultural labor, and diffusion changing yearly, in addition to each country's characteristics of GNP level per capita and average number of available newspapers per 1,000 citizens across time. The diffusion is measured as role modeling on democratic countries by non-democracies and is depicted as the number of democracies in a region weighted by population size and the level of democratization of each democratic country. In accordance with the literature on diffusion (Rogers 1995, Wejnert 2002b) and on diffusion and democracy (Wejnert 2005), I was able to prove the expected assumption that the greater the number and the size of democratic countries in a region, the greater the impact of democracies on non-democracies.

In summary, in this study, based on the above-described dataset, I conducted an analysis of the evolution of democracy in the world over the past two centuries, applying multilevel regression models. I examined the variation in the democracy score at three levels: variation over time in each country's democratization, variation of democracy within regions, and variation of democracy between regions. For the statistical analysis, I selected multilevel modeling, specifically Hierarchical Linear Models (HLM), because this method allows for studying the processes of longitudinal changes and depicts the nested character of outcomes.

Consequently, I use the three-level growth model to measure the longitudinal effect of time in addition to the socioeconomic and diffusion indicators for level of democracy and the temporal rate of democratic growth within each country – the *within-country democratic growth* (whether countries become more or less democratic over time) in the world. In addition to evaluating the *means* for the intercept and slope, I calculated the variance (marked difference) in the level (the intercepts) and the rate (the slopes) of democratic growth between regions, the variance for the intercepts and slopes (as well as a covariance for intercepts and slopes between countries), and the within-country residual. The error variance-covariance matrix in the model was specified as a UN (unstructured) structure.[8]

Keeping in mind that this study intends to assess the growth of democracy in the world and variance between countries and between regions in that growth, as being influenced by countries and regional characteristics, the cross-national dataset is organized as a hierarchical structure of changing yearly predictor values within each country, nested within 168 countries and nested within the regions of Europe, the Americas, Africa, the Middle East, Asia, and Oceania.[9] In this sense, democratic growth is viewed as a joint hierarchical function of the characteristics of countries and of regions, which are analyzed *simultaneously* via *hierarchical models*. These models were developed to analyze data with a hierarchical structure (Bryk & Raudenbush 1993; Coenders & Scheepers 2003).

Conceptually, the HLM models can be viewed as a hierarchical system of regression equations, where longitudinal hierarchical data with one dependent variable is measured at the lowest level but some of the explanatory variables are measured solely at higher levels (Goldstein 1986; Singer & Willett 2003). In this case, the longitudinal data set allowed me to measure the dependent variable of democratization at the country-year level, which was the lowest level in these analyses, and explanatory variables were measured at the country-year, country, and region level. Indeed, to assess the temporal rate and trajectory of the world democratization, three focal points were considered: time

---

[8] The UN structure indicates that the model does not place any structure on the variance for intercepts and variance for slopes, and neither is any structure imposed on the covariance between these two.

[9] Within each region countries in sub-regions, as listed in the Appendix 1, are also assessed.

effect, which means the effect of yearly changes in each country's democracy score; effect of country-level variance, which means the variability of democracy score between countries across time; and the effect of regional variance, which means the effect of variance in each region's democracy level across time. In other words, the interpretation of the research results contains a three-level model in which level-1 expresses evolution of democracy in each country since 1800 (or the year that the country was established/gained sovereignty) across all years of study, level-2 expresses variation in parameters from the evolution model as a random effect unrelated to any country-year level covariates, and level-3 represents the tracking of individual countries nested within regions over the past 200 years.

Viewing democratization processes as being affected by multilevel determinants vindicated the selection of the HLM as the appropriate methodology for this study (Peffley & Rohrschneider 2003). This method accounts for subjective differences in the democracy growth of each individual country and each region, and at the same time presents an objective assessment of their democratization. An additional justification for the application of the multilevel modeling was my assumption that all observations are not independent. Indeed, I expected that the dataset observations in the same group (e.g., within countries or within regions) would be more similar than observations between different groups (e.g., between countries or between regions). I expressed this lack of independence as a correlation coefficient: the intra-class correlation. Multilevel modeling allowed me to take these correlations into account when modeling democratization as a function of variables at the regional level and at the country level, in addition to variables that change over time within each country.

In the study, thus, there are three levels of analysis: within country or a country-year level, across countries, and across regions. Each of these levels adds a source of variability in the description of the evolution of democratization. Multilevel modeling was implemented in "SAS proc mixed," a procedure that allows for the added variability introduced by the multiple levels of analysis. To assess the added importance of the variance estimates at different levels, the Likelihood ratio test was performed.

World democratization. In a three-level model of the evolution of democracy in the world, this study independently examines three increasingly complex models. First, the model specifies only fixed effects of time to assess the temporal effect on world evolution of democracy (Model A in Table 3.1); second, countries are added as a random effect to examine the impact of countries within regions and countries' democracy scores on world democratization over time (Model C in Table 3.1), and third, the model additionally includes region as a second random effect to estimate the impact of regional and countries-within-regions democratization on the world evolution of democracy over time (Model D in Table 3.1). The model that better explained world democratization had lower residual value. To assess how much of the variation of world democracy is explained by added effect, I computed how much the variance component for each term has diminished between those three models (Bryk & Raudenbush 1992, 65; Singer & Willett 2003).[10] In addition, I compared those obtained results with the results obtained in the three-level individual growth model specifying time as a predictor of democracy growth and random effects of time, country, and regional effects (Model UN).

Regional democratization. In a separate sub-study, I examined the longitudinal democratization of individual regions, applying a two-level individual growth model where level-1 indicated yearly growth of democracy in each country and level-2 the variation in countries' parameters as a random effect unrelated to any country-year level covariates (Model UN). In this model, I specified temporal fixed effects – the predictor (democratization of countries within a region over time), and two random effects for the intercepts (representing each country within a region's variation in democracy score) and the slopes (representing the relationship between time and democracy score for each country within a region). The third random effect of relationship between intercepts and slopes was included by default.

Using fit statistics of –2 RES Log Likelihood, AIC, AICC, and BIC, I selected the unstructured (UN) structure of the variance–covariance matrix for the intercepts and slopes as best fitting the dataset that

---

[10] As discussed by Bryk and Raudenbush (1992, 65), Singer (1998), and Singer and Willett (2003), I compute this by subtracting the residual of one model from the residual of the other model divided by the value of the first residual. However, following Singer, I want to explain that this percentage is not the same as the traditional R^2 statistic because it only talks about the fraction of explainable variation that is explained. If the amount of variation between regions in the world is small, this could be explaining a part of very little (Singer 1998, 333; Snijders & Bosker, 1994).

represents the assumed heterogeneous impact of time and other covariance on regional democratization. The UN allows all three parameters: intercepts, slopes, and relationship between intercepts and slopes to be determined by data.[11] Moreover, I comparatively assessed the fit of Model UN with the multilevel means model that was used in the analysis of world democratization. For this study, the two-level means model with fixed effects of time (a predictor) and random effects of country (Model C in Table 3.3) was specified.

The obtained results were validated by comparing the estimated values of democratization over time with the observed values of democratization over the same time intervals. If the models are correct and if I discount for unbalanced data, the obtained values should correspond with observed values. Furthermore, I validated our models with a test on balanced data – data that included only countries that were members of the international community since the early nineteenth century, comparing the obtained results with observed values. As shown in Figure 3.4 above, the created statistical multilevel models were assessed as correct since the estimated and the observed values were almost identical.

Mathematical description of a two-level model

In this study, I use the three-level growth model to measure the longitudinal effect of time in addition to the socioeconomic and diffusion indicators for the level of democracy and the temporal rate of democratic growth within each country – the *within-country democratic growth* (whether countries become more or less democratic over time) in the world.

The modeling was implemented in "SAS proc mixed," a procedure that allows for hierarchical modeling (Singer 1998). It should be noted that in subsequent models, the fact that observations within the same country are

---

[11] I run the models for all countries across 200 years, as well as separately for all countries in each region across 200 years. Using fit statistics of –2 REs Log Likelihood, AIC and AICC and BIC we assessed the UN, AR, ARH, CS, CSH, and HF models. The best (lowest) parameters were obtained for the UN, ARH, CSH, and HF models (54654.8) as compared to 59058.2 obtained for the AR and CS models. In addition, unstructured (UN) models allow all three parameters: intercepts, slopes, and relationship between intercepts and slopes to be determined by the data. Accordingly, I selected UN models as the best fitting our data set.

more similar than observations among different countries creates depend-ence. This lack of independence was expressed as an intra-class correl-ation. Multilevel modeling takes into account these correlations, both when modeling democratization as a function of variables at the within-country level (country-year level covariates) in addition to variables that are characteristic to each country (country-level covariates), and by ana-lyzing variance components. Multilevel models are rarely used in assess-ments of countries' democratization (an exception is the study by Yang, Goldstein, and Heath 2000) but, as this study demonstrates, they provide a stronger and more parsimonious assessment of the longitudinal trends of the complex development of democracy worldwide.

The mathematical description of two-level modeling, i.e., when democratization is modeled separately for each region with consider-ation of each country level and within-country level variability, is as follows:

$$Y_{ij} = (\beta_{00} + \beta_{10}Year_{ij}) + (e_{0j} + e_{1j}Year_{ij} + r_{ij})$$

Where $e_{oj} \sim N(0, \tau_{00})$ $e_{1j} \sim N(0, \tau_{10})$ $r_{ij} \sim N(0, \sigma^2)$

β_{00} represents an average democracy level in the world in 1950

$\beta_{10}Year_{ij}$ represents an average slope of democratic growth in the world

τ_{00} represents variation in the democracy level between countries (between countries' intercepts)

τ_{10} represents variation between countries' temporal rate of demo-cratic growth (between countries' slopes)

σ^2 represents the within country residual

The dependent variable Y (growth of democracy) is explained with an intercept β_{00} and a slope $\beta_{10}Year_{ij}$. The fixed part of the model contains fixed effects for the intercept (β_{00}) and for the effect of time ($\beta_{10}Year_{ij}$). The random part contains three estimates of variance: the intercept e_{oj} representing variation in the democracy level between countries in the world; the slope of time ($e_{1j} Year_{ij}$) representing variation in the slope of the temporal rate of democratic growth between countries in the world, and the within-country residual r_{ij} representing variation in the democracy level within countries or the departure from the predicted score of the ith country's actual score in 1950 on the democ-racy scale.

To explore whether the variations within a country, or the intercepts and slopes, are related to covariates, independent variables were added to this unconditional model, where a variable X_{ij} represents the level-1 (within countries) predictor and a higher level X_j represents the level-2 (country or region-level) predictor. For example, a model with a level-1 and level-2 covariate is summarized by the following equation:

$$Y_{ij} = \left[\beta_{00} + \beta_{10}Year_{ij} + \beta_{01}X_{ij} + \beta_{11}(X_{ij})(Year_{ij}) + \beta_{01}X_j \right.$$
$$\left. + \beta_{11}(X_j)(Year_{ij}) \right] + \left[e_{0j} + e_{1j}(Year_{ij}) + r_{ij} \right]$$

This model is also expressed as the sum of two parts of fixed and random effects. The fixed effects for the intercept (β_{00}) represent an average democracy level in the world in 1950; the slope $\beta_{10}(Year)_{ij}$ represents the average slope of democratic growth; the predictor of democracy level $\beta_{01}X_{ij}$ and $\beta_{01}X_j$ captures the relationship between the covariates and the status of democracy in 1950, and the predictor of slope $\beta_{11}X_{ij}(Year_{ij})$ and $\beta_{11}(X_j)(Year_{ij})$ captures the relationship between the covariate and the growth rate of democracy. As in the unconditional model, the random effects represent a variation in the intercept, the slope, and the within-country variation (residual). The two-level growth model is used to assess democratic growth in each region. With the variance in democratic level between regions and the rate of democratic growth between regions added to this model, the above two-level model became a three-level growth model to which more covariates were added. The three-level model is used to assess democratic growth in the world.

Therefore, delineating the HLM methodology step by step:

1. At the first step, country/year level democracy was assessed as:

$$DEMOC_{tj} = \beta_{0j} + \beta_{1j}X_{tj} + e_{tj} \tag{1}$$

Where:
  j represents the countries $(_j = 1...J)$
  i represents the individual country/years $(_i = 1...N_j)$
  t represents the time
  $DEMOC_{tj}$ represents the scores of democratization for each year in the jth country
  β_{0j} is the intercept coefficient for each country
  β_{1j} *is* the slope coefficient of X_{tj} for each country at the country-year level

X_{tj} represents an explanatory variable

E_{tj} is random error in the country-year

2. In the next step, the model predicts the variation of the regressions β_j by introducing explanatory variables at the country level:

$$\beta_{0j} = \gamma_{00} + \gamma_{01}Z_j + u_{0j}, \tag{2}$$

and

$$\beta_{1j} = \gamma_{10} + \gamma_{11}Z_j + u_{1j} \tag{3}$$

where:

Z_j represents an explanatory variable of each country

γ_{01} is the intercept coefficient

γ_{11} *is* the slope coefficient of Z_j

u_{1j} is random error in the country associated with the slope Z variable

Thus, rearranging terms from equations (1), (2), and (3), we obtain:

$$DEMOC_{ij} = \gamma_{00} + \gamma_{10}X_{tj} + \gamma_{01}Z_j + \gamma_{11}Z_jX_{tj} + u_{1j}X_{tj} + u_{0j} + e_{tj} \tag{4}$$

3. Because we have P explanatory variables X at the lowest level, indicated by the subscript p (p $= 1...P$); likewise, we have Q explanatory variables Z at the higher (second) level indicated by the subscript q (q $= 1...Q$); the equation (4) becomes the more general equation:

$$DEMOC_{ij} = \gamma_{00} + \gamma_{p0}X_{ptj} + \gamma_{0q}Z_{qj} + \gamma_{pq}Z_{qj}X_{ptj} + u_{pj}X_{ptj} + u_{0j} + e_{tj} \tag{5}$$

I extended the model described above by modeling all regions together. This translates in the mathematical model by adding another random component representing the regional variation.

What are now needed are empirical studies that attempt to statistically evaluate predictive schemes of democracy growth as a stepping stone to understanding (a) the complexities of the process of worldwide democratization, especially in terms of linkage between political factors and countries' economic performance; (b) the predictive power of the contribution of endogenous vs exogenous factors to the world's democratization; (c) the temporal rate and growth of democracy, and (d) the global and domestic trends that modify the temporal rate and countries' openness toward democratic principles. Ideally, future studies should bridge the subfields of comparative (relying on domestic characteristics) and international (referring to shifting international trends) analyses.

Operationalization of predictor-type factors

In addition to defining an index of democracy level, using the discussion above on theoretical frameworks explaining democracy growth, two sets of factors predicting democracy growth were selected representing endogenous (herein called development) or exogenous (herein called diffusion) factors. Each set of factors – the development and diffusion – emphasizes differing sets of variables that are expected to influence a country's democratization. In the remainder of the chapter I compare the *relative* predictive power of the two factors in accounting for countries' variation in democratic growth – a change in the level of countries' democratic growth over time, as well as variance in democratic growth between countries and between regions.

Using prior empirical research on democratization (Bollen 1979; Crenshaw 1995; Starr 1991; Lipset 1994) and theoretical accounts of diffusion as a guide (Wejnert 2005), five indicators representing the strongest predictors of *countries' development* on democratic growth and four of the strongest predictors of *diffusion* of many types of phenomena, including political, were selected from the database. In addition, to account for the effect of historical events, a *historical events* variable was created and tested in the study. The indicators were assessed yearly for each country for the past 200 years, or for the time when a country became sovereign or the indicator started to be recorded (e.g., Banks' [1993] dataset records GNP per capita (GNP/c) since 1825).

Grouped by their categories, the indicators are:

Countries' socioeconomic and political development
(i) GNP per capita measured in $1,000 units (Banks 1993); (ii) urbanization measured as a percentage of the population living in cities to the total population in a country; (iii) literacy rate measured as a percentage of each country's population that is literate; (iv) yearly measured mean regional level of labor force in agriculture depicted as a percentage of agricultural labor force to the total labor force, and (v) a country's world-system position. The socioeconomic variables included in

Nations, Development and Democracy (Wejnert 2007) were derived from Banks' (1993) dataset and extended by variables from World Bank (2009). To test the comparability of the merged variables, correlation of each variable from Banks and from World Bank was performed on overlapping years, and correlation scores ranging from 0.9 to 0.95 were obtained. The variable GNP/c is assessed at market prices, where gross national product at market prices is the market value of the product, before deduction of provisions for the consumption of fixed capital, attributable to the factors of production supplied by normal residents of the given country. It is identically equal to the sum of consumption expenditure and gross domestic capital formation, private and public, and the net exports of goods and services plus the net factor incomes received from abroad (Banks 1993; World Bank 2009). This variable is also included in Wejnert's (2007) database.

Variable urbanization in the database *Nations, Development and Democracy* (Wejnert 2007) is measured as a percentage of a population living in cities of 10,000 or more to the total population in a country (Banks 1993). This measure is extended using comparable indicators from World Bank (2009). To test comparability, correlation of each variable from Banks and World Bank was performed, with obtained correlation scores ranging from 0.9 to 0.94 on overlapping years.

The variable of regional agricultural labor allows assessment of the effect of regional level development on democratic growth. It is likely that location in a region that is economically underdeveloped rather than affluent alters opportunities to meet the criteria of democratic transition by a country residing in that region. The regional level of development is also likely an additional factor explaining the regional clustering of democratic growth, e.g., democracy increase followed by its rapid decline in Western Europe from 1870 to 1939 (Moore 1966; Stephens 1989). A complete description of the variables is provided in Appendix 1. A theoretical framework for the selection of variables to assess the democratization of the world and its regions is presented in Figure 3.5.

Finally, countries' world-system positions were recorded in the database *Nations, Development and Democracy* (Wejnert 2007), following Snyder and Kick (1979) and Bollen and Appold (1993), as well as using supplementary data (World Bank 2009). Supplementary data were derived according to Bollen and Appold's specification as each

REGIONS

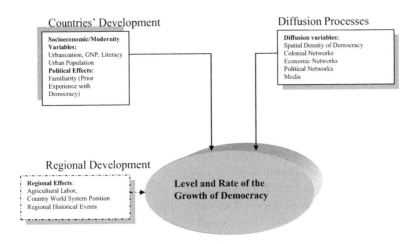

Figure 3.5 A theoretical framework for the selection of variables to assess the democratization of the world and its regions

country's average urbanization level defined as mean GNP/c and percent of agriculture labor. Also, the created world-system measure depicts the world-system position of countries as fixed at its 1950 level, which, considering arguments about the dynamic nature of countries' position in international trade (e.g., Smith & White 1992) presents a limitation to the analysis. Nonetheless, three factors support my study. First, many scholars of the world-system approach (e.g., Wallerstein 2001) indicate that it is not easy for an economically dependent country to move from a peripheral to a core position. Second, to my knowledge, there is no available dynamic measure of countries' position in the world system for all sovereign countries across the past two centuries; hence, such a study needs to be conducted in the future. Third, to test further my finding, I conducted the same analysis with a modified variable of the world system position that reflected, indicated by Smith and White (1992), dynamic changes in the measurement between 1960 and 1989. The control analysis yields similar results (the coefficient of the variable "world position" changed from −.8 (s.e. =.3) in this study to −.9 (s.e. =.4) in the control study). I used measurement of countries' position in the world system to test whether the position alters a country's chances to become democratic. Countries were recorded as either *core* (18 countries), *semi-peripheral* (31 countries), or *peripheral* (112 countries) (see Appendix 1).

Diffusion processes

(i) spatial density of democratic countries; (ii) membership in economic networks; (iii) membership in political networks; (iv) membership in colonial networks, and (v) media. The indicator of spatial density depicts the density of democratic countries within sub-regions. To derive this indicator, countries were recorded according to location in sub-regions – geographically proximate areas within regions of Europe, the Americas, Africa, the Middle East, Asia, and Oceania. Then the sum of democratic countries was divided by the total number of countries in each sub-region and presented as percentage. Using data from the World Trade Organization, the following geographically proximate sub-regions were recorded in the database *Nations, Development and Democracy* (Wejnert 2007): the *Americas*: North America, South America, Central America, the Caribbean; *Europe*: Western Europe, Central and Eastern Europe; *Africa*: Central Africa, East Africa, South Africa, West Africa; the *Middle East*: Middle East, North Africa; *Asia*: East Asia, Southeast Asia, the Indian subcontinent, Central Asia (see Appendix 1).

As shown in the database by Wejnert (2007), the indicator of *economic and political networks* was constructed by coding each country's year and duration of membership within an economic or political network, which was then weighted by the number of democratic members in each network. To create the indicator of a country's membership in networks, I used Osmanczyk's (1982) encyclopedia supplemented by the *Statesman's Yearbook* (2000). Countries' membership in the following networks was recorded: Union of Central African States, American Union, Union Africana et Malgache de Cooperation Economique, Council for Mutual Economic Assistance (CMEA), Nordic Council, Council of Europe, Council of Asian Industrial Development, Council of Arab Economic Unity, Arab League, Organization of Central American States, Organization of African Unity, Union Liga Confederacion Permanente, International Union of American Republics, Warsaw Pact, NATO, Asian Assistance, and the

Organization of American States. Most existing and historical networks were included in the data, with the exception of bilateral economic and political networks and networks that included almost all sovereign countries, such as the League of Nations and the United Nations (see Appendix 1).

To delineate *colonial networks*, a country's former colonial status was recorded in the database *Nations, Development and Democracy* (Wejnert 2007) as a dummy variable following the *Statesman's Yearbook* (2000) and Osmanczyk's (1982) encyclopedia. Accordingly, the colonies of the largest colonial empires of Britain, France, Portugal, and Spain were depicted. Based on the literature on democratic transition in the former communist countries (Przeworski 1996; Wejnert 2002b, 2002c), recently democratizing post-communist states were also believed to follow paths of democratic growth that are more typical of post-colonies than non-colonized states. Hence, these states were considered part of a semi-colonial network of Soviet alliance (see Appendix 1).

The last diffusion indicator of *media* was also drawn from Wejnert (2007), supported by the World Bank (2009) datasets. To represent societal *access* to media communication, this indicator was coded as the mean number of TVs, radios, and newspapers a citizen in each country has access to each year. Since TV was invented in the late 1920s but was not broadly produced for commercial sale until 1950, missing data for this variable for the nineteenth century and the first four decades of the twentieth century were coded as zero. Similarly, zero was coded for the missing data for radio per capita for the period before radio became publicly used (prior to 1920).

As demonstrated in the theoretical part of the analyses above, democratic development is also a latent function of *historical events*. Therefore, key historical events were recorded as dummy variables, where one represents years in which a historical event took place and zero represents non-event years. A value of one was assigned to the following years: (a) 1918–1922 – the end and aftermath of World War I; (b) 1933–1939 – the Great Depression; (c) 1945–1950 – the aftermath of World War II; (d) 1955–60 – the United Nations decolonization act; (e) 1962–1967 – the collapse of fragile democracies in many African post-colonies; (f) 1975–1985 – the effects of the worldwide oil crisis; and (g) Gorbachev's call for *perestroika* reform in the Soviet Union and, in 1989–1991, the collapse of the communist bloc. It is expected that many of these events facilitated worldwide democratic growth/decline but, on average, had a positive impact on the cross-world level of democratic growth.

The descriptive statistics of correlation of indicators used in the analyses of world and regional democratization with the indicator of democracy are presented in Table 3.5. The descriptive statistics assess correlations of dependent and independent indicators from 1800 to 2005.

Empirically developed threshold model of democracy's growth and sustainability, and retreat from democracy

The goal of this chapter is to empirically define the narrow intervals of democratization scores that demonstrate a threshold of the transition to sustainable democracy status, as well as the threshold of the loss of democracy status. Use of these two thresholds will help to define the unique set of endogenous and exogenous variables that modulate countries' transition to growth, sustainability, or loss of democracy status.

In the first part of this chapter I presented an empirical model of democracy adoption by non-democratic states. This presentation complemented prior empirically described models of democracy adoption. However, the primary focus of this study is a statistical model of the growth and sustainability of democracy via an assessed threshold model of democracy. In the existing scholarly work, such models are rather uncommon. The most commonly available index of the stages of countries' progress in democratization was established by Gurr et al. (1990) and followed by Wejnert (2007) who, on a democracy scale of 0–10, arbitrarily designated a score of 7 or more as representing *coherent, stable democracies*, with scores ranging from 1 to 6 representing incoherent or *transitional democracies*. Therefore, this research, by creating a threshold model of sustainability and growth of democracy, represents an empirical extension of the existing knowledge about the processes of democratization.

A threshold of democracy growth after democracy is adopted (TG_t) is a hypothetical construct that represents a weighted value of a country's characteristics of *socioeconomic and political development* (S_t) and external factors of diffusion (D_t) (see Figure 3.6). The relation between D_t and S_t is shown as a trade-off function, where pairs of

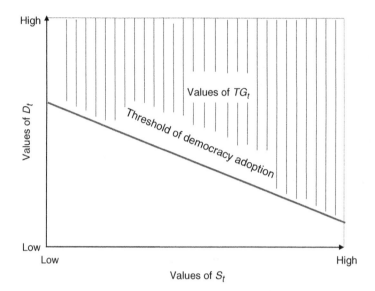

—— Represents Countries' Values of Thresholds of Democracy Adoption

Figure 3.6 The threshold of democracy growth after democracy is adopted (TG_t)

values of D_t and S_t specify a diagonal representing the minimum threshold value for the transition from adoption of democracy to low-level democracy, and low-level democracy to sustainable democracy (as represented in the field "Values of TG_t").

Within the combinatorial weighting of these factors, the threshold is viewed as being weighted most strongly by the joint function of two main variables: D_t and S_t. In future research, other variables that contribute to the threshold need to be defined, and their relative influence along with the variables of S_t and D_t needs to be statistically evaluated. Thus, for any country that adopted democracy, the movements to sustainable or low-level democracy at any point in time are dependent on whether the interaction of D_t and S_t produces a value that exceeds a country's threshold of adoption in the depicted range of TG_t values (values above the line representing countries' values of thresholds of democracy adoption). Because the two input variables (D_t and S_t) are interactive, independent variation in either one of the variables modifies the probability of democracy growth. Therefore, if there were a change in the value of a country's socioeconomic level S_t, for example, a country might go through the transition at lower diffusion (D_t) levels. Similarly, an increase in the value of (D_t) would increase the probability of democratic growth for countries of a specific range of S_t values (Figure 3.6).

To create threshold growth models, I argued, as explained above and elsewhere (e.g., Jagger & Gurr 1995a; Wejnert 2005), that democracy is best understood not simply as a dichotomy, where a country is considered either democratic or not, but as a continuous developmental process from non-democracy to some achieved level of democracy (Dahl 2000; Kissinger 2001; Tilly 2007). Using the established database (Wejnert 2007), it was possible to assess three sets of variables characteristic to all countries: (a) level of democracy assessed annually over 200 years on Jagger and Gurr's (1995a) scale of 0–10 adopted by Wejnert (2005) (where 0 means no democracy and 10 fully developed democracy) as the outcome variable; (b) the influence of countries' socioeconomic and political characteristics (development factors), and (c) the societal context of diffusion (diffusion factors) as predictors of democratization. We will use the established database and select countries based on the criteria of a country becoming democratic within the past half century or not being democratic, or losing democracy within that period. Based on previous findings (Wejnert 2005), across that period we will assess annually each selected country's level of socioeconomic development as indicated by the GNP per capita, level of industrialization and literacy, and its diffusion context as indicated by access to media information, membership in international networks with democratic countries, and neighboring with democratic countries. The interactive impact of socioeconomic development (S_t) and diffusion effects (D_t) at specific points in time when the selected country either moved from a score of 0 (non-democracy) to a score of 1 or more (democracy), or when it moved from a score of 6 (incoherent democracy) to a score of 7 or more (sustainable democracy), or when a democratic country retreated to non-democracy are measured. In this sense, the study empirically determines what interacting pairs of values of D_t and S_t produced conditions under which a country became democratic, became a sustainable democracy, or lost democratic status, i.e., produce a value that defines a country's threshold of democracy (TG_t) and assesses it according to the range of democratic threshold values. Empirical data are analyzed using the HLM models described above.

In the initial step, I provide a demonstration of preliminary analyses of D_t and S_t combinational weights in defining a threshold of democracy growth of a few selected countries. The results are shown in Figure 3.7, where the time point of a country reaching democratic status is matched to its actual D_t x S_t values. For example, low-developed Sierra Leone became a democratic country in 1961 mainly due to imposed democratization by its former colonial power, Britain (representing a strong diffusion effect). However, the democratic government was replaced by a totalitarian regime within 6 years. It took Sierra Leone more than 30 years of socioeconomic development to achieve a developmental level that, integrated with the diffusion effect of Britain and with *familiarity* with the democratic system, allowed the country to re-democratize in 1995. In contrast, the 1970s history of Poland demonstrates that the strong economic development of Poland was not sufficient for its transition to democracy when the existing communist regime extensively censored the media, thereby preventing diffusion of democratic ideas within the country and from outside of the country. However, in the 1980s, despite stagnant economic development, the attention of the international media to the Solidarity movement, the election of a Polish pope, and the demise of the Soviet Union all reduced censorship and opened opportunities for the diffusion of democratic ideas, leading to the democratization of Poland in 1989. Additionally, in the early 1980s, Saudi Arabia was as wealthy as the

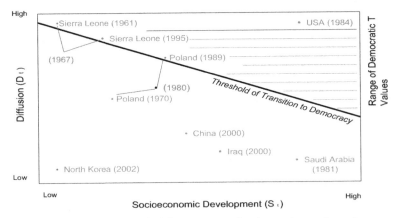

Figure 3.7 Threshold model of democracy's adoption and growth, and regression from democracy

US, but was located in a non-democratic region (a negative diffusion context) and hence never democratized. In contrast, the democratization of much poorer Poland occurred in part due to its location in the democratically-supportive context of Europe (a strong diffusion effect). Thus, results based on data derived from the database *Nations, Development and Democracy* (Wejnert 2007) in Figure 3.7 begin to delineate threshold TG_t values (D_t x S_t) for countries at the point of their transition to democracy or retreat from democracy. As these analyses are extended to additional countries, it is possible to define the interacting sets of values that demarcate a threshold in greater detail than that derived in Figure 3.7. Such an empirically derived threshold supersedes the development of a first-approximation model of transition to, sustainability of, and loss of democracy status presented in Figure 3.7.

Models of worldwide democratization

Before conducting an assessment of particular predictors, the validity of the selected three-level analyses was measured for all countries across the past two centuries. In these analyses the predictive power of the unconditional model, Model A (a model without predictors except the predictor of time), the two-level model, Model 2 (a model with added predictors that characterized countries), and the three-level model, Model C (where predictors at country and regional level interactively influence democracy growth), was measured. The average level of a country in the world at year 1950 and the rate of average growth of democracy level of a country and a region, as well as the rate of the growth over time of an average country and an average world region, were estimated to assess the evolution of democracy in the world from 1800–2005. The estimated effects of unconditional Model A, two-level Model B, and three-level Model C are presented in Table 3.4a.

In addition, covariance parameter estimates of the evolution of democracy in the world in 1800–2005 were assessed to confirm that the three-level model is the most accurate statistical model to use in the assessment of democracy growth across the last two centuries. As presented in Table 3.4b, the covariance/variance analyses further confirmed the correctness of using the three-level regression model for the longitudinal analyses of democracy growth across the world. As the

Table 3.4a *Fixed effects estimates of evolution of democracy in the world, 1800–2005*

Model	Fixed effects estimates		
	Intercept	Year	Year^2
A: Unconditional model	3.8074[1]	.008877[1]	−.00012[1]
p	<.0001	<.0001	<.0001
B: Two-level model	3.2128[1]	.01581[1]	.000092[1]
p	<.0001	.002	<.0001
C: Three-level model	3.7095[1]	.01014[1]	.000093[1]
p	.018	.247	<.0001
SE	(1.07)	(.008)	(.0078)

Data obtained while using two- and three-level growth models.
Model A: Hierarchical growth model depicting residual.
Model B: Hierarchical growth model depicting variance between countries and residual.
Model C: Hierarchical growth model depicting variance between countries and regions. Goodness of fit parameters of Akaike's Information Criterion (AIC), Akaike's Information Criterion corrected for a sample size (AICC), Bayesian Information Criterion (BIC), and Log Likelihood (−2LL) for the models:
Model A: AIC = 72583.6, AICC = 72583.6, BIC = 72591.1, −2LL = 72581.6 (df = 12000)
Model B: AIC = 54526.9, AICC = 54526.9, BIC = 54539.5, −2LL = 54518.9 (df = 12000)
Model C: AIC = 54488.9, AICC = 54488.9, BIC = 54487.4, −2LL = 54474.9. (df = 12000)
The smaller the obtained value, the better is the fit of the model to the data (SAS Manual, 1996).
1 −2LL used to assess probability *p* by comparing the difference in −2 RLL between two competing models to a χ^2 distribution (Singer 1998).

results of the assessed covariance/variance parameters demonstrate, over the last two centuries significant variation between regional levels of democracy can be depicted (variation of 6.9 points of democracy score on a scale of 0–10), and significant variation in democracy level between countries as well as between the rate of countries' democratic growth can be depicted. Interestingly, negative covariance between countries' level and rate of democratic growth attested that over the last two centuries countries that were less democratic in 1950 (the center year) democratized much faster than those countries that were more democratic in 1950 (see Table 3.4b).

Table 3.4b *Covariance parameter estimates of evolution of democracy in the world, 1800–2005*

Model	Covariance parameter estimates						
	Variation between regions' intercepts	Variation between regions' slopes	Covariance regions' intercepts/ slopes	Variation between countries' intercepts	Variation between countries' slopes	Covariance countries' intercepts/ slopes	Residual
A: Unconditional model							6.2048[1]
p							<.0001
B: Two-level model				14.3447[1]	.00322[1]	−.09822[1]	3.1925[1]
p				<.0001	<.0001	<.0001	<.0001
C: Three-level model	6.938[1]	.0003[1]	.000983[1]	10.9957[1]	.0029[1]	−.1046[1]	3.1879[1]
p	<.0001	.2	.9754	<.0001	<.0001	<.0001	<.0001
SE	(5.251)	(.0003)	(.03194)	(1.302)	(.0004)	(.02257)	(.03968)

Data obtained while using two- and three-level growth models:

Model A: Hierarchical growth model depicting residual.

Model B: Hierarchical growth model depicting variance between countries and residual.

Model C: Hierarchical growth model depicting variance between countries and regions. Goodness of fit parameters of Akaike's Information Criterion (AIC), Akaike's Information Criterion corrected for a sample size (AICC), Bayesian Information Criterion (BIC), and Log Likelihood (−2LL) for the models:

Model A: AIC = 72583.6, AICC = 72583.6, BIC = 72591.1, −2LL = 72581.6 (df = 12000)

Model B: AIC = 54526.9, AICC = 54526.9, BIC = 54539.5, −2LL = 54518.9 (df = 12000)

Model C: AIC = 54488.9, AICC = 54488.9, BIC = 54487.4, −2LL = 54474.9. (df = 12000)

The smaller the obtained value, the better is the fit of the model to the data (SAS Manual, 1996).

[1] −2LL used to assess probability *p* by comparing the difference in −2 RLL between two competing models to a χ^2 distribution (Singer 1998; Singer & Willett 2003).

The effect of time on democratic growth

Model 1: No Predictors. In this model, I obtained an estimate of an average country's democratization level at the centered time (1950) – the intercept. The obtained variance components demonstrate significant differences in the average democratization level between countries and between regions. Importantly, differences in democratization level within each country are also depicted, indicating that amore accurate assessment of the intercept could be obtained in models with added predictors. The first added predictor is time.

Predictor of Time. As shown in Table 3.6 (Model 1), time is a strong predictor of democratization worldwide, indicating that for an average country in the world the democracy score is increasing .02 each year and .0002 each quadratic year. The low p values of the slope and the intercept of democratic growth, and a significant difference in obtained values of −2LL between Model 1 as compared to the χ^2 distribution ($df = 6$, $p <.0001$), confirm a strong relationship between time and democratic growth. In Model 1, significant differences in the average status of democratization and the rate of democratization between countries and between regions are observed. These findings confirm the analyses presented in Table 3.4 above, demonstrating that there is evidence that the rate of democratic growth depends on the status of world democratization and is higher for countries that obtained lower democracy scores in 1950 (the covariance of countries' intercepts/ slopes is −.08), while it is lower for countries that attained higher democracy scores in 1950.

The unconditional model characterized the level and rate of growth of democracy in the world in 1950, and estimated the variance in the democracy level and the rate of democratic growth between regions and between countries, as well as the within-country variance. Accordingly, in 1950, closely resembling the observed data, the average country in the world had a level of democracy of 2.85 (on a scale of 0–10), and the rate of democratic growth was upward curvilinear (Figure 1.2). A significant variance in democracy level between regions of 4.9 (on a scale of 0–10) was depicted, as was variance in the level of democracy and the rate between countries (of 11.2 and .004, respectively), and a significant residual of 3.9. Importantly, the depicted negative covariance of countries' intercepts and slopes indicates that in 1950 non-democratic or low-democratic countries increased their

Table 3.5 *Descriptive statistics for indicators used in analyses of world and regional democratization, 1800–2005*

Variable	Mean	Standard deviation	Minimum	Maximum	N *	Correlation score with democracy**
Democracy level	3.17	3.87	0	10.00	13264 (1306)	
Year (centered at 1950)	−22.03	54.77	−150.0	49.00	14570 (0)	.544
Industrial labor (%)	32.65	32.84	.00	99.63	10027 (4543)	.567
Literacy (%)	56.00	36.98	.03	100.00	13644 (926)	.554
GNP/c ($)	2,780.0	3,479.0	62.43	20,849.0	10006 (4564)	.452
Spatial proximity	3.23	2.6	0	10.00	14440 (130)	.369
Networks	.663	.861	.0	4.00	12189 (2381)	.552
Democratic experience	.536	.435	.0	1.00	9919 (4651)	.64
TV/c (mean)	0.75	2.13	.0	6.20	14570 (0)	.379
Urbanization (%) (mean)	30.66	26.63	0	100.00	14570 (1350)	.44
Regional agricultural labor (%)	48.6594	16.49	13.4	82.00	14570 (0)	−.41
Regional democratic history	23.42	10.58	1	42.00	14570(0)	.117

* Missing values are indicated in parentheses.
** Pearson correlation coefficients, correlation is significant at 0.01 level (2-tailed).

level of democracy faster than countries that had high democracy scores. This finding signals that low-level democracies must differ from high-level democracies in characteristics that made them more vulnerable to a speedy democratization in the second half of the twentieth century. To search for those characteristics, I added sets of predictors of development and of diffusion, one set at a time, in consecutive models (see Table 3.5). The descriptive statistics of correlation of indicators used in analyses of world and regional democratization with the indicator of democracy are presented in Table 3.5. The descriptive statistic assesses correlations of dependent and independent indicators from 1800 to 2005.

Added predictors of democratic growth

To predict world democratization and world democracy growth step by step, several models were designed, following an order from least to most complex. As the obtained results show, with each added covariate the model better explained the process of democratic growth (see Table 3.6, the variance part). In the first analytic step, this study assessed worldwide democratic growth using the previously described three-level HLM growth model. Initially a model that did not include predictor variables (Model 1, an unconditional model) was created that served as a baseline for comparing models that are more complex. To each consecutive model were added sets of predictors of (a) development in Model 2; (b) diffusion in Model 3, and (c) historical events in Model 4. Note that the comparison of the unconditional model with Model 1 and Model 2 versus the comparison of Model 1 with Model 3 constitutes an essential part of the study, as it assesses the relative predictive power of socio-economic versus diffusion variables.

Overall, the modeling demonstrates that countries with higher urbanization, higher GNP per capita, a stronger diffusion effect, broader access to media (availability of newspapers, TV, radio, and internet), and a lower percentage of illiteracy result in a higher level of democratization. Also, a higher percentage of the labor force engaging in non-agricultural production in a region leads to a higher level of democratization (see Table 3.6).

The analyses of the results require, however, more parsimonious interpretations.

Effects of development

In Model 2 I assessed the impact of development predictors on democratic growth in the world (the level and the rate) and judged how much of regional and country variance is explained by variables of countries' development in comparison to the unconditional model. In

Table 3.6 Development and diffusion predictors of democratic growth in the world, 1860–2005

	Model 1		Model 2		Model 3		Model 4	
	Unconditional		Development		Diffusion		Historical event	
Fixed Effects								
Model 1. Unconditional model								
1. Intercept (Democracy level)	2.85**	(.8)	7.3*	(1.3)	2.2*	(.9)	2.1*	(.9)
Year	.02**	(.008)	.05*	(.02)	−.01	(.02)	−.005	(.02)
Year² (curvilinear slope)	.0002*	(.00002)	.001**	(.00008)	−.0009**	(.00008)	−.0006**	(.00008)
Model 2. Development predictors								
Country-year predictors								
GNP/c			.04*	(.009)	.01	(.008)	.02*	(.008)
(GNP/c*year)/100			.9**	(.2)	−.5*	(.1)	−.5*	(.2)
(GNP/c *year²)/1000			−.02**	(.0004)	−.02**	(.0004)	−.02**	(.004)
Literacy			−.6**	(.1)	.14	(.1)	.18	(.1)
Literacy*year			.02**	(.004)	.005	(.003)	.002	(.004)
Literacy*year²			.0009**	(.00006)	.0003**	(.00006)	.0003**	(.00006)
Urbanization			.02	(.01)	.02	(.01)	.02	(.01)
Urbanization*year			.00005	(.0002)	.00005	(.0002)	.00005	(.0002)
Country-level predictor								
World position			−1.9**	(.4)	−.8*	(.3)	−.8*	(.3)
World position*year			−.02*	(.007)	.0004	(.006)	−.00005	(.007)
World position*year²			.0004**	(.00002)	.0002**	(.00002)	.0001**	(.00003)

189

Table 3.6 (*cont.*)

	Model 1		Model 2		Model 3		Model 4	
	Unconditional		Development		Diffusion		Historical event	
Region-level predictor								
Regional non-agricultural labor			.01**	(.001)	.0002	(.001)	.0003	(.001)
Reg. non-agric. labor*year)/100			.05**	(.004)	.02**	(.004)	.01*	(.004)
Model 3. Diffusion predictors								
Country-year predictors								
Spatial density					6.6**	(.2)	6.6**	(.2)
(Spatial density*year)/100					.3	(.4)	.3	(.4)
(Spatial density*year²)/100					.05**	(.007)	.05**	(.007)
Network					18.2**	(.7)	18.2**	(.7)
Network*year					.1*	(.02)	.1**	(.02)
Network*year²					.001*	(.0005)	.001*	(.0005)
Colonial network					-.5*	(.1)	-.5*	(.2)
(Colonial network*year)/100					.01	(.4)	-.01	(.3)
(Colonial network*year²)/100					.005**	(.001)	.00004	(.001)
Media					-.07*	(.02)	-.07*	(.02)
(Media*year)/100					-.7**	(.09)	-.7**	(.1)
(Media*year²)/100					-.01**	(.002)	-.01**	(.002)
Model 4. Historical events predictor								
Historical events							-.06*	(.03)
(Historical events*year)/100							-.6**	(.09)

	Model 1		Model 2		Model 3		Model 4	
(Historical events^3·year^2)/100							.02*	(.003)
Random part								
Estimates of Variances								
Variance between regions' intercepts	4.9*	(2.1)	2.4*	(1.3)	.8	(.5)	.8	(.5)
Variance between regions' slopes	.0005*	(.0002)	.0005	(.0003)	.0003	(.0003)	.0003	(.0002)
Variance between countries' intercepts	11.2*	(1.3)	10.3**	(1.3)	6.5**	(.8)	6.5**	(.8)
Variance between countries' slopes	.004**	(.0004)	.004**	(.0005)	.003**	(.0004)	.003**	(.0004)
Covariance between countries' intercepts & slopes	−.08**	(.02)	−.11**	(.02)	−.11**	(.02)	−.11**	(.02)
Residual	3.9**	(.05)	3.8**	(.05)	2.8**	(.04)	2.75**	(.04)

Values in parentheses depict standard errors. For the predictor of urbanization and the regional predictor non-agricultural labor force the linear slope (year) was assessed as best fitting observed data.

Number of observations across countries over time (N_1) =12189; number of countries (N_2) = 161; number of regions (N_3) =17. The fit statistics of −2RLL, AIC, AICC, BIC of 52693.3, 52705.3, 52704.0 in Model 1, as compared to 52243.9, 52255.9, 52255.9, 52254.6 in Model 2 and 48409.8, 48419.8, 48419.8, 48244.0 in Model 4 (df = 1200), indicate a better fit of each consecutive model to the data.

* p <.05, ** p <.0001

191

this model, the democratic growth was explained by controlling for indicators of countries' socioeconomic development, i.e., GNP per capita (GNP/c), literacy, urbanization, and position in the world system, and for the regional variable percentage of non-agricultural labor force. As the results denote, only the GNP/c, world-system position, and regional non-agricultural labor force are robust predictors of democratic growth (see Table 3.6).

First, a higher GNP/c correlates with the higher level of democracy, but a marked *decline* of economic growth predicts an increase in the temporal rate of democratic growth. This result is concordant with the findings of Przeworski et al. (2000) and Tilly (2007) that a high GNP/c is found in sustainable, high-level democracies with a score 7 and above, and validates it with a continuous scale of measurement, which increases its predictive validity (Jagger & Gurr 1995a).

The continuous measurement of the democracy level also extends the prior findings of Przeworski et al. (1996) who argued that a reduction in democracy level takes place at times of economic crisis. As shown, the positive correlation between a decline in the GNP/c and an *increase* of the rate of democratic growth indicates that economic crisis *also stimulates* the development of democracy. It could be because it creates a breeding ground for the onset of democratic transitions (as depicted by studies on democratic movements, e.g., Markoff 2003; Ruschmeyer, Stephens, & Stephens 1992; or by studies on democracy: Dahl 2000; Sedaitis & Butterfield 1991; Tilly 2007) or adds political strength to pro-democratic constituencies that demand greater democratization of countries. Future studies should be conducted to further delineate this issue.

Second, when controlling only for socioeconomic variables, literacy did not correlate significantly with democracy level, indicating that high literacy can be found in totalitarian as well as democratic regimes. However, an *increasing rate* of literacy predicts an increase in the rate of democratic growth. This finding might explain why democratic transitions were not initiated in the highly educated societies of the former Soviet regimes until an economic crisis sparked pro-democratic movements (Wejnert 1988, 2002c), and why recently in many African countries an increase in education level is depicted together with increases in democracy level (Kapstein & Converse 2009; World Bank 2009).

Third, the significant influence of the variable of the *world-system position*[12] supports Wallerstein's (2001) argument that a country's position in the world's trade system strongly affects its democratic growth. Indeed, peripheral countries that are poor and disadvantaged in trade composition are generally low-level democracies. However, there is also a "benefit" to being a peripheral country – the rate of their democratization accelerates faster than in other countries. Some light is shed on the possible explanation of this trend by regional analyses (see below), with the potentially greater vulnerability of peripheral countries to the influences of diffusion leading the explanations. Another possible explanation could refer to the conditions of international aid, such as funds from the International Monetary Fund or the World Bank, which frequently favor aid giving to countries that are sustainable democracies. However, according to more recent arguments, foreign aid negatively affects the economic growth of countries in the developing world by limiting the internal motivation of people to work hard and to succeed in these societies (Moyo 2009).

Fourth, it is shown that limited regional industrialization, measured by a high level of agricultural labor force, inhibits democratic growth in countries located within that region. This finding demonstrates that it does make a difference where a country is located, and being located in a poor region delays or inhibits democratic growth. Therefore, characteristics of regions are important contributors and should be accounted for in research on democratization. For example, focusing only on country-level predictors could lead to mistaken explanations as it would if we attempt to predict democratic growth with GNP/c alone. For example, in 1993 Mexico, located in less-developed Central America, had a GNP/c of $4,230, whereas Portugal, located in well-developed, industrialized Europe, had a GNP/c of $2,020 in 1976. Using the GNP/c alone (as many studies thus far have done), we would predict that Mexico would have a greater chance to become a high-level democracy than Portugal. In reality, Portugal was highly democratized in 1976, whereas Mexico had a low-rated level of democracy in 1993. Regional location must interfere with the impact of GNP/c.

---

[12] The *world-system position* is a country-level indicator and does not change yearly, as do other included indicators. Its value is fixed at the 1950 level, which creates limitations in the findings (see also the description included in Appendix 1).

I argue that economically affluent regions provide economic opportunities, incentives, and protective strategies that help fragile democratic regimes to sustain their system at times of economic crisis. This finding is particularly important when we consider arguments that economic crisis is one of the leading causes of the breakdown of democratic regimes (Przeworski et al. 1996) as well as non-democratic regimes (Przeworski 2009), and when we consider the fragile African democracies of the first decade of the 2000s (Kapstein & Converse 2009). The latter two variables of world position and regional agricultural labor suggest that especially in low-level democracies the effect of GNP/c might be modulated by additional socioeconomic variables that elevate the chances a poor country has to become a high-level democracy.

Effects of diffusion

Model 3 includes predictors of diffusion to account for the growth of the democratic level in the world. These indicators measure exposure to democratic principles resulting from: (a) spatial density of democratic countries in a geographically close region; (b) membership in economic and political networks containing at least one democratic country; (c) membership in colonial networks, and (d) access to media communication.

Overall, as shown in Table 3.6, a country's exposure to democratic principles facilitated by diffusion processes – modeling of democratic countries, learning how democracy works, or spreading information about democratic principles – is a critical predictor of the growth of democracy worldwide. In fact, once the diffusion predictors were added to the model, the significance of development predictors faded. Especially with added spatial density and proximity and countries' membership in political and economic networks, other predictors almost do not matter (the coefficient of spatial density is 6.6 with s.e. = .2 and t = 33; and the coefficient of network is 18.2 with s.e. = .7 and t = 26).

Spatial density and proximity of democratic countries in a sub-region strongly positively affects the mean level of democracy of countries located in that sub-region, where an increase in the number of democracies in a sub-region by 1 percent increases the level of democracy of an average country in that sub-region by .06 (on a scale of 0–10).[13] This finding supports and extends O'Loughlin et al. (1998), Wejnert (2005), and Diamond and Plattner's (2010) argument showing that neighboring with a democratic country increases the democracy level of a country, but also that merely being located in a sub-region containing at least one democracy is an equally important predictor. I believe that the sub-regional structural similarity of countries generated by, for example, similar cultural and economic structures, by trade relations or religious ties, strongly affects democratic growth. An example of the significance of structural similarity providing democratization is the former Soviet bloc in the early 1990s, when Poland initiated the wave of transitions to democracy but its first follower was not one of its neighbors but structurally similar Hungary. At the same time, East Germany, which shared a border with Poland, democratized after democratic transition was initiated in Hungary, the Czech Republic, and Yugoslavia. Another Polish neighbor, the Ukraine, democratized after the democratic transition was initiated in all of the Eastern European countries (Wejnert 2002b, 2010). Following the logic and the findings, it would be correct to assume that democratized Iraq could enhance democratization processes throughout the Middle East in addition to its positive effect on neighboring Iran. At the same time, the impact of democratic but religiously dissimilar Israel on the democratization of non-democratic countries in the Middle East is much weaker due to vast cultural and socioeconomic differences between Israel and the Muslim countries of the Middle East.

Economic and political networks are robust predictors of democratic growth. The increase in membership of democratic countries in an *economic and political network* by 1 percent increases the level of democracy of an average country in that network by .18 (on a scale of 0–10) (s.e. = .007). This result is illustrated by the observed data. For example, since 1963 Chad has been a member of two economic and political networks with a low mean level of democracy. In 1995, the mean level of democracy in its networks increased from a 2.98 score in a previous year to a score of 6.10, and in that year Chad initiated democratic transition. The

---

[13] Considering that in most sub-regions there were from five to ten countries, each new democracy increases the number of democratic countries by approximately 10–20 percent. Thus, with each new democracy established in a sub-region, the democracy level increases by .7 to 1.4 points on a scale of 0–10.

case of Rumania follows the same pattern. Rumania became a low-level democracy in 1990 when the continuously low mean level of democracy in its networks increased five times (from .29 in 1989, to a 1.29 score in 1990). Moreover, Kuwait demonstrated the same pattern when it became a low-level democracy in 1995, after being a member of low democratized networks since the 1960s. Starting with 1993, however, the networks' level of democratization gradually increased to a score of 5.31 by 1995, and in that year Kuwait became a semi-democratic state. Furthermore, the close network of Arab countries enhances societal calls for more political rights across the Gulf states, particularly vocal since the Arab Spring of late 2010. Simultaneously it provides a platform for communication between ruling royal families, concerned that democratic protest in one country becomes a role-model for democratic action in other Gulf countries (Kinninmont 2012).

On the other hand, supporting the arguments of the representatives of a conflict theory of democratic growth (e.g., Wallerstein 2001), membership in a colonial network has a negative impact on countries' democracy level, lowering democracy it by −.5 point on a scale of 0–10; nonetheless, it has affected positively democratic growth over time, where a country's membership in a colonial network positively influenced democracy's growth within the country by .005 point each quadratic year (on a scale of 0–10).

The assessment of the effect of *media* since the 1800s did support the argument of Gunther and Mughan (2000) that societal exposure to *media communication* increases democratic growth (the level and the rate). Such a finding contrasted with my pilot analyses conducted for the years 1800–2005, where the effect of the media indicator was negative. It does not mean, however, that the media's role in the promotion of democracy was incorrectly depicted by pilot studies. Rather, this finding indicates that the effect is generated by modern media technology, especially TV, radio, and the internet, and their existence is too short relative to the time span of our study to overbalance the negative effect of the recorded dummy of 0 for the years when TV, radio, or the internet did not exist. Separate analysis conducted for the last half century demonstrates an even stronger positive media effect on the democratic growth of an average country in the world. This effect increases, however, with the broadening of societal access to media communication, not just with the availability of media technology. Indeed, no variable of existing media technology (newspaper, radio, TV, or the internet) had a significant effect on democratic growth until societal access to media was assessed.

Colonial Dependency. In contrast to prior analyses showing a positive effect of colonial dependency on countries' democratization (e.g., Crenshaw 1995), results indicate that, while *colonial dependency* leads to a higher rate of democratization, post-colonies in general have *lower* levels of democratic growth. The variation of the current results with previous findings may be due to the fact that prior studies tested only the level, but not the temporal rate, of democratization and in mainly British colonies, whereas the current study assessed both the level and the rate in several colonial empires. Importantly, however, the results indicate that the hegemonic imposition of a democratic regime on newly independent colonies (e.g., in British colonial dependencies) did not lead to a strong democracy; nonetheless, it provided experience with a democratic system that, as indicated by increasing democratization over time and by diffusion theory (increase of the familiarity with democratic system), helped to boost re-democratization processes. Separate analysis conducted for each colonial network showed that post-colonies of democratic empires had higher and increasing levels of democratic growth, while colonial dependencies of non-democratic empires had negative democratic growth. For instance, democratic growth of the colonial dependencies of autocratic Spain, Portugal, and Soviet Russia were negatively affected by colonial history, whereas dependencies of democratic Britain were positively affected, while those of France showed no significant effect. Unlike other imperial powers, France had limited interest in imposing or preparing political institutions in newly independent colonies. Thus, membership in the colonial network of democratic Britain increased a country's democratic growth by 2.9 on the democracy scale. At the same time, membership in a French colonial network had a negative, albeit not significant, effect. Subsequently in regions with the influence of one predominant colonial power, the impact of the colonial network reflects the character of the colonial influence. Thus, as the analyses in the next section demonstrate, in regions mainly influenced by British colonial power, such as Asia, the effect of colonial dependency on democracy growth was positive, while in Africa, dominated primarily by French and British powers, the effect was not significant (the positive effect of Britain was balanced by the negative impact of France). In Europe, dominated by the colonial-type impact of the communist Soviet Union, the effect of colonial impact on democracy growth was negative.

Variance Estimates. The most important results for the purpose of this study are estimates of variance, because they demonstrate the relative predictive power of socioeconomic versus diffusion variables in world democratization. Variance estimates are listed at the bottom of Table 3.6, where first are listed the variance parameters of the unconditional model – between regions, between countries, and within-country variance. To this baseline are compared the variance effects of the model with socioeconomic indicators (Model 2), and later with diffusion indicators (Model 3). The comparison of the variance estimates of each model allows judgment as to which model is a stronger predictor of democratic growth (Singer & Willett 2003).

Variance estimates demonstrate *markedly stronger relative predictive power of diffusion than socioeconomic variables* in world democratization. Relative to socioeconomic predictors, predictors of diffusion (when controlling for socioeconomic variables) explained:

1. almost *twice* as much variance in democracy level between regions (84% vs 51%) (albeit not significant);
2. 34% more variance in democracy level between countries (8% vs 42%);
3. 22% variance in the rate of democratic growth between countries, versus *zero* explained by development indicators;
4. *eleven* times the within-countries variance (the residual) (28% vs 2.5%).

In sum, diffusion variables accounted for much more of the variance in the *level* and *growth* rate of democratization than socioeconomic variables (see Table 3.6).

As Table 3.6 demonstrates, the fit statistics of -2RLL, AIC, AICC, and BIC of 52693.3, 52705.3, 52705.3, and 52704.0 in Model 1, as compared to 52243.9, 52255.9, 52255.9, and 52254.6 in Model 2, 48736.4, 48746.4, 48746.4, and 48745.4 in Model 3, and 48409.8, 48419.8, 48419.8, and 48244.0 in Model 4 ($df = 1200$), indicates a better fit of each consecutive model to the data.

Effect of major historical events

Observation of patterns of the evolution of democracy over time in comparison to historical events in the world (see Figure 1.4 in Chapter 1) leads to a conclusion that democratic growth is greatly influenced by historical events, especially the events of the twentieth century. It is also apparent that most of the historical events perpetuate democratic growth. Hence, in the last part of the world analysis, I tested the effect of world-scale historical events on democratic growth in the world while controlling for socioeconomic and diffusion predictors (see Model 4, Table 3.6).

First, comparing Model 4 with Model 3 (Diffusion Predictors), historical events have a moderate effect on the democratization of the world, and the effects were primary at the regional level. As the results indicate, the added predictor of historical events further explained the level of democratic growth of an average country in the world (slightly reduced residual means explained variance in the level of countries' democracy), but did not add any further explanation regarding differences in democracy level between countries or between regions (significant variance of the level of democracy between countries and between regions remains about the same). Second, interestingly, the effect of historical events on the level of democratic growth was negative but led to an increase in democratic growth over time (this indicator's impact on the rate of democratization was positive). In other words, historical events caused an immediate *drop* in democracy level, but subsequently these events over time stimulated democratic growth in the world. These seemingly puzzling results become clear when one refers to the observed data that are presented in Figure 1.4 in Chapter 1. For instance, during World Wars I and II many democracies collapsed, but subsequent spurts in democratic transitions occurred in the aftermath of post-World War I and post-World War II peace treaties. At the end of World War I, newly born countries in Europe were established as democratic states, and so were newly established countries resulting from the aftermath of the World War II.

Conversely, the Great Depression of the 1930s led to the outbreak of totalitarianism and a reduction in the democracy level worldwide, and so did the onset of World War II, when foreign occupation precluded countries' sovereignty, which resulted in the abolition of many democracies and inhibited development of democracy, as shown in Figure 1.4, when the level of democracy rapidly declined worldwide. The events of decolonization were associated with the democratic transition of part of the former colonies in Africa and Asia, but this democratization was for the most part brief, leading to an upward curve followed by a downward trend in worldwide democracy growth. Two upward trends coexist with the last wave of democratic movements in 1970–1980 in South America and in the 1990s in the countries of the former Soviet bloc and Asian countries receiving Western economic aid (a complete discussion of the various historical events that shaped the democratic history of the world is presented in earlier chapters of this book).

It is broadly believed that democracies do not start wars with other democracies (e.g., Dahl 2000; Karatnycky 1997); hence, as the findings indicate, the end of world-scale wars encouraged the international community to undertake new initiatives to build peace. On the other hand, similar to a national economic crisis, a global economic crisis leads to an *onset* of democratic transitions, as societies experiencing economic hardship demand broader inclusion in governing and decision-making processes. In sum, although global wars and economic depression cause destruction to democratic systems, paradoxically, the negative historical events can have overall long-lasting positive effects on worldwide democratic growth.

Models of regional democratization: the effects of development and diffusion

Analyses of each world region were conducted, starting with the construction of an unconditional model with no predictors (Model 1A), followed by a model adding socioeconomic predictors (Model 2A), and then by a model adding predictors of diffusion (Model 3A), and finally by a model with added historical events while controlling for all other indicators (Model 4A). The results of the regional analyses are presented in Table 3.7, demonstrating that different indicators differently affect democratic growth in different regions. Moreover, to provide a more meaningful statistical assessment of regional indicators, the regional indictors are depicted as within sub-regions of the main world regions, to account more strongly for the potential effect of indicators such as spatial density and proximity, or networks.

Western Hemisphere. Accordingly, in the Western Hemisphere, assessed for the years 1820–2005 with adjusted Model 1A, the upward curvilinear slope of the temporal rate of democratization depicted as a quadratic function of time was similar to the observed upward trend of democratic evolution over time, indicating that an average country in a region gained .0002 score on the democracy scale each quadratic year (see Table 3.7). The intercept value was similar to the observed value

Table 3.7 Development and diffusion predictors of democratic growth across the world's regions, 1800–2005

	Americas				Europe				Africa			
	1820–2005 N = 3,066				1800–2005 N = 3,693				1949–2005 N = 1,648			
	Model 1		Model 4		Model 1		Model 4		Model 1		Model 4	
Fixed Effects: (Model 1A)												
Intercept	3.76*	(.58)	−.4	(3.0)	5.05*	(.47)	.6	(1.3)	1.92**	(.87)	−8.03*	(3.93)
Slope: year	.027*	(.005)	−.03	(.06)	.03*	(.005)	−.01	(.02)	.203*	(.58)	.8**	(.2)
Slope: year^2	.0002*	(.00002)	−.002**	(.0002)	.0003*	(.0001)	−.0008**	(.0002)	−.013*	(.002)	−.014**	(.002)
Slope: year^3									.0003*	(.00002)	.00009	(.00001)
Socioeconomic predictors (Model 2B)												
Country-year predictors												
GNP/c			.03*	(.01)			.06*	(.02)			−.16	(.09)
(GNP/c*year)/10			.01*	(.004)			−.01**	(.003)			.2*	(.09)
(GNP/c*year^2)10			−.00004	(.00007)			−.0004**	(.00007)			−.009**	(.002)
Literacy			1.7**	(.3)			−.1	(.2)			18.0**	(2.2)
Literacy*year			−.01	(.01)			.02**	(.006)			−.9**	(.14)
Literacy*year^2			.0004*	(.0001)			.0007**	(.0001)			.01**	(.002)
Urbanization			.03	(.03)			.05*	(.02)			.05	(.05)
(Urbanization*year)100			−.02	(.07)			.028	(.0003)			−.6*	(.2)
(Urbanization*year^2)100			.002**	(.0001)			.0004*	(.0001)			.02**	(.003)
Country level predictor												
World position			.08	(.8)			−.99	(.6)			1.5	(1.1)

Table 3.7 (*cont.*)

	Americas 1820–2005 N = 3,066		Europe 1800–2005 N = 3,693		Africa 1949–2005 N = 1,648	
(World pos.*year)/10	−.02	(.1)	.005	(.1)	−1.9**	(.5)
(World pos.*year²)10	.006**	(.0005)	.003**	(.0005)	.03**	(.006)
Diffusion predictors (Model 3C)						
Country-year predictors						
Spatial density	4.9**	(.4)	7.02**	(.5)	6.2*	(1.74)
Spatial density*year	.007	(.008)	−.01	(.01)	.04	(.1)
Spatial density*year²	.0001	(.0001)	.0007*	(.0002)	−.0002	(.002)
Network	27.8**	(1.2)	15.4**	(1.5)	12.5	(25.5)
Network*year	.3**	(.03)	−.4*	(.10)	2.5	(1.7)
Network*year²	.002*	(.0008)	.009*	(.003)	−.04	(.026)
Colonial network	−.4	(.4)	−1.1*	(.3)	.19	(.6)
(Colonial netw.*year)/10	.03	(.08)	−.08	(.05)	−.4	(.3)
(Colonial netw.*year²)/10	−.002**	(.0002)	.002**	(.0003)	.0048	(.004)
Media	.09*	(.03)	.1*	(.04)	.9*	(.39)
Media*year	−.01**	(.001)			−.1*	(.04)
Media*year²	−.0002**	(.00003)	.0007*	(.0002)	.0023*	(.001)
Historical events predictor (Model 4D)						

Historical events		-.1* (.05)		-.05 (.06)		-.16 (.3)
(Hist. events*year)/10		-.04* (.01)		-.05* (.02)		.1 (.2)
(Hist. events*year²)/10		.0008 (.0006)		.002* (.0007)		-.002 (.003)
Random part						
Estimates of variances						
Variance between countries' intercepts	10.5* (2.2)	5.5* (1.7)	10.7* (2.3)	5.4*** (1.4)	21.1* (5.3)	11.7** (2.8)
Variance between countries' slopes	.01* (.0002)	.002* (.0005)	.001* (.0003)	.002* (.0004)	.008* (.002)	.009** (.002)
Covariance between intercepts & slopes	.038* (.018)	-.06* (.02)	.04** (.01)	-.004 (.02)	-.36 (.1)	-.3* (.07)
Residual	4.28* (.09)	1.9** (.09)	4.3* (.04)	4.1** (.094)	2.29* (.08)	2.2** (.08)

Values in parentheses depict standard errors. The temporal rate (slope) of democratic growth is assessed as a year, year squared or year quadratic dependent on the region. The explanation of assessment of slopes was provided in the first part of Chapter 3.

* $p < .05$,
** $p < .0001$.

Table 3.7 (*cont.*)

	Middle East 1917–2005 N = 1,124				Asia 1900–2005 N = 1,602			
	Model 1		Model 4		Model 1		Model 4	
Fixed effects: (Model 1)								
Intercept	1.97*	(.6)	3.78	(1.98)	3.402*	(.78)	7.2*	(3.2)
Slope: year	−.026**	(.013)	.06*	(.03)	−.086*	(.02)	−.007	(.1)
Slope: year²	−.0016*	(.0003)	−.002*	(.0005)	.0006*	(.0001)	−.0009	(.0008)
Slope: year³	.00005*	(.00001)	.00004*	(.0018)	.00003*	(.000003)	.00006*	(.00002)
Socioeconomic predictors (Model 2)								
Country-year predictors								
GNP/c			−.01	(.01)			−.01	(.02)
(GNP/c*year)/10			−.003	(.01)			−.02*	(.009)
(GNP/c *year²)10			.0002**	(.003)			.0004	(.0002)
Literacy			−1.8*	(.6)			3.2**	(.3)
Literacy*year			.1*	(.03)			−.2**	(.02)
Literacy*year2			−.001*	(.0005)			.002**	(.0005)
Urbanization			−.05*	(.02)			−.02	(.03)
(Urbanization*year)100			−.02	(.03)			.008	(.08)
(Urbanization*year²)100			.001*	(.0005)			.0006	(.0006)
Country level predictor								
World position			−.3	(.6)			−2.7*	(1.1)
(World pos.*year)/10			−.2*	(.08)			.03	(.3)
(World pos.*year²)10			.003*	(.001)			.003	(.003)
Diffusion predictors (Model 3)								

Country–year predictors				
Spatial density			4.6** (.5)	7.3** (.5)
Spatial density*year			-.06* (.03)	-.02 (.02)
Spatial density*year²			.0004 (.0007)	-.0005 (.0005)
Network			48.5** (2.5)	26.4* (11.2)
Network*year			-.2 (.2)	3.6** (.8)
Network*year²			.005 (.004)	-.04* (.01)
Colonial network			.3 (.7)	1.2* (.5)
(Colonial netw.*year)/10			-.8* (.2)	-.5* (.2)
(Colonial netw.*year²)/10			.01* (.004)	.006* (.003)
Media			-.2* (.05)	-.002 (.06)
Media*year			.003 (.004)	-.01** (.002)
Media*year²			-.0001 (.0001)	-.0002* (.00008)
Historical events predictor (Model 4)				
Historical events			-.03 (.05)	-.2* (.06)
(Hist. events*year)/10			.01 (.02)	.0002 (.02)
(Hist. events*year²)/10			.00004 (.0007)	.001* (.0007)
Random part				
Estimates of variances				
Variance between countries' intercepts	6.86* (2.3)	12.4* (3.6)	3.6* (1.3)	7.4* (2.2)
Variance between countries' slopes	.002* (.0008)	.005* (.0016)	.0004* (.0002)	.007* (.002)
Covariance between intercepts & slopes	-.056 (.03)	-.16* (.065)	-.01 (.01)	-.2* (.06)
Residual	2.37** (.11)	2.3* (.09)	.8** (.03)	1.45** (.05)

Note: Values in parentheses depict standard errors. The temporal rate (slope) of democratic growth is assessed as a year squared.
* $p < .05$,
** $p < .0001$.

(3.89 as compared to 3.76, respectively). The null hypothesis that either of the parameters was 0 in a population was rejected (see Table 3.7). Similarly, in other regions, there is evidence that the temporal rate of countries' democratic growth depends on each country's democracy score at time 0, which means the year 1950. In Model 1A with no predictors added (this model accounted only for the impact of time on democracy growth within the region of South and North America), countries that were lower democracies in 1950 democratized slower over time than countries that were highly democratic. However, this trend reversed as soon as we controlled for development and diffusion predictors (p <.05 for the correlation intercept/slope). The correlation between rate and level as depicted by slopes and by intercepts of countries changed from positive to negative.

The results of statistical analysis are supported by observed studies as they reflect on the main part of the Third Wave of Democratization that started in Latin American in the late 1970s (Hagopian & Mainwaring 2005). The obtained significant residual value suggested that part of the variance of democratic growth is still not explained. To better explain the variance in democratic growth and to reduce the observed variance in countries' intercepts and slopes, additional predictors were added to the model.

The addition of the selected predictors significantly improved the statistical modeling of democratization over time; the fit statistics demonstrated that models with development and diffusion predictors more closely corresponded to observed data, and the null hypothesis that the parameter of any predictor was 0 in a population was rejected (see Table 3.7). As expected, the obtained results demonstrated that the higher the mean GNP, the access to media and the number of democratic states with a large portion of a region's population living in them, the greater the democratic growth in the region. Also, the higher the literacy level and increasing literacy over time, the greater the democratic growth. At the same time, contradicting expectations, the effect of the mean level of urbanization on democracy level was insignificant, which indicates that during the non-democratic rule of colonial powers as well as during democracy the size of urban population did not relate to countries' democracy level. However, increase in urbanization positively affected the growth of countries' level of democracy over time. To explain this result I will first look at the causes of countries' urbanization. The causes of urbanization are multiple; among them is increasing education level (that was indicated by the increase of literacy and its positive effect on an average country's democracy level) that opens opportunities to educated rural youth to migrate to cities in search of clerical, service jobs that are available primarily in cities (Hagopian & Mainwaring 2005). Another reason could be the development of cities by colonial rulers as administrative and trade centers of goods produced on rural plantations. City jobs required educated and trained workers that were in excess in rural places (overall increasing literacy level); therefore, rural–urban migration became a form of upgrading individual status and a motivational tool for large movement to cities.

Also unexpectedly, the positive impact of an increasing number of democracies in a region and the effect of an increasing number of democracies within the political and economic networks of Latin American countries was highly significant. Networks and spatial density of democracies within sub-regions of the Americas facilitated modeling on democratic countries by neighboring non-democracies or non-democratic members of networks. The only exception was the negative impact of colonial networks on countries' democratic growth over time. Two explanations of such a situation are plausible. First, the results are consistent with literature findings attesting that most colonial powers (except for Britain) did not help to establish government in their former colonies during the decolonization period. As a result, due to countries' transformation, the governments of newly independent countries were headed by authoritarian rulers. Second, colonial dependencies, economically exploited by colonial powers, were much less developed, and development significantly affects democratic growth.

Added predictors also explained additional variance of the region's democratic growth with diffusion predictors yielding the highest reduction (1.8% and 2%, respectively). Most of the predictors also significantly reduced variation in countries' intercepts, with the GNP per capita and media reduction by as much as 43.5 percent (the GNP/c) and 37.6 percent (media) contributing to the model's more accurate estimate of the intercept of democratization in the region. Indeed, when the GNP/c was added, the estimated democracy level (indicated by the intercept parameter) of 2.29 was closer to the observed democracy score of 2.95 at year $= 0$ than the intercept parameter obtained in the model without added predictors. Most of the predictors contributed also to a closer assessment of the slope of the temporal rate of democratization in the region by reducing variance between slopes, where the

GNP/c and media yield the highest reduction of 3.3 percent (GNP) and
2 percent (media) of variance (see Table 3.7).

Importantly, the model with added predictors of development
explained an additional 17 percent of variance in the democracy level
of countries in the region in 1950, while additional added indicators of
diffusion explained 36 percent of this variance in comparison to the
predictor of time alone. Interestingly, the added predictors of development explained 70 percent of variation between the level and the rate
of democratic growth in countries. All added predictors explained an
additional 80 percent of variance in democratic growth over time,
20 percent of variance in countries' intercepts, and reduced unexplained variance in countries' democratic growth by 55 percent, results
that led to obtained closer parameters of the intercept, the slope, and
the variance/covariance parameters (see Table 3.7). Interestingly, less
covariance between countries' intercepts and slopes was explained
when indicators were added. Such findings indicate that contacts
between democratic and non-democratic countries more strongly
facilitate democratic growth than the impact of countries' development. In the case of the Americas, the selected predictors did not
explain the relationship between the level of countries' democracy in
1950 and the rate of their democratization (the covariance between the
rate of growth and the level of democracy is not significantly predicted). The fit statistics attested that models with added development
and diffusion predictors, as well as the model with all added predictors,
better fit our data than the original Model 1A assessed with a predictor
of time (see Table 3.7).

Europe. In Europe, assessed for the years 1800–2005 with the
adjusted Model 1A, the obtained intercept of 5.05 (means the democracy level in an average country in Europe in 1950) and an upward
curvilinear slope of a quadratic function of time, or the rate of democratic growth, depicting that an average country in the region gained
.03 in democracy score each quadratic year, closely corresponded to
the curvilinear slope of observed data and the democracy score at time
0 of 5.74. We reject the null hypothesis that either of the parameters is
0 in a population (see Figure 1.4 depicting observed data). The correlation between the intercept and the slope parameters for each country
in a region is positive and significant, indicating, *according to statistical
significance*, that the relationship between countries' temporal rate of
democratization and their democracy score at centered time are

positive, which means that for an average country the higher the democracy score was in 1950, the faster the country democratized. This effect might change when development and diffusion predictors are added. In sum, however, the significant residual (means unexplained differences between countries in their democracy's growth) indicates that added covariates might explain more variation in the evolution of democracy over time.

Most of the added predictors improved the modeling of the democracy growth in the region either by explaining more variance of democratic evolution over time, by reducing variance of countries' intercepts, or by reducing the correlation between the intercept and the slope. The largest portion (4.6%) of an unexplained variation in democratic growth (the residual) was explained by *diffusion* indicators vs 0% explained by development indicators. Also, the greatest reduction of variance between countries' intercepts (means the reduction of unexplained differences between countries' level of democracy) was also explained by diffusion indicators (49 percent of variance) versus 0 percent by development indicators. The reduction of differences in the rate of democracy's growth between countries was also obtained by diffusion predictors, where 33 percent more reduction of variance was obtained when indicators of diffusion were added to the predictors of development. The predictor of time alone did not explain any variance of rate of democracy development across European countries (the variance of slope was statistically insignificant).

Assessing particular predictors, the significant impact of GNP/c was detected, where each increase of GNP by $600 per year in an average country, increased the democracy level by 1 on a scale of 0–10. Interestingly, an increase of GNP/c over time had a negative effect on democracy's growth, which could explain the plateau of democracy's increase in the highly democratic but still economically developing countries of Western Europe. An increase in urbanization also generated a higher level and rate of democracy growth per country. A similarly positive effect was caused by an increase in literacy over time, where with a literacy level increase of .0007 percent each quadratic year, democracy increased by one score on a scale of 0–10. An increase in *literacy level*, however, did not generate a significant impact on countries' democratic growth, which would be typical for the nondemocratic but highly educated communist countries of Eastern Central Europe. It could explained by saying that the highly literate and highly democratic societies of Western Europe attained the optimum level of democratic development, hence any further literacy had no effect on the democracy level of already fully democratic societies. Moreover, the positive impact of literacy on the rate of democratization but not on the level could also indicate that perhaps literacy is not so much a cause but a result of democratization.

Moreover, variables of diffusion had a much stronger effect than development predictors, and the effect of each variable was positive. Importantly, all predictors of diffusion – spatial proximity, networks, and media – were significant predictors of the level *and* the rate of democratic development in Europe. In particular, being part of a political or economic network of countries with at least one member being democratic enhanced the chance of each non-democratic country to become democratic as well as increasing the democratic growth of an average democratic country. As demonstrated by the positive effect of the predictor of spatial density (depicting the number and density of democratic countries within each European sub-region; the list of European sub-regions is provided in Appendix 1), an increase in democracies within sub-regions of Europe led to an increase in democracy growth. As supported by the literature, membership in the colonial-type dependency network of the Soviet Union had a negative influence on countries' democracy level (especially visible in the case of Eastern European countries). Contrary to what was expected, the result indicated that membership in the colonial network accelerated the rate of democratic growth by .002 points each quadratic year (also most likely depicting democratization of eight Eastern European states within a couple of years).

Also importantly, as obtained results show, due to limited variance in world position (all countries were well developed or semi-developed), world position did not have an effect on the level of democratic growth. However, it had a positive impact on the rate of democratic growth over time, demonstrating that core countries democratized faster than semi-peripheral (less developed) countries. We may deduce that the communist East European countries were less developed and democratized later and slower than Western European countries, which is confirmed by the observed data. Furthermore, considering European history, it is not surprising that over time historical events, especially events of the post-World War I and post-World War II periods, increase the level of democracy of an average country,

Regarding reduction of variance by individual predictors, the predictor of GNP/c decreased the variance of countries' intercepts by 64.1 percent, followed by media (28 percent reduction). Interestingly, contrasting Model 1A, with the added predictor of time alone, with Model 4A, with all added predictors, indicated *negative* dependence of the temporal rate of democratization on the value of democracy at time 0, which means that nondemocratic or low-democratic countries in 1950 democratized faster than highly democratized countries at that time.

Africa. Analysis of Africa assessed for the years 1949–2005 with Model 3 adjusted to this region's data and time span parameters shows that when only the predictor of time is added, the estimated democracy score for an average country in the region is 1.9 The slope of yearly changes is curvilinear, assessed as a cubic function of time (year^3) with an average country in this region *gaining .0003 score* on the democratic scale each cubic year. Both the intercept and slope parameters are statistically significant ($p = .87$ and $p<.0001$), indicating statistical significance of the relationship between time and democracy score for an average country in the region.

The variance parameters demonstrate that the intercepts are strongly variable across countries; in other words, countries differed in average democracy score after controlling for the effect of time. The slopes are also variable and significant, suggesting that countries are varied in the rate of democratic growth over time. However, when accounting for time parameter alone, the correlation between the intercept and slope parameters for each country is negative but not significant, *suggesting* that countries with a lower average democracy score at time 0 (1950) will experience overall faster growth of democracy than countries with a higher average democracy score in 1950, i.e., countries that were democratic before or at the centered time will decrease their level of democratization over time. The relationship between democracy level and the rate is nonetheless not significant. Indeed, the historical development of Africa closely supports such findings. On one hand, the former colonies that gained independence in the 1950s and 1960s became either weak democracies that shortly withdrew to non-democratic regimes (e.g., Senegal, Benin, Mauritania, or Sierra Leone) or non-democracies (e.g., Togo, Gabon, Zaire, Chad, or Cameroon). It was not until the end of the 1990s that many of these countries democratized. On the other hand, old, sovereign since the nineteenth century countries were usually democratic in the nineteenth century but became non-democratic regimes in the twentieth century. The classic examples are Liberia and Ethiopia. Both established in the 1840s–1850s as independent, strongly democratic states but became non-democratic at the beginning of the twentieth century, then established democratic governments again only at the end of the 1990s.

We reject the null hypothesis that any of the parameters are equal to 0 in the population (see Table 3.7). Also, the significant residual indicated a partial explanation of variance of democratic growth in a region. Indeed, models with added predictors better explained variation in the growth of democracy, demonstrating that higher urbanization over time (rate of urbanization), literacy level and increase over time, mean access to media and the increasing rate of this access, and the diffusion process of spatial density of democratic countries, as well as the temporal effect of a country's world position, lead to an increase in democratic growth over time. In the model with added variable of literacy, the literacy level strongly, positively affects the level of democracy where higher literacy is found in more democratized countries. The effect of the literacy variable on the rate of democratic growth in Africa was also significant.

Interestingly, GNP per capita had no significant impact on democracy level, attesting perhaps to relatively low GNP/c across most African countries, contrasting with a few very well developed states, such as southern African or northern African countries. These findings are further supported by the variable world position, which indicates that poorer countries democratized sooner (low world position had a positive effect on the rate of countries' democratic growth).

Contrasting with assessments of Europe and the Americas, countries' membership in economic or political networks had no effect on democratic growth. Similarly, being part of the colonial network had no significant effect on the level or rate of democratic growth, which is also supported by prior scholarly studies showing vast differences in the preparedness of colonies to sustain a democratic form of rule.

In Africa, where large percentages of the population still live in a rural environment, the significant impact of urbanization on democratic growth is observed only in the rate of democratization. In other words, although the rate of democratization negatively depends on an average level of democracy in this region, the dependence is reduced when the covariate of urbanization level is added to the model.

Historical events did not have significant effect on regional democratization, its level or rate.

The strongest effect demonstrated the process of diffusion of spatial proximity and density on the region's democratic growth. The added variable increased the level of democracy and the rate of democratic growth. The greatest reduction of variance between countries' democratic scores at time 0, and hence, the closest estimate of the region's intercept parameter, was obtained in models with variable development, where development indicators decreased variance in the differences of countries' democracy levels by 48 percent, while added diffusion variables decreased these differences by 43 percent. At the same time, the model with variables of diffusion provided the best explanation of the region's slope by reducing variation between countries' slopes by .08 percent. The best explanation of regions' patterns of democratization, however, was provided by a model with all covariates added, reducing unexplained variance of democratic growth by 3.9 percent, and reducing variation between countries' intercepts by 43 percent and covariance between countries' slopes and intercepts by .08 percent. All models with added predictors and Model 1A with the predictor of time were statistically significant with $\chi^2 <$ 1000.00 ($df = 3$, $p < .0001$).

The analyses of the last two regions are somewhat similar to each other but distinct from analysis of any region described above.

Middle East. The analysis of the Middle East assessed for the years 1917–2005 demonstrates that the curvilinear slope of the temporal rate of democratization estimated as a cubic function of time (year^3) is statistically significant (p <.005), and an average country in the region gained .00005 on democratic score each cubic year. The intercept parameter was borderline significant ($p = .06$), indicating *some statistical significance* of relationship between time and democracy score for an average country. Since there is no democratic tradition in the region and most of the countries were not democratic during their historical development, one could expect that democratic growth over time will be slow and unsteady in the region. The null hypothesis that any of the parameters equals 0 was rejected (see Table 3.7). The obtained significant residual and significant variance between countries' intercepts and slopes suggested that in addition to time, added predictors could better explain the pattern of democratization in the region. (I expect, however, that because the variance between countries' scores of democracy at time 0 is large (6.86) compared to the residual value (2.3), not all predictors would be significant.)

Out of the added predictors only three attested as statistically significant (urbanization, literacy, access to media, and diffusion due to spatial density and proximity, and due to networks) while the remaining GNP, world position, and historical events were not significant ($p =.67$ and $p=.66$, respectively). The covariate of urbanization was significant, but due to limited variance in urbanization over time (by the end of the 1980s, in most countries, nearly 30–40 percent of the labor force was still engaged in agricultural production and was living in rural communities not showing a significant decrease since the first decades of the twentieth century), it indicated opposite to expected effects (lower level of urbanization suggested increase in countries' democratization level). Nonetheless, the urbanization positively affected the rate of democratic growth in the region.

Since the literacy and GNP level are considered to be two of the main predictors of democratization, I attempted to assess their impact in interaction with other highly predictive variables in the model, e.g., GNP with urbanization, and literacy with access to media. In the tests the effect of GNP was not significant, while literacy remained negatively significant. The results are not surprising when we consider the special character of the region, with its high albeit very unequally distributed GNP generated by the oil industry (e.g., Saudi Arabia or Kuwait), and high illiteracy rate with limited variance in illiteracy rate over time (e.g., by 2000 near three-quarters of the population in Yemen and nearly half of the population in Egypt was still illiterate, with much higher than average illiteracy among women). The negative impact also suggests that obtained literacy is mainly provided within religious teaching that is not sympathetic to democracy (e.g., the madrassa schools).

Unlike in the previously discussed regions, only five out of eight predictors contribute to an explanation of regional patterns of democratization, and mainly they were predictors of diffusion. The model with added development predictors lowered the residual by only 3 percent, while the model with all of the significant predictors of diffusion lowered it by 66 percent. Development predictors, however, explained 48 percent more variance between countries' intercepts than the model without the added predictor of time, in comparison to the 43 percent explained by diffusion indicators. The power of diffusion predictors was demonstrated in the reduction of unexplained differences in the rate of democratic growth by 80 percent (the development predictors did not have an impact on the rate). Overall, Model 4A with all added predictors better fit the data (see fit statistics parameters in last column, Table 3.7).

Asia. Finally, the last assessed region, Asia, was also atypical as compared to the first three analyzed regions. In Asia, assessed for the years 1943–2005, the estimated democracy score of 3.4 for an average country was similar to the observed democracy score of 2.38, and an average country increased its democratic score by 0.0003 each cubic year. The intercept and slope parameters were strongly significant, indicating the statistical significance of the relationship between time and democracy score for an average country in the region. Similar to the analyses of all prior regions, the modified for Asia Model 4A depicted variance between countries' intercepts and slopes, and significant residual. We rejected the null hypothesis that the obtained parameters are 0 in population (see last section, Table 3.7).

The small value of the residual of 2.3 without added predictors (the smallest of all regions) as compared to the variance between countries' intercept (12.4) (the largest intercept value except for Africa) indicated difficulty with depicting covariates that would lower the residual or the variance in the intercepts. Indeed, added predictors show that only one out of three development predictors were statistically significant (urbanization and the mean GNP were not significant). Much better were the effects of predictors of diffusion, where three out of four were significant (the only insignificant predictor was media effect), and the effects of diffusion predictors on democratic growth in the region were dissimilar to the effects in any prior region. The largest effect of literacy was depicted in reduction of variance between intercepts, with the largest reduction of 33 percent depicted in Asia (the impact of literacy was positive on the level and the rate of countries' democratic growth). A very strong and positive impact of economic and political networks on democratization was also depicted, as well as colonial networks where the strong impact of networks may suggest regional cohesiveness of countries via networking and direct communication or contacts.

The dissimilarity of this region to well-developed Europe or the Americas rests in, first, the effect of the predictor of media, which, although strongly important in all prior regions, was not significant in

Asia, suggesting that the effect of the media on role modeling of democracies by non-democratic countries was not important to democratic growth in this region. Second, unlike any prior region, neither of the models with added significant predictors largely reduced the residual obtained in a model without added covariates. Third, contrary to the results of the analyses of all prior regions (except for Africa), the model with all significant predictors, although it better fit our data (see fit statistics parameters, the bottom of each column in Table 3.7), largely did not reduce the residual parameters. Its only addition to the explanation of the region's democratization pattern was a reduction of the intercept variance estimate as compared to the intercept variance estimate in a model without added predictors (from 12.4 to 7.4) that more closely corresponded to the observed democracy rate (see Figure 3.4).

Moreover, across all regions there is some evidence that country-to-country democratic growth over time differs depending upon each country's average democracy score (see Table 3.7). Similarly, the variance between slopes, with the exception of the weakly democratized Middle East, is higher in the last three regions in comparison to the first two regions (see Table 3.7). These results suggest that the trajectories of democratization in the Western Hemisphere and Europe are more similar than the paths of democratic growth across the countries in Africa and Asia. Furthermore, a strong negative correlation between intercepts and slopes, depicted in the last three regions, indicates that countries' democratic growth differs *depending* on their democracy score, which was not the case in the regions in the first group.

Furthermore, the obtained *residuals* were lower in Africa, the Middle East, and Asia, suggesting that democratization patterns were explained to a greater extent in the last three regions than in Europe or the Western Hemisphere (see Table 3.7).

Congruent to the analysis above, the obtained results demonstrate significant region-to-region differences in covariates' effects on democratization level.

As shown in Table 3.7, the effects of GNP are statistically significant across the first two regions and suggest that an increase of GNP increases the democracy score for an average country in each region over time. Europe and the Western Hemisphere were the only regions in which GNP explained obtained unexplainable variance in democratic growth, reducing the residual from 3.42 to 3.4 in the first region and from 2.89 to 2.7

in the latter. However, GNP is not the strongest predictor of democratic growth in the Middle East, Africa, and Asia, since the effect of GNP was not significant across these regions and only the temporal rate of increase of GNP additionally explained the unexplained variance in democratic growth (reducing the previously obtained residual from 2.36 to 2.08 in the Middle East and from 2.31 to 2.14 in Asia). The effect of the growth of GNP is much smaller in Europe in comparison to the Western Hemisphere. In Europe, GNP reduces the residual, but only when we added the effect of labor force in agriculture. Considering that over the last two centuries, European countries split into those that approached the industrial revolution at the turn of the nineteenth century and became industrial states that needed educated workers for service and industrial labor, and those that remained a bread basket for the European region until the last decades of the twentieth century and hence had less need to focus on education until the last part of the twentieth century, the joint influence of both covariates is not surprising.

Considering labor force, concordant with the literature (e.g., Kapstein & Converse 2009), in Africa, where dispersion of the labor force from agriculture to industry or services did not reach the same level as in more developed regions, the significance of the covariate of labor in agriculture is not significant. In Asia, while the shift of labor force from agriculture to industry is observed in more recent decades (e.g., in Southeast Asia), a majority of the Asian population is still engaged in agricultural production (e.g., a majority of the Indian, Pakistani, North Korean, Afghani, and Chinese populations), the effect of the labor force in agriculture on democratic growth was contrary to expected means and obtained positive instead of negative effect values, where the lower labor force in agriculture reduced, instead of increasing, democracy growth. However, the increase of labor force in agriculture over time is not significant. In the Middle East, a region with predominantly developed oil industry but without rich agricultural areas, the effect of labor force in agriculture on democratic growth over time is contrary to expected means and obtained positive instead of negative effect values, where the higher labor force in agriculture increased, instead of decreasing, democracy growth.

Europe was the only region in which literacy did not explain the unexplainable variance in democratic growth, reducing its residual. In Africa, Asia, and the Middle East the literacy level and rate of its growth reduced the dependence of the temporal rate of democratization on an average country's democracy score by about 8 percent.

Table 3.8 *Hierarchical growth models with socioeconomic and diffusion predictors of democratic growth, 1800–2005*

	Americas: 1820–2005 (N = 3,066)			Europe: 1800–2005 (N = 3,693)			Africa: 1949–2005 (N = 1,648)		
	Uncon	Dev	Diff	Uncon	Dev	Diff	Uncon	Dev	Diff
Variance estimates									
Residual	4.28*	3.2*	1.9*	4.3*	5.07*	4.1*	2.29*	2.6*	2.2*
SE	(.09)	(.07)	(.04)	(.9)	(.1)	(.09)	(.08)	(.09)	(.08)
Variance between countries' intercepts	10.5*	7.1*	5.5*	10.7*	12.7*	5.4*	21.1*	10.9*	11.7*
SE	(2.2)	(2.2)	(1.7)	(2.3)	(2.9)	(1.4)	(5.3)	(2.6)	(2.8)
Variance between countries' slopes	.01*	.0009*	.002*	.001	.003*	.002*	.008*	.008*	.009*
SE	(.0002)	(.0003)	(.0005)	(.0003)	(.0006)	(.0004)	(.002)	(.002)	(.002)
Covariance countries' intercept & slopes	.038*	−.01	−.06*	.04**	.04	−.004	−.36	−.22*	−.3*
SE	(.018)	(.02)	(.02)	(.01)	(.2)	(.017)	(.1)	(.07)	(.07)
Fit statistics									
AIC	14579.5	9854.7	8046.3	18425.2	9711.7	7821.1	5634.4	3383.4	1163.0
AICC	14587.5	9862.7	8054.3	18433.2	9719.7	7829.1	5642.4	3391.4	1171.0
BIC	14587.5	9862.7	8054.3	18433.2	9719.7	7829.1	5642.4	3391.4	1171.1
−2LL	14592.4	9867.6	8059.1	18441.0	9725.9	7835.0	5649.2	3398.2	1176.4

	Middle East: 1917–2005 (N = 1,124)			Asia: 1900–2005 (N = 1,602)		
	Uncon	Dev	Diff	Uncon	Dev	Diff
Variance estimates						
Residual	2.37*	2.3*	.8*	2.37*	2.4*	1.45**
SE	(.11)	(.09)	(.03)	(.09)	(.08)	(.05)
Variance between countries' intercepts	6.86*	3.5*	3.6*	12.4*	11.9*	7.4*
SE	(2.3)	(1.3)	(1.3)	(3.6)	(3.4)	(2.2)
Variance between countries' slopes	.002*	.002*	.0004*	.005*	.008*	.007*
SE	(.0008)	(.0006)	(.0002)	(.0016)	(.002)	(.002)
Covariance countries' intercept & slopes	−.056	−.01	−.01	−.16*	−.3*	−.2*
SE	(.03)	(.02)	(.01)	(.065)	(.08)	(.06)
Fit statistics						
AIC	3895.2	2509.6	1006.9	5525.4	2744.5	966.1
AICC	3903.2	2517.6	1014.9	5533.4	2752.5	974.1
BIC	3903.3	2517.7	1015.0	5533.4	2752.5	974.2
−2LL	3907.4	2521.6	1018.4	5538.8	2757.0	978.1

Uncon = unconditional model; Dev = development model; Diff = diffusion model. The temporal rate (slope) is assessed differently for different regions: for Europe it is year, for Americas it is $year^2$ and for Africa, Middle East, and Asia it is $year^3$.
* $p < .05$.

The variance estimates for each region's unconditional model, model with added development indicators, and model with added diffusion indicators for the selected years suggest that in each region added predictors explained more variance in democratic growth across time. In each region, the values of residual, variance between countries' intercepts, and variance between countries' slopes, as well as covariance of countries' intercepts and slopes decreased with added predictors. Also the parameters of Fit Statistics: AIC, AICC, BIC, and $-2LL$, decreased with added predictors in each region (see Table 3.8).

To assess the reliability of this model, I created a more balanced dataset by preselecting in each region only countries that existed from the mid nineteenth until the end of the twentieth century. I compared the obtained results in our multilevel regression model with a summary of individual regressions for each country in each region's balanced dataset. I noticed that the results obtained in our model corresponded to the variance/ covariance estimates obtained with the individual regressions.

Moreover, we tested the validity of Model 1A by comparing plotted estimated values of level of democratization in each region over years with observed average democracy scores for each region for the same years and, as presented in Figure 3.4, obtained estimates that closely corresponded with the observed scores of democratization.

To summarize the above detailed discussion about the effect of many indicators on democratic growth in each region, and keeping in mind the main purpose of this study, a brief review of the major findings of the importance of added indicators to democratic growth across the world and across each region are illustrated as a percentage of change of explained variances and presented in Table 3.9a and 3.9b.

Thus, considering variance effects, in each region, adding predictors significantly reduced residual variance, and the variance between countries and regions (see Table 3.9b). However, similar to world analyses, across all regions variance analyses demonstrate the robustness of diffusion predictors. Relative to socioeconomic predictors, diffusion predictors, while controlling for socioeconomic predictors, explained:

(1) from 63% (Middle East) to 39% (Asia) and 30% (Europe) more unexplained variance in democratic growth within countries over time than socioeconomic predictors;

(2) up to 49% (Europe) and 36% (Asia) more variance in democracy level between countries;

Table 3.9a *Importance of democratic growth in the world and the world's regions, 1800–2005*

Estimates of Variances	Percent of explained variances	
	The World	
	Development	Diffusion[2]
Variance between regions' intercepts	51%	83.7%[1]
Variance between regions' slopes	0%[1]	40%[1]
Variance between countries' intercepts	8%	41.9%
Variance between countries' slopes	0%	25%
Covariance between intercepts & slopes	0%	0%
Residual	2.5%	28.2%

[1] Parameters were not significant.

[2] This diffusion variance is explained in comparison to development predictors in all models.

(3) and in some regions up to 80% (Middle East) more unexplained variance in the growth rate of democracy.

To simplify and amplify the summary of the predicted changes in the level of democratization across regions, the findings are abbreviated with symbols, where the symbol 'greater than' indicates a positive effect and the symbol 'less than' a negative effect on an indicator of democracy growth in each region (see Table 3.10).

First, observing patterns of the impact of indicators across regions, it is evident that diffusion predictors of the *spatial proximity* of democratic countries and membership in *networks* containing democratic members predict growth of democracy both in the world (see above) and across all regions. The only exception was the insignificant effect of networks in Africa, mainly because until recently there were not many economic or political networks with democratic members operating in this region (see Table 3.10). Considering that on average, countries are low-level democracies across all regions except recently for Europe (Figure 3.4), the result indicates that spatial proximity and networks facilitate democratization of the world and across world regions prior to obtaining sustainability of the democratic system.

Second, in most regions, exposure to media positively affected democratic growth, but there were two exceptions: out of all regions in Africa, media exposure had the strongest positive effect on democratic

Table 3.9b *Importance of democratic growth in the world's regions, 1800–2005*

	Percent of explained variances									
	Americas		Europe		Africa		Middle East		Asia	
Estimates of variances	Dev	Diff	Dev	Diff	Dev	Diff	Dev	Diff	Dev	Diff
Variance between countries' intercepts	32.4%	47.6%	0%[1]	49%	48%	43%	49.4%	47.5%	4%	40.3%
Variance between countries' slopes	91%	80%	0%	33[2]	0%	0%	0%	80%	0%	0%
Covariance between intercepts & slopes	73.6%[1]	57.8%	0%	0%	38%	16%	0%[1]	0%[1]	0%	0%
Residual	25.2%	55.6%	0%	4.6%	0%	3.9%	3%	66.2%	0%	38.8%

Dev = development model; Diff = diffusion model. The predictive power of the development model was calculated by subtracting the estimate of variances of the development model from variances of the unconditional model and dividing this by the value of the variance of the development model, and multiplying by 100 (see bottom of Table 3.6 and 3.7). The same procedure was applied to estimate the power of diffusion.

[1] Parameters were not significant.

[2] This diffusion variance is explained in comparison to development predictors in all models.

growth, while in the Middle East, the effect was negative. First, according to diffusion theory (explained in the first part of the book), media exposure markedly reduces the need for actors to engage in direct communication in order to adopt democracy or any other political system. In regions where network connectedness with democratic members is weak, as was shown by an insignificant impact of networks on democratic growth in Africa, media became one of the main promoters of democratic principles. On the other hand, in the Middle East, where network connectedness with democratic members is stronger than in Africa but weaker than in other regions (insignificant

Table 3.10 *Summary of the predicted changes in the level of democratic growth across regions*

	Diffusion				Socioeconomic				
Regions	Spatial proximity	Networks	Colonial dependency	Media	GNP	% Urban	Literacy	Peripheral position
Americas	+	+		+	+		+	
Europe	+	+	−	+	+	+		−
Africa	+			+			+	
Middle East	+	+		−	−		−	
Asia	+	+	+				+	−

The temporal rate (slope) of democratic growth is assessed as a year squared.
+, increase in level of democratization.
−, decrease in level of democratization.

effect of networks on rate of growth of democracy) (Table 3.10), and where, due to religious beliefs, anti-Western and anti-democratic images are often spread via media, and religious authorities frequently with political regimes (e.g., in Iran) censor and resist the influence of Western democratic thought, media effects were significant but negative. Accordingly, Lipset's (1994) and Gunther and Mughan's (2000) arguments that modern communication facilitates the spread of democracy should be modified to reflect the fact that media variables are robust predictors of democratic growth only if, under circumstances of censorship or anti-democratic propaganda, countries' domestic conditions allow for the promotion of democratic principles. Such conditions, for example, existed in communist Poland, which underwent a transition to democracy sooner than other communist states in part due to its active underground and alternatives to the ruling regime press (Wejnert 1988, 2002c).

Third, socioeconomic variables have different predictive patterns in different regions. The variance is especially visible in the effect of GNP per capita, where in the low-developed regions of Africa, the Middle East, and Asia, the correlation of GNP/c with level of democracy was not significant. This is in contrast to the significant positive effect of GNP/c on the level of democracy in more economically developed Europe and the Americas (skewed by the US and Canadian economies). This regional result further validates Przeworski and Limongi (1997), Przeworski et al.

(2000), and Tilly's (2005) argument that stable democracies, which are mainly found in Europe and North America, have high GNP/c.[14] Since economies of poorer regions are less stable, withdrawal from democracy followed by re-democratization is frequently experienced by such countries, resulting in a net insignificant correlation between the two variables. As was mentioned in earlier chapters, by stable democracies, also called high-level democracies, scholars understand democracies of a score of 7 or above on the scale of democracy 0–10 (Jagger and Gurr 1995a).

Fourth, except in Europe, *literacy* predicted an increase in the growth of democracy but a decrease in the Middle East. The difference in the effect of literacy indicates that democratic growth oscillates between positive and negative as a function of education spreading both democratic and anti-democratic messages. For example, in the Middle East, education, provided for the most part by anti-democratic religious extremists promoting ideologies that inhibited democratic development, when left unbalanced by non-religious sources of education, led to a negative effect of education on democratic growth (Finn 2003).

In summary, the differential effect of socioeconomic and diffusion predictors could be assessed according to phase of democracy development depicted by democracy level. Although some exceptions on specific indicators occurred, overall the observed differences serve to define two major patterns of the effects of predictors: *Pattern I*, containing the stable democracies of well-developed Europe and recently the Americas (overweighed by North American economies), and *Pattern II*, encompassing transitory democracies and autocracies in less developed Africa, to some extent Asia, and the Middle East. In *Pattern I*, countries' GNP/c dominates as a predictor of democratization, while diffusion effects play a supportive role. Moreover, considering only the indicators of socioeconomic development, GNP/c is the most significant in developed regions, whereas the effect of literacy dominates in *Pattern II* regions. In contrast, in *Pattern II* diffusion processes appear to play a more dominant role in increasing democratic growth or generating democratic transitions (depicted only in those regions having a significant positive influence from colonial networks). In addition, the effects of *networks* and *spatial proximity* are especially important in less-developed regions (*Pattern II*) because the impact of

---

[14] As stated earlier in Chapter 3, the region of Australia and Oceania is not accounted for in regional analyses.

socioeconomic indicators is weaker with no effect of GNP/c. Thus, different patterns of effects of indicators as a function of region portray how the growth of democracy may differ depending on the socio-economic conditions of a region.

Comments on regional patterns of democratization

As was expected *diffusion effects* prove to be more influencial indica-tors of patters of countries' democratization. Among the processes that influence the temporal rate of world democratization were regional connectedness and the effects of role modeling on coherent democra-cies. Indeed, the estimated temporal rate of world and region-to-region democracy growth resembles the slope and curve of a temporal rate of diffusion. Plotted estimates of the temporal rate show an upward curvilinear slope, the typical shape of diffusion rate (Rogers 1995). Furthermore, these results demonstrate that the development of dem-ocracy occurred initially in regions in which the first democracies were established. The intercept variances and the variances of slopes dem-onstrate similarity of slopes and intercepts between countries located in older regions (Europe and Western Hemisphere) and diversity of slopes and intercepts between countries in the remaining three new regions of Africa, the Middle East, and Asia (i.e., in those regions most countries gained sovereignty at the turn of the nineteenth century). This suggests that patterns of regional democratization across countries within older regions were more similar than across countries within the new regions. Considering that the first democracies were established in Europe and the Western Hemisphere we deduce that, among other factors, strong inner regional role modeling on first democratic coun-tries by non-democracies occurred among countries within the older regions, processes that are assumed to generate diffusion. Perhaps that is why the three consecutive waves of democratization took place between countries located in the two oldest regions (post-World War I Europe – wave I, Latin America and Southern Europe – wave II, and Eastern Europe and Russia – wave III).

It is also evident that in both regions the temporal effects of diffusion were closely correlated with proximity and density of democratic countries. In Europe, close geographic proximity of non-democratic countries to the first democracy in the region, i.e., to France, and an overall close spatial proximity of all countries in the region, resulted in diffusion of democracy in the early years of the nineteenth century, lowering the slope and the intercept variance over time. Also, the risk of democracy adoption by non-democratic countries was additionally increased by the density of democratic countries during the nineteenth century. Thus in Europe, as shown by the temporal rate of democratization, the critical mass in the diffusion process occurred in about 1880 when the upward curve of the temporal rate rapidly peaked up. The influence of long-term positive outcomes of French democratization, further enhanced by close geographic proximity between countries, increased the anchoring effect of diffusion processes, i.e., anchoring on the observed experience of the first democratic countries. As results show, the critical mass was observed again at the end of the twentieth century (in the 1990s), affecting mainly countries that were established during the twentieth century.

In addition, the conclusion that, on average, there is little relationship between time and an average democracy score in Europe suggests that temporal effects were not always critical to European democratization. With democracy development over time, diffusion processes reached a *post critical mass* phase leading to democracy consolidation, where only a few laggers remained non-democratic. This trend was depicted by the high but steadily flat curve of the temporal rate of democratization from the end of the 1940s until the collapse of the Soviet Union and the liberation of the Eastern European Soviet dependencies in the late 1980s and early 1990s.

Neither geographic proximity nor density of democracies was the same among countries in the Western Hemisphere. Distanced geographic location from the first democracy – the United States – and overall significant geographical distance between countries slowed down the modeling effect and, in turn, the temporal rate of diffusion. The diffusion processes were weak and delayed, resulting in higher intercepts and slopes variance. As I assume, it was not until the twentieth century, when modern mass communication effectively reduced the geographical distance between countries, that the anchoring effect and critical mass effect played significant roles in the diffusion of democracy in this region. As a result, the critical mass of democratized countries, depicted as the sharp upward trend in the temporal rate of democratization, was obtained in this region in 1980. Incidentally, the timing of the critical mass closely corresponds with Wave II of democratization, the democratization of Latin America in the 1980s.

In Africa, the Middle East, and Asia, although the first democratic countries were also established in the nineteenth century, due to the very limited number of independent countries the diffusion of democracy did not occur until the late twentieth century, when more countries were formed. This delay led to a greater variance in the intercepts and slopes, and, we believe, moderate diffusion effects. The shown strong relationship between time (the critical effect in diffusion processes) and an average democracy score across those regions again suggests the high relevance of diffusion processes to future studies on democratization patterns across the world's regions.

Conversely, we could assume that role modeling also affects modeling on weak democracies by stable, high-level democracies, leading to an escalation of crises in liberal democracies. Analysis of this reverse role of modeling should be valuable to recent scholarly and policy discussions concerning crises of liberal democracies and the future of democracy in the world (Kissinger 2001; Kagan 2008; Wallerstein 2001). The potential studies on the transition to democracy and low-level democracies (the most tangible phase of democratic growth), rather than those that are consolidated democracies, should shed light on scholarly issues relating to democratization and challenges to its sustainability, as well as pragmatic issues of public and scholarly concern about the recent crisis of liberal democracies. The transition to democracy, its challenges and processes, should receive special consideration in policy and scholarly analysis if we expect the democratic system to prevail in the future.

4 | Democratic or autocratic future of the world?

Implications of the assessment of democracy's growth for future research

The assessment of the level of a country's development and the level of exposure to factors of diffusion are important processes in the development of a threshold model of democratization and democratic growth. To assess the threshold model and democracy's growth statistically in terms of the specific values of the development and diffusion determinants of democratization, each potential determinant of a country's democratization was correlated with a country's democracy level at the year a country underwent a transition from a non-democratic to a democratic system. The value of each indicator is presented in Table 4.1.

As shown in Table 4.1, across the world the most influential indicators of a country's transition from non-democratic to a democratic system are literacy, population access to media (both newspapers and radio programs), impact of colonial powers, and a country's position in the world of developed versus developing and undeveloped countries. In contrast to a positive impact of *media* and *world position*,[1] where the greater is a country's population's access to media information and more affluent (closer to the core) their world position, the greater is a country's likelihood of change from non-democracy to democracy, other indicators show the opposite to the expected results. Particularly interesting are the results of a country's literacy level, historical events, and worldwide economic crisis.

Seemingly opposite to what was expected, results for *literacy* level suggest that countries undergo a transition to democracy when their population is not highly educated. At the same time, literacy and education level are higher in democratic than nondemocratic countries,

---

[1] As explained in Appendix 1, the world position is depicted as a dummy variable where the lower the number indicated the higher the world position of a country.

Table 4.1 *The value of socioeconomic and diffusion indicators and regional characteristics at the time a country became democratic, across the world, 1800–2005*

Indicators conditioning democratic transition	Correlation of each indicator with democratic transition	Significance level
GNP/c for each country	−.023	(.087)
Literacy (%) of population	−.049**	(.001)
Urbanization (% of urban)	−.018	(.108)
Political and economic networks	.00001	(.971)
Spatial density of democracies	.003	(.688)
Colonial network[2]	−.237**	(.000)
World position of a country[3]	−.117**	(.000)
Regional labor in agriculture	−.084**	(.000)
Regional media (radio, TV, internet, newspaper)	.039*	(.05)
Media: newspaper	.04**	(.002)
Media: radio	.017*	(.074)
Shift in hegemonic power	.013	(.1)
Worldwide economic crisis	−.019**	(.023)
Historical events	−.032**	(.000)

* $p < 0.01$ (2-tailed),
** $p < .005$.

[1] The value of each indicator is depicted at the year each democratic country experienced democratic transition from non-democracy to a democratic system.

[2] Colonial network is a dummy variable indicating being a part or not of colonial dependencies, where a country is a part of a colonial network is depicted as 1, and not a member of a colonial network as 0.

[3] The world position of a country is also assessed as a dummy variable where score 0 depicts core position, while a peripheral and semi-peripheral position is depicted as 1.

with a high correlation between low literacy and low economic development. Moreover, in the low-developed countries democracies are rare. These seemingly contrasting results indicate that the higher literacy is an outcome rather than a cause of democratic transition. It is most likely an outcome of higher investments of democratic governments in education and in training the educated labor force, especially since democratic countries often aspire to incorporation into a global market economy characterized by modern economic production, global trade, and international collaboration. Incorporation into the global market and global international relations is also associated with the development of science and technology, possible only within educated populations and a highly educated labor force.

Also interesting is an outcome of a *world crisis* indicator, suggesting that world crises do not lead to countries' transition to democracy, unlike within-country economic crises. Hence, many countries are transitioning to democracy when the population is relatively poor, but the world-scale crisis may disguise the responsibility of totalitarian leaders for internal, within-country poverty, delaying democratic changes. The focus of the media on world crises could silence domestic economic problems and governments' responsibility for their solutions.

In contrast to prior findings on the indicators of the growth of democracy attesting to an impact of historical events on countries' democratization, historical events are not the causes of democratic transition. Perhaps democratic transitions and democratic growth are the aftermath of rapid world-scale events such as world-wide wars, rather than the necessary factors that induce and ignite democratic transitions (see Table 4.1).

The confusing result also presents an indicator of *colonial network*. Although Britain imposed a democratic system on former colonies as a part of the decolonization policy, most colonial powers did not prepare their colonies for self-governing. At the time of liberation, the new political powers were usually leaders of nationalistic movements, replacing former colonial powers by totalitarian rule over societies unprepared for self-governing. Democracies were born frequently after a period of domestic turmoil, civil wars, and civil unrest, as was the case with many fragile post-colonial democracies in Africa.

Assessed development, diffusion and a threshold model of democratization

The high correlation between many of the indicators and world democratization does not attest to the causal relations between the indicators and democracy. To determine whether an indicator is causative, versus being merely an effect, of increasing democratization, cross-lagged correlation analyses (using lags from one to twenty-five years) were performed on all indicators in two ways: first, with the indicator predicting by one to twenty-five years the level of democracy, vs second, with the level of democracy predicting by one to twenty-five years the indicator value.[2] The resulting two series of correlations were judged to be causative on the joint basis of a number of criteria, including (a) the number of correlations in the series that significantly predicted a variable above zero; (b) the mean of all correlations in the series; (c) the magnitude of the slope of the correlations in the series, and (d) the numerical closeness of the intercept of the slope of a variable to the correlation at lag 0.

As shown in Figure 4.1, across all indicators, the correlation at lag 0 was bounded in both directions (on the left, the indicator predicting democracy, on the right by democracy predicting the indicator) by a window of almost identical correlations. The breadth of this window varied between indicators, ranging from one year for the indicator of networks, up to four years for the indicator of industrial labor. Within this window of similar correlations, no causal relation could be determined.[3] But beyond this window, when the value of the series of correlations varied markedly on the left versus the right side of lag 0, the predictive direction between the two variables became clearer. For instance, if the series of correlations on the left versus the right of lag 0 in Figure 4.1 was of greater magnitude across a greater number of correlations, had a steeper slope, and an intercept of the slope closer to the correlation at lag 0, then the indicator would be judged to be more causative of democratization than to be the effect of democratization.

Applying this judgment, indicators showing causal relations to world and regional democratization were those of (a) socioeconomic status, including industrial labor force and GNP per capita (GNP/c); (b) diffusion, including spatial proximity and networks, and (c) TV per capita (TV/c) representing media. On the other hand, the regional indicators of agricultural labor and democratic history and the diffusion indicator of familiarity showed no clear indication of causality versus outcome of democratization, while literacy was visibly a stronger outcome of democratization than its cause (Figure 4.1). Thus, the

---

[2] The lag of twenty-five years was selected to roughly represent one generation of each country's population, the distance of time that should permit any outcomes of democratization to be clearly demonstrated.

[3] Another way to control for potential autocorrelation would be to perform analyses with a lag of 1 of each indicator; however, it is believed that due to the depicted window of almost identical correlations in both directions, the lag of 1 in either direction will lead to less conclusive results.

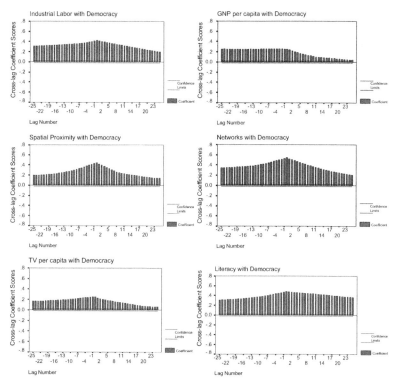

Figure 4.1 Cross-lag correlations of indicators showing causal relations to world democratization

Note: Literacy is visibly more of an outcome of democratization than a cause, whereas other variables, of industrial labor, GNP per capita, TV per capita, networks, and spatial proximity, are more outcomes than causes of democratization. The indicators of regional agricultural labor and democratic history show no clear indication of causality or outcome, and hence are not included in this figure.

obtained parameters and their graphic presentation suggest that with higher GNP/c and a higher percentage of the labor force engaged in industrial production, as well as more open access to TV (representing and symbolizing a higher exposure to modern media communication),[4]

---

[4] Since this longitudinal study spans approximately two centuries, it is assumed that studies conducted solely across the last couple of decades would indicate a prediction of the same impact of internet communication on democratization as had TV communication since its inception in the middle of the last century.

a country is more susceptible to democratization. Moreover, each additional democracy emerging in geographically close regions, and each additional democratic country becoming a member of the international network, enhanced the predisposition of non-democratic countries to democratize (the effect of spatial proximity and networks).

Discourse of future political trends until year 2050

The presented assessment of the development of democracy for the past two centuries stimulates thought on the potential future trajectory and trends of the worldwide political order. Recent academic debates are dominated by two contrasting points of view: on one hand, scholars believe that the future world will be democratic – the prevalence of democracy is inevitable because democracy marks an era of modern prosperity and of human rights; on the other, it is argued that democracies are failing and that their decline is visible because the economy grows faster in many autocratic regimes.

First, according to the first position, the democratic era is characterized by the cultural values of independence, individuality, and freedom. This political system is founded on two main principles, liberty and equality, that are the qualities most desired by all societies (Fukuyama 1992; Inglehart & Welzel 2005, 2009). Moreover, the democratic system will dominate the world's future because it supports people's "struggle for recognition." People desire equality, being valued, respect, appreciation and recognition for their accomplishments, democratic rights, and support for their aspirations to succeed. These desires characterize human nature and stimulate societal progress. They are critical to modern development. Therefore, democracy, being a political system that is founded on respect for civil rights and equality, will prevail and expand in the future. The recent democratic era marks the end of human history and the end of the last man (Fukuyama and McFaul 2007; Deudley and Ikenberry 2009; Mandelbaum 2004, 2008).

Second, democracy is a political system that supports people's desires and struggle for economic improvement by its embeddedness in a free, global market economy that was instituted by democracies and that meets consumers' material and emotional needs. The high economic position of developed, democratic countries in the world stimulates role modeling on existing democracies and promotes democracy's diffusion. More importantly, the growth and development of democratic societies is embedded in market liberalism and the rule of law that governs market economy and international trade (Deudley and Ikenberry 2009). Market economic systems require that countries follow established, uniform, international trade laws which include legitimate production of goods, respect for patent laws, and lawful economic management. Classic examples of disregard for international rules of economic cooperation are the production of illegally copied goods of Western manufacturers by Chinese industry, the nationalization of international joint-venture oil companies in Putin's Russia, or Chinese production of contaminated food. If laws are not respected, a country could face the renouncement of trade relations within the international market. Since autocratic regimes are routinely known for lawlessness and corruption, in the long term autocratic governments will need to change and be accountable and, if corrupted, be replaceable to continue engagement in global trade. A continuous, long-term prevalence of lawless autocracies, some of which have never established the universal rule of law – such as, for instance, China – is questionable. Although presently autocracies with capitalistic economies like China or Russia support market economies and international trade, the absence of law in these countries could prevent foreign investment by international companies in the future. Companies whose industry was nationalized (for instance, the investment of Shell companies that was nationalized in Putin's Russia [Herspring 2003]) could perceive trade with autocracies as too risky and potentially too costly to engage in. In the long term, such conditions could limit the economic prosperity of countries that do not follow universal trade rules.

Third, importantly, democracies require that one of the conditions of a country's participation in international trade is respect for human rights. Though autocracies often do not respect human rights in regard to their own citizens and are often known for abuse of power by the ruling elite, international trade is conditioned by respect for human rights as a precipitating factor for incorporation and continuation of economic cooperation within the global economic order (Politkovskaya 2007). Therefore, existing autocracies need to support the liberal political order in order to continue being embedded in the existing market structure of the global world, and to prosper economically. The international embargo on trade with Iran in the 2000s and the United States' embargo on trade with Cuba are prime examples of international sanctions imposed on an autocratic regime by a democratic world.

Fourth, the diffusion of modern communication has provided less developed societies with global exposure to the living conditions in modern, developed countries. This knowledge of lifestyles and life comforts stimulates modeling on well-developed democratic countries. Knowledge about high living standards in Western democracies enhances people's desires for such lifestyles. Under these conditions, autocratic revival in societies with open access to modern communication and spreading information technology is unlikely. The example of Eastern Central Europe demonstrates how an illiberal and centrally controlled political system was replaced by democracy in most of the former communist states at a time of open access to global mass communication and to global trade. Among other examples are 2010's Chinese government censorship on the use of Google that met with protests from the Chinese people, or the recent popularity of microbloggers in China, like Ms Hung, who post uncensored, sometimes subversive commentary on various rich and powerful Chinese authorities and are followed by millions of Chinese readers (Epstein 2012). The organization and spread of the Arab Spring protests in 2011–2012 was also possible because of the use of text messaging, blogging, and Facebook, i.e., modern media technology.

Fifth, education across all societies is one of the primary agendas of modern development. As theory on democracy teaches (e.g., Dahl 2000), the enlargement of the educated, young middle class in developing states leads to greater social diversity and the formation of various political parties and organizations that demand participation in the decision-making process and inclusion in governing. Educated citizens thus demand the replacement of autocratic political constituencies by a liberal political system that opens the possibility for political engagement. The fast-developing autocratic regimes of China or Russia are also characterized by a growing educated middle class that, according to prior studies on democracy, will necessarily give birth to a strong, large civil society demanding political inclusion. The expanding civil disobedience in 2011–2012 in China and Russia, societies with a large educated young population, exemplifies the formation of strong civil society. As some scholars believe, the democratic future of China is also inevitable because of the increasing level of GDP per capita, which exceeded a threshold that stimulates the development of democracy (Pei 2006).

Sixth, autocratic regimes are characterized by excessive corruption that is very difficult to control and, as European newspapers comment, regimes like Putin's are eventually alone. The regimes of democratic societies are not free from corruption, but their governments and ruling elites are accountable for their actions and, hence, corruption in these societies is much easier to control (Kapstein & Converse 2009). Open access to media exposes corruption and stimulates educated societies to demand accountability of the ruling elite and the replacement of corrupt economic and political elites – leading to the development of a democratic system. Educated society therefore demands the institution of democracy (Dahl 2000).

Seventh, political scientists have found very limited evidence of war conflicts between democratic states. "A world made up of liberal democracies, then, should have much less incentive for war, since all nations would reciprocally recognize one another's legitimacy" (Fukuyama 1992, xx). In part this is because the competition for territorial expansion which was the model of world expansion in the pre-global market economy era is replaced by a global market competition. The new form of international competition defines world powers based on economic development, level of education, trade relations, ownership of patents and new technologies as well as scientific discoveries. Thus, global leadership in technology, scientific expansion, and technological competition replaces the need for war to conquer new territories using military force. Military forces are needed mainly for defense reasons. Such a change on the global political scene stimulates governments' focus on the development of science, education, individual creativity, and innovativeness in place of an expansion of military forces. In the future, cooperation in trade and economic competition could be a path for peaceful existence and is a path to create a democratic future.

Consequently, according to Inglehart and Welzel (2005, 2009), Fukuyama and McFaul (2007), and others, the comparability of democracy with basic societal needs, its focus on peaceful coexistence, and market competition makes this political system irreplaceable in today's world. Moreover, increasing access to media and increasing education levels in societies leads to the development of an educated middle class and an increase in societal well-being, both of which support the prosperity and survival of democracies. A contrasting point of view is expressed by scholars who focus on the contemporary economic crises of modern liberal democracies and believe that democracies are failing. According to some, the time of world-wide democratization is coming to an end and is exemplified by the 2000s economic crisis in Europe, East Asia, economic regression in the United States and other well-developed democracies.

First, scholars like Kagan, Welzel, and Gat (Kagan 2008; Gat, Inglehart, & Welzel 2009) believe in the revival of autocracies, arguing that the economic crisis experienced by Western democracies provides a convincing argument for the worldwide dominance of autocracies in the future. In the early 2000s, the faster economic growth in countries with autocratic regimes, such as Russia, China, or the oil-exporting Middle East states, in comparison to the rate of economic growth of the United States or Britain, attests to a decreasing rate of development and modernization in democratic countries and to a downward trajectory of democratic development in the future. Nevertheless, some scholars contradict such points, believing that the recent fast tempo of the development of alternative sources of energy is leading to a steady but permanent reduction in worldwide dependence on oil reserves. Since the inflow of wealth to autocracies like Russia, Iran, or Venezuela is mainly generated by natural resources – oil and gas – future rapid economic development of autocracies is problematic. The recent temporal rate of expansion of the use of alternative sources of energy would cause lowered dependence on oil reserves across the world, challenging the wealth of oil exporters.

Second, proponents of a revival of autocracy also believe that the economic structure of the global world is founded on a worldwide dependency of under-developed countries on well-developed states (Inglehart & Welzel 2009; Wallerstein 2001). In part, this dependency is based on the exploitation of the natural resources of under-developed states by developed countries (most of which are democratic states) and, in part, by unequally shared benefits from global trade and the global market economy between developed versus under-developed countries. This inequality leads to objections to the economically dominating, developed countries of Western democracies. Western democratic models, therefore, would not be copied by less-developed non-democracies, and this would eventually change the trend of diffusing democratization in the world (Kagan 2008). Wallerstein (2001) correctly argues that in post-colonial African democracies in former British colonies, economic inequality within economically and politically fragile African dependencies eventually resulted in the abolition of democracy. A few decades later, in the 1990s, however, many of the African autocracies reinstituted democratic rule. Waller-stein's argument could be questioned, since economic dependency dates to before the colonial time; nonetheless, over time the cross-world trend of the development of democracy has been upward. Also, despite growing resentments toward the economic supremacy of wealthy, democratic states at the end of the twentieth century, the world continues to be dominated by an increasing number of demo-cratic states.

Third, the failure of democratic growth could also result from economic inequality and economic difficulties within each democratic country. According to Przeworski (1991, 2009), however, economic progress prevents the change of any political system, be it autocracy or democracy. Consequently, economic regression could lead to the abo-lition of any political system, either autocracy or democracy, as long as the system is opposite to a country's system during the regression. Importantly, it is predicted by other scholars (e.g., Dahl 2000) that economic inequality within a country, for instance inequality between rural and urban environments, or between rich and poor, has a strong impact on the establishment of a civil society that demands democratic rights and inclusion in decision making.

Considering the growing popularity of demands for democratic systems across societies worldwide, a future world political order led by the supremacy of autocratic regimes is rather distant and question-able. Not a revival of autocracy (Gat 2008; Gat et al. 2009; Kagan 2008) but rather a continuation of diffusing democracy might be a common trend in the future development of the world. Unless a new alternative political system evolves, Fukuyama's statement about the democratic system: "there would be no further progress in the devel-opment of underlying principles and institutions, because all of the really big questions had been settled" (1992, xi), appears to be strongly valid, and so is his belief that "The most remarkable development of the last quarter of the twentieth century has been the revelation of enormous weakness at the core of the world's seemingly strong dictatorships, whether they be of the military authoritarian Right, or the communist-totalitarian Left ... Liberal democracy remains the only coherent political aspiration that spans different regions and cultures around the globe" (Fukuyama 1992, xiii). It may be short-sighted to announce a crisis and a diminishment of democracy, since it took almost two centuries to achieve a high level of democracy and to implement liberty and equality in contemporary relatively stable democracies. Moreover, in practice, democratic societies are not completely democratic but rather are in the process of evolution toward greater democracy.

Nonetheless, democracies need to combat the economic crisis and rebuild their diminishing global role by cooperative engagement in global problems: environmental devastation, poverty, global safety, the spread of disease. Democracies need to become more attractive to the societies of autocratic regimes so countries desire to model liberal democracy (Deudney & Ikenberry 2009). This would require revisiting the modern capitalistic economy, making it more equal and to the benefit of the majority of societies. It would require the attention of civil societies and political regimes to the divergence of interests of plural polity, inclusive participation in decision making, and open and fair elections.

Consistent with the results presented herein, capitalistic development triggers democracy, as higher income per capita leads to a higher level of education, greater access to modern technology and therefore global media information, greater awareness of civil rights and the need for civil law to govern the competitive economy. These factors stimulate the diversification of society, plurality of organizations, and the growth of civil society that demands inclusion in political governance and initiation of pro-democratic reforms. Capitalistic development, thus, by default leads to the eventual change of autocratic regimes to democracies, although the replacement of autocratic rule is not immediate since, as Fukuyama (1992) argues, the authoritarian systems are inadequate to create complex post-industrial economies that are governed by information and technological innovation. Thus for example in China, with its GDP per capita of $4,000–$6,000, a threshold beyond which scientists believe countries will democratize (Pei 2006), capitalistic development will soon trigger democracy (Epstein 2013), but it takes time to change societal practices and culture to allow for democracy's implementation (Fukuyama 2004).

Empirical prediction of the future development of democracy

The advantage of using statistical modeling is that it offers the possibility of statistically predicting the growth of democracy in the world and across world regions. Therefore, as an extension of the world and regional analyses, I attempted to predict estimated *world* and *regional* patterns of democratization until 2050 by applying the three-level and two-level modeling described above. Understandably, however, this predictive analysis can serve as an overview of potential trends only if I discount the incidence of rapidly occurring large-scale crises in liberal democracies or economic or other crises in currently democratic or non-democratic regimes, or unplanned world-scale events that could influence democratic trends.

The predictive analysis used data from the past two centuries and, hence, accounted to some degree for the impact of unexpected world-scale events that rapidly changed world or regional historical development. The predictive analyses, however, do not take into consideration the growing crisis within liberal democracies broadly discussed in the literature, which could lead to mass withdrawal from the democratic system (Wallerstein 2001). Such a possibility is disputed by some scholars (Deudney & Ikenberry 2009); nonetheless, as other researchers argue, it is a possibility that should not be discounted (Gat 2008). Therefore, the reliability of such findings is very limited. Nevertheless, according to the literature, the likelihood of the survival by liberal democracies of any crisis-like event is higher for consolidated than for non-consolidated democracies. Hence, fragile democratic systems are more likely to undergo a future crisis within democratic polity (Dahl 2000). To account for a potential significant difference in the estimated future levels of democracy in the world, I conducted a retest in the consecutive analysis, where I included only consolidated, stable democracies in the dataset (democracies with a score of 7 and above). In addition, due to the changeability of economic and historical conditions over time, I conducted the study analyzing data from the past five decades, an approach consistent with other studies (Dahl 2000; Tilly 2007).

Interestingly, *in the world* when these study limitations are considered in terms of predictability over the future half-century, the assessment of all countries presented in Model 1 shows the overall trend of democracy to be increasing (upward trend of worldwide democratization), which attests to the growth of the democratic levels of existing democracies and/or the new establishment of democratic regimes in the near future (see Figure 4.2, Model 1). By the mid twenty-first century, democracy in the world is expected to reach an average score of 6.08.

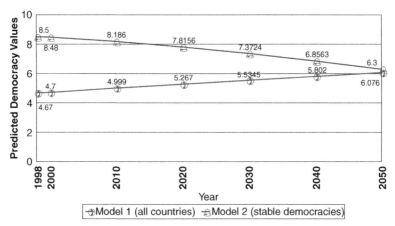

Figure 4.2 Predictive analyses of democracy growth worldwide vs stable democracies until 2050

At the same time, the assessment of only stable democracies until the mid twenty-first century, i.e., democracies with a democracy score above 7 on a scale of 0–10 (Model 2), demonstrates a downward trend. Regardless of the initially much higher average democracy level score of stable democracies than the average cross-world democracy score of all countries (8.2 versus 4.5), it is predicted that, longitudinally, stable democracies will decrease their democracy level to an average score of 6.3. This score is below point 7 for stable democracies. Thus, according to the assessment of only stable democracies, the average level of the democracy score of stable democracies in the world is higher than the general worldwide average at the beginning of the twenty-first century (the average level is above 8.2 points, whereas the average worldwide score of all countries is near 4.5). However, the level of presently stable democracies will decrease over time, reaching the same level as the general worldwide democratic growth (score of about 6 in both cases).

What is the conceptual meaning of these findings? We may assume that, within the next half century, the number of stable democracies will decrease or the level of presently stable democracies will decrease regardless of the overall growth of the level of democracy in the world. The recent example of the loss of many citizens' rights and freedoms in the post-September 11 United States attests to the vulnerability of democratic systems to outside threats and the insecurity of democratic governments in terms of the provision of societal safety, as many historical examples of developing democracies show (e.g., the slow increase of democracy within England, France, or the United States). However, this does not mean that democracy will be replaced by an autocratic regime. On the contrary, recent autocratic regimes have been losing political power as soon as modern communication exposes societies to the living conditions in well-developed and liberal democratic states. Libya and Syria are the most recent examples of such changes.

The worldwide growth of democracy may be generated by an increasing number of new democracies that will be low-level, unstable democracies. Such a conclusion is consistent with the observed long-term trajectory of the development of democracy, which is characterized by the slow growth of the "democraticness" (level of democratization) of countries before any state reaches a stable level of democracy. An interesting result is also the similarity between the levels of world-wide democracy of stable democracies and all countries in the world by 2050. It means that democratization of the world is likely to persist, but the existing highest-level democracies will diminish their impact on the overall average democracy level worldwide, due to economic problems or cultural diversities or any world-wide crisis. The concept of failing democracies (Kagan 2008; Wallerstein 2001) may be correct, not in terms of the replacement of democracies by autocratic revivalism, but rather by the decreasing level of liberties within world democratic powers and the lowering significance of the few most powerful democratic regimes in the world polity. In the future, democratic countries most likely would be the most important players in the international polity, but the impact of recent stable democracies could be shared with the influence of less stable democracies. According to the empirical analyses, the probability of the survival of democracies is high, but the supreme role of some of the most influential democratic forces most likely would be replaced by the combined effect of low and stable democracies (see Table 4.2).

When *regional* democratization is looked at, all regions will continue the trend toward democratization. Democratic growth, however, is estimated to be more rapid in regions that democratized in the twentieth century vs regions that have a long-term history of democratization. It is simply due to the fact that responsiveness to democratic models by new, low-level democracies is higher in the era when democracy is perceived as equal with modernity and a higher standard of life and,

Table 4.2 *Estimated values of democracy across regions, 1990–2050, and observed values of democracy across regions, 1990–2005, while using three-level growth of democracy model. The data are centered at 1950.*

	Estimated values of democracy (on scale 0–10)*						Observed values of democracy (on scale 0–10)					
	World's regions						World's regions					
Year	Western Hemisphere (Americas)	Europe	Africa	Middle East	Asia	World	Americas	Europe	Africa	Middle East	Asia	World
1800		1.0837				2.8992		0.3				.73
1810		1.3085				2.7921		0.6				.95
1820	2.9130	1.5389				2.7033	2.5	0.25				.60
1830	2.8035	1.7749				2.6327	1.91	0.33				.85
1840	2.7246	2.0165				2.5805	1.41	0.79				.98
1850	2.6764	2.2636				2.5466	1.58	1.5				1.43
1860	2.6587	2.5163				2.5309	1.56	1.6				1.79
1870	2.6717	2.7746				2.5335	2.2	1.94				2.14
1880	2.7153	3.0385				2.5544	2.75	2.84				2.67
1890	2.7895	3.3079				2.5936	3.0	3.53				2.93
1900	2.8943	3.5829			5.9345	2.6511	3.1	3.95				3.13
1910	3.0298	3.8635			6.1428	2.7269	2.95	4.69				3.56
1917	3.1623	4.0599			5.9709	2.7622	3.26	6.1			1.0	4.35
1920	3.2167	4.1462		−.2624	5.8332	2.823	3.33	6.7		0.0	1.0	4.77
1930	3.3925	4.4413		1.3687	5.1662	2.933	3.47	6.04		0.0	.86	4.11
1940	3.6198	4.7386		2.0133	4.3023	3.064	2.59	3.16		0.83	1.71	2.83
1943	3.6940	4.8289		2.0311	4.0162	3.1067	2.59	4.31		0.83	1.0	2.96

242

Year												
1948	3.8237	4.9804		2.0126	3.5774	3.1817	3.25	5.84		3.22	2.23	4.09
1950	3.8777	5.0415		1.9875	3.4021	3.2129	2.95	5.74		3.9	2.38	4.04
1955	4.0182	5.1950	2.7594	1.8220	2.9886	3.2942	3.1	5.81	3.5	3.42	2.74	4.13
1960	4.1663	5.3499	2.7515	1.6075	2.6262	3.3801	4.23	5.75	2.83	1.14	3.39	3.69
1970	4.4854	5.6639	1.9112	1.1896	2.1349	3.5656	3.76	5.54	1.69	1.29	2.67	3.21
1980	4.8352	5.9835	1.1521	1.0497	2.0889	3.7694	3.96	6.57	1.53	0.63	1.65	3.13
1990	5.2156	6.3086	1.8908	1.5043	2.6488	3.9915	7.16	8.48	1.42	1.47	2.87	4.4
1998	5.5419	6.5728	4.5122	2.5083	3.6407	4.1823	6.6	7.76	4.07	2.56	3.92	5.07
2000	5.6266	6.6393	5.5439	2.8693	3.9749	4.2319	6.7	7.89	4.26	2.46	3.73	5.32
2005	5.750	6.7789	6.4086	2.8971	4.3598	4.6756	6.4	7.64	4.002	3.01	3.89	5.64
2010	6.0682	6.9756	10.000	5.4611	6.2279	4.9905						
2020	6.5404	7.3175		9.5957	9.5683	4.7675						
2030	7.0433	7.6649		10.000	10.000	5.3627						
2040	7.5768	8.0179				5.7621						
2050	8.1408	8.3765				6.076						

Source: Research based on database *Nations, Democracy and Development: 1800–2005* (Wejnert 2007).

* The estimated democracy values were obtained with Multilevel Growth Model of Linear Regression with specified UN (unstructured) variance/covariance structure of the intercept and time.

hence, very desirable to societies. Older democracies, on the other hand, are mostly well established and within reach of the phase of political equilibrium and relative stability. In such circumstances, revolutionary changes are replaced by negotiated slower reforms that compromise needs along the social spectrum. It is somewhat similar to the economic concept of diminishing returns, when the increase of some production input does not add to but decreases attainable output.

Thus, in the most stable democratic region of Europe, democracy is predicted to continue to increase with a steady upward rate, eventually reaching higher levels than the threshold score for a stable democracy of 7 on a scale of 0–10. The same trend is observed in another region of long-term democratic history, the Americas. The Americas will be democratizing across the next half century, reaching a stable democracy level score of 8.1 by 2050. An interesting trend is observed in regions that democratized later, meaning the regions of Africa, the Middle East, and Asia. Due to a shorter observed democratization period, the trajectory of democratic development goes upward at a steeper rate. According to empirical estimates, these regions will reach the maximum democratization score of 10 before 2030. Such a scenario is highly unlikely, since the high estimates result from a mathematical prediction that does not include any potential crises or political obstacles to the development of democracy. As the history of existing long-term democracies teaches, the initial fast growth of democracy in new unstable democracies is frequently disturbed by economic or political crises, unstable political parties, growing diversified voting constituencies, and the emergence of new polities and institutions with diverse interests. The rapidly changing diversified societal structures are associated with the emergence of new interest groups competing for political power, which causes retreat from democracy followed by re-democratization. The positive upward trend in the level of democracy across all regions, however, suggests that the final outcome is an overall increase in the level of democracy in every region of the world. In some regions that are highly democratic, the rate of growth is slower as it might result from an increasing number of low-level democracies lowering the average rate of regional democracy, while in recent less democratized regions, the emergence of new democracies or an increase in the democracy level of existing democracies would positively increase the existing democracy score. Such an example is found, for instance, in the region of Africa.

Is the future of the world's regions predicted to be democratic, or is a revival of autocracy inevitable? According to the estimated statistical analyses, the world is slowly democratizing, which supports the argument that the democratic system offers more benefits to societal well-being than an undemocratic system. Hence, most societies that are exposed to the living conditions in existing, well-established and well-developed models of democracy will model democracy when planning a future political system for their own countries. Democracy will prevail, as Fukuyama and others argued. This does not mean, however, that the world and its regions will be moving quickly into stable democracy levels. As the literature assures, and this empirical analysis predicts, the democratic system builds slowly but with an upward trend, projecting a trajectory of increasing worldwide democratization. According to this research result, although not perfect, the world's future most plausibly is going to be increasingly democratic, and economic competition will continue to replace the territorial expansion of countries and competition for political dominance.

Democratization of the world: policy and scholarly ramifications

Overall, this study provides significant scholarly and policy-relevant results, extending our understanding of democratic processes in four ways. First, since most prior studies derived their predictors exclusively from the socioeconomic characteristics of countries, the *relative* predictive power of socioeconomic indicators is difficult to judge from their results. In this study, socioeconomic predictors are compared with diffusion predictors. The latter have long been expected by researchers to influence democratic growth, but they have rarely been tested in a comprehensive manner, while to my knowledge, their predictive power relative to socioeconomic indicators has not been tested empirically. Significantly, supporting the prior findings of Crenshaw (1995), Lipset (1994), Dahl (2000), Przeworski et al. (2000), and Tilly (2007) that developed countries are more predisposed to democratization, in both world and regional analyses, diffusion factors were markedly stronger predictors of democratic growth than socioeconomic factors. Indeed, indicators of diffusion explained much more of the unexplained variance in countries' democratization over time and more variance between countries in democratic growth than did socioeconomic indicators. In particular, the diffusion predictors of *spatial proximity* and *networks* were robust predictors of democratic growth *both* in the world and across all regions. In contrast, *no* socio-economic indicator was a significant predictor across all regions (see Tables 3.7 and 4.1).

Moreover, the results demonstrate that diffusion variables affect democratic growth jointly with socioeconomic indicators when the two sets of variables are interactive. Such interactive relations represent a trade-off function, where the effect on democratic growth is dependent on independent variation in both variable sets as a function of regional and country characteristics.

Second, it is suggested that world analyses are only the first approximation to understanding democratic growth, since regional patterns of democratization are evident. While this study expected some differences in democratic growth between regions and the world, different patterns of effects of indicators as a function of the socioeconomic, cultural, and historical conditions of a region portray how the growth of democracy in a country may differ depending on regional characteristics.

Third, this study introduced *hierarchical models* in the form of *growth models* that are rarely applied in research on the longitudinal growth of democracy.[5] Considering the hierarchical nature of data incorporating country-level and region-level variables, hierarchical models proved to be quite informative. The obtained statistical fit parameters demonstrated that multilevel regression models fit data on longitudinal worldwide democratization better than the simple regression models used in the analytic approach of most previous studies on democratization. Neglecting the hierarchical structure of the data might lead to an underestimation of the standard errors of the coefficients and to the conclusion that effects are significant when they are not.

Fourth, different patterns of effects of indicators as a function of region portray how the growth of democracy may differ depending on the socioeconomic conditions of a region. In all regions, *networks* and *spatial proximity* affect democratization processes, but the effects are especially important in less developed and less democratized regions,

---

[5] Among a few exceptions are the applications of HLM in studies on voting patterns (Yang, Goldstein & Heath 2000), political tolerance (Peffley & Rohrschneider 2003), and space-time autocorrelations of democratization (O'Loughlin et al. 1998)

where the impact of socioeconomic indicators is weaker. In future studies, it will be important to assess the rate of the adoption of democracy between countries within the same network. For instance, although Poland and Albania were both former members of the Warsaw Pact and the Council of Mutual Assistance, Poland nevertheless was first to democratize, while Albania lagged markedly behind in democratic growth (Wejnert 2002c). The manner in which Poland and Albania, for instance, interacted within their networks may help to explain such variation. Thus, the regional analyses indicate that worldwide analyses that do not consider the separate effects of regions may actually lead to distorted views on the course and patterns of democratization. The underlying discrepancies between the regions suggest that world analyses should be treated only as first approximations of an explanation of the democratization processes in the world, followed by more detailed regional analyses.

From the *policy* point of view, since the increase in democratization results from the interplay of socioeconomic and diffusion factors, where the diffusion effect is greater, strong policy attention should be devoted to the spatial closeness or network connectedness of democratic and non-democratic countries. Also, results indicate that media communication, which is a facilitator of the spread of democracy, requires the attention of policy-makers. The recent breakdown of communist regimes is a vivid example of the impact of Western media on the development of democratic movements in formerly communist countries. Consistent with a focus on media, special attention should be devoted to broad cultural diplomacy to balance antidemocratic education in countries governed by radical totalitarian regimes or influenced by radical organizations. Relative to the years under President Reagan, the US, following the fall of the Soviet threat, currently invests only one-eighth the resources in cultural diplomacy (Finn 2003), thereby undermining the powerful effect diffusion processes can play in democratization. The results suggest at least three strong policy implications concerning the growth of democracy, as well as referring to the sustainability of democracy and to the potential crisis of liberal democracies: (a) the effect of time, (b) the effect of diffusion, and (c) the effect of regional development.

While this study demonstrates that *time* is a strong predictor of democratic growth, a simple assumption that, given the democratization trends already set in motion, with time the world will democratize, does not hold. Each progressively added predictor altered the impact of time, decreasing its value or changing its parameter from positive to negative, indicating that world democratization depends as much on countries' socioeconomic and political conditions as on the effect of time. Not time alone but countries' and regions' level of development should be the main concern of policy-makers if the democratic system is expected to prevail in the future.

Considering *diffusion*, the strong effect of diffusion of democracy within a region is indicated by the obtained strongly significant parameter of diffusion across all tested models and by its progressive increase with each added diffusion variable (e.g., network or density and proximity), while the impact of other variables decreased. According to the constructed diffusion variables, the diffusion effect of a democratic country is especially strong if the democratic country has large population and a stable democratic system. Hence, while policy-makers concerned with the increase of democratization across the world's regions should devote special interest to supporting democratization processes in the largest countries within each region, they should also be aware that any new democratic country significantly increases the potential of cross-regional democracy expansion; this valid point was also made by Fukuyama (Fukuyama 1992; Fukuyama & McFaul 2007).

The effect of regions' development indicates that a large percentage of the population engaging in agricultural production is a strong deterrent to regional democratic growth. Perhaps due to the difficulty in mobilization of democratic movements in sparsely populated rural communities (Barro 1999; Ramos & del Mar Delgado 2003), or because the geographic distance of rural communities confines channels of communication with other social strata, making it more difficult to establish political alliances, the impact of agrarian groups on political regimes is limited (Ramos & del Mar Delgado 2003). Thus, from a pragmatic point of view, helping to develop an industrial/post-industrial economy within regions not only leads to new consumer markets or trading partnerships but in fact paves a path to world-wide democratization.

This latent function of regions' development should encourage the international community (e.g., the United Nations) and the governments of well-developed Western liberal democracies to sponsor programs aimed at regional development if the progress of world democratization is to be secure. Such initiatives sponsored by the international community might also reduce the currently uncontrolled profits of multinational companies that use the natural resources of developing countries while not caring for the well-being of citizens. In addition, it might solve some of the broadly criticized problems of economic dependency that are especially visible in the recent era of economic globalization.

Contrasted with the common focus of policy-makers on social and economic conditions within individual countries, this study's results demonstrate that, in addition to countries' characteristics, the economic development of regions presents a serious challenge to the sustainable development of democracy in the world; this same point was made earlier by Wallerstein using theoretical discourse (Wallerstein 2001). In addition to increased scholarly attention, the gap in development between regions and regional variance in democratization requires critical attention from policy-makers. Such findings might lead to future studies assessing whether too-low levels of democracy account for frequent dissatisfaction with the democratic system during the early stages of democracy's development, and why liberal democracies that are considered to be the ultimate political system of the future of mankind (Fukuyama 1992) are undergoing crises.

In sum, the results of this study call for (a) intensification of studies on diffusion; (b) greater attention paid to regional versus individual countries' development; (c) specific study of the distinctiveness of democratization patterns within the second half of the twentieth century; and (d) incorporation of methods that could simultaneously assess the world and regional patterns of democratization and the differences between them, and the world and countries' patterns of democratization and the differences between them.

When considering pragmatic ramifications, the results of the current study can be grouped into five major findings. *First*, since most prior studies derived their predictors exclusively from the socioeconomic characteristics of countries, the *relative* predictive power of socioeconomic indicators is difficult to judge from their results. Therefore, herein the socioeconomic predictors were compared with diffusion predictors that were long expected, but rarely tested, to influence democratic growth. Significantly, this study demonstrated a remarkably stronger effect of exogenous indicators of diffusion on world and regional democratization than the broadly studied indicators of social and economic characteristics of countries. Indeed, indicators of diffusion explained much more of the unexplained variance in countries' democratization over time and more variance between countries in democratic growth than did socioeconomic indicators. Also, increases in the value of diffusion indicators were significantly correlated with increases in democratic growth (level and rate) in the world and across regions.

The influence of indicators of GNP, media, and the diffusion indicators of spatial proximity and networks attested to a strong dependence of democratic growth on their level. Thus, high levels of these indicators may be among the main preconditions for the successful implementation of democracy. Perhaps countries low in these indicators are either not likely to democratize or, if they approach democratic transition, the democratic system cannot sustain itself (see also Wallerstein 2001). This may explain why democratic systems in many African countries that democratized in the 1960s, the majority of which had low GNP and a limited urban infrastructure, did not withstand the economic challenges faced by the newly independent colonies, and thus were replaced with authoritarian regimes. This may also explain why the poorest and least developed countries of the former Soviet states, Albania and Belarus, shortly retreated from democratic principles in the 1990s, and why Poland, which had the least severe censorship of media of all communist states, regardless of being less developed than many Eastern European countries, was the first country to adopt democratic changes within the former Soviet bloc states.

Moreover, rather than past colonial heritage, the diffusion variables of networking within political and economic pacts and within spatially close areas are the strongest predictors of future cross-regional democratic growth, especially in regions that traditionally are not democratic. Future analyses of diffusion focusing on networking, colonial dependency, and role modeling should shed light on variations in the characteristics of networks that affect the rate of adoption, as in, for example, the almost simultaneous transition to democracy across the countries of the former Soviet bloc (Wejnert 2002d) vs the initial resistance to democratization in the Middle East (Piscatori 1991) followed by the spread of democratic movements after 2010 stimulated by role-modeling on demands for political rights in some Gulf states (Kinninmont, 2012). Future analyses should also shed more light on the interactive effects of diffusion indicators, e.g., it is strongly believed that it was not until the second half of the twentieth century that modern communication (Gunther & Mughan 2000; Markoff 1996), especially the internet, effectively reduced the distance between countries, promoting the rapid diffusion of democracy across each region. The re-democratization of African countries and the rapid spread of democracy in Eastern Europe, all in the 1990s, overlapped with the growth of the internet, suggesting potentially important contributions of broad access to world-wide information on the growth of democratization. Perhaps internet availability will reduce the strong impact that spatial proximity has had in previous eras. Indeed, ongoing research by our group shows a strong correlation between the growth of the internet and democratization, as well as a causal relation (via cross-lag analysis) of internet access on democratization in the world and in most regions.

Second, while this study expected differences in democratic growth between the regions of the world, the differential effect of socioeconomic predictors according to a dichotomy of developed/under developed is an important extension of the understanding of socio-economic effects. Similarly, there were also stronger diffusion effects in less-developed and less-democratized vs well-developed, democratized regions. In sum, regional differences in the patterns and temporal rate of democratization illuminate different *paths of democratization* that reflect variance in economic, social, and cultural development. Although some exceptions on specific indicators occurred, overall this variance serves to define two major patterns of democratization: *Category I*, containing Europe, the Western Hemisphere, and to some extent Asia, and *Category II*, encompassing Africa and the Middle East. These two categories were defined on the basis of development level, as shown by two major findings. *First*, in less economically developed regions, diffusion processes appear to play a predominant role in democratic growth, in contrast to the joint effect of diffusion and socioeconomic characteristics in more affluent regions. In regions with a high level of development, the dominant effect of GNP in reducing the variance of democratization is observed relative to less developed regions, where the effect of literacy dominates. This finding is further supported by research presented above on the causation effect of indicators of democracy growth, where the higher level of literacy is more an outcome of democracy and not vice versa. Since less-developed regions are more likely young democracies, i.e., democracies that are evolving in the second half of the twentieth century, the democratization has not led to a high literacy level yet. Thus, different patterns of effects of indicators as a function of region portray how the growth of democracy may differ depending on the socioeconomic conditions of a region. *Second*, in all regions, networks and spatial proximity affect democratization processes, but the effects are especially important in less-developed and less-democratized regions, where the impact of socioeconomic indicators is weaker. In future studies, it will be important to assess the rate of adoption of democracy between countries within the same network. Finally, the regional analyses indicate that worldwide analyses that do not consider separate effects of regions may actually lead to incorrect assessments of the course and patterns of democratization.

Third, this study uses the methodological approach of Multilevel Regression Models, especially their application in longitudinal studies that has proved to be quite informative but so far has been only rarely applied in research on democratization. Specifically, this research extended an application of Multilevel Regression Models (Individual Growth Models) to the study of trajectories and the rate of world and regional democratic growth. The obtained statistical fit parameters demonstrated that multilevel regression models fit data on longitudinal world democratization better than simple regression models. Therefore, it appears to be more beneficial to assess the indicators of democratization in a multilevel regression context.

Fourth, this study also attests to the importance of longitudinal approaches to analyzing democratization as compared to the use of one year or only a few years. For instance, prior arguments that British power had a positive impact on the democratization of many colonies through imposing democratic transitions are not totally supported when longitudinal assessment beyond one year of transition is considered. This study showed that, for example, in Africa this argument is correct when only a very short historical period is considered, but it is not supported when half a century of post-colonial history is analyzed. The democratic initiatives imposed by Britain, after only brief democratization efforts in Africa, were subsequently replaced by autocratic regimes. Our separate analyses of the British colonial network in Africa[6] suggest that British intervention alone had only an indirect positive effect on long-term democratic growth in this region, probably

---

[6] Separate analyses of the British colonial networks were conducted for Africa. The results are included in Appendix 2.

due to a modeling effect from previous years of democratic development (referred to in the prior section on democracy adoption as a familiarity with democracy). This potential indirect impact was indexed by the insignificant, negative effect of British colonization across a half century of African post-colonial history: there was a positive impact of this indicator in the first decade (1955–1965), but a negative impact in the second decade (1965–1975) of post-colonial history. Powerful trends in the world, including diffusion processes, networking, or development of media were probably more robust factors in instituting African re-democratization a quarter of a century later. Thus, it is suggested that comprehensive investigation of democratization processes requires analyses with a long-term lens.

Fifth, the results of this study have at least two strong policy implications concerning democratization. First, according to the current findings, the growth of democracy should be accomplished much sooner via networking than via increases in economic well-being, especially for countries located within non-democratic regions. This finding could be an important counterpoint to policies focusing on the provision of economic aid rather than on the facilitation of mutual economic and political cooperation which, according to these results, enhances role modeling on democratic countries and increases understanding of democratic principles within the polity. Second, when considering which predictive societal factors to engage in order to facilitate democratization, a neglect of differences in paths to democratization as a function of region may distort conclusions and may lead to (a) a bias toward a Western perspective in the evaluation of the deterministic power of democratization predictors, and (b) reaching conclusions that are applicable to the Western world but are not applicable to less-developed regions.

Considering *ramifications of this research for scholarship* the obtained assessment of the impact of predictors on the differences in regions' and countries' patterns of democratization over time leads to important conclusions relevant to scholars' concerns that were not indicated when we interpreted the impact of predictors on democratic growth in the world. *First*, this study supports the prior findings of Lipset (1994), Dahl (2000), Tilly (2007), and others that economically developed countries with higher literacy, GNP and urbanization level; a lower percentage of the labor force engaged in agricultural production; and broader access to media are more predisposed to democratization.

However, prior studies predicted world democratization focusing exclusively on the characteristics of countries. The current study extends those results by demonstrating that an increase in worldwide democratization depends equally on the characteristics of regions, including a decreasing labor force in agriculture and a longer history of a region's democratization, as on the socioeconomic characteristics of countries (e.g., industrial labor, literacy, GNP, media, and urbanization). This study also observed vast regional differences in the patterns and temporal rate of democratization. For instance, overall, indicators representing access to media information, such as TV per capita, radio per capita, and societal access to newspapers, were strong predictors of democratization in the world. Marked regional differences, however, were observed. Moreover, variance in the effect of media suggests that regional characteristics conditioned the impact of this indicator on regional democratization. Similar processes were observed in the case of other indicators.

Second, based on the literature (Rogers 2003, Wejnert 2001a) and on estimates of the temporal rate of democratic growth in the world depicted as the slope of a curvilinear quadratic function of time – which is the typical shape of the temporal rate of diffusion (Rogers 2003; Rogers & Shoemaker 1971) – we expected some influence of indicators of diffusion. However, the strength of the impact of diffusion effects was surprising. This study demonstrated that the strongest predictors of all the selected indicators are those related to processes of diffusion, particularly the indicators of spatial proximity, networks, and familiarity. Indeed, after the country-level predictors of socioeconomic status and the regional predictors of agricultural labor force have been considered, diffusion indicators still had the strongest impact on the level of democratization in the world and across regions. These findings are important because indicators of diffusion have thus far been largely ignored in empirical research on democratization. Therefore, the current results significantly contribute to the discussion of mechanisms of the spread of democracy worldwide, and suggest that analyses of world and regional democratizations also need to be considered as processes of diffusion.

Third, when considering the results of cross-lag analyses, the primacy of the diffusion indicators of spatial proximity and networks over socioeconomic/media indicators in predicting democratization is once again strongly supported. For example, as the observed data indicate (Figure 1.4), the development of democracy was initiated in

Europe and the Western Hemisphere, and it was not until about a century later that democratization was observed in other regions. This regionalization of trends in democratic growth only in part resulted from the greater socioeconomic development of Western Europe and North America in comparison to other regions. As this study shows, social proximity was strongly involved in democratization, as indicated by the geographic location of the first liberal democracies, France and the United States, that became role models of democratization within European and North American regions. Moreover, the shorter geographical distances between countries in Europe as compared to the Western Hemisphere resulted in the initially rapid growth in the democratization of Europe until its stabilization in the beginning of the twentieth century. At that point, diffusion reached the phase of "post-critical mass," characterized by democratization of the entire region with the exception of a few lagging countries that retreated to autocratic regimes and remained non-democratic until the 1970s (countries of southern Europe) and 1990s (Eastern Central Europe) (see Figure 1.4). In contrast, in the Western Hemisphere larger geographic distances from the first democracy – the United States – and large distances between countries decreased the role of *modeling* on existing democracies, which resulted in an initial slow increase in the temporal rate of diffusion within this region. The rapid peak in this rate observed in the 1980s during the Second Wave of world democratization is assumed to have resulted from socioeconomic conditions (Rueschmeyer, Stephens, & Stephens 1992), but based on this study, likely the impact of socioeconomic conditions has been enhanced by processes of diffusion.

Another predictor of diffusion that refers to countries' connectedness within international economic and political networks, as the results of this study showed, had an especially significant effect on democratization. Networks serve as a source of democratic ideas, so the incorporation of strongly democratic countries as members of international networks stimulates democratization processes among nondemocratic members. Therefore, networks of countries exert not only economic influence (due to, for example, the frequent provision of international economic aid by relatively better-developed democratic countries), but also political influence via the diffusion of ideas, principles, and institutions. Importantly, in contrast to many studies emphasizing the effect of socioeconomic variables on democratization processes, so far the effects of processes of diffusion have been largely ignored in empirical research. This book's claim of a strong relationship between democracy expansion throughout the world and the effect of diffusion significantly contributes to the discussion on the mechanisms of the spread of democracy worldwide.

Fourth, the findings of causal relations in the cross-lag analyses between specific indicators and world and regional democratization shed light on important scholarly and pragmatic considerations for understanding the expansion of democracy. For example, as this study demonstrated, the stimulation of the growth of literacy by democratization processes adds to the prior understanding of societal outcomes of democratization processes (e.g., Wejnert 2002a). At the same time, the causal relation between the indicators of socioeconomic status of GNP per capita, industrial and agricultural labor, and media attested to a strong dependence of growth of political democracy on the level of socioeconomic development as well as a degree of societal access to media. It could be assumed that high levels of industrial labor, GNP per capita, and a broader access to media are among the main preconditions of successful implementation of democracy in any individual country. We can thus extrapolate that only countries with higher GNP, a higher level of industrial labor, and open access to media are ready to accept democratic systems, while other countries either are not likely to democratize or, if they approach democratic transition, the democratic system will not sustain. Perhaps that is in part why the democratic system in many African countries that democratized in the 1960s, the majority of which had low GNP and quite limited industrial labor, did not withstand the political and economic challenges faced by newly independent colonies, and were replaced by totalitarian regimes.[7] This would also add to the explanation of why Poland, having the least severe censorship of media democratized as the first within the former Soviet bloc states.

The *fifth* conclusion relates to differences in cross-regional and cross-national patterns of democratization over time, specifically with respect to the covariance parameter of the status (intercept) and rate (slope) between countries; in other words, the interrelation between the rate and the level of democracy. Every constructed model indicates

---

[7] Of course, in some cases, the imposition of a democratic system by the British Empire added to the weakness in sustainability of democracy.

dependence of countries' rate of democratization on the status of democracy at the centered time, i.e., in 1950. The negative parameter of the covariance suggests that the rate of countries' democratization was lower when democracy scores in those countries were higher in 1950 and, vice versa, the rate of democratization was higher when obtained democracy scores were lower in 1950. Indeed, as presented in Figure 3.4, the results of the observed data demonstrate such a pattern, where regions with countries that democratized in the second part of twentieth century had, on average, lower democracy scores at the centered time, and regions with countries that democratized sooner had, on average, higher democracy scores at the centered time. Hence, we can assume the existence of potentially large differences in the slope of the temporal rate of democratization between the regions in which many earlier democratized countries are located vs the regions with mainly newly democratized states. Specifically, we expect that in the former regions the slope of the rate of democratization would be almost linear, only slowly increasing over time, while the slopes in the latter regions would demonstrate a sharp curvilinear curve in the second part of the twentieth century. However, as the results of the model with all predictors show, this trend weakens when all our predictors are added (the correlation intercept/slope between countries decreased by 7 percent in the model with all predictors as compared to the model with the predictor of time only).

Sixth, significant also is the impact of media. It was not until the second half of the twentieth century when, among other factors, modern mass media – especially the internet – effectively reduced the distance between countries across each region, which helped in the promotion of democracy (Fukuyama & McFaul 2007). For example, in African countries that re-democratized in the 1990s, after only short-lived democratization efforts in the 1960s, the spread of democracy overlaps with the popularity of the internet, suggesting the important contribution of media to democratic growth. Indeed, our research shows that the effect of diffusion slightly increases when the predictor of access to media was added to the final model. Future studies on the effects of access to a broad range of media (e.g., cell phones, internet) should shed more light on the combined impact of media and diffusion on the expansion of democracy in the world.

Seventh, when applying these findings to world and regional democratization, visible economically and politically profitable outcomes are recognized; among them are a steady progressive development of freedoms, and a controllable, non-violent civil society (Inglehart & Welzel 2009; Kapstein & Converse 2009). These benefits of democracy need to be considered as assets if we intend to work on the prevalence of the democratic system in the future. Also, considering that diffusion effects are expressed by countries' connectedness within international economic and political networks, countries' networking is especially significant for the development of democracy. Within this context it is significant that the well-developed democracy of the United States has stable well-developed trade with non-democratic China, which hopefully will lead to grass-roots democratic changes within China and civil protestors demanding democratic freedom. As Chapter 6 suggests, recent daily strikes in various Chinese regions may signal the start of democratization processes.

Eighth, scholars of the theory of democratization argue that the characteristics of each country delay or add momentum to democracy growth. These should not only include concentration on the change of democracy level over time plus one or two other covariates that change yearly, such as GNP per capita or degree of urbanization. To fully account for the complexity of the conditions influencing the development of democracy, factors that do not vary yearly should be also considered. For instance, the development of *political culture* and *democratic beliefs* that are believed to be a result of a strengthened working class and the middle class of intelligentsia are among such factors. The strong working class was the essential ingredient in bringing democracy about in Europe and Latin America (Burton, Gunther, & Higley 1992; Maravall & Santamaria 1986; Ruschmeyer, Stephens, & Stephens 1992; Stephens 1989). Similarly, the growth of private capital and its industrial convergence with foreign capital led to interrelated, multi-country economic production that is more difficult for authoritarian regimes to control (Derber 2003, Rosenau 2003). Such situations intensified the opportunity for the development of pro-democratic movements (Schwartzman 1998, 167) that, as shown in this study, directly relate to the initiation and growth of democracy.

Indicators that measure the level of development of the working class, intelligentsia, and capitalist economy, e.g., the mean level of urbanization and industrialization, should then explain some of the variation in countries' patterns of democratization. In other words, according to prior scholarly work, it makes a difference in the temporal rate of democratization when a country generates most of its revenues from agricultural production and the sale of raw material vs industrial production, even when the overall level of wealth, measured, for example, by average GNP per capita or per capita GDP, is the same (Simpson 1990). Therefore, conducting tests for world-wide development of democracy needs to include specified covariates in the model that signify differences in regional historical development, cultural differences, and unequal economic development that distinguish a region from other regions (Arbena 1988).

Ninth, this study attests to the importance of *longitudinal analyses* of democratization, as compared to short temporal analyses. Longitudinal analyses provide historical perspective that allows focusing on long-term causes and consequences of democratization, often disputing previously acclaimed findings. Good examples are studies on initiation of democracy in colonial dependencies by prior colonizers (Bollen and Jackman 1985a) that according to this book's longitudinal studies, lead only to unsustainable democracies. The grass-roots based re-democratization of Africa in the early 1990s looks more sustainable (Mustapha & Whitfield 2009).

Finally, *tenth*, this study developed and successfully applied a new multilevel, multidimensional methodology to the analysis of longitudinal data on the expansion of democracy. Specifically, this research extended an application of Multilevel Regression Models (Individual Growth Models) to the study of trajectories and the rate of democratic growth in the world. The obtained statistical fit parameters demonstrated that multilevel regression models fit data on longitudinal world democratization better than simple regression models, as represented by Model A in the table presenting a selection of potential models (Table 3.2) and by the analytic approach of most previous studies of democratization.

In the future, more attention should be devoted to multilevel models and longer-term longitudinal studies in analyses of democratization. In this context, additional indicators of democratization will also need to be assessed. As analyses of the recent democratic changes in the Middle East indicate, not only do modern media, such as twitters, blogging or facebook, facilitate expression of societal desires for political rights, but they also activate support for democratic causes (Seib 2009). Media also facilitate the spread of global modernity including countries' connectedness via international diplomacy, economic market and global response to economic booms and busts (Diamond & Plattner 2012, Gelvin 2011). New studies should shed more light on the interrelations of media and the expansion of democracy.

In summary, this study supports the prior findings of Bollen (1983), Crenshaw (1992), Lipset (1960, 1981), Dahl (2000), and Przeworski et al. (2000) that developed countries are more predisposed to democratization when measuring the effect of development alone. In both the world and regional analyses, however, the importance of development faded with the inclusion of diffusion variables due to the diffusion factors' markedly stronger predictive power for democratic growth than the factors of development. In particular, the diffusion predictors of spatial proximity and networks were robust predictors of democratic growth both in the world and across all regions. In contrast, no socioeconomic indicator was a significant predictor across all regions. In light of these findings, the common strategy of American and other Western policy-makers of attempting to promote democratic development by providing economic aid to totalitarian regimes should not inevitably lead to democratic transitions. Indeed, in most countries – notably Iraq – it did not yield democratization. The belief that a developed, modern, and educated society of a totalitarian country will abolish non-democratic regimes via, for example, pro-democratic movements, does not hold for many non-democratic countries, since development is found in sustainable totalitarian as well as democratic regimes (Przeworski and Limongi 1997). It is proven, nonetheless, that the networking of democratic with non-democratic states enhances the process of democratization by increasing the level of pro-democratic popular sovereignty, ready to use power to demand inclusion in political decision making. Therefore, the provision of economic aid to less-developed, authoritarian regimes facilitates economic contacts between democracies and non-democracies and, in turn, adds to democracy promotion via modeling on established democracies.

Thus, at the broadest conceptual level, this study serves as an integration of two major theoretical approaches to democratization, one focusing on *endogenous* characteristics of countries as agents of democratization, the other on *exogenous* or external structural modulation of countries by variation in the macro environment, such as by diffusion effects. It provides integrative analyses of the *micro* social processes of a country with the *macro* processes embedded in an external societal context. In this sense, the study extends current attempts to rediscover a micro-macro connectedness in social phenomena that was a focal concern of many historical thinkers in sociology (e.g., Weber, Simmel, Marx, and Durkheim) and is visible in the contemporary work of Giddens, Collins, Coleman, Habermas, and Alexander.

5 | Why is *democracy desirable?* Outcomes of democracies and autocracies

Since the 1980s, the number of democracies across the world has approximately doubled. This rapid spread has brought substantial changes to people's lives, and most studies have shown that democratic development leads to increased levels of literacy, education, industrialization, urbanization, and the overall well-being of citizens. Other positive outcomes of democratization have been demonstrated to include a middle class of educated professionals and intelligentsia, the principal carriers of democratic values, who foster civic engagement and the development of a civil society. The sentiment of liberal democracy persists in today's world. Countries are required to democratize in order to receive financial aid or be able to open up to foreign investment (Robinson 2004; Wolf 2001). Colonial empires imposed democracy and market economies on former colonies (Bollen and Jackman 1985a; Crenshaw 1995), and economic problems are believed to be solved with the adoption of democracy (Lederer 1992; Tarrow 1991a). Thus, it seems that the diffusion of democracy is important for the development of societies. Why is this so? What are the outcomes of democracy? Do the benefits of democracy outpace those of non-democracy? To finalize discourse on worldwide democratization, this chapter presents the results of studies accounting for democracy's outcomes from 1970 to 2005 for countries worldwide. A particular focus is designated: to understand the impact of democracy on the Empowerment of Women – one of the goals set up by the United Nations in the Millennium Development Initiative.

Scholarly interest in the outcomes of democratization has visibly intensified since the beginning of the Third Wave of world democratization that encompassed the democratization of southern Europe in the 1970s, Latin America in the 1980s, and the former Soviet bloc in the early 1990s, and the re-democratization of post-colonial Africa in the mid 1990s (Bermeo 1991; Bratton & Mattes 2001; Higley & Gunther 1992; Linz & Stepan, 1996; O'Donnell, Schmitter, & Whitehead

1996; Pridham 1990; Stark & Bruszt 1998; Spears 2003). The beginning of the new millennium, however, has brought a renaissance of scholarly investigations on processes and consequences of democratization. Many of these analyses emphasize the negative impact of power of money on the democratic process and democratic culture (Cowen et al. 2012); the consequences of democracy and democratic transitions to global poverty and social inequalities (Fukuyama, Diamond, & Plattner 2012); the interaction of foreign aid with Chinese political, economic, and cultural impact on African countries (King 2013); the predictive power of diffusion versus development on democratic growth (Wejnert 2005); discourses on the impact of development on democratization (Przeworski & Limongi 1997); the emergence of a global democracy and unified global market economy (Kellner 2002); an association of democratic growth with the transition to a market economy (Cardoso 2005; Przeworski 1991; Tenue 2002); simultaneous transitions to democracy and market economy across the former Soviet bloc (Wejnert 2002d); and the relations between people's quality of life and the global free market and democracy (Inglehart 1997, 23). Broadly, democratic growth is considered a sign of modernity, and democratic transitions are understood as a synonym for improvement of the societal standard of living (Lipset 1960, 1994). Hence, many studies have focused on the positive impact of democratization on development and societal well-being (Garrett 2004; Shafer 1994).

One might assume, then, that the growth of democracy would also improve the well-being of women, as reflected by an increase in their representation in the workforce, equal pay for equal jobs, equal educational opportunities, improvement in women's health care, and longer life expectancy. However, during the transition to democracy in the former Soviet countries, the data show that women's employment declined substantially. So did their inclusion in politics, and unemployment rose faster among women than men. In some countries, a decline in the provision of women's health care, especially medical assistance at birth, led to an alarming increase in maternal mortality (Wejnert & Spencer 1996; Wejnert 2003). It is, therefore, uncertain whether democratic growth leads to the expected increase in standard of living and in life opportunities both for men and women.

To understand the relationship between democracy and gender equality in terms of the costs and benefits of democratization, I turn to viewing democratic growth through the lens of countries' economic development and its impact on women. I posit that in addition to the benefits, there are also costs associated with democratization. Especially when coinciding with the growth of a capitalistic economy (Henisz, Witold, Zelner, & Guillen 2005), democratization leads to major transformations in socioeconomic structures, as expressed by a redistribution of available resources, restructuring of class systems and employment structure, and adjustments in life opportunities and culture (Wejnert 2002a). These changes empower some societal groups while disempowering others (Chua 1995), and women seem to be bearing the costs disproportionately.

The impact of democratic growth and the global free market economy on women relative to men is rarely studied in a comparative way and on a large scale – one of the few exceptions is a book by Chua (2003); however, the author addresses the outcomes of global democracy and free markets in terms of ethnic inequality.[1] Responding to this paucity and adding to the ongoing discourse on the synergy of democratic growth and the transition to a market economy,[2] I test whether democratic growth, defined as a dynamic process of "democraticness," or changing level of democracy (Gurr, Jagger, & Moore 1990; Wejnert, 2005), equally benefits men and women in the well-developed, semi-developed, underdeveloped, and post-communist countries.

Again, using Hierarchical Growth Models (a type of hierarchical linear model – HLM), which were used in prior sections of this book to assess the factors contributing to the development of democracy, I examine 147 countries that were independent from 1970 to 2000, at the time of the Third Wave of democratization and the beginning of an expansion in the global market (Huntington 1992; Rosenau 2003).[3] The HLM analyses are complemented by data collected in 1999–2004 using questionnaire interviews with men and women in six recently

---

[1] Chua addresses the unexpected outcomes of global democracy and free markets in terms of ethnic inequality and argues that free markets have concentrated wealth in the hands of resented ethnic minorities, including the US as a "market-dominant minority." "Market-dominant minorities" include the Chinese in Southeast Asia, Croatians in the former Yugoslavia, Whites in Latin America, Lebanese in West Africa, and Jews in post-communist Russia and the Middle East.

[2] Herein, synergy is understood as the combined action of democratic growth and market economy that is greater than the sum of their effects individually.

[3] I focus on only two aspects of global change – the spread of democracy and its assistance in the globalization of a market economy – understanding, however, that the complete process of globalization also incorporates social and cultural dimensions. I examine the social and cultural dimensions only insofar as they interact with the discourse on global democratization.

democratizing countries of Europe (Hungary, Poland, and the Ukraine), Asia (Kyrgyzstan), and Africa (Mali and Senegal). In each country, the interviews were conducted approximately ten years after the democratic transition or re-democratization was initiated. The data were collected by Wachowiak and Wejnert in Poland in 1999 (306 respondents); in Hungary by Lakocsa, Stycos, and Wejnert in 1998 (369 respondents); in the Ukraine by Wejnert, Plisovskaya-Muller, and Borisovna in 2000–2002 (200 respondents); in Kyrgyzstan by Wejnert and Djumabaeva in 2003–2004 (400 respondents), and in Senegal and Mali by Wejnert and Lo in 2004 (200 respondents).

Democracy, development, and societal well-being

Although scholars acknowledge that democracy enhances development and societal well-being, they disagree as to what extent and in what types of societies the enhancement is sufficiently visible. The many positions can be roughly placed into four views.

Following a neo-Marxist approach, scholars representing the first view argue that growth in the level of democratization mainly benefits societies in the well-developed, *core* countries, further enhancing these countries' position in the world system. Accordingly, they believe that development, articulated via urbanization, industrialization, and an increase of standard of living is a function of a country's historically determined position in the world system, and that level of development alters the processes of democratization. Due to the structure of the world's capitalistic economy, poorer countries (*semi-peripheral* and *peripheral*) are disadvantaged in world trade and hence are unable to catch up with the modernized, well-developed world. This disadvantage alters the level and rate of each country's democratization by delaying democratization processes (Hechter 1984; Snyder & Kick 1979; Wallerstein 1999, 1998, 2001)[4] and by reducing the sustainability of a democratic system during times of economic difficulties (Brown et al. 1992; Herspring 2003).

The second view posits that the poorest and least developed states are benefiting from the global market economy, and frequently assisting in democratization, as much as the most developed states, but developmental improvement in the semi-developed "middle-level

---

[4] The evidence regarding the world system approach is mixed (e.g., Bollen & Appold 1993).

economies" is not sufficient. One of the reasons for this effect is the distribution of foreign direct investment (FDI). As shown, the outcomes of foreign investment are determined by countries' strength of economy and by the economic sector the investment is placed in. Since foreign investment is mainly in raw material and standardized manufacturing, the low manufacturing profit is sufficient to benefit poor peripheries where workers' wages are low. Peripheries also harvest from manufacturing technology developed in richer nations that, as the result of FDI, is transferred to poor countries (Shafer 1994). In sum, global growth is good for the poor (Dollar & Kraay 2000).

More technologically advanced middle economies contain a labor force that is trained in services where foreign investment is inhibited by limited world-scale need for a service economy. To gain sufficient benefits, the service-oriented labor force of middle economies would need to compete with core countries for a knowledge economy, but is not skilled enough to win the competition. Thus, as argued by Garrett (2004), across semi-peripheries, the improvement in societal well-being and development is largely conditioned by the readiness of foreign investors to invest in knowledge technology, which rarely happens. Opinions regarding the benefits of foreign investments to the host economy versus the economy depending on foreign capital, however, are mixed.[5]

The third approach sees democratic growth as a symbol of progress, wealth, high standard of living, liberalization, freedom, and happiness. It is a force advancing technological and cultural progression that operates across all types of countries. With the proliferation of modern technology, media, and the internet, international and cross-national political discourse on democracy intensifies its growth and is enhanced by international collaboration and the improvement of the market-driven economy (Castels 2000; Hutton & Giddens 2000; Henisz, Zelner, & Guillen 2005). Opened channels for political discourse form a base for the creation of trans-national alliances between groups demanding social and political justice, and democratic freedom

---

[5] While one group of scholars argues that dependence on foreign investment is detrimental to countries' economies (Chase-Dunn 1975; Dixon & Boswell 1996), another forcefully argues the opposite (Firebaugh 1999). To solve the problem, Kentor and Boswell (2003) show that in the middle-economies insufficient foreign investment initially negatively affects countries' economic development; however, it also stimulates within-country economic initiatives and innovation that contribute to the reversal of this trend within fifteen years.

(Kellner 2002). Democracy is thus the inevitable final destiny of world history and the modern man (Fukuyama 1992). Globalization and democracy are brought together in the general theoretical concept of development understood as the process of integration of social and economic systems into more encompassing ones, and as bringing individuals into common systems of collective action and the consideration of the principles of equality and accountability (Kearny 2001; Teune 2002). The future danger in the globalization era could be, however, a battle between democratic liberalism expressed as cosmopolitan tolerance versus fundamentalism and authoritarianism (Gibson & Gouws 2003).

The last approach understands that democracy's diffusion is facilitated by countries' collaboration and closeness of communication within economic and political networks, influence of democratic neighbors on non-democracies (the "neighboring effect"), role modeling of non-democratic countries on well-established democracies, and an imposition of democratic principles by economically powerful countries. The diffusion is further augmented by modern media communication that facilitates the spread of democratic ideas and promotes global economic ties (Wejnert 2005). Democratic growth facilitated by diffusion aims for modernity and a higher standard of living, leading to much-improved societal well-being.

Democracy, development, and gender equality

As feminist scholars posit, democracy and modern development entail the enhancement of women's social status and position (Beneria 2003; Beneria & Bisnath 2004). The opening of economic and political opportunities to women, according to the UN Ambassador Muhammad Yunus, not only yields the improvement of women's economic situation, but also empowers women's involvement in family decision making, increases women's political and legal awareness, reduces domestic violence, and enhances the social mobility of their children.[6]

---

[6] Professor Muhammad Yunus, an economist from Bangladesh, set up "Village Bank" (micro-credit) and promoted the formation of local government based on the participation of rural people. He was appointed by the UN Secretary General to the International Advisory Group for the Fourth World Conference on Women in Beijing from 1993 to 1995, served on the Global Commission of Women's Health (1993–1995), and in 2002 was appointed UNAIDS Ambassador.

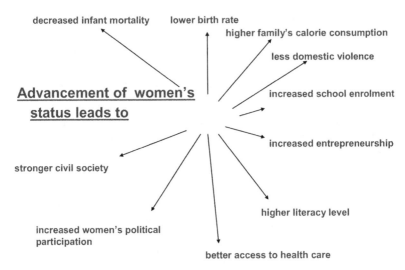

Figure 5.1 The importance of women's empowerment

Hence, numerous studies demonstrate that a stronger position of women leads to a stronger civil society, growth of women's political participation, and in turn, an increase in women's entrepreneurship, higher female literacy, lower birth rate, lower infant mortality, less domestic violence, and more nutritious family diets (Coleman 2004; Sawa-Czajka 2012). Therefore, as illustrated in Figure 5.1, the empowerment of women leads to numerous benefits for society.

Studies also show that the inclusion of women in the top decision-making political structures redresses the imbalance in policy investments, because women policy-makers tend to invest in areas frequently over-looked by male policy-makers yet relevant to families, such as educational institutions, public health facilities, and social and child welfare institutions. Investment in those infrastructures is intrinsically important, especially in light of recent findings showing (using simulation analyses) that the closing of the gender gap in education by increasing girls' education by three years would result in a lower birth rate by one child. In turn, it would lead to an increase in the GNP per capita by 25–30 percent within one generation in any given country (Coleman 2004).

Contrastingly, it has been shown that frequently in non-democracies large gender gaps in the literacy of men versus women are associated with skewed gender ratios of boys to girls (more boys than girls) that indicate discriminatory practices of inadequate nutrition and health care for female children, sex-selective abortions, female infanticide, and insufficient health care for mothers (Murthy 2001; Harriss-White 1996). Coleman (2004), following other studies, thus concluded that when substantial gender inequality exists, democracies are rare because equal rights and freedoms are replaced by the prevailing notion of male dominance and brotherhood. Male-dominated culture is difficult to substitute by democracy, but it can be modified to incorporate limited women's rights (Coleman 2006).

One may assume then that democratizing countries emphasizes and promotes gender equality. However, studies on the position of women relative to men in democratizing post-communist Eastern Europe and Russia demonstrate an *increase* in gender inequality in comparison to prior non-democratic periods (Hauser, Heyns, & Mansbridge 1993; Wejnert & Spencer 1996). At the time of democratic growth, women, because of their dual roles as producers and mothers, and due to more tenuous employment status, faced a plethora of problems not experienced by men. Among these problems were a higher unemployment rate relative to men, unequal access to economic and political resources, and the feminization of poverty (Issraelyan 1996; Lissyutkina 1993; Wejnert 1996 a, b). Specifically, by the late 1990s, women's unemployment skyrocketed to 60–70 percent in Russia and the Ukraine, while rates for men were also high but reached only 40–50 percent (Kholodkovskioi 1998; Zherebkina 2000).

This contrasted sharply with the communist period, when the female employment level was one of the highest in the world (e.g., as early as the 1970s, the percentage of women 15 years of age and over in the labor force, on average 63 percent, substantially exceeded that of the USA [42 percent], and far exceeded that of most Western European countries, including Italy [28 percent], Spain [18 percent], and West Germany [39 percent]) (First-Dilic 1973; Bodrova & Anker 1985). The disadvantaged position of women in the labor market was further amplified by gender discrepancies in earnings and by state propaganda encouraging women employees to return to domestic duties (Paradowska 1992). Subsequently, in the first decade of the transition to democracy, women's status declined vis-à-vis that of men (Wejnert 2003). For Eastern European and Russian women, the political and economic gains of democratic and market economic transitions were overshadowed by negative consequences that women seemed to bear disproportionately (Drakulic 1993; Reading 1992).

Therefore, this study poses questions regarding whether democratic growth necessarily leads to the improvement of quality of societal well-being and gender equality, and whether, for women, the outcomes of democratization vary depending on the level of a country's socioeconomic development and the level and phase of democratic development. To test this hypothesis, the study presents analysis of the balance of costs and benefits of democratic growth on women relative to men and to society at large, using empirical data. First, the study investigates the effects of democratization on women's health and well-being across the world, and comparatively across the well-developed, under-developed, semi-developed, and post-communist countries, applying multilevel analyses. Second, the statistical analyses are supported by analyses of data collected during field studies in countries experiencing democratic transitions.

To conduct the study I use empirical data derived from the same database, *Nations, Development and Democracy* (Wejnert 2007), applying Multilevel Regression Models that were used in the earlier statistical analyses of this book. The indicators of women's well-being and of gender equality were derived from the database.[7] Three key sets of variables were depicted from the database: (a) level of democratization, (b) socioeconomic variables, and (c) gender equality variables. Based on theoretical and empirical accounts of socioeconomic development and gender equality, as well as prior research on democratization (Crenshaw 1995; Lipset 1994), several indicators (measures) of *socioeconomic development* and *gender equality* were depicted for this study.[8] The yearly measures of each indicator for each country allowed us to observe changes in the indicators as a function of time as well as changes corresponding to democratic growth. Level of democratization was recorded in the database *Nations, Development*

---

[7] The data were derived from the database *Nations, Development and Democracy* (Wejnert 2007), particularly its subset of indicators on gender, democracy, and development from *The World's Women 1970–2000: Trends and Statistics* (UN 2001); supplemented by data from volumes of the *Statesman's Yearbook*; the *World Handbook of Political and Social Indicators* (Taylor & Jodice 1982); Osmanczyk's (1982) *Encyclopedia of the United Nations and International Relations*, and the journal *Freedom Review*, published by Freedom House.

[8] Most researchers studying democratization are focusing on its impact on society-at-large; therefore, to demonstrate the distinctiveness of the effects of democratization on women, this study compares effects on society-at-large with impact on women.

and Democracy (Wejnert 2007) that was derived from existing database *Polity IV*.

Grouped by their categories, the socioeconomic and gender indicators are:

Socioeconomic development: (i) *GNP per capita* (GNP/c) measured in $1,000 units;[9] (ii) non-agricultural *labor force* participation, and (iii) *literacy*. Although GNP per capita is the main measure of a country's economic development, in order to incorporate poorly developed countries with a high GNP level (e.g., oil-producing Saudi Arabia), additional measures are used that reflect level of development. In this study, literacy rate is measured as the percentage of each country's population that is literate, and non-agricultural *labor force* is measured as the percentage of the population who were part of the paid labor force in industry and services.

Gender equality: (i) paid *women's labor force* participation, measuring women's labor force as a percentage of the total labor force in each country; (ii) *women's literacy* rate as the percentage of adult females 15 years and older who are literate; (iii) *men's literacy* rate as the percentage of adult males 15 years and older who are literate; (iv) ratio of women's to men's *primary education* as the percentage of girls among pupils in elementary schools; (v) ratio of women's to men's *secondary education* as the percentage of girls among pupils in secondary schools; (vi) *maternal care*, measured as the percentage of births attended by professional health staff as the number of total births;[10] (vii) the *fertility rate*, depicting the total number of births per woman of a reproductive age; (viii) *maternal mortality*, representing the ratio of maternal mortality per 100,000 live births; and (ix) women's *life expectancy* as the duration (number of years) of a women's life calculated at birth.

To complement the results of multilevel regressions, this monograph includes a study of the perceived effects of democratization on quality of life as reported by women and men in recently democratizing countries.

---

[9] GNP per capita (GNP/c) is the gross national product, converted to US dollars using the World Bank Atlas methods, divided by the mid-year population. GNP is the sum of gross value added by all resident producers, plus any taxes (less subsidies) that are receipts of primary income (employee compensation and property income) from non-resident sources. Data are in current US dollars. For more information see World Bank (2009).

[10] The category of professional health staff accounts for all medically trained professionals, including doctors, nurses, and midwives.

The first two countries, Poland and Hungary, are similar in many ways: they are both located in Eastern Central Europe and hence are influenced by European culture and gender roles; before democratization both were communist states with enforced gender equality and women's rights; both had compatible average levels of development; both had about the same ratio of men to women and a similar mean population age, and were about the same size. Ukraine and Kyrgyzstan used to be republics of the communist Soviet Union, but are located on different continents and are developed differently: Kyrgyzstan is a peripheral country, and is located in more traditional Central Asia, while the more affluent Ukraine is in the Eastern part of Europe. Kyrgyzstan, being a predominantly Muslim country, is culturally similar to the African countries of Senegal and Mali, but is influenced by its communist past in terms of rights for women. Senegal and Mali, both former French colonies, follow different developmental trajectories than Kyrgyzstan, but by the end of 1980s their average level of development was about the same.

To depict the similarities and differences between countries, the research in this study was conducted using the same interview questionnaire that was initially developed by Stycos, Wejnert and Tyszka (2001, 2002), and translated into four languages: Polish, Hungarian, Russian, and French. The interviews were conducted with married women, ages 18–49, and, to control for the reliability of the assessment, with 25 percent of their husbands (every 4th husband). In all six countries, the research was conducted in villages located near large cities that were capitals of geographical and administrative regions.[11] In the Polish study, the selected villages were located near Poznan and Konin (the capitals of the central and west districts), and in the second round, near Zielona Gora (the capital of the southwest district); in the Ukraine near Kiev, Ukraine's capital, and Kharkov, the industrial center and the second largest city in the Ukraine; in Hungary near the town of Gödöllo, northeast of the Hungarian capital Budapest; in Kyrgyzstan, south and north of the country's capitol Bishkek; in Senegal and Mali, near the capitals Dakar and Bamako. Rural communities

---

[11] The data were collected by Wachowiak and Wejnert in Poland in 1999 (306 respondents); in Hungary by Lakocsa, Stycos, and Wejnert in 1998 (369 respondents); in the Ukraine by Wejnert, Plisovskaya-Muller, and Borisovna in 2000–2002 (200 respondents), in Kyrgyzstan by Wejnert and Djumabaeva in 2003–2004 (400 respondents), and in Senegal and Mali by Wejnert and Lo in 2004 (200 respondents).

experienced greater economic hardships during the democratic transitions than urban communities (Brown & Bandlerova 2000), but in villages located near cities, the urban influence was expected to enhance women's economic opportunities, e.g., possibilities for selling farm products or crafts in city markets or commuting to jobs in the cities; as well as their well-being, e.g., closeness to medical facilities. In sum, it was assumed that in these villages, women would have a higher satisfaction with life domains than would women in remote villages.

In the study, respondents were asked to assess their own quality of life (also called subjective quality-of-life – QOL) prior to and after democratic growth in each country. Based on studies carried out over the past forty years, perceived well-being, or QOL, is best assessed by specific life concerns (also called life domains) such as jobs, housing, family, or income (Andrews & Inglehart 1979; Andrews & Robinson 1991). The predictive power of these life concerns probably derives from the fact that they appear to apply relatively equally to both rural and urban dwellers, men and women, young and old adults, renters and homeowners, and homemakers and working women (Campbell 1981; Haavio-Mannila 1992; UNESCO 1983; Veenhaven & Ehrhardt 1995; Veenhaven 1996).

The subjective QOL correlates with demographic and social classification variables (such as income, level of education, age, and sex), and current living conditions, but when examined together, these factors typically do not explain more than 10 percent of the variance in people's assessment of life domains and their satisfaction with life-as-a-whole (life in general) (Andrews & Robinson 1991). Similarly, social psychological research has demonstrated that subjective perception of one's QOL is associated with personality traits such as self-esteem, locus of control, depression, or alienation (Costa & McCrae 1980). Moreover, strong religious feelings are one of the determinants of QOL (Campbell 1981; Campbell, Converse, & Rogers 1976). Nonetheless, at the level of population studies, psychological traits and religiosity are only weakly correlated with subjective QOL.

To assess the factors that account for globally rated perceived QOL, US scholars have developed and refined a special type of questionnaire method containing a list of 123 life concerns (domains) that could be integrated into 30 meaningful clusters of life activities (Andora 1980; Andrews & McKennel 1980; Andrews & Robinson 1991; Andrews & Withey 1976; Campbell, Converse, & Rogers 1976; Stycos, Wejnert, & Tyszka 2001). Because of possible differences in the most significant life concerns between other countries and the US, all 30 concern clusters are often included in comparative international studies.

The questionnaire used in this study was built according to specifications designed by prior research on perceived well-being and contained standard clusters of life concerns. These clusters were grouped into fifteen main categories depicting women's degree of satisfaction with (a) their family life, (b) their own housing, (c) the availability and quality of free time, (d) their health and the health care system, (e) political freedom, (f) cleanness of their environment, (g) the activities of religious institutions, (h) the performance of the economic system, (i) the activities of the government and the political system, and (j) their own income.

Each category of concern was rated by each respondent on a 7-point word-anchored scale (where 1 means very dissatisfied and 7 very satisfied with a life domain) of Andrews and Withey (1976) which has been shown to provide high retest stability (Andrews & Robinson 1991).[12] At the end of the questionnaire, respondents were also asked for their degree of general satisfaction with life-as-a-whole, which employed the same 7-point rating scale. In addition, respondents were asked for the depicted *changes* in their well-being since democratization had been introduced. In order to assess the reliability of the interviews, respondents were interviewed by trained interviewers and asked to respond twice to each question: (a) how their life is currently, and how it was in the past using the 7-point word-anchored scale of Andrews and Withey (1976); and (b) select a picture of "face measure" – emotional face measure of satisfaction (Andrews and Withey 1976).[13] To control potential bias of order effects, respondents were counterbalanced for response time-period order, half reporting on the past first, half on current time first. Accordingly, recall periods of up to ten years have been used reliably in assessing QOL (Andrews 1991; Andrews & Withey 1976).[14]

According to the study, as shown in Table 5.1, the comparative assessment of some of the most important indicators of women's

---

[12] Life satisfaction is reported on the 1–7 scale with 1 as completely unsatisfied.

[13] Respondents were asked to select a picture of a face that comes closest to expressing how they feel about a particular life domain.

[14] In the case of the longer period of recall, interviewers can follow the Brown recall method by asking respondents to first give concrete examples for their responses prior to providing their ratings. This method increases test–retest reliability significantly for recall periods of 3–7 years ($r = .77$ with method vs

Table 5.1 The effects of the growth of democracy on women's well-being in democratic vs non-democratic countries in the world in 2005

Countries	INDICATORS OF WOMEN'S WELL-BEING					
	Female literacy (%)	Male literacy (%)	Female labor force (%)	Fertility rate	Medical assistance at birth	Maternal death*
Democratic						
Belgium	.1	.1	39	1.6	100	8
Sweden	.1	.1	47	1.8	100	8
Austria	.2	.2	40	1.4	100	11
France	.03	.03	43	1.75	100	20
Australia	.1	.1	37	2.2	98	6
Mean**	.1	.1	41	1.76	99.5	10.6
Non-democratic						
Afghanistan	85	52.8	27.5	6.9	8	820
Algeria	51	26.1	22.2	4.4	....	150
United Arab Emirates	–	–	7.8	4.5	46	30
Ethiopia	74.5	54.5	38	7	9	1800
Mean**	61	39	23	5.6	34	750

Source: Database *The World's Women 2000: Trends and Statistics* (United Nations 2002); Wejnert (2007).
* Maternal death is measured as number of maternal deaths per 100,000 births per given year.
** mean represents the mean value of an indicator across all democratic and across all non-democratic countries specified in the database Wejnert (2007).

quality of life across countries in the world indicates that, on average, women's quality of life, their economic position, and gender equality are higher in democratic than in non-democratic states:

(a) Fertility rate is three times lower (1.75 vs 5.6);
(b) Women's health care provisions are better as measured by availability of maternal care (99.5 percent vs 34 percent) and by maternal mortality rate at birth (10.6 vs 750 maternal deaths per 100,000 births);
(c) Women's labor force participation is twice as high (41 percent vs 23 percent);
(d) Illiteracy rates are radically lower (0.1% vs 61.0%) and equal for men and women, while in non-democratic countries, women's illiteracy rates are an average of 22 percent higher than men's (see Table 5.1).

For illustrative purposes, a few countries representing each category and an average level of each indicator for well-established democracies and for non-democratic countries are presented in Table 5.1. The demonstrated differences in women's well-being are not longitudinal projections and attest only to differences between democratic and non-democratic countries. The data do not accurately depict the position of women in countries that are in the process of transition to democracy or in countries where the democracy level is fluctuating. A strong example is Russia, which had a democracy level of 2 (on a scale of 0–10) in the early 1990s, became more democratic with a score of 4 in the mid 1990s, and moved to a democracy level of 0 by the early 2000s, and where changes in democracy level correlated with the varying social position of women. The interaction between democratic growth and the well-being of women is illustrated on a comparative, world-wide scale in the empirical analyses presented below.

Tables 17 and 18 show results from multi-level models for the world, as well as comparatively for the developed, semi-developed,

$r = .56$ without method, $p<.01$). Retest stability is often assessed in the study: 40% of each cell of the sample (total n $=$ 40) is randomly selected and re-interviewed by a different interviewer within two weeks of the first interview. Retest stability is indexed by interclass correlation, which reflects both rank order of respondents and magnitude of ratings. The retest reliability was tested in the pre-test of the study, showing high stability of responses. The pre-test was conducted in Poland by Stycos, Wejnert, and Tyszka in 1996 (50 respondents).

underdeveloped, and post-communist countries, with each row of the table presenting the results for a different outcome measure. In order to provide information on the general time trends in the sample and compare them with the effect of democratization, each outcome measure is presented as an unconditional model that includes time effect, and as a conditional model, which includes democratization and time effects.

Cross-world models: The results of a broader world community support the common assumption of scholars, policy-makers, and the public alike that democratization improves societal well-being and thus is beneficial to countries' modern development. When looking at the effects of time in comparison to the additional effect of democratic growth on indicators of societal development, it is evident that democratic growth further enhances the temporal trend of increase of societal development, i.e., correlates with an increase of GNP per capita (in the equation of democracy and time with GNP/c) and an increase in literacy rates (in the equation of democracy as well as democracy and time).[15]

In regard to women's well-being, at first glance it seems that there are no discrepancies in the positive effects of democratic growth on women in comparison to the society at large, because indicators specific to women's health are improving, i.e., fertility rate is reduced, maternal care is improving, and maternal mortality is declining over time. However, a closer investigation of the findings points to unexpected effects.

First, women's labor force participation is negatively associated with the growth of democracy (negative covariate estimates in the equation of democracy with women's labor force in Model 1, Table 5.2), where a yearly increase in the level of democracy by one *reduces* women's labor force participation by −.11 percent, while no effect on the labor force in society at large is depicted. In the equation of time with women's labor force, however, women's participation in the labor force is indicated to increase over time. Considering that from 1970

---

[15] Notably, these findings contradict earlier arguments that a high correlation of women's literacy and democracy refers to an increase of literacy among women either causing countries' democratization or spurring democratic growth (Almond & Verba 1989; Lipset 1960). Rather, an increasing female literacy rate seems to support prior the findings in this study showing that an increase in literacy is a function of democratic growth and contrasts the effect of socioeconomic development that leads to democratic growth (Wejnert 2002b).

Table 5.2 Predicted effects of the growth of democracy on women and society-at-large across the world, 1970–2005

MODELS	Intercept and time effects		Democracy effects		Log-likelihood
	Intercept	Intercept * year	Democracy	Democracy over time (democracy * year)	−2RLL
Women					
I. Women's labor force (%)					
A. Unconditional	35.9* (.98)	.27* (.03)			18163.2
Conditional	36.2* (.98)	.27* (.03)	−.11* (.02) (−)	.001(.002)	18153.0
II. Women's literacy (%)	62.69* (3.1)	.7* (.1)			6154.6
A. Unconditional					
Conditional	62.7* (3.06)	.7* (.1)	−.009 (.12)	.0007(.01)	6014.2
III. Females in elementary school	30.17* (.85)	1.3* (.04)			32093.4
A. Unconditional					
Conditional	30.17* (.91)	1.5* (.06)	.07 (1)	−.06*(.009) (−)	32067.3
IV. Females in secondary school	27.3* (1.06)	1.28* (.046)			32109.3
A. Unconditional					
Conditional	27.24* (1.1)	1.48* (.06)	.1 (.1)	−.055*(.009) (−)	32092.2
V. Fertility					
A. Unconditional	4.07* (.15)	−.02* (.004)			12114.9
Conditional	4.25* (.15)	−.005 (.005)	−.053* (.01) (+)	−.002*(.0008) (+)	12085.6

VI. Maternal mortality					51742.2
A.Unconditional	135.7* (18.7)	15.4* (1.7)			
Conditional	144.4* (19.2)	17.9* (1.8)	−1.99 (1.76) (+)	−.6* (.17) (+)	51719.5
VII. Maternal care					33882.4
A.Unconditional	35.2* (2.9)	2.29* (.17)			
Conditional	33.16* (2.98)	2.03* (.18)	.58* (.21) (+)	.055* (.019) (+)	33849.1
VIII. Female life expectancy					31300.4
A. Unconditional	57.08* (1.19)	0.95* (.059)			
Conditional	57.17* (1.25)	1.3* (.07)	.03 (.13)	−.048* (.01) (−)	31290.8
Society					
IX. GNP/c					14771.3
A.Unconditional	2.73* (.3)	.15* (.028)			
Conditional	2.74* (.31)	.12* (.027)	−.01 (.01)	.008* (.001) (+)	14755.4
X. Literacy					4057.7
A.Unconditional	50.5* (2.69)	.0037* (.001)			
Conditional	48.4* (2.68)	.0009 (.001)	.006* (.001) (+)	.0006* (.0001) (+)	4006.2
XI. Labor force					8840.6
A.Unconditional	55.22* (2.4)	.53* (.035)			
Conditional	55.18* (2.4)	.54* (.035)	.01 (.01)	−.0025 (.0016)	8825.3
Men's literacy					4822.0
A. Unconditional	78.1* (2.4)	.5* (.04)			
Conditional	78.3* (2.5)	.5* (.35)	−.04 (.08)	.003 (.006)	4733.6

* Coefficient at least twice its standard error. Values in parentheses depict standard errors. Yearly assessed countries in the world (N = 3869), number of countries (n = 149).

to 2005 in economically developed stable democracies the percentage of women incorporated into the labor force either did not change or slightly increased[16] (Bodrova & Anker 1985; United Nations 2001; Wejnert 1996a), the depicted decrease must reflect a change in either new or transitional democracies of less-developed countries. I return to this hypothesis when discussing the results of countries categorized by the level of their development.

Second, a decline in primary and secondary schooling of girls, measured as a ratio of girls to boys in primary and secondary schools, is depicted with the growth of democracy over time (see Models 3 and 4, Table 5.2). It could be that the indicated decrease of women's labor force participation caused a decline in the status of women in families and lowered women's influence on decision making within families, which eventuated in the low enrolment of female children in schools.[17]

Third, unexpectedly and contradicting the comparative statistical assessment of democratic and non-democratic countries (presented in Table 5.2), female life expectancy is indicated to decrease with an increase of democracy, i.e., the increase of democracy by a score of 1 per year correlates with the decrease of women's life expectancy by $-.05$ year. Considering that according to the literature, life expectancy in well-developed, strongly democratic countries is either stable or steadily increasing, mainly lower-developed democratizing countries must influence the decrease. I expect analyses of groups of countries to shed more light on these findings.

Models of groups of countries: To assess whether the general findings are similar for all countries regardless of differences in their development level, the same models were assessed in cross-regional analyses of the well-developed (core), semi-developed (semi-peripheral), under-developed (peripheral), and post-communist countries (see Table 5.3).

Core countries: In core, well-developed countries, democratization is positively associated with most of the indicators of women's well-being. Female labor force participation increases with an increase in democratization over time. Female health improves, as indicated by the decline in fertility rate, improvement in maternal care, maternal

---

[16] In 1970, in most highly democratic countries the percentage of women 15 years of age and over in the labor force did not exceed 40% (US 43%, Germany 39%, Italy 28%); by 2005, with the exception of the United States, whose rate had increased to 50%, other democratic countries showed little improvement.

[17] Such an assumption is concordant with Coleman (2004) and other studies.

Table 5.3 Predicted effects of the growth of democracy on women and society-at-large in core, semi-peripheral, peripheral, and post-communist countries, 1970–2005

MODELS **	INTERCEPT		EFFECT of TIME		DEMOCRACY EFFECTS			
	Intercept		Intercept * year		Democracy		Democracy*year	
CORE COUNTRIES								
Women								
Women's labor force (%)	37.17*	(1.06)	.17*	(.06)	−.02	(.05)	.02*	(.005)
Women's literacy (%)	98.1*	(.25)	.019*	(.01)	1.3	(1.5)	−.2	(.2)
Females in elementary school	48.4*	(.25)	.013	(.02)	.039	(.025)	−.0009	(.002)
Females in secondary school	50.7*	(.8)	.16*	(.07)	−.1	(.08)	−.009	(.008)
Fertility	2.03*	(.11)	.01	(.011)	−.019	(.01)	−.004*	(.001)
Maternal mortality	90.88*	(2.52)	.6*	(.07)	−.13*	(.05)	−.029*	(.005)
Maternal care	99.13*	(.19)	−.035*	(.01)	.05*	(.01)	.005*	(.0008)
Female life expectancy	76.6*	(.42)	.17*	(.02)	.07*	(.02)	.005*	(.002)
Society								
GNP/c	13.08*	(2.35)	1.17*	(.25)	−.27	(.22)	−.03	(.02)
Literacy – society %	88.7*	(2.2)	.002*	(.001)	.007*	(.002)	−.0002	(.0001)
Labor force	90.88*	(2.52)	.6*	(.07)	−.13*	(.05)	−.029*	(.004)
Men's literacy (%)	97.63*	(.33)	.11*	(.02)	.17*	(.02)	−.009*	(.002)
SEMI-PERIPHERIES								
Women								
Women's labor force (%)	30.7*	(1.86)	.42*	(.049)	.037	(.02)	−.016*	(.002)
Women's literacy (%)	74.5*	(4.7)	.65*	(.17)	−.1	(.11)	.007	(.009)
Females in elementary school	46.96*	(.74)	.11*	(.026)	−.05*	(.02)	−.007*	(.002)

Table 5.3 (cont.)

MODELS **	INTERCEPT		EFFECT of TIME		DEMOCRACY EFFECTS			
	Intercept		Intercept * year		Democracy		Democracy*year	
Females in secondary school	49.06*	(1.76)	.29*	(.06)	-.1*	(.05)	-.015*	(.005)
Fertility	3.87*	(.3)	-.07*	(.008)	-.017*	(.006)	.0007	(.0006)
Maternal mortality	110.9*	(32.5)	-.6	(2.2)	1.4*	(.7)	-.01	(.07)
Maternal care	79.9*	(4.87)	.4	(.28)	.48*	(.21)	-.02	(.02)
Female life expectancy	69.42*	(1.27)	.37*	(.047)	.01	(.01)	-.009*	(.001)
Society								
GNP/c	4.23*	(.85)	.103*	(.05)	-.09*	(.03)	.015*	(.004)
Literacy – society (%)	76.6*	(3.6)	.01*	(.001)	.001	(.001)	-.00045*	(.0001)
Labor force	69.9*	(3.98)	.61*	(.096)	.03	(.01)	-.0016	(.002)
Men's literacy (%)	90.09*	(2.7)	.11	(.11)	-.002	(.03)	-.004	(.003)
PERIPHERIES								
Women								
Women's labor force (%)	38.3*	(1.13)	.19*	(.03)	-.14*	(.02)	.005*	(.002)
Women's literacy (%)	53.39*	(3.95)	.78*	(.15)	.013	(.21)	-.001	(.018)
Females in elementary school	43.68*	(.67)	.17*	(.02)	.04	(.03)	-.017*	(.003)
Females in secondary school	40.23*	(1.18)	.39*	(.039)	-.01	(.05)	-.01*	(.004)
Fertility	5.13*	(.17)	-.055*	(.005)	-.01	(.008)	-.0013*	(.0007)
Maternal mortality	432.0*	(55.8)	2.79	(4.16)	-3.03	(2.6)	.38	(.24)
Maternal care	55.86*	(3.8)	.51*	(.18)	.015	(.35)	-.0009	(.02)
Female life expectancy	59.27*	(1.16)	.34*	(.023)	.007	(.019)	-.007*	(.001)
Society								

GNP/c	1.67*	(.22)	.027	(.019)	−.0087	(.01)	−.0003	(.001)
Literacy – society (%)	57.4*	(3.04)	.009*	(.0006)	−.0009	.0008	−.000005	(.00007)
Labor force	44.3*	(2.68)	.54*	(.04)	−.018	(.01)	.0004	(.002)
Men's literacy (%a)	70.46*	(3.37)	.5*	(.13)	−.11	(.17)	.008	(.014)
POST-COMMUNIST COUNTRIES								
Women								
Women's labor force (%)	42.6*	(3.1)	.03	(.06)	−.25*	(.07)	.02*	(.006)
Women's literacy (%)	95.4*	(2.5)	.08	(.08)	.01	(.05)	−.002	(.005)
Females in elementary school	18.2*	(4.2)	1.8*	(.2)	2.01	(1.2)	−.4*	(.09)
Females in secondary school	17.4*	(4.8)	1.4*	(.2)	1.6	(1.4)	−.21*	(.1)
Fertility	2.7*	(.2)	−.03*	(.007)	.09*	(.02)	−.01*	(.002)
Maternal mortality	19.7*	(3.6)	2.6*	(.3)	−1.09	(1.3)	−.07	(.1)
Maternal care	77.04*	(8.3)	−.09	(.15)	−3.2	(.1)	.27	(.15)
Female life expectancy	58.0*	(4.3)	1.9*	(.4)	−4.3	(1.3)	.2	(.6)
Society								
GNP/c	1.98*	(.3)	.01	(.01)	.17	(.09)	−.02*	(.007)
Literacy	97.0*	(.008)	.002*	(.0006)	.001	(.001)	−.0001	(.001)
Labor force	72.1*	(3.09)	.4*	(.07)	−.8	(.7)	.06	(.07)

* Coefficient at least twice its standard error. Values in parentheses depict standard errors.

** For clarity, only conditional models that predict the effect of democratic growth on outcome variables are reported here.

Total number of observations in core countries N = 436, number of countries n = 17; in semi-peripheries N = 747, number of countries n = 32; and in peripheries N = 2480, number of countries n = 100, post-communist countries N = 426, number of countries n = 20.

[1] In addition to being a separate category, post-communist countries are also included in peripheries and semi-peripheries.

mortality decline, and an increase in life expectancy. The coefficient of democracy in the fertility equation is $-.004$; the coefficient of democracy in the maternal mortality equation is $-.13$, and the coefficient in the interaction equation is $-.029$; the coefficient of democracy in the maternal care equation is $+.05$ and the coefficient in the interaction variable of maternal care is $+.005$; and the coefficient of democracy in the female life expectancy equation is $+.07$. At the same time, women's education increases, as indicated by the positive coefficient of democracy in the elementary schooling equation (albeit not significant, perhaps due to limited variance in already achieved relatively high levels of education). In sum, in well-developed countries, democratization benefits women by increasing their job opportunities, schooling, and health, and by expanding their life span.

The positive effect of democracy on indicators of societal well-being is also depicted. Of the tested indicators, the societal literacy level is expected to increase while the impact on the already high GNP per capita is not significant. At the same time, the societal non-agricultural labor force was shown to decline, suggesting an even stronger positive impact of democratic growth on the expansion of women's non-agricultural labor force (see Table 5.3).

Positive effects of democratic growth are also indicated in the analysis of democracy predicting indicators of women's well-being by 1 and 5 years of democratic growth (see Table 5.4).[18] Specifically, models with democracy effects lagged by 1 year conform to the initial decline of the women's labor force, but the decline is reduced from $-.11$ to $-.09$ ($p < .0001$). In the model with democracy effect lagged by 5 years, the negative effect is eliminated, yielding a positive coefficient of $.011$ ($p < .0001$) (see Table 5.3). Maternal care is also indicated to improve with time; life expectancy is increasing (the indicator of life expectancy increases in the variable of democracy and in the interaction variable of time and democracy); fertility is continuously decreasing in models predicting fertility by 1 and 5 years of democratic growth; maternal mortality is indicated to decrease; and there are no negative effects on girls' schooling. Similar positive effects on indicators of societal well-being are depicted in lagged analyses.

[18] The long-term effects were measured in models with dependent variables (indicators) lagged by 1 and by 5 years.

Table 5.4 *Predicted effects of the growth of democracy on women and society-at-large after 1 and 5 years of democratic growth in core, semi-peripheral, peripheral, and post-communist countries, 1970–2005*

Models[1]	Indicators lagged by 1		Indicators lagged by 5	
	Democracy	Democracy*year	Democracy	Democracy*year
CORE COUNTRIES				
Women				
1. Women's labor force (%)	−.01(.06)	.015* (.004)	−.19 (.17)	.04 * (.14)
2. Women's literacy (%)	1.3 (1.5)	−.2 (.2)	1.3 (1.5)	−.2 (.2)
3. Females in elementary school (%)	.05 (.03)	.004 (.003)	.03 (.02)	−.0009 (.002)
4. Females in secondary school (%)	−.048 (.03)	−.003 (.003)	−.05 (.05)	−.005 (006)
5. Fertility rate	−1.07* (.3)	.07* (.04)	−.006 (.01)	−.006* (.001)
6. Maternal mortality	−.038* (.01)	−.01* (.004)	−.3 (.5)	−.1 (.16)
7. Maternal care	−.002 (.003)	.00036 (.0004)	.02* (.006)	.003* (.0003)
8. Female life expectancy	.04 (.03)	.01 (.007)	.18* (.07)	.02* (.005)
Society				
1. GNP/c	−.02 (.03)	.003 (.004)	.4 (.21)	−.04 (.03)
2. Literacy	−.16 (.3)	.08* (.04)	.008*(.002)	−.002 (.001)
3. Labor force (%	.02 (.15)	.01 (.02)	.15* (.05)	.03 (.005)
4. Men's literacy (%)	.17* (.02)	−.009* (.02)	−.003 (.03)	−.0049 (.003)
SEMI-PERIPHERIES				
Women				
1. Women's labor force (%)	.05 (.04)	−.001 (.003)	.035 (.045)	.002 (.007)

Table 5.4 (cont.)

Models[1]	Indicators lagged by 1		Indicators lagged by 5	
	Democracy	Democracy*year	Democracy	Democracy*year
2. Women's literacy (%)	.02 (.09)	−.01 (.016)	.03 (.16)	−.007 (.01)
3. Females in elementary school (%)	.029* (.01)	.001 (.002)	−.025 (.02)	−.005* (.002)
4. Females in secondary school (%)	−.028*(.01)	−.001 (.001)	−.08 (.06)	−.015* (.007)
5. Fertility rate	−.5* (.17)	−.06*(.019)	−.036* (.017)	−.001 (.001)
6. Maternal mortality	−.0005 (.001)	.0001 (.0003)	−2.8 (2.3)	.25 (.23)
7. Maternal care	.001 (.004)	.003* (.0006)	.3 (.2)	−.01 (.02)
8. Female life expectancy	−.02* (.01)	−.01 (.003)	.06 (.05)	−.001 (.005)
Society				
1. GNP/c	−.076* (.036)	−.002 (.005)	−.1* (.03)	.01* (.004)
2. Literacy	−.63 (.8)	−.24* (.08)	.001 (.001)	−.0005* (.0001)
3. Labor force (%)	−.56 (.45)	.32 (17)	.038* (.02)	−.001 (.003)
4. Men's literacy	−.1 (.14)	.008 (.01)	−.003 (.002)	.008 (.01)
PERIPHERIES				
Women				
1. Women's labor force (%)	−.02*(.01)	−.001 (.001)	−.1*(.04)	.006 (.004)
2. Women's literacy (%)	.0003 (.01)	−.0007 (.003)	.07 (.2)	.017 (.016)
3. Females in elementary school (%)	.003 (.004)	.001* (.0006)	.026 (.23)	−.01* (.003)
4. Females in secondary school (%)	.001(.004)	−.0015* (.0006)	.19* (.06)	−.017* (.006)
5. Fertility rate	−.13* (.06)	−.017*(.006)	−.02 (.1)	−.003* (.001)
6. Maternal mortality	−.0001(.0001)	.00003 (.000028)	−3.1 (4.2)	−.15 (.36)

7. Maternal care	.003 (.002)	−.0007* (.0002)	.57 (.36)	−.04 (.03)
8. Female life expectancy	−.015*(.005)	−.00001 (.0005)	.01 (.04)	.005 (.004)
Society				
1. GNP/c	.029 (.03)	.003 (.003)	−.002 (.012)	−.0002 (.001)
2. Literacy	−.09 (.4)	−.07* (.03)	−.0004 (.0008)	−.00005 (.00008)
3. Labor force (%)	.01 (.01)	−.003 (.002)	−.009 (.01)	−.003 (.002)
4. Men's literacy	−.1 (.14)	.008 (.01)	−.1 (.14)	.008 (.01)
POST-COMMUNIST COUNTRIES				
Women				
1. Women's labor force (%)	−.02 (.17)	.014 (.01)	−.05* (.027)	−.0009* (.0001)
2. Women's literacy (%)	.0011 (.001)	−.0001 (.00009)	−.0016 (.001)	−.0001 (.0002)
3. Females in elementary school (%)	.08* (.04)	−.009* (.003)	.007 (.006)	.0002 (.001)
4. Females in secondary school (%)	.24 (.7)	−.04 (.06)	−.009 (.001)	−.00007(.0001)
5. Fertility rate	.14* (.06)	−.015* (.005)	−.4* (.01)	.005* (.0012)
6. Maternal mortality	1.1 (5.4)	−.08 (.4)	.006 (.02)	.00009 (.00001)
7. Maternal care	.036 (.09)	−.008 (.007)	.007 (.006)	−.0004 (.001)
8. Female life expectancy	.14 (.22)	−.006 (.02)	.02* (.01)	−.0002* (.0001)
Society				
1. GNP/c	.29* (.09)	−.024* (.007)	.02 (.018)	.004 (.01)
2. Literacy	.001 (.001)	.06* (.03)	.02* (.01)	−.24 (.1)
3. Labor force (%)	−.8* (.3)	.06* (.03)	−.6 (.5)	−.04 (.1)
4. Men's literacy	.0013 (.001)	.0009 (.002)	.008 (.009)	.0002 (.001)

* Coefficient at least twice its standard error. Values in parentheses depict standard errors. In the table conditional models are presented.

Total number of observations in core countries N = 436, number of countries n = 17; in semi-peripheries N = 747, number of countries n = 32; in peripheries N = 2480, number of countries n = 100; in post-communist N = 426, number of countries n = 20.

In addition to being a separate category, post-communist countries are also included in the peripheral and semi-peripheral groups.

[1] Dependent variables (indicators) are lagged by 1 and by 5 years.

Semi-peripheries: In contrast, negative effects of democratic growth on women's well-being in semi-peripheries are depicted. Women's participation in the labor force is predicted to decline with increasing democratization in the interaction equation, contrasting the depicted increase in the women's labor force over time (the coefficient of the effect of time on women's labor force is $+.17$). Women's education is also indicated to decline. In an average country, the percentage of females among students in elementary and secondary schools is indicated to decline by $.05$ percent and $-.1$ percent respectively. Moreover, these indicators also show decline in the interaction variable of time and democracy, with coefficients of $-.007$ percent in the elementary and $-.015$ percent in the secondary education equation. The negative effects are even stronger in light of the absence of influence of democratic growth on men's literacy (in the equation of neither democratic growth nor democracy with time).

The depicted increase in maternal mortality is also disturbing, especially that it coincides with a decline in female life expectancy. With an increase in democracy level by a score of $+1$, female life expectancy is expected to decline on average by $.009$ per year and maternal mortality to increase by 1.4 maternal deaths per 100,000 live births. These negative outcomes on women's well-being are expected to continue over time, as indicated by the negative coefficients in the equations of democracy and time with labor force and life expectancy indicators.

The only positive impact of democratic growth is the decrease in fertility rate and the increase in maternal care. As the literature indicates, during democratic growth, modernization of medical facilities and better training of medical personnel takes place in part due to the increase of foreign aid and professional contacts with medical personnel in well-developed countries. An increase in maternal care attests to the possibility of reversing the negative trend in maternal mortality and life expectancy, under the condition of sustainability of democracy. However, the sustainability of democratic growth in countries that are not well-developed is uncertain, as new fragile democracies often revert to totalitarianism or became dangerous democracies (Herspring 2003; Owen 2005; Przeworski et al. 2000).

At the societal level, the results of the impact of democratic growth on societal development are mixed in semi-peripheries. As shown, democratization does not lead to an overall higher societal standard of living; the coefficient of the interaction of democracy with GNP per capita (GNP/c) is negative and significant (−.09), but positive in the equation of democracy and time. The initial negative trend is consistent with the economic decline in transitional democracies described in the literature (Herspring 2003), and with prior investigations on the dis-advantaged position of semi-peripheral, middle economies in the pro-cesses of the global diffusion of democracy and market economy (Garrett, 2004). The impacts on other indicators of societal well-being are not significant except for the indicated decline in societal literacy over time, which in part accounts for the shown decline in female enrollment in elementary and secondary schooling.

The analysis of democracy predicting women's and societal well-being after one and five years of democratic growth indicates a further reduc-tion in women's well-being after one year of democratic growth and only in some indicators a limitation of the negative effects after the fifth year. Specifically, female life expectancy is predicted to decline in the first year of democratic growth, with no improvement indicated by the fifth year. The ratio of girls to boys in primary and secondary schooling is predicted to decline across five years. The negative effects on women's labor force are eliminated but not reversed to a positive effect. Contrastingly, the societal non-agricultural labor force is predicted to increase by the fifth year of democratic growth, but the decline in the GNP/c is not eliminated. In addition, the negative effect on female schooling is correlated with a decline in societal literacy level across the five years (see Table 5.4).

Peripheries: It seems that women in peripheral countries do not benefit from democratic growth either. However, in contrast to semi-peripheries, some indicators of women's well-being become positive in the interaction models of democratic growth and time.

First, the observed decrease in women's labor force participation weakens over time; the coefficient on democracy is negative (−.14), while the interaction of democracy with time is positive (+.005). Second, in contrast to semi-peripheries, a negative effect on maternal mortality rate is not detected. Third, the regression in the ratio of girl to boy students over time is indicated (the coefficient on the interaction variable of democracy with time is −.01 and −.13, respectively), but the coefficients are not significant. Fourth, democratization positively influences fertility levels (with an increase in democracy level by one, women's fertility rates decreased by .0013% over time). Fifth, in the life expectancy equation, the coefficient of the interaction variable is still negative (−.007) and significant.

Particularly alarming is the negative effect of democratic growth on female life expectancy in semi-peripheries and peripheries. Although more research needs to be conducted to explain the phenomenon, a plausible explanation could be a correlation between traditionalism and diffusing models of a small family. At the time of the democratization and modernization of the economy, practices of family planning diffuse (e.g., indicated by the decline in fertility rate) (see also Bongaarts 1994; Bongaarts & Watkins 1996; Rosero-Bixby & Casterline 1993). In poorer countries, small family models coincide with the traditional cultural preference for male offspring, and the new expectations often lead to sex-selective abortion, female infanticide, and inferior infant girls' nutrition and health care (Murthy 1996). Thus, on one hand, declining fertility indicates improvement in the future women's health; on the other, in traditional, poorer countries, declining fertility could signal deliberate sex-selective practices, indicating a latent negative function of democratization and diffusing models of small families (Coale & Banister 1996; Sabu 1997; Shin et al. 1981).[19]

In respect to societal development, no negative relations between democratic growth or democracy in interaction with time and socioeconomic indicators were found. The positive effect of democratic growth over time on women's labor force participation; no negative effects on maternal mortality; positive albeit not significant impact on schooling; and no negative effects for a society at large, attest to the validity of Garrett's (2004) hypothesis that peripheries are better off during democratic growth than semi-peripheries and are consistent with arguments that the outcomes of globalization are determined by the local developmental conditions of each country (Rosenau 2003).

Similar to semi-peripheries, the analysis of democracy predicting women's and societal well-being after one and five years of democratic growth indicate a persistent decline in women's well-being. The

---

[19] For example, in China, evidence suggests that the practice of female infanticide was the cause of the high female mortality rate in the 1930s and 1940s. This practice declined subsequently, and the ratio of females to males in successive cohorts increased. Enhanced female mortality in the 1950s was due to the great famine in which female children suffered more than males. The introduction of birth control in the 1970s did not affect the sex ratio at birth but led to the voluntary cessation of childbearing after the birth of a male child. The escalation in the ratio of male-to-female births in the late 1980s when ultrasound testing became widely available was largely due to the increased number of sex-selective abortions of female fetuses (Coale & Banister 1996).

women's labor force is indicated to decrease after one and five years of democracy growth; female life expectancy declines after the first year and shows no improvement after the fifth year of democratic growth; the ratio of girls relative to boys in elementary and secondary schools decreases; maternal care is indicated to decrease by the first year with no improvement indicated by the fifth year. However, the positive effect on the fertility rate sustains. This worsening women's well-being contrasts with no negative impact of democracy growth on societal quality of life (see Table 5.4).

Post-communist countries: Being an aggregate of mixed low- to middle-level economies with a high literacy rate and a high provision for women's health, post-communist countries follow their own path when reacting to global democratic growth and the free market economy (see the last parts of Tables 5.3 and 5.4).

First, in sharp contrast to the results for countries worldwide and across prior groups of countries, a number of women's health indicators are negatively associated with an increasing level of democracy. Female life expectancy is negatively associated with democratization (the coefficient on democracy in this model is negative and statistically significant), and the decline is observed with the increase of democracy level rather than in the equation on democracy and time, suggesting an *immediate* negative effect of democratic growth that fades with time (albeit insignificantly).

Second, unexpectedly, the fertility level increases where the coefficient on democracy in the fertility equation is positive and statistically significant, but this effect is reduced over time (the coefficient on the interaction of democracy and time is negative). According to the literature, the fading with time negative effect may depict substantial differences in women's attitudes about fertility before and after the mid 1990s. There is some evidence that newly democratic governments promote larger families in order to solve the problems associated with growing unemployment, but years after the initiation of a democratic transition, women facing economic difficulties decided to move back into the labor market and forgo larger families (Albanese 1996; David & Titkov 1994; Kligman 1992; Kurczewski 1990).

Third, similar to the peripheries and semi-peripheries, the coefficient of women's labor force participation and democracy equals −.25 and is statistically significant. This indicates that an increase in the level of democracy by a score of +1 (on a scale of 0–10) is associated with a decline of .25 percent in women's labor force participation. However, the positive coefficient in the interaction of time and democracy suggests that, with time, the negative association between women's labor force participation and democracy becomes less strong. In contrast, the relationship between democracy and measures of the societal labor force was not significant, but the coefficient was negative. Considering a strong negative effect on women's labor force participation, we may expect that females largely drove the non-significant, negative correlation in the equation of democracy and the societal labor force.

Fourth, former communist countries used to provide equal educational opportunities to men and women, which led to gender equality in education (Stycos, Wejnert, & Tyszka 2002; Wejnert 1996a). As indicated by a declining ratio of girls to boys in elementary and secondary schools over time, this equality may be lost during democratic transition. It is plausible that the rebirth of cultural traditionalism is one of the causes of the declining school attendance of girls in these countries. Democratizing former communist countries often express their newly gained freedom by returning to traditional gender roles that were banned during communism. Consequently, early marriages of girls are being promoted, motherhood is prioritized over women's employment, and women's domestic duties are glorified, which reduces parental interest in the schooling of girls (Wejnert & Djumabaeva 2004).

On the societal level (see the last rows of Table 5.3), the only significant effect is depicted in the interaction of democratic growth with the GNP. The coefficient in the equation of democracy and time with the GNP per capita was negative (−.02) and significant, suggesting a decline in countries' economic development as the processes of democratic and market economic transitions unfold. These relationships are consistent with the literature discussions of the economic decline experienced by transitional democracies of the former Soviet bloc (Herspring 2003; Kolodko 2001, 2002), which, I assume, in part caused the depicted increasing gender inequality.[20]

In post-communist countries, many of the negative effects of democratic growth on women's lives are constant by the fifth year of

---

[20] Considering the limited foreign investment in many of the post-communist countries, it is expected that the decline will change into positive growth in the future (Kentor and Boswell 2003).

democratic growth. Women's labor force decreases in the democracy and democracy with time equation. A regression is indicated in the ratio of girl to boy students in primary education over time (despite a depicted increase of the coefficient in the democracy equation). By the fifth year of democratic growth, female life expectancy increases (the coefficient of democracy in the female life expectancy equation is $+.02$), but the coefficient in the interaction equation is $-.002$.

The impact of democratic growth on societal well-being fluctuates between the positive and negative coefficients, but the negative outcomes prevail. The negative coefficients are depicted in the interaction of democracy with GNP per capita (GNP/c) and the societal non-agricultural labor force, as well as in the interaction of democracy and time with GNP/c. The positive coefficient, however, is indicated in the equation of democracy and time with literacy (see Table 5.2).

In all models reported in Tables 5.2 and 5.4, the low p values for the effect of democratic growth and a significant difference in the obtained values of $-2LL$ between models with and without democracy variables confirm the statistically significant relationship between indicators of societal and women's well-being and countries' democratization. The statistical significance of this study also confirms the variance estimates of the Hierarchical Growth Models, and the random parts of the models are presented in Table 5.5.

To summarize the results, Table 5.6 demonstrates the effects of democracy on indicators of women's well-being and women's empowerment, depicting the positive outcome of democracy as a sign "+" and its negative impact as "−".

The final part of this study on democracy outcomes supports the findings of multilevel regression models assessing subjective, perceived changes in women's quality of life in democratizing, semi-peripheral, and peripheral countries, using the questionnaire interviews conducted in Poland, Hungary, the Ukraine, Kyrgyzstan, Senegal, and Mali. Table 5.7 provides results from the questionnaire interviews conducted on perceived satisfaction with quality of life in the recently democratizing Poland, Hungary, Ukraine, Kyrgyzstan, Senegal, and Mali. During the interviews, women and men subjectively assessed social, economic, and political changes, as well as changes in women's quality of life since the initiation of democratic reforms in their countries.

Table 5.5 *Variance estimates of hierarchical growth models predicting the effects of growth of democracy on women and society at large across the world and across groups of countries, 1970–2005*

					WORLD	
VARIANCE ESTIMATES	Women's labor force		Women's literacy		Females in elementary school	Females in secondary school	Fertility
Residual	4.2*	(.1)	2.8*	(.1)	204.8* (4.8)	201.4* (4.8)	1.06*
Variance between countries' intercepts	143.5*	(16.6)	13.3*	(1.5)	99.9* (13.1)	156.9* (19.8)	3.09*
Variance between countries' slopes	.13*	(.02)	1.5*	(.2)	.16* (.04)	.3* (.05)	.001*
Covariance countries' intercepts & slopes	−1.6*	(.4)	−30.1*	(4.8)	2.2* (.5)	4.2* (.8)	.001
FIT STATISTICS	18161.0		6022.2		32075.3	32100.2	12093.6
−2LL	18161.0		6022.3		32075.3	32100.2	12093.6
	18173.0		6034.3		32087.3	32112.3	12105.6
	18153.0		6014.2		32067.3	32092.2	12085.6

						CORE COUNTRIES	
Residual	.3*	(.02)	.3	.2	.08* (.006)	.99* (.07)	.02*
Variance between countries' intercepts	14.3*	(5.1)	3.2	1.7	.06* (.03)	1.05* (.4)	.03*
Variance between countries' slopes	.03*	(.01)	.0004	.0004	.0003* (.0001)	.012* (.005)	.0003*
Covariance countries' intercepts & slopes	−.27	(.17)	−.05	.03	.002 (.001)	.004 .03	−.001
FIT STATISTICS AIC	981.4		427.5		185.5	1208.0	218.4
AICC	981.5		427.3		193.5	1208.1	218.3
BIC	984.7		427.2		193.7	1211.3	215.1
−2LL	973.4		435.5		196.9	1200.0	226.4

						SEMI-PERIPHERIES	
Residual	.82*	(.04)	.8*	(.08)	1.08* (.06)	5.04* (.27)	.04*
Variance between countries' intercepts	109.4*	(27.9)	684.1*	175.9	16.4* (4.3)	93.8* (25.1)	2.9*
Variance between countries' slopes	.06*	(.01)	.8*	(.22)	.01* (.004)	.09* (.03)	.001*
Covariance countries' intercepts & slopes	−1.25*	(.5)	−17.6*	(5.4)	−.27* (.1)	−2.2* (.74)	−.04*
FIT STATISTICS AIC	2378.4		991.3		1992.9	3480.7	207.0
AICC	2378.4		991.5		1993.0	3480.7	207.1
BIC	2384.2		997.2		1998.8	3486.5	212.0
−2LL	2370.4		983.3		1984.9	3472.7	199.0

	Maternal mortality		Maternal care		Female life expectancy		GNP/c		Literacy–society		Labor force	
(.02)	29267*	692.9	274.5*	(6.5)	15.6*	(.3)	1.9*	(.04)	.01*	(.0003)	.6*	(.01)
(.36)	50030*	5989	1267.2*	(149)	20.5*	(2.5)	14.4*	(1.7)	.1*	(.01)	824.1*	(98.2)
(.0003)	407.3*	(50.1)	4.15*	(.5)	.4*	(.06)	.1*	(.01)	.0003*	(.00003)	.17*	(.02)
(.007)	2698.8*	(442.9)	−34.9*	(6.7)	−1.7	(1.01)	1.07*	.13	.0004	(.0004)	.5	(1.02)
	51727.5		33857.1		31298.8		14763.4		3998.2		8833.3	
	51727.5		33857.1		31298.8		14763.4		3998.2		8833.4	
	51727.1		33869.2		31310.8		14763.4		3986.1		8845.4	
	51719.5		33849.1		31290.8		14755.5		4006.2		8825.3	
(.002)	438.5*	42.04	.02*	(.002)	.06*	(.004)	4.9*	(.4)	.002*	.0001	.09*	(.008)
(.01)	806.7*	308.6	.4*	.17	2.2*	(.8)	10.2*	(3.8)	.002*	.0007	104.3*	36.9
.0001	10.2*	3.9	.0007*	(.0003)	.002*	(.0009)	.15*	(.05)	.00001*	(.000001)	.06*	(.02)
(.0009)	−91.1*	(34.4)	−.02*	(.002)	−.018	.02	1.07*	(.42)	−.00004*	(.0008)	−2.2*	.85
	2274.3		158.8		234.3		1946.2		893.5		431.9	
	2274.5		58.6		234.4		1946.3		893.3		432.0	
	2277.6		158.4		237.6		1949.5		890.1		434.3	
	2266.3		166.8		226.3		1938.2		901.5		423.9	
(.003)	126.1*	(9.7)	16.1*	(1.3)	.2*	(.01)	2.8*	(.15)	.002*	(.0001)	.57*	(.03)
(.7)	32148.1*	8308.1	657.7*	(176.4)	51.3*	(13.1)	21.1*	(5.5)	.03*	(.01)	44.4*	(12.1)
(.0005)	147.1*	(38.2)	1.8*	(.5)	.07*	(.02)	.07*	(.02)	.00004*	(.00001)	.25*	(.06)
(.01)	−239.4	405.1	−23.1*	(8.3)	−1.2*	(.43)	.23	(.23)	−.0009*	.0003	−2.2	(.2.1)
	3457.8		2332.7		1367.1		3031.2		1935.6		1794.9	
	3457.9		2332.8		1367.2		3031.2		1935.6		1795.0	
	3463.7		2338.6		1373.0		3037.1		1929.8		1800.0	
	3449.8		2324.7		1359.1		3023.2		1943.6		1786.9	

Table 5.5 (*cont.*)

									PERIPHERIES
VARIANCE ESTIMATES	Women's labor force		Women's literacy		Females in elementary school		Females in secondary school		Fertility
Residual	1.78*	.05	4.3*	(.29)	3.1*	(.1)	5.3*	(.17)	.07*
Variance between countries' intercepts	12.5*	(1.8)	145.2*	(21.4)	42.3*	(6.3)	128.2*	(19.1)	2.8*
Variance between countries' slopes	.09*	(.01)	1.9*	(.3)	.04*	(.006)	.11*	(.02)	.003*
Covariance countries' intercept & slopes	−2.3*	(.4)	−34.8*	(6.9)	−.68*	.15	−2.2*	(.5)	.003
FIT STATISTICS AIC	9557.3		4082.9		8178.2		10351.4		1131.4
AICC	9557.3		4083.0		8178.2		10351.4		1131.5
BIC	9567.7		4093.3		8188.5		10361.7		1141.8
−2LL	9549.3		4074.9		8170.2		10343.4		1123.4
									POST-COMMUNIST COUNTRIES[1]
Residual	.3*	(.02)	.12*	(.01)	180.1*	(13.2)	246.7*	(17.8)	.02*
Variance between countries' intercepts	199.7*	(65.1)	123.1*	(41.1)	305.7*	(138.3)	422.7*	(163.4)	1.1*
Variance between countries' slopes	.07	(.05)	.12*	(.02)	1.2*	(.5)	.7*	(.3)	.001*
Covariance countries' intercept & slopes	−3.6*	(1.8)	−3.8*	(1.3)	15.6*	(7.8)	11.2	(6.0)	−.03*
FIT STATISTICS AIC	948.9		327.8		3521.5		3640.0		53.2
AICC	949.0		328.0		3521.6		3648.1		53.0
BIC	952.9		331.6		3525.5		3651.9		49.4
−2LL	940.9		319.8		3513.5		3640.0		61.2

* Coefficient at least twice its standard error. Values in parentheses depict standard errors.
Total number of observations in core countries N = 436, number of countries n = 17; in semi-peripheries N = 747, number of countries n = 32; in peripheries N = 2480, number of countries n = 100; in post-communist N = 426, number of countries n = 20.
[1] In addition to being a separate category, post-communist countries are also included in peripheries and semi-peripheries.

	Maternal mortality		Maternal care		Female life expectancy		GNP/c		Literacy–society		Labor force	
(.004)	427.9*	(18.3)	25.7*	(1.1)	1.17*	(.03)	.42*	(.01)	.002*	(.0001)	.63*	(.02)
(.4)	274.6*	(42.1)	132.3	(19.7)	13.08*	(1.8)	4.5*	(.6)	.08*	(.01)	682.3*	(99.6)
(.0009)	14.9*	(2.36)	2.3.5*	(4.3)	.05*	(.008)	.03*	(.005)	.0003*	(.0001)	.16*	(.02)
(.009)	−11.1*	(.2.5)	−30.5*	(7.4)	−.35	(.2)	.23*	(.04)	−.0007*	(.00002)	2.6*	(1.1)
	15373.1		8410.7		8410.7		5482.3		5983.1		6134.9	
	15373.1		8410.7		8410.7		5482.3		5983.1		6135.0	
	15383.4		8421.0		8421.0		5492.6		5972.8		6145.3	
	15365.1		8402.7		8402.7		5474.3		5991.1		6126.9	
(.002)	372.1*	(26.6)	351.7*	(24.7)	3.17*	(.2)	.5*	(.03)	.0001*	(.000006)	.28*	(.02)
(.4)	208.1*	(75.1)	1292.0*	(445.0)	2.7*	(1.1)	1.07*	(.4)	.0009*	(.00003)	153.6*	(.56.1)
(.0003)	1.6*	(.6)	.5	(.6)	1.8*	(.7)	.003*	(.001)	.000005*	(.000002)	.08*	(.03)
(.38)	16.9*	(6.2)	−2.8*	(5.6)	−17.6*	(8.4)	−.008	(.02)	−.00007	(.00003)	−1.1	(.9)
	3799.4		3782.0		3730.1		827.6		1763.6		774.6	
	3799.4		3782.1		3730.4		827.8		1763.5		774.7	
	3803.3		3782.1		3731.3		831.4		1759.8		778.3	
	3791.4		3782.9		3731.7		819.6		1771.6		766.6	

Table 5.6 Summary of outcomes of the predicted effects of growth of democracy on women and society-at-large in the world, as compared to core, semi-peripheral, peripheral, and post-communist countries, 1970–2005

	WORLD		CORE COUNTRIES		SEMI-PERIPHERIES		PERIPHERIES		POST-COMMUNIST	
	Democracy	Democ/time	Democracy	Democ/time	Democracy	Democ/time	Democracy	Democ/time	Democracy	Democ/time
Women										
Women's labor force (%)	(−)			(+)	(−)		(−)	(+)	(−)	(+)
Women's literacy (%)		(−)			(−)	(−)		(−)		(−)
Females in elementary school			(+)	(+)	(−)	(−)				
Females in secondary school			(+)	(+)	(−)	(−)		(−)		(−)
Fertility	(+)	(+)	(+)	(+)	(+)	(+)		(+)		(+)
Maternal mortality	(+)	(+)	(+)	(+)	(−)					
Maternal care	(+)	(+)	(+)	(+)	(+)					
Female life expectancy		(−)	(−)	(+)		(−)	(−)	(−)		(−)
Society										
GNP/c	(+)	(+)	(+)		(−)					
Literacy–society (%)	(+)				(+)	(−)				(−)
Labor force		(−)	(−)	(−)						
Men's literacy (%)		(+)	(+)	(−)						

Table 5.7 Level of satisfaction and dissatisfaction with selected life domains as expressed by women in Poland, Hungary, the Ukraine, Kyrgyzstan, Mali, and Senegal at the end of the 1990s and early 2000s

LIFE DOMAINS	COUNTRIES					
	POLAND	HUNGARY	UKRAINE	KYRGYZSTAN	MALI	SENEGAL
Mean satisfaction with life domains (on a scale of 1–7; where 1= very dissatisfied, 7= very satisfied)						
Life in general	3.65	3.89	3.71	3.57	4.75	4.08
Family	3.99	5.87	4.81	5.05	4.49	4.78
Housing	3.64	4.55	4.42	4.67	4.61	4.36
Free time	3.08	4.25	2.98	2.88	4.05	4.95
Health	3.16	4.22	3.96	3.26	4.92	4.41
Life accomplishment	3.23	4.76	3.43	3.47	4.27	4.67
Political freedom	3.35	2.15	3.07	2.86	4.08	3.64
Environment	2.63	5.14	2.12	4.00	4.45	3.63
Economy	2.15	2.57	2.11	2.88	3.91	3.39
Government	2.08	2.59	2.48	2.99	3.75	3.70
Church activity[1]	2.94	4.59			4.63	4.34
Own income	2.75	3.33	2.87	2.81	4.17	3.90
Strong satisfaction with … (as % of very satisfied, scores of 6 and 7)						
Life in general	29.8	37.3	46.0	37.5	39.8	32.0
Family	47.2	64.3	34.0	49.0	39.8	58.0
Housing	31.8	45.0	56.0	39.5	34.9	41.0
Free time	18.5	34.1	34.0	38.0	16.8	35.0

Table 5.7 (cont.)

LIFE DOMAINS	COUNTRIES					
	POLAND	HUNGARY	UKRAINE	KYRGYZSTAN	MALI	SENEGAL
Health	21.6	34.9	20.0	38.0	33.8	36.0
Life accomplishment	21.5	42.8	40.0	25.0	19.3	41.0
Political freedom	26.3	20.4	14.0	14.0	22.9	26.0
Environment	14.0	53.6	6.0	29.0	42.2	24.0
Economy	6.6	7.2	4.0	8.0	24.1	19.0
Government	11.8	10.6	12.0	15.5	21.7	23.0
Church activity[1]	15.3	49.2	42.0		42.2	39.0
Own income	13.1	13.4	8.0	13.0	28.9	32.0
Strong dissatisfaction with .... (as % of very dissatisfied, scores of 1 and 2)						
Life in general	6.3	1.6	8.0	10.5	7.2	11.0
Family	10.7	6.5	18.0	10.0	3.6	14.0
Housing	8.5	18.0	14.0	12.0	6.0	21.0
Free time	15.8	24.6	24.0	25.0	15.6	16.0
Health	16.4	25.4	24.0	21.0	4.8	10.0
Life accomplishment	14.2	15.0	20.0	23.0	8.4	5.0
Political freedom	14.8	18.3	34.0	55.5	7.2	14.0
Environment	32.4	12.7	70.0	44.0	14.5	25.0
Economy	38.1	41.3	72.0	69.5	14.5	23.0
Government	44.6	36.5	70.0	54.5	13.2	18.0
Church activity[1]	20.6	7.2	8.0		2.4	9.0
Own income	21.4	35.7	58.0	48.0	9.6	19.0

Change in satisfaction with life domains**

	Poland 1999	Hungary 1998	Ukraine 2000–2002	Kyrgyzstan 2002–2004	Mali 2004	Senegal 2004
Life in general	1.93	1.67	2.41	2.81	1.53	1.94
Family	2.07	1.99	2.14	2.31	1.60	1.66
Own employment	2.34	1.68	2.54	2.56	1.01	1.88
Free time	2.16	2.11	2.40	2.24	1.95	2.00
Political freedom	1.70	1.59	1.36	2.47	1.44	1.57
Environment	2.66	2.87	2.87	2.34	1.34	2.07
Availability of goods	1.67	1.32	1.91	2.44	2.03	1.34
Government	2.50	1.21	2.68	2.70	1.13	1.88
Church activity	2.33	1.80	1.19	1.27	1.48	1.65
Own income	2.23	1.53	2.56	2.76	1.68	2.17
Life in the past	1.36	1.87	1.75	1.58	2.18	1.22
Past women's position[2]	1.80	1.24	1.30	1.24	2.27	2.3
Women's employment[2]	2.10	1.89	1.80	1.80	1.78	1.75

Sources: Questionnaire interviews conducted by the author and collaborators in Poland in 1999 (N = 306), Hungary in 1998 (N = 369), Ukraine in 2000–2002 (N = 200), Kyrgyzstan in 2002–2004 (N = 400), Mali and Senegal in 2004 (N = 200).

* Subjective assessment of Quality of Life of women. Percent of women who are strongly satisfied are reported as score 6–7 (on a 1–7 satisfaction scale with 7 depicting very strong satisfaction), and strongly dissatisfied as a 1–2 score (on the same 1–7 satisfaction scale).

** Change in satisfaction with life domains is reported on a scale of 1–3; where 1 depicts better, 2 = same, 3 = less satisfaction.

[1] Due to freshly gained religious freedom and religious activity being a still-sensitive issue, the data on satisfaction with the activity of religious institutions were not collected in Kyrgyzstan.

[2] To avoid bias in assessment, the change in women's position and women's employment was measured according to assessment by women and men and recorded as a mean of both scores.

Although reported assessments vary across people's life history, as well as across life domains and countries, a few conclusions can be drawn in light of the depicted similarities of responses.

First, the cross-state comparison reveals a clear pattern of pair-like clustering of responses: Poland and Hungary versus Kyrgyzstan and the Ukraine versus Senegal and Mali. This pattern overlaps the paths of the countries' economic and political developments, suggesting that the economic and political situation of a country determines satisfaction with the result of transition (Rueschmeyer 1998; Saleci 1992) more than, for instance, shared historical and cultural roots.[21]

Second, satisfaction with life in general varies across countries, but the level of satisfaction seems to be most strongly determined by countries' *economic performance*. Kyrgyzstan and the Ukraine have experienced a downward trend in economic development since the time of democratic growth (Kolodko 2002), where respondents reported the lowest satisfaction with life in general (3.57 and 3.71, respectively, on a scale of 1–7 with 7 meaning "very satisfied"). In the economically progressing countries of Senegal and Mali, democratic growth coincided with the highest life satisfaction (4.75 and 4.08, respectively). Furthermore, only in Mali, the poorest of the selected countries, did respondents believe that their life prior to democratic growth was worse than during the years following the democratic transition. An argument that democratic growth is less costly for low developed states and that the least developed countries gain more from the transition to a global market economy and democracy than semi-developed countries was supported (Dabrowski & Antczak 1996; Garrett 2004; Kearny 2001).

This finding was complemented by reports on satisfaction with the national economy and the activity of the new democratic government, where low satisfaction was reported in economically declining post-communist countries, while satisfaction was much higher in economically progressing Mali and Senegal. Accordingly, the depicted mean in satisfaction with the state economy ranged from 2.11 to 2.15 in post-communist Ukraine and Kyrgyzstan, was slightly higher in Poland and Hungary (2.57 and 2.88, respectively), but in the postcolonial African states ranged from 3.91 to 3.39. Satisfaction with the activity of democratic government ranged from 2.08 to 2.99 across post-communist

---

[21] Grouping these countries according to shared historical and cultural roots, e.g., as being the old statehoods of Poland, Ukraine and Hungary vs the newly created post-colonial/post-tribal states of Mali, Senegal and Kyrgyzstan, or as Christian vs Muslim countries, would create a distinctly different pattern.

states, while in Senegal and Mali it was 3.75 and 3.70; satisfaction with political freedom ranged from 2.15 to 3.35 in post-communist countries while in Senegal and Mali it was 4.08 and 3.64, respectively. The satisfaction with macroeconomic and political changes was similar to satisfaction with personal income, which ranged from 2.75 to 3.33 in post-communist states, while it was 3.90 and 4.17 in Senegal and Mali.

Third, in addition to the division of countries into two groups of respondents – more versus less satisfied with democratic changes – the less-satisfied post-communist countries were further divided into subgroups: Poland and Hungary, where nearly 40 percent of respondents claimed to be either very dissatisfied or dissatisfied with the economic and political activity of democratic government, and Kyrgyzstan and the Ukraine, where almost 70 percent of respondents were dissatisfied (see Table 5.7).

In particular, while in Poland and Hungary respondents were particularly satisfied with gains in *political freedom*, this was not the case in the Ukraine and Kyrgyzstan, where the reported satisfaction level was near 2.00. One explanation could be that in the former republics of the Soviet Union, the concept of political freedom was frequently misinterpreted as the complete elimination of governmental accountability to its citizens, shown by, for example, the falsification of elections, as well as limited crime control. The lack of control led to excessive corruption, lack of accountability of regimes, drug trade, the spread of the Mafia and other crimes, all of which, according to public opinion, resulted from the extreme leniency of the democratic government (Wejnert 2003).

The reported satisfaction with gains in political freedom was similar to the perception of gains in *civil rights*. As expressed by the early 2000s grass-roots protests, the impeachment of presidents and re-run elections, the depicted societal dissatisfaction was a sign of germinating societal revolt against the ruling elites in the Ukraine and Kyrgyzstan that, in the public eye, were not democratic.

Environmental conditions were one of the major areas of concern in the Ukraine and in Poland, but in Hungary, where the democratic government focused on the protection of the natural environment, 54.3 percent of respondents reported they were very satisfied with environmental conditions. Furthermore, relative to Hungary, the Ukraine, and Kyrgyzstan, Polish respondents reported low satisfaction with *religious* life and the activity of the church. During the communist period, Poland, unlike any other Soviet bloc country, placed fewer restrictions on religious practices, and the Polish church played a strong role in the initiation of democracy. Therefore, gains in freedom of religion were not as visible as in other countries, and, hence, not as appreciated.

Fourth, regardless of the limited rights for women in predominantly Muslim African states and their relatively low income, African women were much less critical of newly democratic states' governing, and state policies. The limited criticism observed in Senegal and Mali sharply contrasted with the reports in post-communist countries. Specifically, only 10–20 percent of women in Senegal and Mali were dissatisfied with the economy, government, and environment, a striking contrast to the 40–70 percent of women in post-communist countries. Less than 20 percent of African women were dissatisfied with their own income, compared to more than twice as many in the former communist states. Comparison of these results with economic progress further supports the hypothesis of a greater gain of democratization experienced by peripheral than semi-developed countries.

Fifth, across all countries, the most satisfying elements were the domains of private life, such as one's family, life accomplishments, personal health, relationships with others, the amount and quality of free time, community life, and housing. These domains were assessed at equally high (4.00–4.5 on a scale of 1–7) levels of satisfaction *across all countries*. Any assumption of differences in the psychological or cultural predispositions of the more optimistic African respondents versus the more pessimistic European and Central Asian respondents should therefore be excluded (Czapinski 1994). The next part of the analysis contains discourse on plausible causal explanations of the reports.

Reported changes in women's well-being after the transition to democracy were also observed. As Table 5.7 shows, opinions regarding changes in women's societal position after democratic transition significantly differed between the African and former communist countries. Specifically, in Senegal and Mali, respondents reported the enhancement of women's social position, evaluating their social position before the democratization as a score of 2.7 and 2.3 on a scale of 1–3 (where 1 means better and 3 worse). Women's possibilities for employment, income, and satisfaction with life in general were reported to improve (on the same scale of 1–3, these were reported as scores of 1.8, 1.7, and 2.2 prior to democratization) (although according to the literature, employment opportunities are still limited in these countries) (see Table 5.7).

In contrast, respondents in post-communist countries reported a decline in women's social position in comparison to their position prior to democratic transition, indicating scores of 1.2–1.3 on a scale of 1–3, where 1 means better and 3 worse, in comparison to their position prior to democratic transition (only Polish respondents were less critical). In particular, women's income and employment opportunities were perceived to decline (before democratization these indicators were reported as a score of 0.5 on a scale of 1–3, with 3 being much worse), and life opportunities prior to democratic transition were reported to be better under communism (scores of 1.3–1.8, with 1 being worse and 3 better). The exception was Hungarian women, who reported that their life opportunity did not significantly change.

What are the potential causal explanations of the differences in impact?

First, it is plausible that the differences in perceived outcomes of democratic growth on women in selected African countries versus selected formerly communist countries of Eastern Europe could be related to culture. Accordingly, respondents in Senegal and Mali, subdued and accustomed to male dominance, may be more compliant with changes introduced by predominantly male political authorities. In contrast, in post-communist democracies, the more critical attitude toward the changes of democratic transition could result from the ideology of gender equality and women's participation in governing and decision-making institutions introduced by the communist system.

Second, it is also plausible that the differences are caused by factors of political liberty. In African countries, due to limited women's rights prior to democratization, gains made toward women's basic rights to education, inheritance or custody of children in case of divorce (Coleman 2006) could be perceived as significant improvements brought about by democratic change. At the same time, in formerly communist states, gains in freedom of speech made during democratization allowed a previously voiceless society to criticize openly democratic ruling elites (Binyon 1983). Likely women and men wanted to express openly their criticisms regarding political authorities.

Third, in light of this study's findings, the most compelling explanation seems to be a socioeconomic explanation of the influence of the progress of countries' economic development on women's perception of quality of life. Accordingly, substantive opinions of democratic changes seem to be formed in relation to the fluctuation of women's social position which correlated with economic development, where social position would be strengthening or weakening by women's gained (or lost) economic opportunities, services, and rights.

Thus, Senegal and Mali have experienced rapid modernization, specific to women, of medical and other facilities and services relative to the prior democratization period. The modernization was supported in part by foreign aid (conditioned, for instance, by the required provision of schooling for girls and rights for women), which probably effected more positive opinions about the impact of democracy on women's lives. In contrast, negative responses in democratizing post-communist countries correlated with experienced economic difficulties, the limitation of women's employment, and the deterioration of medical, maternal, and women's health services (Romaniuk 2002; Solcova 1984; Stephenson 1998; Titkov 1993).

Overall, the results on the subjective perception of quality of life support the findings of the multilevel regressions, showing that while democratic transitions and the globalization of the free market economy are costly for all developing countries, they are more costly to women than men and are positively influenced by economic progress. By the tenth year of democratic growth, as the results of perceived changes in women's position indicate, in economically progressing countries a reversal of the trend in indicators of women's social position and life opportunities is observed. This reversal occurs independently of the observed average level of development, i.e., it is reported in relatively low-developed Mali and Senegal, and to some extent in Poland and Hungary, but not in the economically declining Ukraine and Kyrgyzstan.

The combined findings allow the formation of a new conceptualization of the outcomes of democracy on society. In regard to women, this framework suggests that in recent decades, democratic growth, assisted by transitions to global market economy, have caused economic instability in all except highly developed countries, with costs disproportionately being born by women. The negative effects on women's well-being appear to follow a biphasic temporal course that is not resolved until at least ten years after the initiation of democratization. In contrast to the frequently observed increase in overall societal well-being that accompanies democratic development, this study demonstrates that such development does not improve immediate societal well-being.

As demonstrated, within the first five years after transition to a democratic system, democratization does not improve the well-being of women by measures of their representation in the workforce, equal pay for equal work, educational opportunities, and health care and life expectancy. These findings unveil a striking societal decline for women that is not resolved until after the tenth year of democracy. In additional analyses, these findings were supported by data collected using standardized interviews with men and women in six recently democratizing countries: Hungary, Poland, the Ukraine, Kyrgyzstan, Mali, and Senegal. These data show that during democratic growth, women's representation in the workforce declines, as does provision for their medical health care – especially medical assistance at birth – and women's life expectancy decreases in all but highly developed countries.

Nonetheless, there is no doubt that women are significantly more empowered in democratic vs non-democratic (authoritarian, totalitarian, military) states. Thus, for future world development and to create the most optimal environment for human development, democracies need to prevail. Without the broad spread of democracy, it would be difficult, if not impossible, to reach the Millennium Development Goals of a much improved world by 2015 – a new world where (a) poverty is cut in half, (b) child and maternal mortality is reduced significantly, (c) gender disparity in education is eliminated, (d) women are empowered, (e) health indicators are greatly improved, and (f) environmental indicators are improved. To obtain some portion of these goals, the democratic system needs to make paths in world development.

Democracy, therefore, is needed to support and provide higher gender equality, and, in turn, could reverse the trends reported by the United Nations Commission on the Status of Women (Morgan 1984) that while women represent half of the global population and one-third of the labor force, they receive only one-tenth of the world's income and own less than 1 percent of world property. Women perform 60–80 percent of all the agricultural work in the world and in developing countries; they produce more than 50 percent of the food (in African countries over 90 percent). Nonetheless, of the 22 million people who die yearly from starvation, the majority are women and children under 5 years old.

The need for special attention to pro-women policies and services can best be summarized by Kofi Annan, secretary general of the United Nations: "study after study has shown that there is no effective development strategy in which women do not play a central role. When women are fully involved, the benefits can be seen immediately: families are healthier; they are better fed; their income, savings and reinvestment go up. And what is true of families is true of communities and, eventually, of whole countries" (Annan 2002).

Gender equality is desperately needed and would greatly honor women's place in the world. It can be obtained with the development of democracy, although positive outcomes might not be visible initially.

6 | Epilogue: the democratic/autocratic world through a journalistic lens in 2013

The key issues on the world political agenda of the early 2010s are the birth of democratic movements in the authoritarian regimes of Libya, Syria, and Tunisia in the Middle East; nationalistic demands for independence in the ethnic regions of well-established European democracies, e.g., British Scotland and Spanish Catalonia; the economic fiasco and regression experienced by many of the Western European countries of the European Union, such as Spain, Greece, Italy, and to some degree France; the economic downturn in the United States; the strict restrictions imposed on civil liberties in authoritarian Russia; rising civil disobedience and protests against corruption and limited freedom in rapidly economically growing China; and the unfulfilled expectations of an increase in societal well-being in democratized African and Latin American countries.

The rapid spread, intensity, and global range of events signal potential change in the political situation of the global world that stimulates journalists' commentaries and experts' debates on the world's future. Similarly to scholarly theoretical predictions on the dominant political systems of the near future, journalists' accounts on the prospects of global political developments are split halfway between democracy and autocracy. Some journalists are certain that democracies are spreading and that this trend will prevail in the future; others have noticed the fast growth of authoritarian regimes in the world's political arena and are estimating its constant progression. While analyzing particular countries, journalistic debates and the news frequently focus on the key players in world politics: the countries of the European Union, the United States, the economic powers of China and Russia, the rich oil producers of the Middle East, and the fragile economies and unstable democracies of Africa and Latin America.

Hence, in 2012 and early 2013 in the news on Russia, the media information focuses on the severe restrictions and limitations on civil liberties imposed by Russian President Vladimir Putin. These restrictions encompass severe punishment for civil disobedience, including long-term imprisonment and quick, unjust, and harsh court sentences for minor disobedience. For instance, speaking unfavorably about members of the Russian government is legally categorized and punished as a crime of treason. The violation of human rights by police officials and ruling elites is common. Civil liberties are banned, including a ban on international marriages, a ban on adoption by international parents, a ban on activity by NGOs (non-governmental organizations) – which are being accused of spreading political upheaval in Russia – and restrictions on travel and study abroad for Russian citizens. Putin's authoritarian rule is characterized by extensive bureaucratic corruption that has been unpunished, uncontrolled, and unattended to, but has been known of and frequently blessed by political powers over the past twelve years of Putin's office.

The anti-democratic internal policies and movement toward autocracy in Russia turn away many international trade partners that are exploring more friendly markets. For example, German Chancellor Angela Merkel, after a visit to Russia in the late fall of 2012, decided to abandon trade with Russia and replace it with trade with more friendly countries. President Putin won election to a third term nonetheless, although international and Russian journalists asserted that "Russia's president [is] alone at the top" and that "his support looks shaky" (*The Economist*, December 2012: 57). Not only did his popular support drop to the lowest approval ratings ever, but also, as Yevgenia Albats, editor of the liberal *New Times*, observes, he is suffering the "typical syndrome of an ageing general secretary" (*The Economist*, December 2012: 57). Thus, when in 2012 Putin decided to publicly punish a few corrupt top governmental leaders, he confused the ruling elite, which in turn weakened its support for Putin. Weak support of corrupted officials, combined with low approval ratings and frequent protests against Putin's regime, develop gradually into, as Alexei Venediktov from the Ekho Moskvy radio station calls it, the giant autocracy (pretending to be a form of democracy) that is like airplane turbulence that shakes the governments, and "the ruling class may know in which direction and with which pilot they are flying . . . but the plane is shaking disconcertingly" (*The Economist*, December 2012: 58).

Another shaking autocracy and economic giant is China. As journalists indicate, since the violent end of the 1989 Tiananmen Square protests, totalitarian rule in China has gradually been shaken. As the *Observer*

News Weekly reported in December 2012, in China the number of protests has risen from 40,000 in the year 2000, to 280,000 in 2010. According to information provided by the independent television network NTD, the number of citizens involved in mass protests increased from over one and a half million in 2000 to nearly 6 million in 2009, and this trend is increasing at an average of 17 percent per year (NTD January 2013). Across years, protesters add new issues to their agendas, from protest against corruption and the regime's violent oppression to protests against censorship (January 2013). Also, new forms of protest are being developed that include blogging, Twitter networks such as that developed by Ms. Hung with millions of followers, and an online mob of protestors. Independent media information includes independent TV networks and internet communication. Movie producers expose the atrocities of Chinese regimes in independent films such as *Free China: The Courage to Believe*, which has won four international film awards. Chinese civil society is expressing that it will not accept corruption, the chronic afflictions of political repression, and cronyism any longer.

In addition to political turmoil, China is losing its rapid speed of economic growth. According to *The Wall Street Journal*, for the first time since the 2009 financial panic, foreign direct investment in China has fallen, and many investors have moved their capital to Vietnam, Indonesia, and Thailand to find cheaper labor costs. Lack of civil rights and the slowdown of economic development are solid indicators of coming political change, and, as some journalists believe, the regime in China is on the verge of change to democracy.

For the past two years we have also been witnessing the birth of a new wave of democratic movements across the states of the Middle East. A series of uprisings against totalitarian rule in the Arab countries of Tunisia, Libya, Syria, and Egypt ended with the peaceful replacement of totalitarian regimes in Tunisia and Egypt (*The Economist* December 2012: 52), and the eventual national election and formal transfer of power to civil government of the elected General National Congress in Libya created a New Libya (Vandewalle 2012). Hence, authoritarian regimes experience difficulties in protecting themselves from democratic influences.

In the early years of the second decade of the twenty-first century, worldwide democratic regimes are not free of difficulties. The economic recession, followed by financial crisis, influenced a global loss of public faith in politicians and the political program in many democracies. This includes the well-developed democracies of Western Europe, which are faced with the declining value of their currency, extensive debt, and a slipping sense of crisis in politics. The push for the peaceful establishment of autonomous nation-states in Europe is an example of economic and political weakness. Using democratic elections and referenda, the societies of Spain and Britain are asked to vote on an independent Catalonia that would separate from Spain, followed by the Scottish independence vote in 2014, attempting to establish an independent state separate from Great Britain. The voters' decisions will concern in part civil liberties and in part economic prosperity that would be determined by whether or not the new states (if established) will be accepted into the European Union (in the case of Catalonia, many policy-makers express concern regarding Catalonia's admission and Spain's readmission to the European Union); and whether the long run-up to the Scottish independence referendum will delay investment in this country (*The Scotsman* 2013, January 27, 2013:1).

Political difficulties are visible in the gridlock politics of the United States that, with the politically polarized Senate and Congress, deter the achievement of bipartisan agreement on many essential issues, including the fiscal policy of 2013 and immigration reforms. National politics is also failing in India, which has slowed its initial rapid development, is overburdened by corruption, and is increasingly polarized politically. Similarly, Japan, another well-developed and stable democracy, experiences many socioeconomic problems, among them soaring public debt that consecutive governments are unable to control.

The trouble in democratic regimes diminishes the strength of democratic countries; nonetheless, no democratic country that has experienced economic or political difficulties has retreated from democracy to autocracy. Rather, the opposite trend is observed. Many non-democratic states are on the march toward democracy, and with this growing popularity, the importance of democratic principles and the rule of law, a democratic future is likely suggested.

Appendix 1 Description of variables of expressed value, risk, and countries' tolerance of democracy adoption

Agricultural Labor per Region allows for assessment of the effect of regional-level development on democratic growth. It is measured as a percentage of the population working in the agricultural sector of the economy per year per country. The average of agricultural labor force in a region constitutes the measurement of the regional agricultural labor force.

Democratic Experience is a variable that depicts the type of political system a country had before becoming democratic. This variable refers to the period between World War I and World War II (the 1920s and 1930s).

Executive Adjustment is defined as a modification in the membership of a national executive body that does not signify a transfer of formal power from one leader or ruling group to another. National executive bodies include cabinets, councils of ministers, presidential offices, and ruling party councils in states in which authoritarian power is wielded by a single party. Modification in the membership of such a body, short of major executive transfer, typically includes "reshuffles" or "shake-ups" in which one or a small number of men are removed from or added to the membership. Executive adjustments always involve the movement of men into or out of the executive body; they do not include acts such as the redistribution of ministerial portfolios within an executive body.

GNP per capita is assessed at market prices, where the gross national product at market prices is the market value of the product, before deduction of provisions for the consumption of fixed capital, attributable to the factors of production supplied by normal residents of the given country. It is identically equal to the sum of consumption expenditure and gross domestic capital formation, private and public, and the net exports of goods and services plus the net factor incomes received from abroad.

Governmental Sanction is an action taken by the authorities to neutralize, suppress, or eliminate a perceived threat to the security of the government, the regime, or the state itself. The category encompasses a diversity of governmental activities, but they share the characteristic of constituting specific responses to a perceived security problem at the national level. The category includes the following types of action: (a) censorship; (b) restriction on political participation, such as the banning of a political party, the arrest of opposition politicians, or the arrest of persons reportedly involved in political protest actions, exiling or deportation of persons for political action; and (c) espionage.

Gross Domestic Product is a variable indicating the value of all final goods and services produced within a nation in a given year divided by the average (or mid-year) population for the same year. It is often considered an indicator of a country's standard of living.

Irregular Executive Transfer is a change in the office of national executive from one leader or ruling group to another that is characterized by actual or threatened violence and by abnormal procedures. The office of national executive refers both to individual leaders, such as presidents and prime ministers, and also to collegial executive bodies, such as cabinets composed of one or more parties or groupings.

Political Strike is defined as a work stoppage by a body of industrial or service workers, or a stoppage of normal academic life by students, to protest against a regime, government leaders, and/or a government policy or action. Strikes that were included in the dataset were judged to have assumed a primary political significance. A political strike may last for many days or weeks and is still counted as a single event. An additional strike is scored, however, at junctures in which the character of the strike changes, e.g., each time a new category of strikers joins the strikes, or each time a new political goal is enunciated.

Protest Demonstrations are indexed as a non-violent gathering of people organized for the announced purpose of protesting against a regime, government, or one or more of its leaders; or against its ideology, policy, intended policy, or lack of policy; or against its previous action or intended action. This variable is intended to encompass peaceful protest outside the formal structures of government and, therefore, excludes election meetings, rallies, and boycotts.

Regular Executive Transfer is a change in the office of national executive from one leader or ruling group to another that is accomplished through conventional legal or customary procedures and is unaccompanied by actual or directly threatened physical violence. The office of national executive refers both to individual leaders, such as presidents and prime ministers, and to collegial executive bodies, such as cabinets composed of one or more parties or groupings.

Relaxation of Sanctions is an event in which government modifies or eliminates restrictions on political action or expression of the type classified as governmental sanctions.

Riots are violent demonstrations or disturbances involving a large number of people. "Violent" implies the use of physical force and is usually evinced by the destruction of property, the wounding or killing of people by authorities, the use of riot control equipment such as clubs, gas, guns, or water cannons, and by the rioters' use of various weapons.

Urbanization, in the database *Nations, Development and Democracy* (Wejnert 2007), is measured as a percentage of a population living in cities of 10,000 or more to the total population in a country.

Appendix 2 Selected predictors of democratic growth

Measurement of development

GNP per capita is assessed at market prices, where the gross national product at market prices is the market value of the product, before deduction of provisions for the consumption of fixed capital, attributable to the factors of production supplied by normal residents of the given country. It is identically equal to the sum of consumption expenditure and gross domestic capital formation, private and public, and the net exports of goods and services plus the net factor incomes received from abroad (Banks 1993; World Bank 2009).

Urbanization is measured as the percentage of a population living in cities of 10,000 or more to the total population in a country (Banks 1976, 1993). This measure is extended using a comparable indicator from the World Bank (2009). To test the comparability, correlation of each variable from Banks and the World Bank was preformed with an obtained correlation score ranging from 0.9 to 0.94 on overlapping years.

A country's *world system position* is assessed based on Snyder and Kick's (1979) data, supplemented by Bollen and Appold's (1993) specification. Accordingly, the following countries were recorded as the *core* countries: Australia, Austria, Belgium, Canada, Denmark, France, Germany (West Germany), Greece, Italy, Japan, Luxembourg, the Netherlands, Norway, Sweden, Switzerland, the United Kingdom, the United States, and Yugoslavia. Recorded as *semi-peripheries* were: Argentina, Burma, Cuba, Cyprus, East Germany, Finland, Hungary, India, Iran, Ireland, Israel, Jordan, Kenya, South Korea, Kuwait, Lebanon, Malaysia, Pakistan, Peru, the Philippines, Portugal, Russia, Singapore, South Africa, Spain, Sri Lanka, Taiwan, Turkey, the United Arab Emirates, Uruguay, and Venezuela. And as *peripheries*: Afghanistan, Albania, Algeria, Angola, Armenia, Azerbaijan, Bahrain, Bangladesh, Belarus, Benin, Bhutan, Bolivia, Bosnia Herzegovina, Botswana, Brazil,

Bulgaria, Burundi, Cambodia, Cameroon, the Central African Republic, Chad, Chile, China, Colombia, Comoros, Congo, Costa Rica, Croatia, Czechoslovakia (Czech Republic), the Dominican Republic, Ecuador, Egypt, El Salvador, Estonia, Ethiopia, Fiji, Gabon, Gambia, Georgia, Ghana, Guatemala, Guinea-Bissau, Guyana, Haiti, Honduras, Iceland, Indonesia, Iraq, the Ivory Coast, Jamaica, Kazakhstan, North Korea, Kyrgyzstan, Laos, Latvia, Lesotho, Liberia, the Libyan Arab Republic, Lithuania, Macedonia, Madagascar, Malawi, Mali, Mauritania, Mauritius, Mexico, Moldavia, Mongolia, Morocco, Mozambique, Namibia, Nepal, New Zealand, Nicaragua, Niger, Nigeria, Oman, Panama, Papua New Guinea, Paraguay, Poland, Rumania, Rwanda, Saudi Arabia, Senegal, Sierra Leone, Slovakia, Slovenia, Somalia, Sudan, Swaziland, the Syrian Arab Republic, Tajikistan, Tanzania, Thailand, Togo, Trinidad and Tobago, Tunisia, Turkmenistan, Uganda, Upper Volta, the Ukraine, Uzbekistan, North and South Vietnam, Yemen Arab Republic (Yemen), Yemen People's Republic, Yugoslavia/Serbia, Zaire, Zambia, and Zimbabwe. Historical states of the nineteenth century that existed for too short a time to determine their world positions were excluded from the study (e.g., Baden, Saxony, or Papal States).

Measurement of diffusion

Spatial Proximity: Using the World Trade Organization data, countries were recorded as members of the following sub-regions: the *Americas*: North America, South America, Central America, the Caribbean; *Europe*: Western Europe, Central and Eastern Europe; *Africa*: Central Africa, East Africa, southern Africa, West Africa; *Middle East*: Middle East, North Africa; *Asia*: East Asia, Southeast Asia, the Indian subcontinent, Central Asia.

Countries' membership in economic and/or political networks

Using data from Osmanczyk and the *Statesman's Yearbook*, in each network of countries its members were recorded according to the time and duration of their membership, as follows: American Union, Arab League, Asian Assistance, Council for Mutual Economic Assistance (CMEA), Council of Arab Economic Unity, Council of Asian Industrial Development, Council of Europe, International Union of American

Republics, NATO, Nordic Council, Organization of African Unity, Organization of American States, Organization of Central American States, Union Africana et Malgache de Cooperation Economique, Union Liga Confederacion Permanente, Union of Central African States, and Warsaw Pact.

Countries' colonial heritage

Following the *Statesman's Yearbook* (2000), *British colonies* were recorded as: Bangladesh, Botswana, Burma, Canada, Ghana, India, Jamaica, Kenya, Lesotho, Malawi, Malaysia, Nigeria, Pakistan, Sierra Leone, Singapore, South Africa, Sri Lanka, Swaziland, Tanzania, Trinidad and Tobago, Uganda, Zambia, and Zimbabwe.

As *French colonies:* Algeria, Benin, Burkina Faso, Cambodia, Cameroon, Central African Republic, Chad, Comoros, Congo, Gabon, Guinea, Guyana, Haiti, Ivory Cost, Laos, Madagascar, Mali, Mauritania, Niger, Senegal, Somalia, Sudan, Togo, and Vietnam.

As *Spanish and Portuguese colonies* (due to similar religion and culture and a relatively smaller number of colonies than the French or British empires, the colonies of the two countries were recorded in the same category): Angola, Argentina, Bolivia, Brazil, Chile, Colombia, Costa Rica, Cuba, the Dominican Republic, El Salvador, Guatemala, Guinea-Bissau, Honduras, Indonesia, Mexico, Mozambique, Nicaragua, Panama, Paraguay, Peru, the Philippines, and Uruguay. As members of the *Soviet alliance*: Albania, Armenia, Azerbaijan, Belarus, Bosnia-Herzegovina, Bulgaria, Czech Republic, Croatia, East Germany, Estonia, Georgia, Hungary, Kazakhstan, Kyrgyzstan, Latvia, Lithuania, Macedonia, Moldova, Poland, Romania, Slovakia, Tajikistan, Turkmenistan, Ukraine, Uzbekistan, and Yugoslavia/Serbia. However, due to missing data on many indicators, the following twenty countries were not included in the analyses: Albania, Armenia, Azerbaijan, Belarus, Bulgaria, Estonia, Czechoslovakia (Czech Republic), East Germany, Georgia, Hungary, Kyrgyzstan, Latvia, Lithuania, Moldavia, Poland, Rumania, Russia, Turkmenistan, the Ukraine, and Uzbekistan.

References

Abbott, Andrew, and Stanley DeViney. 1992. The Welfare State as Transnational Event: Evidence from Sequences of Policy Adoption. *Social Science History* 16: 245–274.

Albanese, Patricia. 1996. Leaders and Breeders: The Archaization of Gender Relations in Croatia. In Wejnert and Spencer 1996

Alexievich, Svetlana. 2006. *Voices From Chernobyl: The Oral History of a Nuclear Disaster.* New York: Picador.

Almond, Gabriel A., and Sidney Verba. 1989. *The Civic Culture: Political Attitudes and Democracy in Five Nations.* Newbury Park, CA: Sage.

Anderson, Ronald E., and Shon M. Magnan. 1996. The Adoption of External Networking by American Schools. *The American Sociologist* 27: 55–64.

Andora, Rudolf. 1980. Long-Term Development of Hungary, Measured by Social Indicators. *Social Indicators Research*, 8: 1–13.

Andrews, Frank. 1991. Stability and Change in Levels and Structure of Well-Being: USA 1972–1988. *Social Indicators Research* 25: 1–30.

Andrews, Frank, and Ronald Inglehart. 1979. The Structure of Well-Being in Nine Western Countries. *Social Indicators Research* 6: 73–90.

Andrews, Frank, and Aubrey McKennell. 1980. Measures of Self-Reported Well-Being: Their Affective, Cognitive, and Other Components. *Social Indicators Research* 8: 127–155.

Andrews, Frank, and John Robinson. 1991. *Measures of Well-Being.* In John Robinson, Phillip Shaver, and Lawrence Wrightsman (eds.), *Measures of Personality and Social Psychological Attitudes.* San Diego, CA: Academic Press.

Andrews, Frank, and Stephen Withey. 1976. *Social Indicators of Well-Being: Americans' Perceptions of Life Quality.* New York: Plenum Press.

Annan, Kofi. 2002. Speech of the Secretary General of the United Nations at the General Assembly of the United Nations. *New York Times,* September.

Arat, Zehra. 1991. *Democracy and Human Rights in Developing Countries.* Boulder, CO: Lynne Rienner.

Arbena, Joseph L. 1988. *Sport and Society in Latin America: Diffusion, Dependency and Rise of Mass Culture.* Westport, CT: Greenwood.

Bakardjiva, Maria. 1992. Home Satellite TV Reception in Bulgaria. *European Journal of Communication* 7: 477–89.

Banac, Ivo (ed.) 1992. *Eastern Europe in Revolution*. Ithaca, NY: Cornell University Press.

Bane, Mandi. 2010. From Clients to Participants? Alternative Local Governments and the Limitations of Participatory Democracy in the Neoliberal Era, Saquisili, Ecuador. *Research in Political Sociology* 18: 111–128.

Banks, Arthur. 1993. *Cross-National Time Series, 1815–1973. Electronic manuscript*. Ann Arbor, MI: Inter-University Consortium for Political and Social Research. www.icpsr.umich.edu/icpsrweb/ICPSR/studies/7412

Barro, Robert J. 1999. Determinants of Democracy. *Journal of Political Economy* 107(S6): 158–183.

Beck, Sam. 1993. The Struggle for Space and the Development of Civil Society in Romania, June 1990. In H. G. DeSoto and D. G. Anderson (eds.), *The Curtain Rises: Rethinking Culture, Ideology and the State in Eastern Europe*. Atlantic Highlands, NJ: Humanities Press International.

Beissinger, M. 1990. Protest Mobilization among Soviet Nationalities. Report Submitted to the National Council for Soviet and Eastern European Research, August.

Beneria, Lourdes. 2003. *Gender, Development and Globalization: Economics as if All People Mattered*. New York: Routledge.

Beneria, Lourdes, and Savitri Bisnath (eds.) 2004. *Global Tensions: Challenges and Opportunities in the World Economy*. New York: Routledge.

Bermeo, Nancy, ed. 1991. *Liberalization and Democratization: Change in the Soviet Union and Eastern Europe*. Baltimore, MD: Johns Hopkins University Press.

Berry, Frances Stokes, and William D. Berry. 1992. Tax Innovation in the States: Capitalizing on Political Opportunity. *American Journal of Political Science* 36: 715–742.

Binyon, Michael. 1983. *Life in Russia*. New York: Pantheon Books.

Bloom, Jack. 2002. A Line of Blood: How December 1970 Prepared Polish Workers for Political Transition in 1989. In Wejnert 2002a.

Bo, Zhiyue. 2010. China's Model of Democracy. *International Journal of China Studies* 1, 1: 102–124.

Bodrova, Valentina, and Richard Anker, eds. 1985. *Working Women in Socialist Countries: The Fertility Connection*. International Labour Office: Geneva.

Boli-Bennett, John, and Francisco Ramirez. 1987. The Political Construction of Mass-Schooling: European Origins and Worldwide Institutionalization. *Sociology of Education* 60: 2–18.

Bollen, Kenneth. 1979. Political Democracy and the Timing of Development. *American Sociological Review* 44: 572–587.

    1980. Issues in the Comparative Measurement of Political Democracy. *American Sociological Review* 45: 370–390.

    1983. World System Position, Dependency, and Democracy: The Cross-National Evidence. *American Sociological Review* 48: 486–479.

    1998. *Liberal Democracy Indicators 1950–1990. Electronic manuscript.* Ann Arbor, MI: Inter-university Consortium for Political and Social Research.

Bollen, Kenneth, and Stephen J. Appold. 1993. National Structure and the Global System. *American Sociological Review* 58: 283–301.

Bollen, Kenneth, and Robert Jackman. 1985a. Political Democracy and the Size Distribution of Income. *American Sociological Review* 50: 438–457.

Bollen, Kenneth, and Robert Jackman. 1985b. Economic and Noneconomic Determinants of Political Democracy in the 1960s. *Research in Political Sociology* 1: 27–48.

Bongaarts, John. 1994. Population Policy Options in the Developing World. *Science* (February 11): 771–776.

Bongaarts, John, and Susan Cotts Watkins. 1996. Social Interactions and Contemporary Fertility Transitions. *Population and Development Review* 22, 4: 639–682.

Borkowicz, Jacek. 1989. Polacy Niemile Widziani. *Gazeta Wyborcza* (September 11): 1.

Boswell, Terry, and Ralph Peters. 1990. State Socialism and the Industrial Divide in the World-Economy: A Comparative Essay on the Rebellions in Poland and China. *Critical Sociology* 17: 3–34.

Bowman, Lehaucq, and Mahoney. 2005. Measuring Political Democracy: Case Expertise, Data Adequacy, and Central America. *Comparative Political Studies* 38: 939–970.

Bratton, Michael, and Robert Mattes. 2001. Support for Democracy in Africa: Intrinsic or Instrumental. *British Journal of Political Science* 31: 447–474.

Braudel, Fernand. 1973. *Civilisation Matérielle, Economie et Capitalisme, XV–XVIII (Capitalism and Material Life, 1400–1800).* New York: Harper Collins.

Braun, Norman. 1995. Individual Thresholds and Social Diffusion. *Rationality and Society* 7: 167–182.

Braunthal, Julius. 1949. The Rebirth of Social Democracy. *Foreign Affairs* 27, 4: 586–600.

Bremmer, Ian. 2009. State Capitalism Comes of Age: The End of the Free Market? *Foreign Affairs* (May/June): 40–55.

Bremmer, Ian, and Preston Keat. 2009. *Fat Tail: The Power of Political Knowledge for Strategic Investment.* Oxford University Press.

Brown, David, and Anna Bandlerova. 2000. *Rural Development in Central and Eastern Europe: Proceedings of Research Conference.* Podbanske, Slovakia.

Brown, Elspeth H. 2005. Popular Culture and Democratic Parties. *Canadian Review of American Studies* 35, 3: 335–344.

Brown, J.F., Robert Hormats, William Luers, and John Lederer. 1992. *Western Approaches to Eastern Europe.* New York: Council on Foreign Relations Press.

Brown, Richard. 1989. *Knowledge is Power. The Diffusion of Information in Early America: 1700–1865.* New York: Oxford University Press.

Bruszt, Laszlo, and David Stark. 1991. Remaking the Political Field in Hungary: From the Politics of Confrontation to the Politics of Competition. *Journal of International Affairs* 45: 1.

Bryk, Anthony S., and Stephen W. Raudenbush. 1992. *Hierarchical Linear Models: Applications and Data Analysis Methods.* Newbury Park, CA: Sage.

Bunce, Valerie. 1989. Soviet Decline as a Regional Hegemon: Gorbachev and Eastern Europe. *Eastern European Politics and Society* 3: 235–267.

1990. The Struggle for Liberal Democracy in Eastern Europe. *World Policy Journal* 7 (Summer).

Burt, Ronald. 1983. *Corporate Profit and Cooptation.* New York: Academic Press.

1987. Social Contagion and Innovation: Cohesion versus Structural Equivalence. *American Journal of Sociology* 92: 1287–1335.

1992. *Structural Holes: The Social Structure of Competition.* Cambridge, MA: Harvard University Press.

Burt, Ronald, and Ilan Talmud. 1993. Market Niche. *Social Networks* 15: 133–149.

Burton, Michael, Richard Gunther, and John Higley. 1992. Introduction: Elite Transformations and Democratic Regimes. In J. Higley and R. Gunther (eds.), *Elites and Democratic Consolidation in Latin America and Southern Europe.* Cambridge University Press.

Campbell, Angus. 1981. *The Sense of Well-Being in America: Recent Patterns and Trends.* New York: McGraw Hill.

Campbell, Angus, Phillip Converse, and Williard Rogers. 1976. *The Quality of American Life.* New York: Russell Sage Foundation.

Cardoso, Fernando Henrique. 2005. Globalization and Democracy. Footnotes. *ASA Bulletin* (February 8–10).

Carrington, Peter, John Scott, and Stanley Wasserman. 2005. *Models and Methods in Social Network Analysis.* New York: Cambridge University Press.

Castels, Manuel. 2000. Information Technology and Global Capitalism. In Will Hutton and Anthony Giddens (eds.), *On the Edge: Living with Global Capitalism.* London: Jonathan Cape.

Chase-Dunn, Christopher. 1975. The Effects of International Economic Dependence on Development and Inequality: A Cross-National Study. *American Sociological Review* 40: 720–738.

Chirot, Daniel. 1996. *Modern Tyrants.* Princeton, NJ: Princeton University Press.

Chu, Yun-Han, Larry Diamond, and Doh Chull Shin. 2001. Halting Progress in Korea and Taiwan. *Journal of Democracy* 12: 122–136.

Chua, Amy. 1995. The Privatization–Nationalization Cycle: The Link Between Markets and Ethnicity in Developing Countries. *Columbia Law Review* 95.

2003. *World on Fire: How Exporting Free Market Democracy Breeds Ethnic Hatred and Global Instability.* New York: Doubleday.

CITUB, 1991. *From Totalitarianism to Democracy.* Sofia, Bulgaria: CITUB.

Coale, Ansley J., and Judith Banister. 1996. Five Decades of Missing Females in China. *Proceedings of the American Philosophical Society*, 140, 4 (December): 421–450.

Coenders Marcel, and Peer Scheepers. 2003. The Effect of Education on Nationalism and Ethnic Exclusionism: An International Comparison. *Political Psychology* 24, 2: 313–343.

Coleman, Isobel. 2004. The Payoff from Women's Rights. *Foreign Affairs* 83: 80–95.

2006. Women, Islam and the New Iraq. *Foreign Affairs* (January/February): 24–38.

Coleman, Isobel, and Tamara Cofman Wittes. 2008. Economic and Political Development of the Middle East. In The Saban Center at Brookings and the Council on Foreign Relations, *Restoring the Balance: A Middle East Strategy for the Next President.* Washington, DC: Brookings Institution Press.

Coleman, James S., Elihu Katz, and Herbert Menzel. 1966. *Medical Innovations: A Diffusion Study.* New York: Bobbs-Merrill.

Computer Aid International. 2000. Where we work. www.computeraid.org/wherewework.htm (Accessed September 20, 2009).

Conell, Carol, and Samuel Cohen. 1995. Learning from Other People's Actions: Environmental Variation and Diffusion in French Coal Mining Strikes, 1890–1935. *American Journal of Sociology* 101: 366–403.

Confederation of Labor Podkrepa. 1990. *Constitution of Podkrepa*. Sofia, Bulgaria.

Coppedge, Michael, and Wolfgang Reinicke. 1990. Measuring Polyarchy. *Studies in Comparative International Development* 25: 51–72.

Costa, Paul T., and Robert R. McCrae. 1980. Influence of Extroversion and Neuroticism on Subjective Well-Being: Happy and Unhappy People. *Journal of Personality and Social Psychology*, 38, 4: 668–678.

Cowen, Tyler, Sebastian Mallaby, Francis Fukuyama, and Robert Reich. 2012. *Plutocracy and Democracy: How Money Corrupts Our Politics and Culture*. The American Interest, Ebook.

Crenshaw, Edward. 1992. Cross-National Determinants of Income Inequality: A Replication and Extension Using Ecological-Evolutionary Theory. *Social Forces* 71: 339–363.

1995. Democracy and Demographic Inheritance: The Influence of Modernity and Proto-Modernity on Political and Civil Rights, 1965 to 1980. *American Sociological Review* 60: 702–718.

Czapinski, Janusz. 1994. Uziemnienie Duszy Polskiej. *Kultura i Spoleczenstwo*: 19–37.

Dabrowski, Marek, and Rafal Antczak (eds.) 1996. *Ukrainska Droga do Gospodarki Rynkowej 1991–1995*. Warsaw: Wydawnictwo Naukowe, PWN.

Dahl, Robert. 1982. *Dilemmas of Pluralist Democracy: Autonomy vs Control*. New Haven, CT: Yale University Press.

1989. *Polyarchy: Participation and Opposition*. New Haven, CT: Yale University Press.

1990. *After the Revolution? Authority in Good Society*. New Haven, CT: Yale University Press.

2000. *On Democracy*. New Haven, CT: Yale University Press.

David, Henry, and Anna Titkov. 1994. Abortion and Women's Rights in Poland. *Studies in Family Planning* 25.

Davis, Gerald. 1991. Agents without Principles? The Spread of the Poison Pill through the Incorporate Network. *Administrative Science Quarterly* 36: 583–613.

Deacon, Bob, Mita Castle-Kanerova, Nick Manning, Frances Millard, Eva Orosz, Julia Szalai, and Anna Vidinova. 1992. *The New Eastern Europe*. New York: Council on Foreign Relations.

DePou, Jeannie Ash. 2005. *10-year Beijing Review*. United Nations, INSTRAW.

Derber, Charles. 2003. People Before Profit: The New Globalization in an Age of Terror, Big Money, and Economic Crisis. New York: Macmillan Press.

DeSoto, Hermine, and David Anderson. 1993. *The Curtain Rises: Rethinking Culture, Ideology, and the State in Eastern Europe.* Atlantic Highlands, NJ: Humanities Press.

Deudney, Daniel, and G. John Ikenberry. 2009. The Myth of the Autocratic Revival. *Foreign Affairs* (January/February).

Dewar, Robert D., and Jane E. Dutton. 1986. The Adoption of Radical and Incremental Innovation: An Empirical Analysis. *Management Science* 32: 1422–1433.

Diamond, Larry, and Marc F. Plattner. 2010. *Democratization in Africa. Progress and Retreat.* Baltimore, MD: The Johns Hopkins University Press.

(eds.) 2012. *Liberation Technology: Social Media and the Struggle for Democracy.* Baltimore, MD: The Johns Hopkins University Press.

DiMaggio, Paul J., and Walter W. Powell. 1983. The Iron Cage Revisited: Institutional Isomorphism and Collective Rationality in Organizational Fields. *American Sociological Review* 48: 147–160.

Dinstein, Yoram (ed.) 1992. *The Protection of Minorities and Human Rights.* Norwell, MA: Kluwer Academic Publishers.

Dixon, William, and Terry Boswell. 1996. Dependency, Disarticulation, and Denominator Effects: Another Look at Foreign Capital Penetration. *American Journal of Sociology* 102: 543–562.

Dollar, David, and Aart Kraay. 2000. *Growth Is Good for the Poor.* Washington, DC: World Bank.

Douglas, Mary. 1985. *Risk Acceptability According to the Social Sciences.* Social Research Perspectives Series. New York: Russell Sage Foundation.

Douglas, Mary, and Aaron Wildavsky. 1982. *Risk and Culture: An Essay on the Selection of Technical and Environmental Dangers.* Berkeley, CA: University of California Press.

Dowding, Keith, Robert Goodin, and Carole Pateman. 2004. *Justice and Democracy.* Cambridge University Press.

Doyle, Michael. 1983. Kant, Liberal Legacies, and Foreign Affairs. *Philosophy & Public Affairs* 12, 3: 205–235.

Drakulic, Slavenka. 1993. Women and New Democracy in the Former Yugoslavia. In Nanette Funk and Magda Mueller (eds.), *Gender Politics and Post-Communism.* New York: Routledge: 123–130.

Edwards, John, Jack Kemp, and Stephen Sestanovich. 2006. *Russia's Wrong Direction: What the United States Can and Should Do.* New York: Council on Foreign Relations.

El-Badri, Abdalla Salem. 2010. Secretary General's Message. Secretary General of OPEC, Abdalla Salem El-Badri of the Socialist People's Libyan Arab Jamahiriya. Organization of the Petroleum Exporting Countries.

Elson, John. 1994. John Paul II: Lives of the Pope. *Time* (December 26): 2.

Emerson, Rupert. 1960. *From Empire to Nation: The Rise of Self-Assertion of Asian and African People.* Cambridge, MA: Harvard University Press.

Epstein, Gady. 2012. China: Hung Verdict. *The Economist* (November 21).

2013. A Giant Cage. *The Economist* (April 6): 490.

Etzioni, Amitai. 2004. *From Empire to Community.* New York: Palgrave Press.

Evans, Peter, Dietrich Rueschemeyer, and Theda Skocpol (eds.) 1985. *Bringing the State Back In.* New York: Cambridge University Press.

Evens, G., and S. Whitefield. 1995. The Politics and Economics of Democratic Commitment: Support for Democracy in Transitional Societies. *British Journal of Political Science* 25: 485–514.

Finn, Helena. 2003. The Case for Cultural Diplomacy. Engaging Foreign Audiences. *Foreign Affairs* (November/December): 15–20.

Firebaugh, Glenn. 1999. Empirics of World Income Inequality. *American Journal of Sociology* 104: 1597–1630.

First-Dilic, Ruza. 1973. Zene u Privrednom I Politickom Zivotu. *Nase Teme* 1: 120–139.

Fish, Steven. 2005. *Democracy Derailed in Russia: The Failure of Open Politics.* New York: Cambridge University Press.

Fliegel, Frederick C. 1993. Diffusion Research in Rural Sociology: The Record for the Future. Westport, CT: Greenwood.

Freedom House. 2000. *Political Freedom Indicators 1994–1999.* New York: Freedom House.

2009. *Freedom in the World 1994–2009. Electronic manuscript.* New York: Freedom House. www.freedomhouse.org/template.cfm?page=363 &year=2009

Fukuyama, Francis. 1992. *The End of History and the Last Man.* New York: Avon.

2004. State Building. Governance and World Order in the Twenty-First Century. Ithaca, NY: Cornell University Press.

2012. The Future of History. *Foreign Affairs* 91, 1: 120–125.

Fukuyama, Francis, and Michael McFaul. 2007. Should Democracy be Promoted or Demoted? *The Washington Quarterly* 31, 1: 23–45.

Fukuyama, Francis, Larry Diamond, and Marc F. Plattner. 2012. *Poverty, Inequality, and Democracy.* Baltimore, MD: The Johns Hopkins University Press.

Galbraith, James K. 2000. *Created Unequal: The Crisis in American Pay* (2nd edn.) Chicago University Press.

Gardawski, Juliusz. 1996. *Poland's Industrial Workers on the Return to Democracy and Market Economy.* Warsaw: Friedrich Ebert Stiftung.

Garrett, Geoffrey. 2004. Globalization's Missing Middle. *Foreign Affairs* (November/December): 84–96.

Gasiorowski, Mark. 1993. *The Polity Change Dataset*. Baton Rouge: Data Center, Louisiana State University.

Gat, Azar. 2008. *War in Human Civilization*. London: Vintage Books.

Gat, Azar, Daniel Deudney, G. John Ikenberry, Ronald Inglehart, and Christian Welzel. 2009. Which Way Is History Marching? Debating the Authoritarian Revival. *Foreign Affairs* (July/August).

Gazeta Wyborcza.1989a. Spotkanie z Opozycja (Meeting with the Opposition). (July 24): 1.

1989b. Kometarz Wiadomosci (Commentary News). (August 21): 2.

1989c. Polska Zaraza (Polish Disease). (September 3–5): 2.

1989d Polacy Niemile Widziani (11 September).

1989e. Premier Solidarny z Havlem (Solidarity of the Prime Minister with Havel). (October 3): 1.

1989f Wiadomosci (News). (October 3): 3.

1989g Czesi i Slovacy Okupuja Wrocław (Czechs and Slovaks Occupying Wrocław). (November 16): 1.

1990. Kanty i Emocje (Tricks and Emotions). (June 8): 1.

Gelvin, James. 2011. *The Modern Middle East*. Oxford University Press.

Gerwin, Donald. 1988. *A Theory of Innovation Process for Computer-Aided Manufacturing Technology*. IEEE Transitions on Engineering Management, 35: 90–100.

Gibson, James, and Amanda Gouws. 2003. Overcoming Intolerance in South Africa: Experiments in Democratic Persuasion. Cambridge University Press.

Gill, Graeme, and Markwick, Roger D. 2000. *Russia's Stillborn Democracy? From Gorbachev to Yeltsin*. Oxford University Press.

Goldfarb, Jeffrey. 1991. *Beyond Glasnost*. University of Chicago Press.

Goldstein, H. 1995. *Multilevel Statistical Models* (2nd edn.) New York: Halstead.

Gordon Ash, Timothy. 2005. *Free World: America, Europe, and the Surprising Future of the West*. London: Vintage Press.

Gore, Al. 2009. *Our Choice: How we can Solve the Climate Crisis*. New York: Rodale Books.

Graf, W., W. Hansen, and B. Schulz. 1987. From the People to One People: Social Bases of the East German "Revolution" and Its Preemption by the West German State. In D. Anderson, J. Lovenduski, and J. Woodall (eds.), *Politics and Society in Eastern Europe*. Bloomington: Indiana University Press.

Granovetter, Mark, and R. Soong. 1983. Threshold Models of Diffusion and Collective Behavior. *Journal of Mathematical Sociology* 9: 165–179.

de Grassi, Davide. 2002. La globalizzazione della democrazia: transizioni agli albori del XXI secolo. *Revista italiana di scienza politica* 1: 3–29.

Gredelj, Stjepan. 2002. Cultural and Civic Movements Prefiguring the Breakdown of the Socialist Regime in Yugoslavia. In Wejnert 2002a: 279–311.

Greve, Henrich R. 1998. Performance, Aspirations, and Risky Organizational Change. *Administrative Science Quarterly* 43: 58–86.

Gunther, Richard, and Anthony Mughan (eds.) 2000. *Democracy and the Media: A Comparative Perspective*. Cambridge and New York: Cambridge University Press.

Gurr, Ted R. 1974. Persistence and Change in Political Systems, 1800–1971. *American Political Science Review* 68: 1482–1504.

Gurr, Ted R., Keith Jagger, and Will H. Moore. 1990. The Transformation of the Western State: The Growth of Democracy, Autocracy, and State Power since 1800. *Studies in Comparative International Development* 25: 73–108.

Haavio-Mannila, Elina. 1992. *Work, Family and Well-Being in Five North and East European Capitals*. Helsinki: Suomalainen Tiedeakatemia.

Hagopian, Frances, and Scott P. Mainwaring. 2005. *The Third Wave of Democratization in Latin America*. New York: Cambridge University Press.

Hannan, Michael T., and John Freeman. 1987. The Ecology of Organizational Founding: American Labor Unions, 1836–1985. *American Journal of Sociology* 92: 910–943.

Harriss-White, Barbara. 1996. Fighting Female Infanticide by Working with Midwives: An Indian Case Study. *Gender and Development* 4, 2 (June): 20–27.

Hauser, Ewa, Barbara Heyns, and Jane Mansbridge. 1993. Feminism in the Interstices of Politics and Culture: Poland in Transition. In Nanette Funk and Magda Mueller (eds.), *Gender Politics and Post-Communism*. New York: Routledge: 257–273.

Havel, Václav. 1985. The Power of the Powerless. In J. Keane (ed.), and P. Wilson (trans.), *The Power of the Powerless: Citizens Against the State in Central-Eastern Europe*. Armonk, NY: M. E. Sharpe.

　1988. Cards on Table. In B. Gwertzman and M. Kaufman (eds.), *The Collapse of Communism: The Correspondents of New York Times*. New York: Times Books.

　1990. Speech in the Polish Parliament. *Gazeta Wyborcza* (January 21): 1.

Hechter, Michael. 1984. Review Essay: Lineages of the Capitalist State. *American Journal of Sociology* 82: 1057–1073.

Hedstrom, Peter. 1994. Contagious Collectivities: On the Spatial Diffusion of Swedish Trade Unions, 1890–1940. *American Journal of Sociology* 99: 1157–1179.

Held, David. 1995. *Models of Democracy*. Stanford University Press.

　(ed.) 1993. *Prospects for Democracy*. Stanford University Press.

Henisz, Witold, Bennet Zelner, and Mauro Guillen. 2005. The Worldwide Diffusion of Market-Oriented Infrastructure Reform, 1977–1999. *American Sociological Review* 70, 6: 871–898.

Herbig, Paul A., and J. C. Miller. 1991. The Effect of Culture upon Innovativeness: A Comparison of the United States' and Japan's Sourcing Capabilities. *Journal of International Consumer Marketing* 3: 1–57.

Herbig, Paul A., and Fred Palumbo. 1994a. India and Japan: A Longitudinal Study of Innovation and Development: 1850–1990. *Asian Pacific Journal of Marketing*.

1994b. The Effect of Culture on the Adoption Process: A Comparison of Japanese and American Behaviour. *Technological Forecasting and Social Change* 46: 71–101.

Herspring, Dale (ed.) 2003. *Putin's Russia: Past Imperfect, Future Uncertain*. Oxford: Rowan & Littlefield.

Herzog, Ben. 2002. Dual Citizenship and the Revocation of Citizenship. In Wejnert 2002a.

Higley, John, and Richard Gunther. 1992. *Elites and Democratic Consolidation in Latin America and Southern Europe*. Cambridge University Press.

Holbrook, Richard. 2008. The Next President. *Foreign Affairs* 87, 5: 2–21.

Holmes, L. 1997. *Post-Communism*. Oxford: Polity Press.

Huntington, Samuel. 1992. *The Third Wave: Democratization in the Late Twentieth Century*. Norman: University of Oklahoma Press.

1997. After Twenty Years: The Future of the Third Wave. *Journal of Democracy* 8, 4: 3–12.

2004. *Who Are We? The Challenges to America's National Identity*. New York: Simon & Schuster.

2011. *The Clash of Civilisations and the Remaking of World Order*. New York: Simon & Schuster.

Hutton, Will, and Anthony Giddens (eds.) 2000. *On the Edge: Living with Global Capitalism*. London: Jonathan Cape.

Hyojoung, Kim, and Emory Morrison. 2010. Shifting Functional Forms in the Relationship between Economic Development and Political Democracy. *Research in Political Sociology* 18: 155–176.

Informacja PAP. 1993. Polska Zbrojna. *Nowy Rozdzial Wspolpracy* (February 26–28): 1.

Inglehart, Ronald. 1997. *Modernization and Postmodernization: Cultural, Economic, and Political Change in 43 Societies*. Princeton University Press.

Inglehart, Ronald, and Christian Welzel. 2005. *Modernization, Cultural Change and Democracy*. New York: Cambridge University Press.

2009. How Development Leads to Democracy: What We Know About Modernization. *Foreign Affairs* 88, 2: 33–48.

Inkeles, Alex, and Larry Sirowy. 1983. Convergent and Divergent Trends in National Educational Systems. *Social Forces* 62: 303–333.

International Labour Organization. 2014. *International Training Centre of the International Labour Organization. Turin School of Development.* www.itcilo.org/en/the-centre/programmes

Issraelyan, Yevgenia. 1996. Russian Women: Challenges of the Modern World. In Wejnert & Spencer 1996.

Jagger, Keith, and Ted Robert Gurr. 1995a. Tracking Democracy's Third Wave with the Polity III Data. *Journal of Peace Research* 32: 469–482.

    1995b. *Polity III: Regime Type and Political Authority 1800–1994. Electronic manuscript.* Ann Arbor, MI: Inter-University Consortium for Political and Social Research. www.colorado.edu/IBS/GAD/spacetime/data/Polity.html

Jarosz, Maria. 1996. *Polish Employee-Owned Companies in 1995.* Warsaw, Poland: PolishAcademy of Sciences.

Joffe, Josef. 1999. Rethinking the Nation-State: The Many Meanings of Sovereignty. *Foreign Affairs* 78, 6: 122–126.

    2007. Überpower: The Imperial Temptation of America. New York: W.W. Norton.

    2009. The Default Power: The False Prophecy of US Decline. *Foreign Affairs* 88, 5: 21–36.

Kagan, Robert. 1999. *The Future of Great Powers: Predictions.* London: Orion Publishing.

    2004. Gulliver Unbound: Can America Rule the World?Occasional Paper 85. Center for Independent Studies, Australia. www.cis.org.au (Accessed August 19, 2009).

    2006. League of Dictators? *Washington Post* (April 30).

    2008. *The Return of History and the End of Dreams.* New York: Vintage Books/Knopf Publishers.

Kahneman, Daniel, and Amos Tversky (eds.) 2003a. *Choices, Values and Frames.* Cambridge University Press.

    (eds.) 2003b. Choices, Values and Frames. In Kahneman & Tversky 2003a: 1–16.

Kaminski, M. 2013. Democracy May Have Had Its Day. *Wall Street Journal* (April 27): A11 (US edn.)

Kapstein, Ethan, and Nathan Converse. 2009. *The Fate of Young Democracies.* New York: Cambridge University Press.

Karatnycky, Adrian. 1995. Democracies on the Rise, Democracies at Risk. *Freedom Review* (January/February): 5–10.

    1997. Freedom on the March. *Freedom Review* 28:3–17.

Karger, Jacob, and David Stoesz. 2009. *American Social Welfare Policy.* New York: Allyn & Bacon.

Karnoouh, Claude. 1991. The End of National Culture in Eastern Europe. *Telos* 89: 133–140.

Kavan, Jan. 2002. McCarthyism Has a New Name – Lustration: A Personal Recount of Political Events. In Wejnert 2002a.

Kearny, A.T. Inc. 2001. Measuring Globalization. *Foreign Policy* 1: 56–65.

Kellner, Douglas. 2002. Theorizing Globalization. *Sociological Theory* 20: 285–305.

Kentor, Jeffrey, and Terry Boswell. 2003. Foreign Capital Dependence and Development: A New Direction. *American Sociological Review* 68: 301–313.

Kholodkovskioi, K.G. (ed.) 1998. *Grazdanskoe Obshchestvo v Rossii: Structury i Sozdanie*. Moscow: Nauka.

King, Kenneth. 2013. *China's Aid and Soft Power in Africa*. Oxford: James Currey.

Kinninmont, Jane. 2012. *Kuwait's Parliament: An Experiment in Semi-Democracy*. Middle East and North Africa Programme Briefing Paper. Chatham House (August). www.chathamhouse.org

Kirby, Eric, and Susan Kirby. 1996. On the Diffusion of International Social Values: Institutionalization and Demographic Transition. *Social Science Quarterly* 77: 289–299.

Kissinger, Henry. 2001. *Does America Need a Foreign Policy?* New York: Simon and Schuster.

Klein, Naomi. 2007. *The Shock Doctrine: The Rise of Disaster Capitalism*. New York: Picador Press.

Kligman, Gail. 1992. Abortion and International Adoption in Post-Ceausescu Romania. *Feminist Studies* 18, 2: 405–417.

Klingemann, Hans-Dieter, Dieter Fuchs, and Jan Zielonka. 2006. *Democracy and Political Culture in Eastern Europe*. New York: Routledge Press.

Knoke, David. 1982. The Spread of Municipal Reform: Temporal, Spatial, and Social Dynamics. *American Journal of Sociology* 87: 1314–1339.

Kolodko, Grzegorz W. 1996. *Poland 2000: The New Economic Strategy*. Warsaw: Poltext Press.

2000. *From Shock to Therapy: The Political Economy of Postsocialist Transformation*. Oxford University Press.

2002. Nouveaux Riches vs Nouveaux Pauvres: Policy Making in Transition Economies. In Wejnert 2002a.

2011. *Truth, Errors, and Lies: Politics and Economics in a Volatile World*. New York, NY: Columbia University Press.

Komitov, Stefan. 1991a. Interview with Dr. Konstantin Tenchev and Other Podrepa Leaders. *C. L. Podkrepa Press* (August).

1991b. Interview with Plamen Darakchiev Activists of Podkrepa. *C. L. Podkrepa Press* (August): 8.

Koralewicz, Jadwiga, and Marek Ziolkowski. 1993. Changing Value Systems. *Sisyphus* 9: 123–139.

Kristof, Nicholas, and Sheryl WuDunn. 2009. *Half the Sky: Turning Oppression into Opportunity for Women Worldwide*. New York: Alfred A. Knopf.

Krueger, Alan. 1991. How Computers Have changed the Wage Structure: Evidence from Microdata: 1984–1989. National Bureau of Economic Research. Working papers series, Issue 3858.

Kubicel, Paul. 2005. The European Union and Grassroots Democratization in Turkey. *Turkish Studies* 6: 361–377.

Kulluk, F. 1993. From the National Question to Autogestion and Perestroika: Controversies in Theoretical and Political Approaches to Nation(ist) Movements. In D. Hermine & D. Anderson (eds.), *The Curtain Rises: Rethinking Culture, Ideology and the State in Eastern Europe*. Atlantic Highlands, NJ: Humanities Press International.

Kurczewski, J. 1990. Carnal Sins and Privatization of the Body. In J. Kurczewski and A. Czynczyk (eds.), *Family, Gender and Body Law and Society Today*. Warsaw University Press.

Kurzman, Charles. 1996. Structural Opportunity and Perceived Opportunity in Social-Movement Theory: The Iranian Revolution of 1979. *American Sociological Review* 61: 153–170.

Lederer, Ivo John (ed.) 1992. *Western Approaches to Eastern Europe*. New York: Council on Foreign Relations Press.

Linz, Juan, and Alfred Stepan. 1996. *Problems of Democratic Transition and Consolidation: Southern Europe, South America and Post-Communism Europe*. Baltimore, MD: Johns Hopkins University Press.

Lipset, Seymour Martin. 1960. Some Social Requisites of Democracy: Economic Development and Political Legitimacy. *American Political Science Review* 54: 69–105.

1981. *Political Man: The Social Bases of Politics*. Baltimore, MD: Johns Hopkins University Press.

1994. The Social Requisites of Democracy Revisited: 1993 Presidential Address. *American Sociological Review* 59: 1–22.

Lissyutkina, Larissa. 1993. Soviet Women at the Crossroad of Perestroika. In Nanette Funk and Magda Mueller (eds.), *Gender Politics and Post-Communism*. New York: Routledge.

Little, R. C., G. A. Milliken, W. W. Stroup, and R. D. Wolfinger. 1996. SAS System for Mixed Linear Models. *The American Statistician* 45: 54–64.

Lityński, Jan. 1992. Solidarity Contacts. *Mazowsze* (Spring).

Lord, Christopher, and Erika Harris. 2006. *Democracy in the New Europe*. New York: Palgrave Macmillan.

Lovenduski, J., and J. Woodall. 1987. *Politics and Society in Eastern Europe*. Bloomington: Indiana University Press.

Lubiejewski, Tadeusz. 1989. Za wczesnie. *Trybuna Opolska*. (August 2): 2.

Madaha, R., and B. Wejnert. (2011). The Declining Health Status as Fuelled by Illusory Internal Migration in Sub-Saharan Africa: Is There any Future? In Barbara Wejnert (ed.), *Democracy: Challenges to Societal Health*. Research in Political Sociology, 19. New York: Bingley; London: Emerald Press (Macmillan).

Mainwaring, Scott, and Aníbal Pérez-Liñán. 2012. *Democratic Breakdown and Survival in Latin America, 1945–2005*. Paper for the conference "Gillermo O'Donnell and the Study of Democracy," Buenos Aires, March 26–27, 2012.

Mandelbaum, Michael. 2004. *The Ideas That Conquered the World: Peace, Democracy, and Free Markets in the Twenty-First Century*. New York: Public Affairs/Perseus Books Group.

    2008. *Democracy's Good Name: The Rise and Risks of the World's Most Popular Form of Government*. New York: Public Affairs/Perseus Books Group.

Maravall, J. M., and J. Santamaria. 1986. Political Change in Spain and the Prospect for Democracy. In O'Donnell, Schmitter, & Whitehead 1986 *Transition from Authoritarian Rule: Latin America*. Baltimore, MD: Johns Hopkins University Press.

Markoff, John. 1996. *Waves of Democracy: Social Movements and Political Change*. Newbury, CA: Pine Forge.

    2003. Margins, Centers, and Democracy: The Paradigmatic History of Women's Suffrage. *Journal of Women in Culture and Society* 29: 85–116.

Marody, Mira. 1991. New Possibilities and Old Habits. *Sysyphus* 7: 33–40.

Marsh, Herbert W., Kit-Tai Hau, and Chit-Kwong Kong. 2000. Late Immersion and Language of Instruction in Hong Kong High Schools: Achievement Growth in Language and Nonlanguage Subjects. *Harvard Education Review* 70: 302–46.

Marshall, Monty G. and Ted Robert Gurr. 2012. *Polity IV Project: Political Regime Characteristics and Transitions, 1800–2012*. www.systemic-peace.org/polity/polity4.htm

Marshall, Monty G., Keith Jagger, and Ted Robert Gurr. 2009. *Polity IV: Regime Authority Characteristics and Transition Datasets, 1800–2009* [Data file]. Available from the Center for Systemic Peace Website: www.systemicpeace.org/inscr/inscr.htm

    2011. *Polity IV Project: Dataset Users' Manual*. Arlington, VA: Polity IV Project.

Mayer, Ann Elizabeth. 2007. *Islam and Human Rights: Tradition and Politics*. Boulder, CO: Westview Press.

McAdam, Doug. 1988. *Freedom Summer*. New York: Oxford University Press.

McAdam, Doug, and Ruth Dieter. 1993. Cross-National Diffusion of Movement Ideas. *Annals of the American Academy of Political and Social Science* 528: 56–74.

McColm, Bruce. 1990. The Comparative Survey of Freedom: 1990. The Challenges of Freedom. *Freedom at Issue* (January/February): 6–17.

Merritt, Richard L., and Stein Rokkan (eds.) 1996. *Comparing Nations: The Use of Quantitative Data in Cross-National Research*. New Haven, CT: Yale University Press.

Meyer, David S. 2007. The Politics of Protest: Social Movements in America. New York: Oxford University Press.

Meyer, John W. 1987. The World Polity and the Authority of the Nation State. In G. M. Thomas, J. W. Meyer, F. O. Ramirez, and J. Boli (eds.), *Institutional Structure*. Newbury Park, CA: Sage.

Meyer, John W., and Brian Rowan. 1977. Institutionalized Organizations: Formal Structure as Myth and Ceremony. *American Journal of Sociology* 83: 440–463.

Meyer, Thomas. 2002. *Media Democracy. How the Media Colonize Politics*. Oxford: Blackwell/Polity Press.

Michnik, Adam. 1990. Politics and Ethics. *Trud* (June 5): 1–2.

Mingst, Karen, and Margaret Karns. 2007. *The United Nations in the Twenty-First Century*. Boulder, CO: Westview Press.

Mizruchi, Mark S. 1993. Cohesion, Equivalence, and Similarity of Behavior: A Theoretical and Empirical Assessment. *Social Networks* 15: 275–307.

Moore, Barrington. 1966. *Social Origin of Dictatorship and Democracy*. Boston, MA: Beacon.

Morgan, Robin. 1984. *Sisterhood is Global*. New York: Anchor Books.

Most, B. A., and Harvey Starr. 1990. Theoretical and Logical Issues in the Study of International Diffusion. *Journal of Theoretical Politics* 2: 391–412.

Moyo, Dambisa. 2009. Dead Aid: Why Foreign Aid is Not Working and How There is a Better Way for Africa. New York: Farrar, Straus and Giroux.

Murthy, Ranjani. 1996. Fighting Female Infanticide by Working with Midwives: An Indian Case. *Gender and Development* 4, 2: 20–27.

2001. A Note on Male Governance of South Indian Family Businesses and Its Implications for Women. *Indian Journal of Gender Studies* 8, 1: 89–96.

Mustapha, A. R., and L. Whitfield (eds.) 2009. *Turning Points in African Democracy*. Oxford: James Currey.

Myrdal, Gunnar. 1968. *Asian Drama*, New York: McGraw-Hill.

Nazir, Sameena, and Leigh Tomppert. 2005. *Women's Rights in the Middle East and North Africa*. New York: Rowan and Littlefield.

Nee, Victor, and David Stark (eds.) 1989. *Remaking the Economic Institution of Socialism: China and Eastern Europe*. Stanford University Press.

Neubauer, Deane. 1967. Some Conditions of Democracy. *American Political Science Review* 6: 1001–1009.

O'Donnell, Guillermo, Philippe C. Schmitter, and Laurence Whitehead. 1986. *Transitions from Authoritarian Rule*. Baltimore, MD: Johns Hopkins University Press.

O'Loughlin, John, Michael Ward, Corey Lofdahl, Jordin Cohen, David Brown, David Reilly, Kristian Gleditsch, and Michael Shin. 1998. The Diffusion of Democracy, 1946–1994. *Annals of the Association of American Geographers* 88: 545–574.

Oakley, R. P., P. G. Hare, and K. Balazs. 1992. Computer Numerically Controlled Machinery Diffusion within the Hungarian Economy. *Science and Public Policy* 19: 241–250.

Oberschall, Anthony. 1989. The Sit-ins: Protest Diffusion and Movement Take-Off. *Research in Social Movement, Conflict and Change* 11: 31–53.

Offe, Claus. 1991. Capitalism by Democratic Design? Democratic Theory Facing the Triple Transition in East Central Europe. *Social Forces* 58: 865–891.

Olujic, Maria. 1990. Economic and Demographic Change in Contemporary Yugoslavia: Persistence of Traditional Gender Ideology. *East European Quarterly* 23, 4: 477–485

Opp, Karl-Dieter, and Christiane Gern. 1993. Dissident Groups, Personal Networks, and Spontaneous Cooperation: The East German Revolution of 1989. *American Sociological Review* 58: 659–681.

Orlikowski, Marian. 1989. Polak Bulgar Przyjazn bez Obowiazku (Polish and Bulgarian Friendship Without Obligations). *Gazeta Wyborcza* (May 21):.1.

Ormrod, Richard K. 1990. Local Context and Innovation Diffusion in a Well-Connected World. *Economic Geography* 66: 109–122.

Osmanczyk, Edmund. 1982. *Encylkopedia ONZ I Stosunkow Miedzynarodowych (UN and International Relations Encyclopedia)*. Warsaw: Wiedza Powszechna.

Ost, David. 1990. *Solidarity and the Politics of Anti-Politics*. Philadelphia: Temple University Press.

———. 1992. Labor and Social Transition. *Problems of Communism* 3: 48–51.

Owen, John. 2005. Iraq and the Democratic Peace. *Foreign Affairs* (November—December): 122–128.

Palmer, Donald A., P. Devereaux Jennings, and Xueguang Zhou. 1993. Late Adoption of the Multidivisional Form by Large US Corporations: Institutional, Political, and Economic Accounts. *Administrative Science Quarterly* 38: 100–131.

Paradowska, Janina. 1992. Kobieta do Domu. *Polityka* (March 21): 5.

Peffley, Mark. and Robert Rohrschneider. 2003. Democratization and Political Tolerance in Seventeen Countries: A Multi-Level Model of Democratic Learning. *Political Research Quarterly* 56: 243–257.

Pei, Minxin. 2006. The Dark Side of China's Rise. *Foreign Policy* 153 (March/April): 32–40.

Pelikan, Jirim. 1989.Wierze ze Polska bedzie miala Wiecej Szczescia. (I Trust That Poland Will Be More Lucky). Interview conducted by Pelikan, former hero of the Prague Spring of 1968 and later a member of the European Parliament, and published by the Polish press. *Gazeta Wyborcza* (November 10–12): 3.

Pellicani, Luciano, and Florindo Volpacchio. 1991. The Cultural War between East and West. *Telos* 89: 127–132.

Petrova, Dimitrina. 1993. The Winding Road to Emancipation in Bulgaria. In Nanette Funk and Magda Mueller (eds.), *Gender Politics and Post-Communism*. New York: Routledge: 22–30.

Piscatori, James (ed.) 1991. *Islamic Fundamentalists and the Gulf Crisis*. Chicago, IL: The American Academy of Arts and Sciences.

Podkrepa. 1990. *Constitution of Podkrepa*. Sofia: Podkrepa.

Polish Ministry of Labor and Social Policy. 1990. Program of visit of the Romanian Ministry of Labor, September 3–7.

Politkovskaya, Anna. 2007. *Putin's Russia: Life in a Failing Democracy*. New York: Owl Books.

2011. *Is Journalism Worth Dying For?* New York: Melville House.

Polska Agencja Prasowa (PAP) (Polish Press Agency). 1989. *Buletyn Zagraniczny (International Bulletin)* (December 5).

1990. *Biuletyn Informacyjny PAP* (September 26).

1991. *Buletyn Zagraniczny (International Bulletin)* (November 10).

Porter, Charles, and Robert J. Alexander. 1961. *The Struggle for Democracy in Latin America*. New York: Macmillan.

Prempeh, Kwasi.2010. Presidents Untamed. In Larry Diamond and Marc Plattner (eds.), *Democratization in Africa: Progress and Retreat*. Baltimore, MD: The Johns Hopkins University Press.

Pridham, Geoffrey. 1990. *Securing Democracy: Political Parties and Democratic Consolidation in Southern Europe*. New York: Routledge.

Przeworski, Adam. 1991. *Democracy and the Market*. Cambridge University Press.

2009. The Mechanics of Regime Instability in Latin America. *Journal of Politics in Latin America* 1, 1: 5–36.

2010. *Democracy and the Limits of Self-Government*. New York: Cambridge University Press.

Przeworski, Adam, and Carolina Curvale. 2006. Does Politics Explain the Economic Gap between the United States and Latin America? In Francis Fukuyama (ed.), *La Brecha entre America Latina y los Estados Unidos*. Buenos Aires: Fondo de Cultura Economica.

Przeworski, Adam, and Fernando Limongi. 1993. Political Regimes and Economic Growth. *The Journal of Economic Perspectives*: 751–769.

1997. Modernization: Theories and Facts. *World Politic*, 49: 155–183.

Przeworski, Adam, Michael Alvarez, Jose Antonio Cheibub, and Fernando Limongi. 1996. What Makes Democracies Endure? *Journal of Democracy* 7: 39–55.

2000. *Democracy and Development: Political Institutions and Well-Being in the World*. Cambridge University Press.

Putnam, Robert D. 1988. Diplomacy and Domestic Politics. *International Organization* 42, 3: 427–461.

Ramos, Eduardo, and Maria del Mar Delgado. 2003. European Rural Development Programmes as a Means of Strengthening Democracy in Rural Areas. *Research in Rural Sociology and Development* 9: 135–157.

Rasler, Karen. 1996. Concessions, Repressions, and Political Protest in the Iranian Revolution. *American Sociological Review* 61: 132–152.

Rawls, J. 1999. *A Theory of Justice*. Boston, MA: Belknap Press of Harvard University Press. Originally published 1971.

Reading, Anna. 1992. *Polish Women, Solidarity and Feminism*. London: Macmillan Academic and Professional Press.

Ritzer, George. 2007. *The McDonaldization of Society* (5th edn.) Thousand Oaks, CA: Pine Forge Press.

Robinson, William I. 2004. Globalization, the World System, and "Democracy Promotion" in US Foreign Policy. *Theory and Society* 25: 615–665.

Rogers, Everett M. 1962. *Diffusion of Innovations*. New York: The Free Press.

1995. *Diffusion of Innovations* (4th edn.) New York: The Free Press.

2003. *Diffusion of Innovations* (5th edn.) New York: The Free Press.

Rogers, Everett M., and D. Lawrence Kincaid. 1981. *Communication Networks: Toward a New Paradigm for Research*. New York: The Free Press.

Rogers, Everett M., and F. Floyd Shoemaker. 1971. *Communication of Innovations: Cross-Cultural Approach*. New York: Free Press.

Romaniuk, Lara A. 2002. A Country in Transition: Health Crisis in Ukraine, with a Focus on Tobacco and Alcohol. In Wejnert 2002a: 241–257.

Rosenau, J. 2003. *Distant Proximities: Dynamics Beyond Globalization.* Princeton University Press.

Rosero-Bixby, Luis, and John B. Casterline. 1993. Modeling Diffusion Effects in Fertility Transition. *Population Studies* 47: 147–167.

——— 1994. Interaction Diffusion and Fertility Transition in Costa Rica. *Social Forces* 73: 435–462.

Rothwell, R., and H. Wisseman. 1986. Technology, Culture and Public Policy. *Technovation* 4: 91–115.

Roy Rosenzweig Center for History and New Media. 2011. *Making the History of 1989. Economies in Transition 2007–2011.* http://chnm. gmu.edu/1989/exhibits/economies-in-transition/introduction (Accessed June 1, 2011).

Rueschemeyer, D., E. H. Stephens, and J. Stephens. 1992. *Capitalist Development and Democracy.* University of Chicago Press.

Rueschmeyer, Marilyn. 1998. *Women in the Politics of Postcommunist Eastern Europe.* New York: Sharpe.

Russett, Bruce M. 1964. Inequality and Instability: The Relation of Land Tenure to Politics. *World Politics* 16: 442–454.

Ruttan, V.W. 1988. Cultural Endowments and Economic Development: What Can We Learn From Anthropology? *Economic Development and Cultural Change* 36: 247–271.

Ryan, B., and Neal Gross. 1943. The Diffusion of Hybrid Seed Corn in Two Iowa Communities. *Rural Sociology* 8: 15–24.

Saban Center at Brookings. 2008. *Restoring the Balance. A Middle East Strategy for the Next President.* Washington, DC: Brookings Institution Press.

Saban Center for Middle East Policy. 2008. *Toward a New US–Middle East Strategy.* Saban Center at Brookings–Council on Foreign Relations Project. Washington, DC: Brookings Institution Press.

Sabu, George M. 1997. Female Infanticide in Tamil Nadu, India: From Recognition Back to Denial? *Reproductive-Health-Matters*: 124–132.

Saleci, Renata. 1992. *Nationalism, Anti-Semitism, and Anti-Feminism in Eastern Europe Democracy.Working Paper Series.* New York: East and Central Europe Program of the New School for Social Research.

Sanderson, Stephen, and Kristopher Proctor. 2009. *World Democratization 1900–2005: Cross-National Test of Modernization, Power Resources, and Diffusion Theories. Paper presented at the Annual Meeting of the American Sociological Association*, San Francisco, August.

Sawa-Czajka, Elizabeth. 2010. *System Polityczny RP 1989–2010 Wybrane Problemy.* Krasnystaw, Poland: Polianna.

——— 2012. Women in Poland: Transition to Democracy and Stereotypes. *Research in Political Sociology* 20: 105–25.

Schmidt, Vivien. 2006. *Democracy in Europe: the EU and National Polities.* New York: Oxford University Press.

Schumpeter, Joseph. 1950. *Capitalism, Socialism and Democracy.* New York: Harper and Row.

Schwartzman, Kathleen. 1998. Globalization and Democracy. *Annual Review of Sociology* 24: 159–181.

Scott, Richard W., John W. Meyer, et al. 1994. *Institutional Environments and Organizations: Structural Complexity and Individualism.* Thousand Oaks, CA: Sage.

Sedaitis, Judith, and Jim Butterfield. 1991. *Perestroika From Below.* Boulder, CO: Westview Press.

Seib, Philip. 2009. *The New Media and the New Middle East.* Palgrave MacMillan Series in International Political Communication. New York: Palgrave MacMillan.

Shafer, D. Michael. 1994. *Winners and Losers: How Sectors Shape the Developmental Prospects of States.* Ithaca, NY: Cornell University Press.

Shin, Eui, Hang Kwon, Tai Hwan Lee, and Hae Young. 1981. Determinants of Fertility Differentials in Korea. *Sociology and Social Research* 65, 2: 211–225.

Simpson, Miles. 1990. Political Rights and Income Inequality: A Cross-National Test. *American Sociological Review* 55: 682–693.

Singer, Judith D. 1998. Using SAS PROC MIXED to Fit Multilevel Models, Hierarchical Models, and Individual Growth Models. *Journal of Educational and Behavioral Studies* 24: 323–355.

Singer, Judith D., and John B. Willett. 2003. *Applied Longitudinal Data Analysis.* Oxford University Press.

Skocpol, Theda. 1979. *State and Social Revolutions.* Cambridge University Press.

    1992. *Protecting Soldiers and Mothers.* Cambridge, MA: The Belknap Press of Harvard University.

    1998. *Democracy, Revolution and History.* Ithaca, NY: Cornell University Press.

Skocpol, Theda, and M. P. Fiorina (eds.) 1999. *Civil Engagement in American Democracy.* New York: Brookings Institution Press.

Slownik, Dysydentow. 2007. *Czolowe Postacie Ruchow opozycyjnych w krajach komunistycznych w latach 1956–1989. (Dictionary of Dissidents. Main Representatives of dissident movements in communist states 1956–1989).* Warsaw: Karta.

Smith, David, and Douglas R. White. 1992. Structure and Dynamics of the Global Economy: Network Analysis of International Trade 1965–1980. *Social Forces* 70: 857–893.

Snijders, T. A., and R. J. Bosker. 1994. Modeled Variance in Two-Level Models. *Sociological Methods and Research* 22: 342–363.

Snyder, David, and Edward Kick. 1979. Structural Position in the World System and Economic Growth, 1955–1970: A Multiple-Network Analysis of Transnational Interactions. *American Journal of Sociology* 84: 1096–1126.

Solcova, Miroslava. 1984. *Postareni Zeny v Socialisticke Spolecnosti*. Prague.

Somers, Margaret. 1993. Citizenship and the Place of the Public Sphere: Law, Community, and Political Culture in the Transition to Democracy. *American Sociological Review* 58: 587–620.

Soule, Sarah. 1997. The Student Divestment Movement in the United States and Tactical Diffusion: The Shantytown Protest. *Social Forces* 75: 855–883.

Spears, Ian S. 2003. Africa: The Limits of Power-Sharing. *Journal of Democracy* 3: 123–136.

Stark, David, and Laszlo Bruszt. 1998. *Postsocialist Pathways*. Cambridge University Press.

Starr, Harvey. 1991. Democratic Dominoes. Diffusion Approaches to the Spread of Democracy in the International System. *Journal of Conflict Resolution* 35: 356–381.

Statesman's Yearbook (138th edn.) 2000. London: Macmillan.

Stephens, John D. 1989. Democratic Transitions and Breakdown in Western Europe, 1870–1939: A Test of the Moore Thesis. *American Journal of Sociology* 94: 1019–1077.

Stephenson, Patricia (ed.) 1998. *Improving Women's Health Services in the Russian Federation: Results of a Pilot Project*. Washington, DC: World Bank.

Strang, David. 1990. From Dependency to Sovereignty: An Event History Analysis of Decolonization 1870–1987. *American Sociological Review* 55: 846–860.

—— 1996. *Inducing a Network Structure from Multiple Diffusion Processes. Technical Report*. Ithaca, NY: Department of Sociology, Cornell University.

Strang, David, and John W. Meyer. 1993. Institutional Conditions for Diffusion. *Theory and Society* 22:487–511.

Strang, David, and Sarah Soule. 1998. Diffusion in Organizations and Social Movements: From Hybrid Corn to Poison Pills. *Annual Review of Sociology* 24: 265–290.

Strang, David, and Nancy Brandon Tuma. 1993. Spatial and Temporal Heterogeneity in Diffusion. *American Journal of Sociology* 99: 614–639.

Straub, Detmar W. 1994. The Effect of Culture on IT Diffusion: E-Mail and Fax in Japan and the US. *Information Systems Research* 5: 23–47.

Strodthoff, Glenn G., Robert P. Hawkins, and A. Clay Schoenfeld. 1985. Media Roles in a Social Movement: A Model of Ideology Diffusion. *Journal of Communication* (Spring): 134–153.

Stycos, Mayone J., Barbara Wejnert, and Zbigniew Tyszka. 2001. Polish Women and Quality of Life: A Preliminary Research Report. *Roczniki Socjologii Rodziny (Annals of Sociology of Family)* 9: 17–29.

Stycos, Mayone J., Barbara Wejnert, and Zbigniew Tyszka. 2002. Polish Women During Transition to Democracy: A Preliminary Research Report. In Wejnert 2002a: 259–279.

Szelenyi, Ivan. 1988. *Socialist Entrepreneurs: Embourgeoisement in Rural Hungary*. Madison: University of Wisconsin Press.

Szelenyi, Szonja. 1996. Interests and Symbols in Post-Communist Political Culture: The Case of Hungary. American Sociological Review 61: 466–477.

Tarrow, Sidney. 1989. *Democracy and Disorder: Protest and Politics in Italy, 1965–1975*. Oxford University Press.

1991a. "Aiming at the Moving Target": Social Science and the Recent Rebellions in Eastern Europe. *Political Science and Politics* 3: 9–10.

1991b. Understanding Political Change in Eastern Europe. *Political Science and Politics* 3: 12–20.

1998. *Power in Movement: Social Movements and Contentious Politics* (2nd edn.) Cambridge and New York: Cambridge University Press.

2005. *The New Transnational Activism*. New York: Cambridge University Press.

Taylor, Charles, and David Jodice. 1982. *World Handbook of Political and Social Indicators #III: 1948–1982. Quarterly Event Data*. Ann Arbor, MI: Inter-University Consortium for Political and Social Research.

Tessler, M. 2002. Islam and Democracy in the Middle East: The Impact of Religious Attitudes Toward Democracy in Four Arab Countries. *Comparative Politics* 34: 337–354.

Teune, Henry. 2002. Democratizing Globalization and Globalizing Democracy. *Annals of the American Academy of Political and Social Science* 581: 22–34 .

Theobold, Robert (ed.) 1960. *The New Nations of West Africa*. New York: H. W. Wilson.

Thomas, George M., and P. Lauderdale. 1987. World Polity Sources of National Welfare and Land Reform. In Thomas et al. 1987: 198–214.

Thomas, George M., J. W. Meyer, F. O. Ramirez, and J. Boli (eds.) 1987. *Institutional Structure*. Newbury Park, CA: Sage.

Tilly, Charles. 2005. *Trust and Rule*. New York: Cambridge University Press.

2006. *Regimes and the Repertoire*. University of Chicago Press.

2007. *Democracy*. New York: Cambridge University Press.

2008. *Explaining Social Processes*. Seattle, WA: Paradigm Press.

Titkov, Anna. 1993. Political Change in Poland: Cause, Modifier, or Barrier to Gender Equality? In Nanette Funk and Magda Mueller (eds.), *Gender Politics and Post-Communism*. New York: Routledge: 253–256.

de Tocqueville, Alexis. 2009. *Democracy in America*. Charleston, SC: BiblioBazaar. Original publication by Cambridge University Press, 1863.

Tolnay, Stewart E. 1995. The Spatial Diffusion of Fertility: A Cross-Sectional Analysis of Counties in the American South, 1940. *American Sociological Review* 60: 299–308.

Trybuna Ludu. 1989. Kwestia stylu i nie tylko (The matter of style and not only). (July 25): 1.

Trybuna Opolska. 1989. Za wczesnie? (Too Soon?). (August 2): 1.

Tuma, Nancy Brandon, Mikk Titma, and Rein Murakas. 2002. Transitional Economies and Income Inequality: The Case of Estonia. In Wejnert 2002a.

Tuttle, Lisa. 1986. *Encyclopedia of Feminism*. New York: Facts on File.

Tversky, Amos, and Daniel Kahneman. 1974. Judgment Under Uncertainty: Heuristics and Biases: Biases in Judgments Reveal Some Heuristics of Thinking Under Uncertainty. *Science* 185: 1124–1131.

1982. *Causal Schemas in Judgments under Uncertainty. In Kahneman, Daniel, Paul Slovic, and Amos Tversky, Judgment under Uncertainty: Heuristics and Biases*. Cambridge University Press.

Tversky, Amos, and Daniel Kahneman. 1988. Rational Choice and the Framing of Decisions. In David Bell, Howard Raiffa, and Amos Tversky (eds.), *Decision Making: Descriptive, Normative, and Prescriptive Interactions*. Cambridge University Press.

Uhlin, Anders. 1993. *Indonesian Democracy Discourses in a Global Context: The Transnational Diffusion of Democratic Ideas. Center for Southeast Asian Studies Working Paper 83*. Clayton, Victoria: Monash University.

1995. *Democracy and Diffusion. Transnational Lesson-Drawing Among Indonesian Pro-Democracy Actors. Lund Political Studies Working Paper 87*. Lund University, Sweden.

UNESCO. 1983. *Quality of Life: Problems of Assessment and Measurement*. Paris: UNESCO.

United Nations, Department of International and Social Affairs. 2001. *The World's Women 1970–2000: Trends and Statistics*. New York: United Nations.

United Nations Development Program. 1992. *Human Development Report*. Oxford University Press.

US Department of State. 2010. *Background Note: Belarus* (August 27). www.state.gov/r/pa/ei/bgn/5371.htm

Valente, Thomas W. 1995. *Network Models of the Diffusion of Innovations.* Cresskill, NJ: Hampton.

Vallinder, Torbjörn. 1962. *In the Front Line for Democracy: The Universal Suffrage Movement in Sweden 1886–1900.* Stockholm: Lund Political Studies.

Vandewalle, Dirk. 2012. After Qaddafi: The Surprising Success of the New Libya. *Foreign Affairs* (November 8): 22–28.

Vanhanen, Tatu. 1990. *The Process of Democratization.* New York: Crane Russak.

Veenhaven, R. 1996. Happy Life-Expectancy: A Comprehensive Measure of Quality-of-Life in Nations. *Social Indicators Research* 39: 1–58.

Veenhaven, R., and J. Ehrhardt. 1995. The Cross-National Pattern of Happiness: Test of Predictions Implied in Three Theories of Happiness. *Social Indicators Research* 34: 33–68.

Verdery, Katherine. 1993. Nationalism and National Sentiments in Post-Socialist Romania. *Slavic Review* 52, 2: 179–203.

Vickers, Miranda, and James Pettifer. 2000. *Albania: from Anarchy to a Balkan Identity.* New York University Press.

Vladislaw, Jan (ed.) 1987. *Vaclaw Havel: or Living in Truth.* London: Faber and Faber.

Vodopivec, Peter. 1992. Slovenes and Yugoslavia, 1918–1991. *East European Politics and Societies* 6, 220–242.

Waldron, Jeremy. 1994. Vagueness in Law and Language: Some Philosophical Issues. *California Law Review* 82: 509.

Walker, Jack. 1969. The Diffusion of Innovations Among the American States. *American Political Science Review* 63: 880–899.

Wallerstein, Immanuel. 1974 (1997).*The Modern World System: Capitalist Agriculture and the Origin of the European World-Economy in the Sixteenth Century.* New York: Academic Press.

1998. *Utopistics: Or Historical Choice of the Twenty-First Century.* New York: The New Press.

1999. *The End of the World as We Know it.* Minneapolis: University of Minnesota Press.

2001. Democracy, Capitalism, and Transformation. In O. Enwezor et al. (eds.), *Democracy Unrealized.* Ostfildern: Hatje Cantz: 96–110.

2004. *The World-Systems Analysis: An Introduction.* Durham, NC: Duke University Press.

Weimann, Gabriel, and Hans-Bernd Brosius. 1994. Is There a Two-Step Flow of Agenda-Setting? *International Journal of Public Opinion Research* 6: 323–341.

Wejnert, Barbara. 1988. Polish Student Movement 1980–1981. *Research on Social Movements, Conflict and Change* 10: 173–183.

1996a. Political Transition and Gender Transformation in the Communist and Post-Communist Periods. In Wejnert & Spencer 1996: 3–19.

1996b. The Quality of Life in Post-Communist Poland. In Wejnert & Spencer 1996: 169–185.

1996c. Family Studies and Politics: The Case of Polish Sociology. *Marriage and Family Review* 22: 233–257.

2001a. Problematyka Subiektywnej I Obiektywnej Oceny Jakosci Zycia w Badaniach Amerykanskich. In A. Wachowiak (ed.), *Jak Zyc: Wybrane Porblemy Jakosci Zycia*. Poznan: Wydawnictwo Fundacji Humanitora.

(ed.) 2002a. *Transition to Democracy in Eastern Europe and Russia: Impact on Politics, Economy and Culture*. Westport, CT: Greenwood.

2002b. A Conceptual Framework for Integrating Diffusion Models. *Annual Review of Sociology* 28: 297–326.

2002c. The Contribution of Collective Protests to the Softening of Communist Regimes in East Central Europe. In Wejnert 2002a: 65–90.

2002d. Integration of the Processes and Components of Transition to Democracy. In Wejnert 2002a: 3–26.

2003. The Effects of Growth of Democracy and Transition to Market-Based Economies on Women's Well-Being. *Journal of Consumer Policy* 26: 465–493.

2005. Diffusion, Development and Democracy1800–1999. *American Sociological Review* 70, 1: 53–81.

2007. *Nations, Development and Democracy: 1800–2005. [Computer file] ICPSR20440-v1*. Ann Arbor, MI: Inter-University Consortium for Political and Social Research. www.icpsr.umich.edu/access/index.html

2010. World Trends and Trajectory of Democratization. *Research in Political Sociology* 18: 5–24.

Wejnert, Barbara, and Almagul Djumabaeva. 2004. From Patriarchy to Egalitarianism: Parenting Roles in Democratizing Poland and Kyrgyzstan. *Marriage & Family Review* 36, 3/4: 147–171.

Wejnert, Barbara, and Metta Spencer (eds.) 1996. *Women in Post-Communism*. Greenwich, CT: JAI Press.

Whitehead, L. 1986. International Aspects of Democratization. In O'Donnell, Schmitter, &Whitehead 1986: 3–46.

Wolf, Martin. 2001. Will the Nation-State Survive Globalization? *Foreign Affairs* (January/February): 178–190.

Woodward, S. 1995. *Balkan Tragedy*. Washington DC: The Brookings Institution.

World Bank. 2009. *World Development Indicators 1960–2009. Electronic manuscript*. Washington, DC: World Bank. http://web.worldbank.org/wbsite/external/datastatistics (Accessed May 15, 2011).

2011. National accounts data and OECD National Accounts data files (for Albania). www.indexmundi.com/facts/albania/gdp-per-capita (Accessed June 1, 2011).

World Economic Outlook. 2011. WEO data, IMF (for Romania). www.econstats.com/weo/V008.htm (Accessed June 1, 2011).

Yang, Min, Harvey Goldstein, and Anthony Heath. 2000. Multilevel Models for Repeated Binary Outcomes: Attitudes and Voting over the Electoral Cycle. *Journal of the Royal Statistical Society Series A (Statistics in Society)* 163: 49–62.

Zakowski, B. 1991. *Zakowski pyta Geremek odpowiada. (Zakowski is asking and Geremek Answers).*Warsaw: PWN.

Zherebkina, Irina. 2000. *Prochti moi zhelanye (Almost My Wishes).* Moscow: Ider Press.

Zhou, Xueguang. 1993. Occupational Power, State Capacities, and the Diffusion of Licensing in the American States: 1890 to 1950. *American Sociological Review* 58: 536–552.

Index

Made in the USA
Las Vegas, NV
10 May 2022